Making Archives in Ea

European states were overwhelmed with information around 1500. Their agents sought to organize their overflowing archives to provide trustworthy evidence and comprehensive knowledge useful in the everyday exercise of power. This detailed comparative study explores cases from Lisbon to Vienna to Berlin to understand how changing information technologies and ambitious programs of state-building challenged record-keepers to find new ways to organize and access the information in their archives. From the intriguing details of how clerks invented new ways to index and catalog the expanding world to the evolution of new perspectives on knowledge and power among philologists and historians, this book provides illuminating vignettes and revealing comparisons about a core technology of governance in early modern Europe. Enhanced by perspectives from the history of knowledge and from archival science, this wide-ranging study explores the potential and the limitations of knowledge management as media technologies evolved.

RANDOLPH C. HEAD is a professor of history at the University of California, Riverside. He has published extensively on democracy, religious conflict, and knowledge systems in early modern Europe, particularly Switzerland. His publications, which were recognized by the Max Geilinger Prize in 2017, include *Early Modern Democracy in the Grisons* published in 1996, *Jenatsch's Axe* published in 2008, and *A Concise History of Switzerland* (with Clive Church) published in 2013.

Making Archives in Early Modern Europe

Proof, Information, and Political Record-Keeping, 1400–1700

Randolph C. Head

University of California, Riverside

CAMBRIDGE
UNIVERSITY PRESS

CAMBRIDGE
UNIVERSITY PRESS

University Printing House, Cambridge CB2 8BS, United Kingdom

One Liberty Plaza, 20th Floor, New York, NY 10006, USA

477 Williamstown Road, Port Melbourne, VIC 3207, Australia

314-321, 3rd Floor, Plot 3, Splendor Forum, Jasola District Centre, New Delhi - 110025, India

79 Anson Road, #06-04/06, Singapore 079906

Cambridge University Press is part of the University of Cambridge.

It furthers the University's mission by disseminating knowledge in the pursuit of education, learning and research at the highest international levels of excellence.

www.cambridge.org
Information on this title: www.cambridge.org/9781108462525
DOI: 10.1017/9781108620659

First published 2019
First paperback edition 2020

A catalogue record for this publication is available from the British Library

Library of Congress Cataloging in Publication data
Names: Head, Randolph Conrad, author.
Title: Making archives in early modern Europe : proof, information, and political record-keeping, 1400-1700 / Randolph C. Head, University of California, Riverside.
Description: Cambridge, United Kingdom ; New York, NY : Cambridge University Press, 2019. | Includes bibliographical references and index.
Identifiers: LCCN 2018061495| ISBN 9781108473781 (hardback : alk. paper) | ISBN 9781108462525 (pbk. : alk. paper)
Subjects: LCSH: Archives–Europe–History–To 1500 | Archives–Europe–History–16th century. | Archives–Europe–History–17th century. | Archival resources–Europe–History–To 1500. | Archival resources–Europe–History–16th century. | Archival resources–Europe–History–17th century.
Classification: LCC CD1001 .H33 2019 | DDC 930.1–dc23
LC record available at https://lccn.loc.gov/2018061495

ISBN 978-1-108-47378-1 Hardback
ISBN 978-1-108-46252-5 Paperback

Additional resources for this publication at www.cambridge.org/delange

Contents

Figures

Tables

Preface
Writing the History of Archives

"Archivorum quoque animam nihil aliud quam ordinem esse, jure dixerimus."
We would rightly say that the soul of archives, too, is nothing else than order.   Baldessare Bonifacio, *Liber de Archivis*, 1632[1]

In 1337, the city of Siena in Italy purchased a cat to protect its archive from mice.[2] The most interesting feature of this minor transaction is the fact that we know about it at all. What possessed the city fathers of Siena, like political actors all across Europe in the late Middle Ages, not only to begin recording seemingly trivial transactions, but also to provide so well for the careful organization and preservation of the resulting documents that we can still unearth them more than 600 years later? Towns and princes all over Europe began preserving and managing an astonishing number of records in the fourteenth century, produced by various authorities and by their citizens or subjects, so that we can today leaf through a register, browse a document bundle, or consult a manuscript index to find out about every kind of public business from the distant past – even about public cats. The proliferation of written records organized and stored for posterity that took off in late medieval Europe continued at a rising pace through the following centuries, and accelerated even more from the nineteenth century right to the present. This "birth of the archive," as Markus Friedrich calls it, amplified the scope of governance through secretarial practices that recorded a wide variety of information, kept the resulting records in more or less organized repositories, and then drew on these repositories to support political authority in various ways. Access to ordered archives allowed rulers to guide their future actions by learning about past circumstances, thus engaging more effectively in contestations over power, privilege, and property.[3]

---

[1] Bonifacius, *Liber de Archivis*, 10. The entire text is translated in Born, "Baldessare Bonifacio."
[2] Koch, "Die Archivierung," 64.
[3] Friedrich, *Birth*. This study complements Friedrich's important synthesis, which situates practices of record-keeping among multiple social contexts.

This book concentrates on one aspect of this sustained development, which became a cornerstone of state power in Europe and in the European colonial world (as it was in many other political systems around the globe): how European secretaries and archivists sought to establish order among the ever-growing mass of stored records, and how their efforts could fail. It examines how those responsible for public records from about 1400 to 1700 developed tools for managing documents and the information they contained, including inventories, storage architectures, and indexes, all taking place within an emerging institution, the state archive. The chapters that follow begin by investigating the work that political authorities imagined that stored records could do, and the enterprises to which such records were relevant. I then turn to a series of detailed case studies of secretarial practice and archival organization to demonstrate the growing differentiation of functions and of spaces that were key to the developments involved.

From about 1400 to about 1700, practices of organizing documents traversed a trajectory, with many variations, that began with repositories imagined as hidden treasuries of material proofs, continued through a phase during which archivists sought to organize records according to their content (a project that turned out to be fraught with difficulties), and began converging around 1700 in new approaches that categorized stored information primarily according to its place in the transaction of political business. This arc of development always proceeded in close correlation with evolving practices of government in Western Europe, referred to by historians as the rise of the early modern state. Changes in archival practice also permeated Europe's larger systems of knowledge as they developed – although with substantial autonomy, as I will argue. Both erudite and popular knowledge horizons were transformed after 1400: Technological changes such as movable-type printing, global changes such as new routes of commerce and conquest beyond Europe, and cultural changes that are captured under the terms "humanism" and "scientific revolution" all had an impact on what and how Europeans knew about their world. Archives were one distinctive site where such changes became manifest.

The arc I have just sketched out was anything but smooth, and a second important finding of this book is that information management practices in archives from the fourteenth to eighteenth century were extremely heterogeneous, even though they rested on a remarkably stable foundation of fundamental media technologies that included the loose-leaf paper or parchment document and the bound book. Manuscript books will play a particularly prominent role in the story laid out in the following chapters, because in the High Middle Ages, they represented a channel through which a sophisticated suite of knowledge tools moved from the world of scholarship to the world of administration. Changing conceptions of what made stored records authentic and authoritative once again drew on the world of erudition in the seventeenth century, ushering in the transformations around 1700 that represent the endpoint of this study, as pathways opened toward the emerging world of administrative states resting on systemic control and deployment of information.

Author's Note and Acknowledgments

The research presented here began with a chance encounter in an archive. While working on an entirely different project on Swiss political culture, I innocently asked a Zurich archivist whether any inventories from the sixteenth or seventeenth century survived. The archivist pointed me toward Johann Heinrich Waser's remarkable *Index archivorum generalis* of 1646, which was so captivating that I have been working on archival history for more than 20 years since. I could never have come this far without the enthusiastic support I have received from many directions. It is a pleasure to thank every person and institution who contributed, though the passage of time and the fallibility of my own archive means that the record here is surely incomplete. I am also grateful to the many scholars of medieval Europe, early modern Europe, and archival science that I cite, and I apologize in advance for every time I have missed their point or overlooked their contribution.

Professional archivists across Europe answered my questions with insight and enthusiasm, and occasionally bent their rules so that I could work more effectively with the material they preserved. Many stepped beyond the requirements of their position to lead me to resources and to help me along my path, and deserve my personal thanks. José Luis Rodríguez de Diego welcomed me to Simancas early in this project, and personally led me on a tour through the spaces of this remarkable facility, in continuous operation since 1540. His enthusiasm convinced me that I might be on to something, while his publications, including his priceless edition of Philip II's *Instrucción* for the operation of Simancas, provided invaluable insight and theoretical depth at a critical phase. Christoph Haidacher in Innsbruck welcomed me for two substantial visits in Innsbruck, and enabled me to inspect materials in the archival stacks. On the second occasion, when unanticipated construction closed the archive's reading room, he went far beyond the call of duty to set up a private reading room with staff on hand. When I met Leopold Auer, director of the Haus-, Hof-, und Staatsarchiv in Vienna, he invited me to come to his archive, and once I was there, directed the staff to help me in every way possible. Finally, during my work in The Hague, Eric Ketelaar not only connected me with a remarkable team of scholars working on Dutch archives, but invited me to his study for penetrating questions and invaluable insight, which has continued since. The following archivists also provided warm welcome and support: Dr. Jens Martin (Würzburg), Dr. Silvester Lacerda (Torre do Tombo), Franziska Mücke and Dr. Jürgen Kloosterhuis (GStA-PK, Berlin), and Dr. Anton Gössi (Lucerne).

I further gratefully recognize the support of the following institutions and their professional staff: Haus-, Hof-, und Staatsarchiv, Vienna; European Reading Room, Library of Congress, Washington, DC; Arquivo Nacional Torre do Tombo, Lisbon; Archivo General de Simancas, Simancas; Archivo General de Indias, Seville; Princeton University Library Rare Books Department, Princeton, NJ; Rutgers University Library, New Brunswick, NJ; Staatsarchiv Würzburg, Würzburg; Tiroler Landesarchiv, Innsbruck; The Newberry Library, Chicago; University of Chicago Rare Books Department, Chicago; Nationaal Archief, The Hague; Stadtarchief Leiden (now Ergoed Leiden), Leiden; Staatsarchiv Zürich; Zentralbibliothek Zürich (Handschriftenabteilung and Alte Drücke), Zurich; Staatsarchiv Aargau, Aarau; Staatsarchiv Graubünden, Chur; Staatsarchiv Luzern; Staatsarchiv Bern; Geheimes Staatsarchiv-Preussischer Kulturbesitz, Berlin.

Many fellow-scholars have provided personal support, from passing citations to help with ideas, grants, and travel. James Amelang, Luann Homza, Jodi Bilinkoff, Marc-Andre Grebe, and Richard Kagan provided advice on Spain, and Geoffrey Parker shared drafts of his work on Simancas. Marjorie "Beth" Plummer provided insight on German archives. Peter Horsman, Rudi van Maanen, and Theo Thomassen provided extensive support in the Netherlands. Constantin Fasolt discussed law and German archives with me in Chicago. James Tracy advised on Belgian archives. Colin Wilder helped me navigate the Latin in Roman Law. Diogo Ramada Curto, Pedro Cardim, and Saul António Gomes all provided insights on Portugal, and Pedro Pinto became a regular correspondent and oracle on the Torre do Tombo, as well as helping with translations from Portuguese. Warren Brown shared the manuscript of an important collection on early medieval archives he co-edited, and E. William Monter exchanged ideas on the Franco-German borderlands and their archives. At the last minute, Matthew Grohowski jumped into help complete this volume's index.

A team of high-powered scholars whose own research is about archives was particularly important. Eric Ketelaar has supported my research since we met at a Radcliffe conference, organized by Ann Blair. Arndt

Brendecke's scholarship has shaped my own in many ways, while Simon Teuscher in Zurich and Regula Schmid in Bern discussed Swiss and medieval matters. During an early phase of the project, Roger Sablonier provided me with workspace and library access at the University of Zurich. Filippo de Vivo and his remarkable ARCHives team at Birkbeck College, University of London, let me learn from their work. Maria de Lurdes Rosa in Lisbon invited me to become an outside member of the Digit.ARQ team on Portuguese family archives. Markus Friedrich and I have been trading ideas and papers for a decade, and he has often corrected me. Anthony Grafton lent me his office at the Princeton University Library one summer as I read up on German registry.

Colleagues, staff, and students at the University of California, Riverside also deserve thanks. Over the years, Michael Cox, Benjamin Esswein, Russell Fehr, Josh Lieser, Colin Whiting, and Katrin Boniface served as research assistants; Colin Whiting, Conrad Rudolf, and Juliette Levy provided assistance in translating particularly thorny passages in Latin and Spanish; and the Interlibrary Loan Department of the Tomás Rivera Library has reached far and wide to fulfill my requests.

Generous funding allowed me the liberty to absorb myself in research and writing, including from the School of Historical Studies at the Institute for Advanced Studies in Princeton, NJ, in 2002; an American Philosophical Association sabbatical grant in 2007–2008; and a National Endowment for the Humanities fellowship at the Newberry Library in 2011–2012, which also brought the inestimable support of Paul Gehl, Paul Saenger, Douglas Knox, Martha Briggs, and Jennifer Thom. In 2015 and 2016, a Senior Stipendiate at the Herzog–August Bibliothek in Wolfenbüttel, Germany, allowed me to bring the manuscript close to completion. Grants from the Academic Senate at the University of California supported research assistants, copying, and the mundane expenses of completing such an extended project.

I have enjoyed many opportunities to speak about my work. Parts of this project have been presented in England (Birkbeck and University Colleges, University of London), France (Institute Universitaire de France), Germany (Herzog–August Bibliothek, Wolfenbüttel; Centre for Manuscript Cultures, University of Hamburg), Portugal (Universidade Nova, Lisbon), and Switzerland (Schweizerische Akademie der Geisteswissenschaften, Monte Verità). I have spoken at conferences including the Sixteenth Century Studies Conference, the American Historical Association Conference, the German Frühe Neuzeitstagung, and the Renaissance Studies Conference. Several American universities have extended a welcome, including the University of California, Berkeley; University of California, Los Angeles; University of California, Riverside;

University of Arizona; University of Chicago; Duke University; Princeton University; Radcliffe Institute; and University of Virginia. In addition, I thank audiences at conferences sponsored by various research institutions for hearing me out, including at the American Philosophical Society, the British Academy, the Clark Library, the Huntington Library, the Institute for Advanced Studies (Princeton), and the Newberry Library.

Material from this project has previously appeared in print in the following venues: Michael Böhler et al., eds., *Republikanische Tugend: Ausbildung eines Schweizer Nationalbewusstseins und Erziehung eines neuen Bürgers* (Geneva: Slatkine, 2000); André Holenstein, Wim Blockmans, and Jon Mathieu, eds., *Empowering Interactions: Political Cultures and the Emergence of the State in Europe, 14th–19th Centuries* (Farnham: Ashgate, 2009); Robin Barnes and Marjorie Plummer, eds., *Ideas and Cultural Margins in Early Modern Germany: Essays in Honor of H. C. Erik Midelfort* (Aldershot: Ashgate, 2009); Karin Friedrich, ed., *Opening Spaces: Constructions, Visions and Depictions of Spaces and Boundaries in the Baroque* (Wiesbaden: Harrassowitz, 2014); Arndt Brendecke, ed., *Praktiken in der Frühe Neuzeit* (Cologne: Böhlau, 2015); Maria de Lurdes Rosa and Randolph C. Head, eds., *Rethinking the Archive in Pre-Modern Europe: Family Archives and Their Inventories from the 15th to 19th Century* (Lisbon: Instituto de Estudos Medievais, 2015); Anne Gilliland, Sue McKemmish, and Andrew Lau, eds., *Research in the Archival Multiverse* (Melbourne: Monash University Publishing, 2016); and Liesbeth Corens, Kate Peters, and Alexandra Walsham, eds., *Accessing the Past: Archives, Records and Early Modern History, Proceedings of the British Academy* (Oxford: Oxford University Press, 2018). I have also published articles related to this project in the *Journal of Modern History* (2003), *Archival Science* (2007), *The Historical Journal* (2013), and *European History Quarterly* (2016).

This project has required long absences from home for travel across the Atlantic and around Europe, as well as to many conferences and workshops. My entire family has helped bear these burdens. My mother was patient even when a fellowship took me away from Southern California just after she moved there, and has not only supported me but constantly expressed her fascination in the project and her pride in my work. Throughout it all, my partner and spouse Chih-Cheng Tsai undertook everything needed for me to get as far as I have. I dedicate this book to him.

1 Introduction
Records, Tools, and Archives in Europe to 1700

Records: Objects, Information, and Artificial Memory

Both the administration of states and the writing of history are possible only because of the human propensity for making and keeping records. As far back as we can trace, humans caught in the flow of time have made records about what they experienced, knew, or valued, using techniques that ranged from marks on bones and walls to the shared structures of mythical recitation.[1] Most significantly, our ancestors developed writing systems that could reproduce their words and ideas in persistent media. Among its many uses, writing from its earliest beginnings allowed the creation of *records* – that is, stable representations that could be activated later for the purposes of providing information and evidence.[2] Early record-making often took place during the management of property, goods, and relationships, and the resulting products were of particular interest to rulers and their agents in the pursuit of power.[3] It is records in this more limited sense, and their accumulation and organization in repositories that we now call archives, that are the focus of this book, particularly in Europe from about 1400 to about 1700. A short discussion of the epistemological, archaeological, and theoretical dimensions that such a study touches on may be useful before turning to specific historical evidence and its analysis.

As the primeval history sketched here suggests, not all records are written, and not all writings constitute records. It is rather the specific purpose of providing evidence about past circumstances for future situations that defines the record – and many different configurations of medium and information can fulfill this purpose. To quote the eighteenth-century Swiss scholar Salomon Hirzel in defining the related German term *Urkunde*:

---

[1] Delsalle, *Histoire,* 9–11.
[2] I owe the term "stable representations" to Yeo, "Concepts of Record (1)."
[3] Posner, *Archives*; Jan Assmann, *Cultural Memory.*

All proofs of actions that have taken place are called *Urkunden*. These are of many kinds, for the things that can prove that an action took place are very diverse. A coin, an inscribed column, a gravestone, the remnants of a building—all of these are witnesses to past actions.[4]

Given the right context, all sorts of phenomena can serve as evidence of past action, and thus serve as a record. Moreover, with the notable exception of oral and performative records, most records by their very nature combine materiality with information. Keeping both the informational and the material dimensions of records in sight is therefore vital, since each aspect has presented its own challenges for the transmission of records through time.

The study of archives resonates with the broader study of memory, both individual and cultural, but is not the same thing.[5] Whereas the investigation of cultural and social memory encompasses a wide variety of media, purposes, and channels by which societies have appropriated the past for present and future use, the study of archives narrows its focus in two ways. First, focusing on archives means concentrating on the accumulation and management of large numbers of records, rather than on individual records and what they conveyed. Second, an archival focus situates such accumulations of records as part of political and legal contention in particular circumstances and according to socially established rules. The term "archive" has a broad range of meanings today, but its genealogy lies firmly within the fields of political power, social authority, and practices of domination, as will be demonstrated at length in this book. Narrowing the field of analysis from the global theme of memory to the highly structured context of archival records (namely, those kept in pre-modern Europe), and to the even more specific question of how such records were preserved and made available to future users, puts the role of archival technologies in the history of Europe and its emerging states at the center of attention in what follows.

Developments since the Middle Ages have made it seem natural to us today that political institutions create, collect, and organize a wide variety of records about their world, their work, and us as their subjects. In reality, however, the emergence of such practices was itself one part of long and contingent processes of political transformation with many names – bureaucratization, the emergence of the modern state, the

---

[4] [Hirzel], "Versuch eines Plans," 37. The attribution of this anonymous text to Hirzel appears in Im Hof and de Capitani, *Die Helvetische Gesellschaft*, 1: 230.

[5] On memory, see Jan Assmann, *Cultural Memory*; Aleida Assmann, *Cultural Memory*, especially 327–43. On the memory in medieval European culture, see Carruthers, *The Book of Memory*.

intensification of dominion – that have drawn historians' attention at least since Leopold von Ranke, Max Weber, and others began defining and exploring them in the nineteenth century. Bureaucratization has occurred repeatedly in quite different global contexts, and record-keeping is just as much part of the history of China, India, the Islamic world, and beyond as it is part of the history of European politics. The material presented in this book addresses only the European case, primarily in the high medieval and early modern periods, which were characterized by rapid change in the volume of records produced and consequential developments in how rulers sought to preserve, organize, and use the resulting accumulations. In earlier medieval Europe, rulers had made limited (though very significant) use of writing as they administered their domains, even as writing and its associated technologies played a vital role in other spheres of medieval culture. In the later Middle Ages, however, "governance on the basis of knowledge" expanded very substantially.[6]

Even if this development was only one part of the changes that led toward modern European states, it represents a vital part whose multiple dimensions deserve close attention. When we look at how record-keeping practices evolved as European states expanded their investment in records and information management, we will see that the path from rare and precious documents hidden away in tightly locked treasuries to the ubiquitous piles of paper (not to mention accumulations of bits) that we experience today was far from simple. Understanding the history of record-keeping depends in part on understanding how states themselves emerged as a central player in political life.

Contemporaries already noted the growing salience of stored records during this period. In an oft-cited decree of 1456 that sought to improve the finances of Venice's secret chancellery, the city's Council of Ten described the chancellery and its records as *cor status nostri*, the heart of their state.[7] Similar expressions abounded by the later Middle Ages, especially in the writings of secretaries and chancellors seeking patronage and funding for their efforts among such accumulations of records. However, closer examination suggests that political leaders often attributed more value to their treasuries of charters and accumulations of administrative records than this material, and the staff responsible for it, could reliably deliver. Fantasies of complete information through

---

[6] The phrase from Max Weber cited in Stock, "Schriftgebrauch." On surveillance practices in early modern Europe, see Groebner, *Who Are You?*

[7] De Vivo, "Heart of the State," noting that the phrase conveyed fragility and dysfunction as well as centrality as the Council sought to bolster their staff.

effortless access to carefully indexed collections usually faced a reality in which disorderly masses of paper, parchment, and books were stuffed into bulging armoires or simply piled on the floor, leaving them vulnerable to fire, flood, and the depredations of rats (not to mention thieves). Nevertheless, the archival image of a collection of treasures persisted, and underpinned most of the efforts analyzed in this study.[8]

Historians, for their part, have been acutely aware of archives for as long as they have been drafting footnotes.[9] In the nineteenth century, Leopold von Ranke's turn away from chronicles and narrative sources and toward archival records as the most authentic source of knowledge about the political past reflected changes in historiography whose roots went back the Reformation, and launched a new discipline that thrived in parallel with the states it investigated.[10] More recently, after a century of work during which historians' faith in archives was reinforced by professional norms, the so-called historical turn and archival turn in the human sciences has increased awareness of archives' complexities among scholars in multiple disciplines – as has the digital revolution over the same decades, which has made archivists out of everyone, willy-nilly.[11] Still, though historians have been working in archives since at least the seventeenth century, and have been questioning how to use archives properly since the nineteenth century, only recently have they begun looking at archives as socially, culturally, and politically situated phenomena in themselves.[12] The chapters that follow take up this approach by looking at particular archives found across Europe from the end of the Middle Ages to the early eighteenth century, investigating and comparing their structure and practices, with particular attention being paid to the registers, inventories, and other finding aids.

Older views of the European Middle Ages sometimes posited an oral culture that only slowly gave way to literacy and written texts during the Renaissance.[13] More recently, medievalists have stressed that both medieval and early modern European cultures were fully literate – that is, written records played a vital role in the circulation of information and

---

[8] For more on the cultural trope of the archive in early modern Europe, see Navarro Bonilla, *La imagen.*

[9] Grafton, *The Footnote*, captures this development.

[10] Leopold von Ranke's programmatic statement to this effect from 1824 is still striking: *Zur Kritik.*

[11] The term "historical turn" gained currency with the publication of McDonald, *The Historic Turn.* On the archival turn, see Stoler, "Colonial Archives," especially 95, and Ketelaar, "Archival Turns."

[12] Recent overviews: Yale, "The History of Archives"; De Vivo, Guidi, and Silvestri, "Archival Transformations."

[13] Ong, *Orality*; Goody, *The Logic of Writing.*

the production of knowledge throughout our period.[14] What is relevant for our purposes is understanding changes in *how* writing was used at various times, by whom, and for what purposes.[15] While some scholars such as Michael Clanchy posit an overall trend "from memory to written record," which they support by exhaustive investigation of medieval documents, others such as Brian Stock have probed the uses of texts by different communities in ways that defy any simple divide between the oral and the literate.[16] Extensive studies of scholastic erudition as it consolidated after about 1100 demonstrate the central role that medieval Europeans assigned not only to writing, but also to the sophisticated analysis and manipulation of texts – developments with major ramifications for record-keeping as well.

The key purpose of this study is to explore from a comparative perspective the practices of record-keeping and record-finding that characterized chancelleries, registries, and similar institutions across Europe from the fifteenth to the eighteenth century. Broad statements about the growing power of written records will remain tenuous until we grasp how record-keepers actually worked, which depended significantly on the framing assumptions that grounded their approaches. "Knowledge is power" remains a vapid abstraction until we understand how actionable information could be produced from specific documents, and indeed which documents could even be found among overfilled chests and boxes. After all, secretaries' complaints about drowning in a sea of records were just as ubiquitous throughout the early modern period as were scholars' laments about too much knowledge.[17] If theories of political change imply that archives were a new source of political power and social capital, then we need to understand how archives evolved, and how they worked in a wide variety of situations, as undertaken in the case studies that follow.

Some Tools and Terminology

Certain terms will be ubiquitous in what follows, and therefore need at least a preliminary definition that takes account of the layers of meaning these terms possess in various disciplines. Along with historiography and

---

[14] Following Teuscher, *Lords' Rights*. Carruthers, *The Book of Memory*, 194, argues: "it will become clear during my discussion that the terms 'oral' and 'written' are inadequate categories for describing what actually went on in traditional composition."

[15] Peter Burke provides oversight on this debate from an early modern perspective: *Popular Culture* and *A Social History*.

[16] Canonical works include Clanchy, *From Memory*, and Stock, *The Implications of Literacy*.

[17] Blair, *Too Much to Know*.

historical ethnography, recent contributions from archival theory are particularly important in establishing such definitions. Although I have greatly benefited from many thinkers' contributions, the main purpose here is to lay out my own usage in what follows.[18] As I have already discussed memory, the first set of definitions concentrates on framing assumptions about the role of media and their configurations in European archival history, and on a pair of centrally important terms for formal record-keeping in Europe – namely, "information" and "proof." The second set of definitions turns to specific terms whose technical definitions derive primarily from archival science, although they also resonate with historians' language and with our broader culture. These latter terms include "document," "text," "record," "repository," and (as a first attempt) "archive" itself.

Information and Media

I treat political information (the genre of information most relevant to this study) as inherently relational and medial.[19] Recorded information is relational because it moves *within* systems of knowledge as one vital element that can emerge from texts in the context of human relationships. What counts as information depends on who is recording, circulating, or retrieving it, and on whose knowledge is, in consequence, informed by it.[20] Information in this sense therefore cannot be reified as something autonomously present or absent in a particular record. In a study that focuses on chancelleries and their practices, this requires that we attend to the techniques available to scribes for recording and organizing various kinds of information, their ability to read older records containing potential information, and the specific tasks that their masters gave them. As users and their needs changed, so did the information they found in chancellery records.[21] In regard to records and their use in the Middle Ages and early modern period, I will argue that one particular category of information from documents – namely, proofs – took a central and defining role.

---

[18] Recent archival theory will be discussed at more length in Chapter 2.

[19] Geoffrey Yeo's illuminating discussion of *Records, Information and Data* appeared after this book was complete, and offers a deeper analysis that I find very persuasive. On broad definitions of "information," see Zins, "Conceptual Approaches," and Brown and Duguid, *The Social Life*.

[20] In Peter Burke's terms, "The classic trinity of problems – gathering, storing and employing information – needs to be subdivided and above all personalized. Historians need to investigate who stores what, loses what, stores where, classifies how, makes accessible to whom, hides what from whom, uses for what purpose and so on" (Burke, "Commentary," 391).

[21] Demonstrated over the *longue durée* in Hildbrand, *Herrschaft*.

Equally, all record-keeping depends on, and is therefore shaped by, the communications media available in a particular context.[22] In any given medium, moreover, human users inscribe and recover information only by relying on shared, culturally specific forms. I define such medial forms as stable technical ensembles that actors in a particular period and region employed when creating records. Different medial forms allowed information to be inscribed differently, and the characteristics of a particular medium – voice, parchment, or paper; icon, text, or image – constrained how (or if) information might be recalled or reconveyed in the future. The practices involved in inscribing political information, and in seeking information from the resulting products, evolved continually in tandem with changes in the larger political world as a changing *gestalt*. In late medieval and early modern Europe, key medial forms included parchment, paper, ink, boxes, sacks, codices, rolls, seals, and so forth. For contrast, one can look at the clay tablet, stylus, and syllabic–ideographic writing of the Ancient Mesopotamian world as another medial *gestalt*, or the bamboo strips inscribed with ideographs of the Ancient Chinese tradition. But while medial forms enable and constrain record-making and record-keeping for any particular society and era, they do not provide differentiating features when looking at archives *within* that society and era, since they tend to be widely shared, and innovations in their use tend to diffuse rapidly. For example, a tradition that employs the medial form of hanging seals will not tightly bundle documents – you cannot bundle the seals – but this constraint will operate throughout the historical environment in which hanging seals are prevalent, rather than distinguishing cases within that space. In northern Europe, the hanging seal was most relevant in the High and Late Middle Ages, leading to the emergence everywhere of archival spaces organized by chests or drawers in which documents could be laid loose. When nonsealed records took on greater salience, however, the fact that these materials could be bundled tightly with string led to a shift to bound or bundled documents, leaving behind the awkward sealed originals as a differentiated subgroup rather than as the core form of stored record.

As this example suggests, basic medial forms created shared practices that founded and supported various specific and fluid medial configurations. In contrast to medial forms, which represent a common resource in any historical moment, medial configurations at various levels of abstraction are critical to understanding *differences* in how records are stored and organized over time. Medial configurations crucial in Europe

---

[22] See Head, "Configuring European Archives."

Table 1.1 *Medial forms underlying medieval and early modern European archives*

Fundamental medial forms occur in various functional realms, including inscription, authentication, methods of gathering multiple records, and technologies for stable storage. The lists in this table are suggestive rather than comprehensive.

Production: paper, parchment, ink, alphabetic writing
Authentication: signatures by issuers and witnesses, seals, signets, notarial signs, chirographs
Multiple-record collocations: rolls, codices, quires, strung groups (*filae*, files), piles
Spatial units of storage: boxes, sacks, strings, armoires, rooms

included, for example, specific practices of *mise-en-page* and *mise-en-livre*, which shaped how a codex could be deployed in an archive; the specific practices and the resulting formation of bundles, *Konvolute*, *liasses*, *legajos*, and other forms of noncodical gathering; and so forth. These configurations and others are discussed in detail in the case studies later. In contrast to the stability of the underlying medial forms, such configurations, I have found, display great heterogeneity across early modern Europe, such that they provide useful comparative tools for differentiating cases and for understanding the practices in play within a given case.[23]

The European discipline of diplomatics founded by Jean Mabillon works with a characteristic set of medial forms and configurations that will be familiar to any student of European history. Table 1.1 includes key medial forms relevant across late medieval and early modern European record-keeping, grouped according to various aspects such as record-making, authentication, storage, and forms of gathering.

These medial forms all appeared ubiquitously across Europe after about 1200, with variations that reflected specific micro-practices in use at particular moments. Often, such micro-practices then remained fossilized within collections – as in the stitching of documents into a roll or in the sewing of particular material into quires – even as new practices emerged to shape the production of subsequent archival material.

Moving from forms to medial configurations, Table 1.2 suggests some specific configurations that form a basis for comparative analysis across European cases. None, to be sure, was exclusive to Europe, and all, with

---

[23] Obviously, no a priori line can distinguish medial forms from medial configurations: Depending on the context, one can place phenomena in either category. Thus, these terms are heuristics for distinguishing which medial features matter for a particular agenda.

Table 1.2 *Common medial configurations in European archives*

Medial configurations can be distinguished within every functional area of the medial and communications technologies in use in a record-keeping system. Relevant functional areas include the core realms distinguished in Table 1.1, but also extend to all other aspects of record-making, record-keeping, and record-using that follow regular structures or forms. As in Table 1.1, the possibilities listed here are suggestive, not exhaustive.

Document genres: privilege, letter, missive, report, and so on
Codex genres: registers, cartularies, bound documents, copybooks, inventories
Mise-en-livre tools: page, opening, folio numbers, sections, tabs, hard or soft bindings, and
  so on
Mise-en-page tools: running heads, blocks, columns, marginal rubrics, bold text, pointers,
  initials, illumination, and so on
Grouping and labeling tools: icons, alphanumeric signs, spatial algorithms; cases,
  storerooms, vaults, towers, and so on
Spatial organizing tools: numbered space, lettered space, named space, ideal-topographic
  spaces, and so on
Organizational practices: alphabetization; chronological ordering; mirroring between
  material and finding aids, and so on

equal certainty, need to be contextualized in relation to the larger circuits of communication and power that produced them (and which we today deduce *from* them). A number of them have long been the subject of formal disciplines such as diplomatics, archivistics, sigillography, and the like, and have therefore been explored and cataloged in loving detail by previous generations of scholars. Viewing them as culturally specific configurations rather than as universal archival forms does not devalue this earlier work, although it may require us to adapt the conclusions we draw. Such configurations exist at multiple levels of abstraction and are usually highly contingent, flexible, and dynamic, as the cases in this book demonstrate. They could be combined and recombined in many ways, leading to very specific local practices, which in turn led to equally diverse practices of placing and finding documents.

The employment of stable medial forms and flexible configurations remains deeply connected to how each society understands the relationships among writing, memory, and power. The way officials collect records has always rested on their understandings of human communication, human obligation, and the reproduction of a culture through time. Clay tablets or inscriptions on stone generated different approaches than did parchment, paper, or thumbnail drives. Moreover, record-keeping in societies using paper and ink can still vary profoundly, as even a brief look at Chinese, Islamic, and European modes of keeping (or not keeping) various records demonstrates. Treating specific repositories as growing out of the interplay of fluid medial configurations therefore helps us understand each repository's characteristics in comparison to others, near and far, and accordingly highlights the implications of organized records for governance in the past and for historical research today.

Attention to mediality also reminds us how *little* actually reached the archives in pre-modern Europe. All sorts of information circulated in medieval and early modern courts – and often also through courtyards, print shops, coffeehouses, and boudoirs. Communication often took place in oral, performative, or textual forms without ever leaving a record in a political chancellery. Consequently, what we find in archives is neither a complete nor an unbiased representation of the information that actors at the time encountered. Entirely aside from the issue of selective preservation of documents over time, political archives were radically limited in their information content even during their formation.[24] As Arndt Brendecke argues,

The knowledge that shaped pre-modern political and social praxis must doubtless be sought primarily outside of libraries and archives. Such knowledge was carried by persons, was guarded and transmitted by families, workers, and guilds, was constituted through conversations at table or in court, and remained embedded in practices that scarcely required written form … the relationship between knowledge within and without an archive must be determined, not simply in quantitative terms but rather in respect to their status and their operative significance within everyday politics.[25]

We must therefore attend with particular care to the capacities and intentions of those who produced or preserved information in written form – and equally to the abilities and intentions of those who sought information from archival records.

Proof and Forensic Thinking in Europe

A particularly salient dimension of records in the minds of medieval and early modern practitioners of record-keeping lay in their culturally conditioned capacity to provide proof (in the forensic sense of testimony or evidence, including as part of formal adjudication) about circumstances in the past. As Chapter 3 will argue, Europeans' conceptualization of public record-keeping revolved around such proofs, and specifically around text-bearing objects intended to provide perpetual memory of the authentic and consequential acts of rulers and other authorities

[24] On selective preservation, see Esch, "Überlieferungs-Chance," especially 51–3.
[25] Brendecke, *"Arca, Archivillo, Archivo,"* 268.

(however fictional the acts, and however fluid the ways such acts were interpreted across time). The quintessential act to be memorialized, as the European political economy emerged out of its post-Roman antecedents, was the granting of a privilege – a transfer of authority over people, places, or other things of value from a higher authority to a lower-placed recipient. Other memorialized acts, such as verdicts, treaties, and contracts, also played important roles in the emerging European culture of proof and found documentary forms that allowed them to become recorded for future use. European legists and scribes adapted the Roman genre of the *instrument* to memorialize such acts. They adapted both written forms and social and visual forms of authentication (such as witness lists, seals, and signatures) in producing elaborate parchment objects (such as charters and diplomas) that carried out important political work through their creation, and that could be reactivated textually or performatively in future contestations. Such instruments, in turn, became the foundations of the earliest European archives.[26] A full theory of documentary acts in this context – one that relates how objects and their texts operated culturally and legally, independently though often in connection with speech acts as identified by John Austin and the subsequent philosophical tradition – would surely contribute to our understanding of the shifting terms under which documents were deployed.[27] For this project, it suffices to recognize that records in archives were always part of larger legal and political contexts that changed according to their own trajectories of development.

Archival Terminology

When we turn to the study of actual accumulations of records that have survived from the past and of the finding tools created to manage them, the vocabulary of archival science provides relatively precise terms that distinguish different aspects of the material involved. The terminology involved is primarily modern, so it must be employed with care in discussing circumstances from the Middle Ages to the eighteenth century. Nevertheless, the clarity and consistency of this terminology help ensure stability across comparisons and across disciplines, and I have

---

[26] *Black's Law Dictionary* (2nd ed., 1910) (https://thelawdictionary.org/instrument/) defines an instrument as "Anything which may be presented as evidence to the senses of the adjudicating tribunal." On the historiography of early medieval instruments, see Koziol, *The Politics of Memory.*

[27] Smith, "Document Acts"; on speech-act theory in archival science, see Yeo, *Records,* especially chapter 6; Hentonnen, "Looking"; from a European medieval perspective, see Bedos-Rezak "Towards an Archaeology"; see also Patrick Geary, "Entre gestion."

been as methodical as possible in applying these terms in the same way throughout this project. It is worth noting that this terminology often does not translate well across European languages: German lacks a clear parallel to the term "record," for example, since *Aufzeichnung* conveys both more and less; likewise, the word "archive" itself covers different semantic fields across languages, not to mention the very substantial changes in meaning it has experienced through time.[28] The terms defined in this section are thus artificially precise compared to general usage at any time since the fourteenth century. Nevertheless, establishing a coherent set of terms is particularly important when evidence in multiple languages and from multiple periods is involved.

In this book, *record* is a broad term used to describe any trace of past action that is produced in some medial form. Such traces could also be reproduced, which allowed them to circulate, accumulate, or evaporate. Written records took physical form through the conjunction of a material substrate, specific medial forms, and a linguistic text. The combination of these elements was a *document* – that is, a material object inscribed with meaning-generating signs, in contrast to an abstract trace of memorialized knowledge. Records in Europe became documents in diverse ways: as original charters, as authenticated or non-authenticated reproductions, as register entries in manuscript books, or as loci in later published collections. Single records were routinely transmediated into multiple documents, usually by reproduction of their *text* (a string of symbols used in writing) into a new medium, although records can also be transmediated as printed or digital images. For example, a medieval record inscribed as a single-leaf charter could be reproduced as a manuscript textual copy in a late medieval cartulary, which could be edited for publication in a nineteenth-century printed book, which is now digitized as scanned images in a research repository.[29]

Depending on the media and modes of reproduction involved, subtractions or additions to what was originally recorded inevitably take place when a record migrates from one medium or document to another. In addition, reproduction changes records' communicative context, since the documentary surroundings of a record (materially, visually, and in who possessed it) were, and are, often as important as the actual text for shaping a record's meaning. Not all medieval and early modern records and the documents that carried them were equal, moreover: Some were carefully preserved and zealously guarded, whereas others might function as traces, memories, or proofs for a shorter or longer

---

[28] Ketelaar, "The Difference."
[29] See Saxer, "Archival Objects," on transmediation of this kind.

time, then be discarded without hesitation. Some records were kept secret and hidden; others were engraved into wooden, metal, or stone tablets and publicly displayed.

Archives, as the term is used in this project, were loci for the collection and preservation of records in diverse documentary forms.[30] The word "archive" did not come into common use until the sixteenth century. It found only scattered use in medieval circumstances, and even after 1500, its meaning was far from stable. To distinguish a major divide in the implications of the term, as originally observed by Robert-Henri Bautier in an influential 1968 article, I use two different forms of the word to describe two distinct ideal types of records repository in what follows: the Latin word *archivum* for what Bautier calls the "treasury of charters," and *archive* for what Bautier calls the "arsenal of authority."[31] In the Middle Ages and well into the early modern period, various institutions designated an accumulation of particularly valuable instruments as a treasury.[32] *Archivum* will be used to refer to accumulations of records understood this way, with the additional observation that their possession was not necessarily connected with the exercise of public authority (given that public authority itself was diffuse in medieval Europe). Often located in the sacristy of a monastery's church or of a town's cathedral or preserved for a royal house in a convent dedicated by their family, an *archivum* was above all a place to preserve precious objects – specifically, documents bearing records that could serve as proofs – that found relatively infrequent active use. Such *archivia* might also contain other precious documentary and nondocumentary objects, such as relics, coins, flags, and other objects of value. Even the documentary objects in actual *archivia* could be heterogeneous, including sacred books, documents with ceremonial or ritual functions, chronicles, and a wide variety of additional material.

Never were all preserved records kept in such treasuries, however. Indeed, as the Middle Ages moved into the early modern period, more and more records found other homes of quite different character, notably

---

[30] Definitional questions are addressed in Lepper and Raulff, "Erfindung," and more briefly in Delsalle, *Histoire*. *Archive* versus *archives* has additional implications in various contexts, but the distinction between the meanings of the singular and the plural is not stable across disciplines or countries, and plays no role here.

[31] Bautier, "La phase cruciale," 140. For a critique of Bautier's periodization, see Friedrich, *The Birth*, 12–14. I view Bautier's phases as overlapping ideal types, rather than distinct periods.

[32] Potin, "Entre trésor," documents how treasuries of records resembled the other French royal treasuries of the fourteenth century.

as resources preserved for the use and information of public authorities. I call such repositories *archives*, as long as they fulfilled one important definitional characteristic: Whereas any person or institution could accumulate records, such an accumulation became archival in early modern terms only to the extent that its possessor exercised some form of dominion.[33] In the High and Late Middle Ages, many individuals, families, and institutions participated in dominion, which produced a correspondingly dense archival landscape by 1500. With the rise of centralized states claiming sovereignty in the sixteenth century, a long struggle over the authenticity and authority of many repositories began, with officials seeking to seize or copy many collections in the territories they ruled, while subjects often resisted such appropriation.[34]

Archives in this second sense frequently overlapped with or grew out of the treasuries I call *archivia*, and could be extraordinarily heterogeneous in their contents, political value, and organization. The term "archives" from the outset applied to three distinct aspects of such repositories: to the documents themselves, to the institution and personnel under whose control they rested, and to the building or space dedicated to their preservation. Many political authorities possessed material conforming to the ideal type of an *archivum* around 1300, but soon accumulated additional material in their chancelleries or in storerooms, basements, or attics that began to form an archive. As traced through the cases presented in this book, these diffuse and heterogeneous collections of material, and the evolving political institutional contexts around them, generated incentives to improve their organization and disposition. Further developments after the sixteenth and seventeenth centuries eventually transformed the concept of archive further, turning the term into a designation for a body of material that was no longer in use but which a political authority wanted to keep for (often poorly conceptualized) future purposes. Particularly in the Germanic world by 1700, the archive in this latter, narrower sense was distinguished from the registry (*Registratur*). After 1700, the archive as dead-storage was often combined with remaining *archivia* to form a new kind of state archive; as an example, such a step took place during the founding of the Habsburg *Haus-, Hof- und Staatsarchiv* in the late 1740s.

---

[33] My research has led me to move away from a universal definition of an archive – a more-or-less ordered intentional collection of documents believed to be important, as I wrote in 2007 – and toward a definition that takes greater account of European legal and material expectations. See Head, "Mirroring Governance," 318.

[34] For example, Soll, *The Information Master*; Menne, "Confession."

Archival Knowledge in Europe, 1400–1700

Three specific questions underlie this book's approach to *archivia* and archives in early modern Europe. First, how did political actors and those charged with keeping political records understand the material in their possession? What purposes could it serve, why was it worth preserving, and what priorities existed in making it findable through new instruments such as inventories or spatial reorganization? Second, how did record-keepers actually organize the materials they had, and the knowledge implicitly present in their collections? What resources could they draw on to improve their ability to find documents (as material objects) and information (contained in the form and texts of such objects)? How did their changing strategies for making records usable reflect changes in the larger political world, and in the world of learning? Third, what consequences did the organizational strategies available to secretaries at various times and places have for political life, and how did these evolve over the early modern period? How did debates over the authenticity and authority of old documents, particularly as these peaked in the later seventeenth century, reframe the emergence of intensified state record-keeping systems before the revolutionary transformation of governance during the eighteenth and nineteenth centuries?

Because the growth of archives after 1400 was a Europe-wide phenomenon, a comparative approach using evidence from many different parts of the subcontinent offers the best path to answering these questions. The legal and political systems of Western and Central Europe shared many political and legal principles throughout the medieval and early modern periods, which left comparable marks on their archival practices, despite local and regional variations. Conducting research on such a broad geographical and temporal scale, however, also required limiting the scope of material that is included. After all, written records accumulated in repositories from Lisbon to Lvov in a vast variety of forms, for multiple purposes, and at different rates, creating a landscape of evidence available today that extends far beyond the reach of any single researcher. For this reason, the discussion here narrows its focus in several ways.

First, this entire study concentrates only on chancellery archives, leaving out at least three major alternative areas of document accumulation: financial records, judicial records, and ecclesiastical records. While the latter three categories appear occasionally, they are not themselves part of the analysis conducted here.

Second, this book concentrates primarily on evidence about how accumulations of political and administrative records were organized. Rather than looking at masses of documents directly, the key sources invoked will be inventories, finding aids, architectural features of repositories, organizational frameworks of storage areas, and similar kinds of evidence.

Finally, this book rests on a finite number of case studies. The core cases are built on in-person research conducted in Lisbon, Seville, Simancas, multiple Swiss archives, Innsbruck, Vienna, Würzburg, Leiden, and the Hague, along with engagement with additional literature. After careful consideration, I did not include primary cases from Italy or from England, each of which offers massive quantities of surviving records, but each of which also involves important structural differences from the core Continental cases I chose. Other European regions, such as Eastern Europe and Scandinavia, perforce remained outside my purview owing to the languages involved.

The book approaches the core questions in four major sections. Part I, "The Work of Records (1200–)," examines the political and cultural ends that their possessors imagined for the records accumulating in their chancelleries, and the organizational tools they created in their efforts (often futile) to reach those ends. Most rulers saw their repositories, whether stored safely in a monastery or carried in sacks along the pathways of itinerant kingship, as providing proof of their legitimacy and evidence about the privileges they had given or received. Towns, monasteries, and nobles across Europe, in turn, saw the chests of charters (genuine or forged) that they kept in their sacristies or town halls as treasuries from which they could draw when a ruler or neighbor made demands on them, or bring to the king's court in defense of their rights. Everyone involved echoed the conviction that their records provided "perpetual memory" of important acts. The great challenge for such paper and parchment memory, however, is that documents are all too easily lost or forgotten, especially as the volume of records increases. In consequence, as Chapter 3 argues, secretaries serving rulers and town councils began organizing records, often by reproducing them, summarizing them, or listing them in new documents that served as finding aids to help future users understand what was held and how it might be retrieved. As a generation of brilliant scholarship by medievalists has shown, the tools of medieval book-learning, particularly the vast work of organizing older knowledge that we call Scholasticism, became a key resource. Secretaries drew on Scholastic techniques as they created new books of various genres, such as the cartulary and the emissions register, that enabled them to find the proofs their masters sought. Chapter 4 turns to a late and particularly splendid example of these book technologies at work in the Lisbon royal chancellery – namely, a project that commenced in 1460 and culminated in a sumptuous set of parchment registers created between 1504 and the 1550s.

Yet proofs were always only a subset of the information that rulers and others sought from records. Particularly when the adoption of paper drastically lowered the cost of records production in the fourteenth century, European chancelleries began recording information in many documentary forms, as discussed in Chapter 5. Although proofs remained paramount, secretaries actually worked with mounting masses of information, mostly on paper and taking many different forms: letters to and from diplomats and other rulers, bodies of statutes and regulations, evidence from investigations and inquests, lists of rights, lists of income and other property, reports from subordinate officers, and many more. The Scholastic tools they had already adopted provided ways to bring order to the material accumulating in chancelleries, and also offered innovative administrators a way to proactively shape the flow of written communication into forms that made it easier to capture, index, and store for systematic access. Research on ecclesiastical inquisitions, particularly the great Inquisition launched against the Cathars in southern France after 1220, is particularly illuminating in showing how scribes learned to use books to gather and organize information. The resulting techniques flowed into secular administration over the following centuries, since clerics served as scribes for many princes, and since Inquisitors' handbooks circulated widely around Europe. Chapter 6 illustrates how secular administrations could manage information just after 1500 through a detailed analysis of a project contemporaneous with, but quite different from, the impressive Lisbon registers – namely, the information-tracking system established in Innsbruck in 1523.

Part II, "The Challenges of Accumulation (1400–)," comprises Chapters 7 through 10 and turns specifically to the techniques and conceptual models that chancelleries adapted or invented to cope with the increasing flood of documents entering or leaving their doors. The chapters look closely at organizational models and specific finding aids created in various sites across Europe after 1350. Chapter 7 tracks the evolution of inventories, including approaches such as listing, alphabetization, and the mapping of concepts to spaces, as secretaries and a new species of functionary, the registrator, created finding tools for the material they held. The remarkable inventory created in Paris by Gérard de Montaigu in the 1370s provides insights into these later medieval medial tools. Montaigu left a precious description of his efforts, which reveals that most of the fundamental principles of organization found in archives through the 1700s were already available at this point.

Chapter 8 examines two large inventory projects carried out in the first half of the sixteenth century, each the life's work of its primary author. In the first case, Wilhelm Putsch took on the *Schatzgewölbe* (treasure-vaults) of the Habsburg family in Austria, creating massive multivolume inventories for tens of thousands of documents, first in Innsbruck and then in Vienna. Meanwhile, his contemporary Lorenz Fries in Würzburg addressed the heterogeneous and spatially dispersed record collections of the Prince-Bishops of Würzburg by developing a remarkable interlinked structure of chancellery books and carefully organized armoires, all made accessible through an encyclopedic index known as the *Hohe Registratur.* Each of these two functionaries reconfigured basic media tools already well known by Montaigu into startlingly powerful finding aids to large masses of documents – though each system also had distinctive weaknesses, as we shall see.

Chapters 9 and 10 turn to a different approach to organizing records: classification of records on the basis of their pertinence or content. Whereas the inventories in Chapter 8 illuminated bodies of records that were already stored, classification sought to structure repository space and the corresponding finding aids so that knowledge about the world could be translated into algorithms for finding relevant records. My analysis builds on the brilliant work of Peter Rück from the 1970s about classification and archival topography, particularly in Savoy in the 1440s. It addresses a series of logically distinct approaches to classification, from the segmented list (which divided material into content-oriented subgroups), through systems of mapping archival spaces against categories in the real world, and finally the emergence of systems that used logical taxonomies of state functions as a template for the placement of records in storage. The way that these approaches to classification could be deployed, combined, and adapted to different political contexts is examined in Chapter 10, which uses multiple cases from the Swiss Confederation after 1500 to illustrate the flexibility and power of early modern record classification.

The evidence in Part II makes clear that record-keeping practices were shifting in complex ways from the late Middle Ages into the sixteenth century. Internally, the growing volume of stored records created incentives to organize spaces and deploy finding aids; externally, growing expectations on the part of rulers, judges, and other political actors affected the strategies that archivists employed. Working together, these forces led to ongoing differentiations of chancellery functions, of record-keeping genres, and of repository spaces, creating a more complex landscape. In case after case, secretaries responded not only by reconfiguring and recombining the basic repertory of tools on which they continued to depend, but also by forming these tools into systems that they hoped would meet the rising external expectations they faced.

Part III, "Comprehensive Visions and Differentiating Practices (1550–)," turns to the interaction of rising expectations and new resources, using the contemporary German term "registry" (*Registratur*) to define the more systemic approaches to stored records that emerged in this period. Chapter 11 presents two case studies of archives established to meet new rulers' demands: the royal archive in Simancas founded by Charles V Habsburg but fully developed after 1560 by his son Philip II in Spain, and the Berlin archive of the Electors of Brandenburg as reestablished in the 1590s. In each of these cases, a history of record-keeping failure drove rulers to invest in new facilities and new staff. Philip's project was by far the most ambitious knowledge management initiative yet seen in Europe, comprising not only the Simancas fortress but also the library at the Escorial and additional organizational nodes in Lisbon, Barcelona, Naples, and Rome. Money and records poured into Simancas, where Diego de Ayala tried to create systems for preserving the realm's most precious proofs in a beautiful and fortified *archivum*, but equally for responding to the king and to private litigants whom the king authorized by providing testimony about past disputes. The Simancas experiment quickly overreached its own capacities, however, and was largely dysfunctional by 1630. In Berlin, a much more modest program survived both the tumult of the Thirty Years' War and the lack of overarching systematic goals, perhaps because of the archive's consistent tight association with the Electorate's most important administrative site, the Secret Council.

Chapter 12 reviews systems of registry, defined by their focus on records' place in the administrative process, under diverse European circumstances. In German and Dutch cities, the early development of book-form protocols as an administrative tool shaped one path of development, since protocols inherently organized records according to the flow of deliberation and decision making. A closer look at the city of Leiden in the late sixteenth century shows how additive improvement to urban book-form records could lead to full-fledged registries with accession and transmission journals for record-tracking. The chapter then turns to the similar evolutionary development of a document-tracking registry in Innsbruck after 1564. Centered on careful registration, storage, and indexing that tracked the flow of loose records in many genres, the Innsbruck *Hofregistratur* operated smoothly for more than a century, yet also displayed characteristic weak points that became more burdensome over time. A look forward to registry systems as they evolved over the eighteenth and nineteenth centuries closes out this section of the book.

Starting in the late sixteenth century, the long dominance of the probative record in thinking about archives and written memory finally began to yield to other perspectives. Part IV, "Rethinking Records and State Archives (1550–)," tracks changes in how records were conceptualized after 1550, leading to a series of debates among jurists and antiquarians about the value and authenticity of the records found in archives and beyond. In

Chapter 13, I describe the radical new methods proposed by Jacob von Ramingen, who in 1571 published Europe's first explicit guides to registry. Ramingen's background lay in the revindication of feudal rights in the Holy Roman Empire, which paralleled the emergence of specialists in feudal records in other regions such as Portugal and France. His books, which were later adapted into a comprehensive manual by Georg Aebbtlin in the 1660s, provided a guide to the purpose and structure of effective registries and archives, while also insisting that each secretary and registrator had to adapt to the particular situation he found.

The second half of the chapter provides a sample investigation into how archival records could be read and interpreted in the early seventeenth century, using a sustained dispute among members of the Swiss Confederation as a case study. The Zurich chancellery adopted, one after the other, three quite different ways of gathering evidence relevant to a single key document, the Swiss *Landfrieden* (Religious Peace) of 1531. For most of the sixteenth century, the city treated the *Landfrieden* as proof of a generally known act by the Confederates. Later, when its rivals began deploying particular sections of the document's text in new ways, the city first sought to record oral testimony as a counterweight, but ultimately returned to the document itself as a text open to hermeneutical dissection that could shift the meaning of its words. The analysis of this case study shows the potential of investigating the use of archival documents in the early modern period, an important current research desideratum.

Chapter 14 focuses on a highly consequential divergence in thinking about records that took place in the late seventeenth century. On one side, debates over the authenticity of Europe's oldest records, the diplomata of the Merovingian and Carolingian periods, led the Bollandist collectors of saints' lives in Belgium and the Benedictine monk Jean Mabillon in Paris to develop a new philological approach to authenticating old records and identifying forgeries. By concentrating on the physical and textual signs that could prove each individual document to be genuine, this approach put archival transmission and authorization in the background. At the same time, several little-known German jurists were developing a detailed theory of archival law (*ius archivi*) that drew on neo-Roman principles to argue that documents' authority depended above all on the kind of repository in which they currently rested. While not inattentive to the seals, notarizations, and other signs of authenticity, the *ius archivi* writers gave the highest credibility to the possessor's sovereignty. Indeed, they denied that anyone not sovereign could even maintain an archive, as opposed to a mere chest of records.

The distinction that emerged around 1700 between philological and institutional approaches to authenticating records ultimately generated two separate disciplines. On the one hand, diplomatics emerged, which combined the Baroque fascination with antiquities with the rigorous philological methods laid out by Mabillon. Diplomatics represented an important applied science as long as the *Ancien Régime* persisted, as Markus Friedrich has shown, but remained extremely useful for the emerging discipline of historiography as a so-called auxiliary science that could authenticate the all-important sources. On the other hand, the *ius archivi* provided a prototype for the authority of state archives in the eighteenth and especially nineteenth centuries, as Elio Lodolini argues, and thus influenced archivistics (more recently redefined as archival science) as a discipline whose primary zone of application lay in administration. Chapter 14 thus outlines one source of distinctions that resonated in complex ways with both the evolving European states and the evolving discipline of history.

The path summarized here begins with Chapter 3. Before diving into that exploration, Chapter 2 provides further discussion of the scholarly literature on the history of archives, including older legal and administrative histories as well as the traditional archival history carried out primarily by working archivists. A revolution in archival science that began in the 1980s – derived in part from post-structuralist theory's energetic appropriation of the category archive in the work of Michel Foucault and Jacques Derrida – spurred archivists' interest in archives as social and cultural phenomena. Work by archival scientists and archival theorists in this later period converged with the concerns of a new generation of historians, also influenced by post-structuralism, who began questioning the way historians treated archives as sites of research practice without any history of their own. Over the last thirty years, a lively body of research has emerged to which this book is intended to contribute. Chapter 2 ends by considering some additional research desiderata. Most importantly, the time is ripe for a comparative approach to archival history that is not limited to Europe, and that recognizes the cultural contingency of the key categories involved, starting with archive itself. I propose the term *archivality* as a way to acknowledge the significant contributions of work on European record-keeping while opening the door to comparisons that do not take European approaches as either self-evident or paradigmatic. In addition, closer connections with the history of information, the history of communication, and the history of scholarly practice are essential to advance our understanding of how European and others made, kept, and particularly used records, as innovative recent work by medievalists has shown. We are beginning to understand the way archives have contributed to changes in governance, knowledge, and relationships with the past in Europe, but much remains to be done in this exciting field of research.

2   Archival History
Literature and Outlook

Introduction

The selective evidentiary base of this study, comprising archival finding tools and evidence about organizational schemes, relates to a surprisingly broad range of fields, ranging from hermeneutics (how do documents found knowledge and transmit information?) and legal history (how do legal theories and practices coevolve with legal record-keeping to produce authentic evidence?) to political sociology (what roles do record-keeping staff and institutions play in political change?) and the anthropology of institutional cultures (how did performative practices shape the meaning conveyed by stored records?).[1] In addition, any history of archives draws intensively on a series of specialized disciplines formerly designated (misleadingly) as the auxiliary sciences of history; these include diplomatics, archivistics, book history with its various subdivisions, and more. These many connections mean that the relevant scholarly literature is voluminous and diffuse: A systematic treatment would require a book in itself. Nevertheless, a review of some key bodies of prior research that help frame the research trajectory found here is essential. In addition, since archival history is a surprisingly new subfield in current historiography, a wide variety of approaches and questions remain open for additional investigation, and indeed for formulation and definition; I address some of particular interest in the second part of this chapter.[2]

The Literatures of Archival History

Scholarly research in the history of archives has been conditioned since the nineteenth century by two ways that both scholars and political

---

[1] "If the question of the political ideas [behind archives] is posed, then fundamental conceptions are involved of justice, memory, speech, comprehension, identity and property, of the public and the private" (Lepper and Raulff, "Erfindung," 2).

[2] For an exposition of key methodological assumptions on comparison, see Head, "A Comparative Case-Study Approach."

practitioners have looked at archives (in Robert-Henri Bautier's formulation): as "arsenals of authority" for national states, on the one hand,
and as "historians' laboratories," on the other hand.[3] This split can be
seen in the durable separation between archivists' handbooks – many
with considerable historical content – and historians' narrative accounts
of political contention and change. It also appears in the way that historical writing has either treated archival history as an element of source
criticism or else relegated discussions of archival history to the subfields
of legal history and the history of administration. Such relegation, while
founded on real connections among archives, law, and administration,
has meant that most historians have paid relatively little attention to how
archives came to be and how they changed over time. Yet as suggested in
Chapter 1, archival history can provide important insights for understanding not just political but also cultural change; its implications for
history writing, meanwhile, go far beyond providing source-critical perspectives on the individual documents that historians find and use for
other projects. Only in the 1980s and 1990s did simultaneous developments in historiography and in archival science change the terrain for
histories of archives, opening up new pathways for understanding archives both as fascinating historical phenomena in their own right and as
phenomena whose history had major epistemological consequences for
historians.

Early Scholarship by Historians

Before World War I, a generation of European scholars meticulously
probed the administrative history of late medieval chancelleries, compiling ordinances and carefully studying the process by which charters were
authorized and issued. Similarly, throughout the nineteenth and twentieth centuries, scholars of the law probed historical aspects of adjudication, including how courts treated charters and other documents as
evidence. The resulting research, while profoundly erudite, generally
embodies several assumptions about the worlds it studies that require
considerable caution on the part of modern readers. First, most of this
research equated the administrative practices of the Late Middle Ages
and early modern period with those found in post-1815 states that
employed rationalistic methods in an elaborate administrative apparatus.
Until destabilized by Max Weber's brilliant critical analyses of how the
administrative practices of governance were in themselves profoundly

---

[3] Bautier, "La phase cruciale."

cultural and social phenomena, much of this work treated prescriptive documents such as chancellery ordinances as descriptions of real administration, and silently assumed that pre-modern chancellery secretaries resembled the selfless state servants idealized in nineteenth-century Prussia.[4] Similarly, the school of German legal history whose enormous output is enshrined in the three series of the *Zeitschrift für Rechtsgeschichte*, founded in 1861, and its equivalents in France and Italy, treated medieval and early modern courts as sites for rational adjudication that followed statutes and used evidence in ways that corresponded to nineteenth-century ideals about law and reason.

The evidence gathered in this extensive literature, while of great value for a study of pre-modern paperwork, must therefore be used with caution so as not to import its governing assumptions along with the material it analyzes. The issue is not that administrative functions did not exist before the Enlightenment, or that courts from the twelfth to the eighteenth centuries did not, by their own lights, apply reason in considering evidence. Rather, it is the unhesitating assimilation of such phenomena in all their complexity to later ideals that threatens to distort our understanding of what it meant to use an archive in Europe before 1800. One core assumption during my own investigation of European archives has been that governance, including governance by means of paper and writing, is a culturally embedded process in which institutions embody cultural assumptions rather than eliminating them. When using the work of authors such as Delaborde, Fellner, and Kretschmayer, or the *Archiv für Urkundenforschung* school in Berlin, one must also attend to the selectivity of such work's evidentiary choices, which implicitly naturalize certain views about the phenomena under study, as well as to their attribution of modern administrative ideals to actors set in performative, symbolic, and political contexts for which administrative efficiency was often only a minor issue.

Older Archivistics and Archival Science

A second body of older research also provides great value to the comparative study of European archives – namely, the long tradition of scholarly works written for archivists, registrators, and secretaries. With

---

[4] Weber's historical studies offer an anthropology and sociology of institutions that undermine any timeless understanding of either state or church; see, for example, *The Religion of China* (1915). His essays on "Politics as a Vocation" (1919) present his pivotal theory of traditional, patrimonial, and rational domination, whose emphasis on legitimacy as a cultural and social process undermines the positivism of earlier approaches.

roots in the sixteenth century in Jacob von Ramingen's works (discussed in Chapter 13) and expanding vastly in the eighteenth century with publications across Europe, archivists' handbooks and manuals reached a high level of sophistication in the nineteenth and early twentieth centuries, often including a historical review of past practices of archiving. While the most influential archivists' handbook of all, the *Handleiding voor het ordenen en beschijven van archieven* (the so-called Dutch Manual) of 1898, has relatively little explicit historical content, other exemplars such as Harry Bresslau's *Handbuch der Urkundenlehre* (1912–1931) contain insightful discussions of medieval and early modern archival history in their introductory material.[5] Twentieth-century handbooks from the Italian school (Eugenio Casanova) and German tradition (Adolf Brennecke) expanded the engagement with the history of archives and provide important points of reference as the first truly comparative approaches to the European archival past.[6]

Following a long discursive tradition, the second body of work continued to focus on archives as repositories of legal evidence that might be useful in a secondary way for historians. It is telling that only well into the twentieth century did archivists taking this approach go beyond charters and instruments and turn their attention to the history of administrative records more broadly. Otto Heinrich Meisner published a first guide to *Aktenkunde* (the science of files) in 1935, with an expanded and systematic version focusing on post-medieval practices appearing in 1950.[7] Further development, including a significant historical component, appears in the work of Johannes Papritz and most recently Michael Hochedlinger, who brings an Austrian perspective to a field previously dominated by exponents of Prussian registry.[8] As with the earlier historical scholarship, however, the centrality of the modern state to these works' consideration of past archives – strong among authors who were practicing archivists within the apparatus of such states – means that respect for this scholarship's empirical breadth must always be accompanied with care about its tendency to assume that earlier forms of governance were identical to, or at least closely linked, to those of

---

[5] The Dutch Manual is translated as Muller et al., *Manual*. On the translation and issues it raises, see Horsman, Ketelaar, and Thomassen, "New Respect." See also Bresslau, *Handbuch*.

[6] Casanova, *Archivistica*; Brennecke, *Archivkunde*, resting on pre-war lectures at the Prussian school of archives. On the persons in Brennecke's sphere, see Eckert, *The Struggle*, 99–120.

[7] Meisner, *Aktenkunde*; Meisner, *Urkunden- und Aktenlehre*.

[8] After a series of contentious articles published in the 1950s and 1960s, Papritz's approach was fully developed in *Archivwissenschaft*. Hochedlinger's *Aktenkunde* consciously builds on and updates Meisner's work; he offers historical perspective in *Österreichische Archivgeschichte*.

modern states. To these broader works must be added the many narrative histories of specific archives, often composed in connection with new published inventories or oversights, which are invaluable for a scholar entering almost any historical archive in Europe, and which have helped me understand the cases presented in this volume.

New Perspectives among Historians

Beginning in the 1970s, two developments began changing the way historians thought about records and archives. The first, which emerged most clearly in the work of European medievalists, began when movements for social history, "history from below," and historical anthropology turned historians' interest toward finding sources about more than the national state and its antecedents. A closer focus on what could be mined from archival records, often resting on new interpretive methodologies derived from literature, ethnography, and other disciplines, spurred historians to reconsider basic issues of how texts were used and read in past eras. An important milestone in this development was Brian Stock's massive study, *The Implications of Literacy* (1983), which argued that reading was not a passive activity, but rather an interpretive activity that took place collectively in communities led by charismatic readers. Meanwhile, medieval intellectual historians began using literary and bibliographical techniques to reconsider the evolution of Scholastic learning, turning their attention toward the material features and conceptual architecture of the material that survived.

An important theoretical approach focusing on records over time is exemplified in Thomas Hildbrand's study of how one monastic archive evolved over four centuries. Hildbrand offers a dynamic approach that connects storage with silencing and preservation with the production of information. His key terms are unlovely but illuminating: we must consider, he argues, how medieval archival conditions led documents to experience *de-semiosis* and – crucially – *re-semiosis* over time.[9] Placing a document into storage, he notes, also removed it from view, thereby silencing it as an immediate source of knowledge. When a record was later retrieved to serve as a focal point for knowledge production, the interpretive context had necessarily changed. Those now reviewing the document viewed it in a different communicative context, weighed its

---

[9] Thomas Hildbrand, "Quellenkritik." This theoretical approach, drawing on Niklaus Luhmann, is applied in Hildbrand's *Herrschaft*, where he explains his terms (*Desemiotisierung, Resemiotisierung,* and *Umsemiotisierung*) as key transformations that occur as documents move through archives.

external characteristics and text according to different practices of interpretation, and inevitably generated situationally specific meaning at least
partly disconnected from earlier contexts. The new significance attributed to the document was never unconstrained, since both traditions of
practice and the words and form of the document bound possible meanings to some extent. Nevertheless, if the meaning of a record could
change from when it entered an archive until a later moment when it
was found and retrieved, Hildebrand argues, its *content* was not a fixed or
predetermined quantity. Retrieval thus necessarily included re-semiosis,
which both recovered old meanings and attributed new meaning to the
documents.

Simon Teuscher extends Hildbrand's analysis by analyzing more precisely the way that changing communicative contexts affected how and
by whom documents were read.[10] One typical context during the High
Middle Ages took place when a community drew on a charter in its
possession, either to reinforce and legitimate the community's existence
or to carry out a conflict with some other actor. Under such circumstances, the community's presence and the (generally oral) commentary
that they contributed were part of a correct reading of the document.
Teuscher contrasts this mode with the fifteenth-century practices of lords
and their bailiffs, who gathered peasant documents and copied them into
their archives. Such copying detached text from document and replaced
the context of a living community with a context consisting of other
records. In the latter space, knowledge grew out of the differences or
similarities among documents and their words, while correct interpretation came to rely on cross-reference and appeals to abstract principles
found in law books.

The second key impulse for historians came from the arrival of new
theories in the 1980s. Whether through the anthropological hermeneutics of Clifford Geertz or in the critical perspectives of post-structuralism,
historians began reconsidering how they used documents as sources.
This drew attention away from existing narratives of the state, and
toward more self-reflective practices of historical interpretation, while
also enabling strategies of reading administrative or judicial records
"against the grain" to recover the experience of historical actors whose
own voices had been silenced. Natalie Zemon Davis's delightful *Fiction
in the Archives* (1987) exemplifies this direction, with specific attention to
archival technology and practices, but similar tendencies characterized
many key works in microhistory. This broad tendency gained particular

---

[10] Teuscher, "Textualising Peasant Inquiries" and "Document Collections."

impact in the history of archives because two key figures in post-structuralism, Michel Foucault and Jacques Derrida, successively seized on *the archive* as a powerful metaphor that they could use for their theoretical arguments.[11]

These impulses resonated in the work of historians who started working on the history of archives in the 1990s, in parallel with three broader developments, generally characterized as distinct turns, that were emerging across the humanities in the same decade. Most broadly, archival history gained tremendous impetus from the cultural turn that was increasingly directing historians' attention to practices rather than to the structures and functions that had been the primary focus of earlier methodologies. More specifically, the so-called spatial and material turns – which themselves can be viewed as reflecting the maturation of cultural history as a major register for contemporary historiography – brought new ways to think about archives, which scholars increasingly recognized as emphatically both spatial and material.[12]

These three turns were highly productive when applied to the historical analysis of archives. First, the cultural turn allowed scholars to view specific archives as sites of practice that transformed archives' contents over time – and thus historians' possibilities for later research as well.[13] Second, the spatial turn highlighted the ways in which archives functioned as assemblages of objects deployed in space, physical as well as metaphorical, in a more or less ordered way. Third, the material turn brought to the fore the many ways that documents as material objects (rather than as disembodied texts) entered political and cultural contestation, while also recognizing that early modern archivists had to deal not only with preservation and organization of texts, but also fire, damp, insects, and mice, not to mention security, cabinetmaking, and the circulation of the material objects in their care. An additional approach in the same register addresses the relationship between legal systems (viewed through a cultural history lens) and stored records.[14]

A first summation of historians' recent efforts to re-envision the history of early modern European archives appears in Markus Friedrich's study,

[11] Foucault and Derrida universalized the term "archive" as a philosophical term, notably in Foucault's *The Archaeology*, and Derrida's *Archive Fever* and *Paper Machine*. Critical theory has also been important in undermining historians' uncritical use of the concept sources. Even though historians of archives express considerable hesitation about whether Foucault's and Derrida's invocation of "the archive" is productive, the larger influence is unavoidable. See Steedman, *Dust*.

[12] Further discussion appears in Head, "Configuring."

[13] Hirschler, "From Archives," 2–3.

[14] Recent studies include Hiatt, *The Making*, and Schulte, "Fides Publica." More broadly and in global context, see the studies of Lauren Benton and Tamar Herzog.

The Birth of the Archive.[15] Friedrich provides an invaluable survey of how historians have interrogated archives as historical phenomena, looking at everything from writing practices to furniture. His critique of earlier periodizations of change in the archives, including Bautier's, problematizes the narrative structure (based largely on continuity since Roman or early medieval times) found in the older scholarship, even if his title evoking "the birth of the archive" still echoes Bautier's conclusions about the "naissance de l'archivistique" in the burgeoning administrative collections of early modern Europe. Francis X. Blouin and William Rosenberg, meanwhile, demonstrated the value of collaborations between archivists and historians in their book-length essay on the tensions between archival and historical understandings of authority.[16] These authors concentrate on the nineteenth and twentieth centuries as they help clarify – especially to historians – the recent differentiations in form, function, and practice that delineate Western archive traditions on the brink of the digital revolution.

These works were accompanied by a flood of new research and interdisciplinary conversations, much of it taking place at conferences and appearing in print as volumes of essays or special issues of journals. Blouin and Rosenberg published a pioneering collection in 2006 entitled *Archives, Documentation and the Institutions of Social Memory,* which presented a wide variety of articles by both archival scientists and historians that had been prepared for a Sawyer Seminar at the University of Michigan.[17] A special issue of *Archival Science* edited by Ann Blair and Jennifer Milligan in 2007 looked primarily at early modern European evidence, with one important comparative discussion about China. Recently, Filippo de Vivo sought to take stock of this growing body of scholarship from a historian's perspective as he edited a special issue of the *European Historical Quarterly* (2016) dedicated to "Archival Transformations in Early Modern Europe." De Vivo identified four major branches of new archival history emerging out of studies of early modern Europe. The first he characterized as "the political history of archives, or the archival history of politics" – a category relevant to the approach taken in this book – with particular attention to "the massive surge in administrative paperwork resulting from the concurrent centralization and expansion of early modern states."[18]

A second major approach derives from current work in the history of science, and more broadly the history of knowledge (*Wissensgeschichte* in

---

[15] Friedrich, *The Birth.*   [16] Blouin and Rosenberg, *Processing the Past.*
[17] Blouin and Rosenberg, *Archives.*
[18] De Vivo, Guidi, and Silvestri, "Archival Transformations."

German). De Vivo lays out a range of approaches that build on current research into how knowledge was produced, circulated, and preserved in Europe, including studies of scientists and their archives, paper technologies for inscription and retrieval, responses to information excess, and the evolution of new knowledge tools. Akin to the approaches that De Vivo mentions – and also connecting to archival science's interest in archival communities – are ongoing developments in the history of erudition, in which scholars such as Ann Blair, Anthony Grafton, and Peter Miller have concentrated on channels of circulation and preservation of knowledge by the learned members of the early modern Republic of Letters.[19]

De Vivo sees a third approach in the social history of archives practiced by Markus Friedrich. Friedrich's work shows that looking at archives encompasses many dimensions, from the social foundations of archival writing through the personnel, spaces, and power of archives in early modern society.[20] Most recently, Friedrich has been concentrating on the emergence of archival specialists, such as the *féodistes* in France, who brought the social power of archives to petty nobles and minor institutions across France during the eighteenth century. An article on this theme appears in a recent special issue of the journal *Past & Present* that is dedicated to the social history of archival record-keeping.[21]

Finally, De Vivo points to the history of historiography as a fourth area where closer attention to archives – and to early modern archives in particular – brings rich rewards. This approach highlights the often unrecognized contributions of archivists and archival science to the work of historians. As De Vivo notes, they "prefigured historiographical activities, preparing compendia, annals, and lists of 'curious and memorable deeds'... whether or not they then were used by historians."[22] In this area, a recent special issue of the journal *Storia della Storiografia* on "Archives and the Writing of History" has opened up new questions for further discussion.[23]

Beyond these issues, the absolutely central (and frequently underexamined) role that archives play have played in history writing over the past two centuries, serving as the place where historians find their all-important sources, means that any study of early modern archives will have important implications for how historians write history, and for how

---

[19] Grafton anticipates the discussion of archival knowledge across cultural boundaries in the latest collection he has edited: Grafton and Most, *Canonical Texts*. See also Miller, *Peiresc's Europe*.
[20] Friedrich, *Birth*.   [21] Friedrich, "The Rise."
[22] De Vivo, Guidi, and Silvestri, "Archival Transformations," 426–7.
[23] De Vivo, Donato, and Müller, "Archives."

they understand the relationship between evidence from the past and the narratives they construct using this evidence.

Archival Science after the 1980s

Like historiography with its successive social and cultural turns, archival science underwent major changes in the 1980s that put the centrality of state service into question as archives' main purpose, and which interrogated the way that recorded information could serve as evidence in both forensic and policy contexts.[24] This turn – whose full richness is beyond the scope of this discussion – coincided with a rising concern among historians that the traditional paradigm of archive-based research effectively marginalized the social actors in whom new historical studies were most interested. Women, the poor, and colonial subjects, along with racial, religious, and sexual "others," if they appeared in traditional archives at all, did so primarily as the objects of surveillance and state control, not as actors and sources of cultural change.[25] Canadian and Australian archival theory have been particularly influential in rethinking the cultural work taking place in archives, which has inevitably raised interest in reconsidering the archival past.[26] The rise of post-structuralist theory across the humanities also contributed very substantially to the way that new approaches in archivistics formulated their understanding of archives as sources of historical evidence – even if the ideas of Foucault and Derrida also pose problems for archival science.[27]

Thus, archivists experienced major challenges to traditional views, theoretically and methodologically, at the same time that historians, particularly medievalists, began thinking deeply about the historical processes that had produced the archives where they did their work. An additional powerful impulse to rethink archives as historical phenomena came from scholars as well as activists working in contexts where the existing archives were highly problematic. Historians looking for subaltern subjects encountered and learned from the efforts of communities

---

[24] A useful retrospective appears in Eastwood and MacNeil, *Currents*, 2nd ed.

[25] After seminal work by Terry Cook, the field developed above all in the pages of the journal *Archival Science*, founded in 2000 by Horsman, Ketelaar, and Thomassen.

[26] Cook, "What Is Past"; McKemmish et al., *Archives*.

[27] Foucault's and Derrida's appropriation of "archive" also galvanized critiques of empiricism in archival science. See Brothman, "Declining Derrida"; Ridener, *From Polders to Postmodernism*; Schenk, "'Archivmacht.'" Rück, "Zur Diskussion," 6, captured the tensions involved in 1975: "Trotz seiner für die engere Archivistik kaum brauchbaren Umschreibung des Archivbegriffs ... scheint mir Foucaults Sicht für die Archivgeschichte wertvoll, denn ihr geht es ja um eine archäologische Abschichtung bestimmter Dokumentationssysteme, um eine Stratigraphie des Archivmaterials."

separated from the sources of their own past (for example, African Americans, lesbians, and gay men from the 1970s onward, or island communities that had passed under multiple distant colonial masters), which sought to build their own archives to secure their memory and identity.[28]

Contemporary archival science in 2018 gives a significant role to such social-critical approaches, which ask how archivists can ensure the memorialization of the subaltern. Developments are also driven by a tension between the well-established conceptual framework going back to the late nineteenth century and the Dutch Manual, on the one hand, and efforts to create an alternative approach for both undertaking and understanding record-keeping as a social phenomenon under the rubric "records continuum", on the other hand.[29] This latter tension has important methodological implications for a study such as this one. The key point is that over a century of refinement and elaboration, pre-1980s archivistics developed a robust set of categories for managing and understanding archives, categories that came to seem natural or even scientific. A core breakthrough in the mid-nineteenth century revolved around problems of archival arrangement – that is, the way that surviving documents should be placed in an archive's space so as to be accessible. Rejecting early modern approaches that looked first to the content of documents or series, the first modern archival revolution proposed that provenance (or the overlapping French expression *respect des fonds*) should govern such placement: Archives should receive documents arranged as they had "organically" accumulated in the custody of their creator. The creator of documents was initially conceptualized exclusively as an office or agency, but later expanded to include individual actors or communities.[30] Changing this original order, archivists had come to realize, would irrevocably disrupt way all the information inherent in the context and relationships among documents.

---

[28] Historians of the post-colonial world played a leading role in this work, while also applying critical theory in particularly fruitful ways. See especially Bastian, *Owning Memory*; Hamilton et al., *Refiguring*; and Stoler, *Along the Archival Grain*.

[29] On the revisionist movement in archival science, see Gilliland, McKemmish, and Lau, *Research*. I am also indebted to Eastwood, "A Contested Realm." Post-custodial archiving and the records continuum are laid out in intellectual context in Oliver, "Managing Records," 89–92.

[30] The online glossary of the Society of American Archivists (2018) provides a definition of archives that links a series of key terms: "*Materials* created or received by a person, family, or organization, public or private, in the conduct of their affairs and preserved because of the enduring *value* contained in the information they contain or as *evidence* of the functions and responsibilities of their *creator*, especially those materials maintained using the principles of *provenance*, original order, and collective control" (emphasis mine).

A second core concept growing out of nineteenth-century practice conceptualized archives as final depositories for documents no longer in regular use by their creators (and thus of interest primarily as evidence in future litigation and to future historians). In this view, archiving revolved fundamentally around custody. Hilary Jenkinson, writing during World War I, most powerfully idealized custodial archives protected by archival custodians, which in turn promoted the idea that only a clear archival threshold, separating documents in use from documents in archives, could ensure the continuity and security of the all-important custody.[31]

The enormous expansion in record production by states in the twentieth century brought about a new focus on the limits of archiving and the importance of efficient records management to national states. Along with formalizing the stages through which a record passed during its life cycle, from initial drafting in an agency through filing, organization, and eventually passage across the archival threshold to permanent storage (or else to disposal after an archivist appraised its permanent value), records management models further discounted the place of historians in archives. Whereas historical training had been required for most archivists well into the twentieth century, the ideal records manager of the later twentieth century needed to study information science and public management. Not surprisingly, state or corporate record creators became the canonical client for records management specialists, with historical research fading as a primary future use that archivists were expected to consider.[32]

In this way, a complete model of archiving matured through the twentieth century, with precise terminology being developed for the various stages of record-keeping and for the key challenges that records managers would face. Despite ongoing debates over many issues, its various elements supported one another and seemed to provide language for discussing all the major questions that practicing archivists might have (while largely excluding historians from its conversations, treating them as clients rather than agents). Two key changes around 1970 began undermining this seemingly stable edifice, however. The first, already discussed, was critical theory's early appropriation of the archive as a key interpretive metaphor, which focused attention on the power dynamics implicit in the existing model while encouraging new approaches to archiving the subaltern and the excluded; the second was the digital

---

[31] Jenkinson, *A Manual*; on the archival threshold, see Duranti, "Archives."
[32] T. R. Schellenberg sketches the canonical distinction between records management and archives management in *Modern Archives*.

revolution beginning in the 1980s, which profoundly undermined the medial forms – above all, paper-based record-keeping – that had provided another implicit scaffolding for canonical archival theory.

The trigger for rethinking not only archival theory, but also how record-keeping could and should work in the post-digital age, came from professional state archivists who were also deeply concerned about justice for communities that had largely been excluded from producing authentic archival records, such as indigenous peoples in Australia and Canada and the African population of South Africa.[33] When such communities sought justice and restoration of traditional rights, they generally lacked records of their past status that could pass muster according to traditional archival canons; even worse, they found themselves forced to argue before courts that accepted colonial or police-state records whose inaccuracy and bias were manifest despite their formally correct archival custody and provenance.[34] Efforts to retheorize contemporary archiving practice, replacing the custodial archive filtered through appraisal and organized by provenance with something more flexible and open, are ongoing under the umbrella terms "records continuum" and "community archives."

An important preliminary outcome is that the older terminology itself has been historicized. The old model's character as the product of historical developments backed by one historically contingent form of state power has become visible, undermining any claim that it represents a neutral framework for the scientific management of records. Once modern terminology and practice have been historicized in this way, moreover, it becomes interesting to trace the emergence of traditional archival theory as a historical product, and to rethink what came before in its own terms – as this study seeks to do – rather than regarding early modern practices merely as imperfect intimations of the perfection that coalesced after 1898. We will return to this issue in the book's Conclusion, since these issues have implications not only for our understanding of archives, but also for how we view law and the state as historical phenomena themselves.

Outlooks for the Future

Given the centrality of archives to historical research, and in light of the information revolution that is transforming record-keeping practices and

[33] Early leaders included Terry Cook in Canada, Sue McKemmish in Australia, and Verne Harris in South Africa.
[34] Lucidly analyzed in Perry, "The Colonial Archive."

technologies today, research that treats archives as subjects rather than sites of research (for which evidence *about* archives is as important as evidence *from* archives) has great potential and implications that extend across multiple disciplines. It raises the question of which future directions will be most important for the historical understanding of knowledge cultures and for clarifying the complex and constantly evolving relationship between human memory, technologies of knowledge transmission, and political and cultural patterns of interaction. Two areas of particular urgency became visible during the research for this book, along with a third fundamental aspect of historical epistemology, already adduced in this chapter, that research about archives makes particularly pressing.

Making, Keeping, and Using – Especially Using

In his influential 1979 study, *From Memory to Written Record*, M. T. Clanchy distinguished three phases in the life-history of the preserved documents that deserve separate treatment: making, keeping, and using.[35] Scholars have long conducted studies of record-making and record-keeping, but focused studies on how records have been used remained rare until quite recently. Medievalists have been at the forefront on this theme and continue to produce some of the most illuminating work. In contrast, systematic analysis of early modern record use (including how records were located and identified, how they were reproduced for different audiences, and what roles they played in various kinds of contestation) has remained diffuse and unfocused until recently. Most of the available work touches on related but somewhat different questions, particularly in the history of historiography and the history of science. Exemplary work by scholars such as Anthony Grafton, Donald Kelley, and D. R. Woolf has looked at how historians used records to make their cases for diverse audiences and patrons.[36] Closer to this book's topic, Jacob Soll provides a profound analysis of the multiple ways that Louis XIV's advisor Colbert sought to control France through systematically collected and organized information, and has also addressed the critical topic of accounting as another archival practice (a topic largely bracketed out here).[37] In *Fiction in the Archives*, Natalie

---

[35] I rely on the second edition of 1993.

[36] Relevant works include Grafton, *The Footnote*; Kelley, *The Foundations*; and Woolf, "A High Road."

[37] Soll, *The Information Master*; Soll, *The Reckoning*. See also Sabean, "Village Court Protocols."

Davis carried out a study entirely about documents' use, in a way, but oriented toward illuminating larger questions of social order and gender rather than processes inside and outside archives and registries. In this book, Chapter 13 presents a case study of how actors in seventeenth-century Zurich changed their strategies for collecting information and reading it as evidence during disputes with their neighbors. Still, the various ways that early modern documents could be used over generations remains a topic whose surface we have only begun to scratch.

Archives and Archivality: From European Paradigms to Global Comparison

Carrying out a comparative study of Western European archives also raises questions about the appropriate scale for various questions about archival history. The more deeply I delved into Europe's history over the course of this project, the more evident it became to me that wider comparisons remain urgently necessary.[38] This is particularly true because the vocabulary of modern archivistics is itself a historically specific product of Western European practices from the High Middle Ages to the mid-twentieth century, as argued earlier in this chapter. As long as we rely uncritically on this language, we risk overlooking important aspects of human record-keeping beyond the European context, which will remain opaque or simply invisible because of the limitations of our categories.

This issue was already addressed by Ernst Posner, the first scholar to undertake a systematic comparative analysis of archives outside the European experience.[39] In the introduction to his path-breaking *Archives in the Ancient World*, Posner asked whether surviving accumulations of cuneiform tablets and other ancient material could legitimately be labeled as archives. Posner argued that archives possessed "significance as components of ... various cultures," such that they varied from culture to culture.[40] How, then, could he decide which textual material from the vast region he was studying should be included? Posner's answer to this question rested on his own background as an archival practitioner profoundly steeped in both German and American traditions: "The archives of the ancient world seem to have much in common with those of our own times," he concluded, because of a series of "constants in records

---

[38] Comparison discussed in Head, "A Comparative Case-Study Approach."
[39] On Posner, see O'Toole, "Back to the Future."   [40] Posner, *Archives*, 1.

creation" that linked the cuneiform and papyrus repositories he analyzed to categories with which he was familiar.[41]

More recently, cultural history as practiced in the last generation has shown convincingly that describing other cultures with categories based on European experience leads to the naturalization of what are, in fact, highly contingent assumptions about human interaction. The same issue arises when comparing record-keeping practices, and we should be careful to take an approach that does not rest uncritically on European-based terms and concepts – above all, on the mutable central category of archives, which is both distinctively European and highly unstable in meaning within Europe across time. Concepts and practices found in Europe do not represent universal constants, as Posner argued, but rather constitute features of what I call European *archivality* – that is, of an ongoing tradition intimately connected (as Posner correctly noted) to European ways of organizing "the governance of secular and religious affairs and ... the individual's conduct of business."[42] Archivality is a comprehensive configurational term for characterizing the way different societies collect documents that record information about dominion, possessions, and power, and thus relativizes European forms while still allowing for useful comparison. Each particular archivality emerges out of phenomena at multiple levels of abstraction, including medial forms and medial configurations, the social trajectories of record-keepers, and connected cultural forms such as law, ceremony, and administration.

Differentiating separate archivalities provides a way to understand how different societies accumulated records, how these records were preserved, and how later actors deployed them across multiple contexts. It allows us to distinguish medieval from early modern archivality within Europe, as well as European from Chinese, South Asian, or Islamic archivalities, which rested on quite different modes of making, keeping, and using records.[43] At the same time, because it retains the root concept of the archive, the term "archivality" signals that important homologies do exist across cultures and eras. The similarities with Prussian practice that Posner discerned in Mesopotamia and Persia are real, because he was comparing record-keeping carried out by the ruling groups in premodern agrarian empires who had similar interests and fears, and who used comparable methods for documenting their possessions and authority. In short, they practiced record-keeping that we can meaningfully describe as homologous to the European case.

---

[41] Posner, *Archives*, 2–3, identifies six such constants.   [42] Posner, *Archives*, vii.
[43] Explored in Hirschler, "From Archives."

Applying the term "archivality" to Europe as well as to other comparable cases therefore seeks to provincialize the European-based terminology that currently predominates in the study of record-keeping. As outlined in Dipesh Chakrabarty's influential collection of essays, *Provincializing Europe*, provincializing existing categories begins by rejecting implicit or explicit assertions that one culture's disciplinary framework can provide a universal approach to phenomena from other cultures.[44] As will be demonstrated later in this chapter, the term "archive" (along with the related terminology of canonical archivistics) is tightly bound to culturally and temporally specific Western conceptions of law, power, authority, and human memory. Posner's approach to ancient archives through modern categories privileged the European prototype not only by assuming that categories such as notarial records were universal, but also by applying an entire complex of expectations based on twentieth-century archival theory to the cases he was considering. Subordinating European archives to comparative archivality, in contrast, avoids Posner's assumptions and accepts the irreducibility of differences among cases, even as it recognizes that record-keeping by political authorities in pre-modern agrarian societies really did share important features.

Archives and Historical Reflexivity: A Disciplinary Predicament

A final consideration involves the reflexive predicament that arises when a historian studies the formation, operation, and use of archives. The cultural foundation of archives in the European tradition lies in their capacity (imagined or real) to provide evidence in various situations. In the Middle Ages, the key form of evidence imagined in archives consisted of proof, particularly of privileges that had been issued, but also of contracts, treaties, and other acts for which an authentic, intersubjective memorialization was of value. In the early modern period, the provision of information about subjects, rivals, and the larger world was added to the tasks of archival managers. Meanwhile, historians began turning to archives as sources of *historical* evidence, particularly after the Reformation and even more in the seventeenth and eighteenth centuries, leading to nineteenth-century historiography's canonization of the archive as the "historian's laboratory" (Bautier) filled with precious sources. It is this last turn that is significant here: Because of the particular place that archives occupy in European historical thinking and writing, writing

---

[44] Chakrabarty, *Provincializing Europe*.

archival history always represents a reflexive examination of an institution that enables and shapes our own scholarly practice.

Not all evidence about the human past is contained in archives, of course. Recall Salomon Hirzel's dictum that "All proofs of actions that have taken place are called *Urkunden*," which not only noted the wide range of phenomena that provide traces of past action – "a coin, an inscribed column, a gravestone, the remnants of a building" – but also assimilated all of these to the paradigmatic form of a charter (*Urkunde*), an archival record.[45] Even in the eighteenth century, one way to conceptualize the role of archives in historical thinking was to turn the phenomenal world into part of the archive, ready to be cataloged and prepared for historians' use.[46] Another thinker from the seventeenth century responded differently to the question of how records could serve as evidence. As cited by Daniel Papenbroeck, the Jesuit Alexander Wilthelmius commented on heated Baroque debates about the authenticity of old records by remarking that "And often, what the judge approved in court, the scholar condemns in his study."[47] Once drawn from an archive, documents and their texts were subject to different readings according to different expectations and criteria. Archival context and transmission history, or provenance, is one important criterion that might differentiate a judge's evaluation from a historian's assessment of a document.

As these varied responses to the relationship between archives and the larger category of evidence reveal, treating archives and other repositories as subjects rather than sites of research inevitably brings an elevated level of reflexivity. Such reflexivity operates in several distinct modes. First, investigating the history of any system of keeping records means using the records that the system preserved (both their content and their architecture) to understand the system itself: Put simply, the means of research and the object of research overlap. Second, particularly for work within the Western tradition, this reflexivity is heightened by the way Western historians give archives a central place in our practice. Since the eighteenth century, and especially since Ranke, archives have been treated as collections of potential *sources*, the raw material that allows historians to reconstruct specific pasts. Yet archives' collective existence and organization remain largely unquestioned, except in highly technical terms or by auxiliary sciences. Historians in this tradition are expected to perform source criticism – that is, intense scrutiny of the individual

---

[45] [Hirzel], "Versuch," 37.

[46] On what counts as archives today, see Ketelaar, "Archival Turns."

[47] Cited from a letter in Papenbroeck, "Ad tomum II Aprilis propylaeum," xvi.

record distilled in textual form – but have generally left the transmission, archival context, and material features of documents to specialized disciplines such as diplomatics, archivistics, and sigillography.[48]

The epistemological challenges that arise whenever historians create narratives of the past point to predicaments that will not be resolved by looking more closely at archives, of course.[49] This book concentrates on much more mundane and empirical challenges to understanding how records of various genres accumulated, soon becoming the concern of specialized personnel who sought to bring some kind of order to the material they confronted. We would do well to remember that we rely on those specialists not only because they helped preserve these records (rather than others), but also because their expectations about the purposes of the material they ordered and interpreted have very significant consequences for the sources we find today.[50] Because no historian reads archival documents in a vacuum, but rather finds them through pathways inflected by the work of archivists past as well as present, the ordering work of making archives leaves marks on every step of our results.[51] In addition to its inherent fascination, the study of archives reminds us that our own interpretive activities are part of the ongoing process of creating, preserving, and using material transmitted in archives, as well as beyond archives.

---

[48] Studies in the intellectual history of these subdisciplines represent a rapidly growing field. For archivistics, see Blouin and Rosenberg, *Processing the Past*; and Saxer, *Die Schärfung*.

[49] See, for example, Popkewitz et al., "Debatte," and responses.

[50] Esch, "Überlieferungs-Chance."

[51] Two recent reflections on historians' practices in archives specifically: Farge, *The Allure*, and Steedman, *Dust*.

Part I

The Work of Records (1200–)

The following four chapters seek to illuminate the work that stored records did for political actors in Europe from the High Middle Ages into the early modern period. From the perspective of record-keeping, I ask why records from different genres were considered worth keeping, and which technologies those charged with keeping them could draw on to ensure the records' physical preservation and accessibility for the purposes that political leaders imagined they might fulfill. A central argument, made both here and throughout the book, is that the records in question had by the thirteenth century largely settled into a limited and stable set of medial forms, and that these medial forms are essential to our analysis of how contemporaries understood records and how they managed them. These medial forms included parchment and paper, inscription with ink applied with quill pens, and authentication through seals, sigils, or signatures. Such tools allowed the creation of diverse medial configurations of documents that included the single-leaf document, usually issued by one authority to its subjects or peers, and the quire or codex, which could accommodate longer records or combine multiple records in a single medial unit. Various genres of record flourished on the foundation of these forms and their many configurations.

Contemporaries understood such records as fulfilling several functions. They could provide authentic testimony about past acts – the most visible *explicit* function, at the time, of the records that this book investigates – and could preserve information about people and communities. They could also embody lordly or communal autonomy or evoke past decisions and resolve. When drawn out of storage, records might be used probatively or informationally, but also performatively and ritually. Over time, uses often diverged from those imagined when the records were initially created and stored. Indeed, processes of meaning loss and meaning establishment (de-semiosis and re-semiosis) ensured that documents functioned differently each time they moved in and out of archives.

The four chapters in this section consist of two pairs. Chapter 3 introduces key aspects of high medieval record-keeping as it evolved after

1100, with attention to both the available media and techniques, but equally to the social and cultural frameworks that shaped both the making and keeping of records. Particular attention goes to Roman-law concepts, adapted or reinvented through European thinkers' contact with Roman law books recovered just before 1100. Roman law provided a way to define written documents as a form of testimony, which opened the door to wider applications of writing to social processes, and equally to the increasing accumulation of the resulting testimonies. Confronted with growing corpora of proofs – in particular, proofs of privileges given and received – rulers and their subjects created treasuries to keep their proofs together with other precious or sacred objects. Chapter 4 describes an extraordinary product of such probative thinking, the Lisbon royal chancellery's *Leitura Nova* registers of the early sixteenth century. These registers were simultaneously precious books enhanced with illumination and beautiful layout, and political tools closely honed to an emerging patrimonial–colonial state with considerable resources to dedicate to establishing its authority.

Chapters 5 and 6 address the way records could be used to document and retrieve information. After reviewing the surveillance techniques of the medieval Inquisition as a model, Chapter 5 considers how book technologies borrowed from Europe's universities led to powerful tools for administration as well as domination. Chapter 6 addresses another major royal project, this one to implement effective information management for the Austrian Habsburg state's operations centered in Innsbruck. As in contemporary Lisbon, political realities intersected with technical and human capabilities to produce an extraordinary set of record-keeping tools.

3   Probative Objects and Scholastic Tools
   in the High Middle Ages

The Probative Imperative from Late Antiquity
to the High Middle Ages

The way political institutions in Europe accumulated records and managed the information that those records provided changed repeatedly and
in profound ways from the sixth to the sixteenth centuries.[1] These
transformations did not take place in a vacuum; instead, new practices
grew out of the ways that Late Antique and medieval European princes,
prelates, and magistrates, on the one hand, and communities, scholars,
and book producers, on the other hand, used writing and texts in various
situations. The starting point for understanding the "nearly revolutionary
technical changes in political and administrative behavior" involving
written records that began *after* 1400, therefore, must be familiarity with
earlier methods used in chancelleries and scriptoria from Late Antiquity
through the twelfth and thirteenth centuries.[2] Many aspects of these
methods looked different in 1600 than they had in 1400, and they looked
different yet again from those employed in 1200 or 800.[3] Visible changes
took place in medial forms (from papyrus and parchment and objects to
paper, files, and printed forms), forms of proof (seals, signatures, notary
authentications, and provenances), and the medial configurations of the
textual objects that were available (loose documents, copybooks,
inventories, and indices). In parallel with such external changes, the ways
that records were conceptualized and the relationship between text-
bearing objects and juridical and political knowledge also shifted, in close
connection with changes in the institutional cultures through which
power and knowledge circulated. Most importantly, the High Medieval

---

[1] The most ambitious effort at periodization for Western Europe remains Bautier's "La
phase cruciale."
[2] The quoted phrase from Keller, "Vom 'heiligen Buch," 1. See also Guyotjeannin,
Morelle, and Parisse, *Les Cartulaires*.
[3] On archival practices in the West in the *longue dureé*, see Geary, *Phantoms*, and Koziol, *The
Politics*, particularly the lucid introduction and review of the recent literature.

reinvention of Roman law and its standards of evidence, proof, and public faith set in place principles for the creation, keeping, and use of records that resonated at least until the eighteenth century.

This chapter consists of three main sections, which introduce key medieval practices that produced documentary accumulations. The first concentrates on practices of producing records and documents in light of the uses that their creators imagined for them, particularly the production of records understood as proofs. Producing probative records embodied a conviction that to be worthy of storage, such records had, above all, to contain trustworthy *testimony* about the specific acts of authorized actors such as kings, lords, or communities. A particular feature of European medieval documentary practice was the way in which free-standing documents, generally referred to as charters or instruments, or by the German term *Urkunden,* became a paradigmatic way to memorialize legally binding acts for the future. Medieval chancelleries produced many other genres of record, including compilations of laws (capitularies), inventories of possessions, records of expenses, and the products of formal inquiries, especially in the thirteenth and fourteenth centuries. Probative records, however, played a particularly important role for the earliest intentional accumulation in special repositories because of their character as authoritative traces of acts recorded *ad perpetuam rei memoriam,* "for the perpetual memory of the matter."

Just as important as recording acts or deeds was providing reasons to believe that the record was authentic and reliable. Material signs such as seals, textual confirmations such as signatures and notarial signets, and formal characteristics all played a role in establishing a document's authenticity. Likewise, institutional evidence, such as placement in the custody of a certain office or among other records of the right kind, could lend a document's content additional authority. Trust in written records, which was essential for preserved documents, came to be understood in the later Middle Ages through the Roman-law term *fides instrumentorum* ("faith in instruments") and the associated term *publica fides* ("public faith"), which became focal points for careful analysis and detailed practices of authentication. Such faith made it possible for royal and lordly privileges as well as private contracts and wills to provide evidence during later disputes over power and property.[4]

The second section of this chapter focuses on two characteristic ways in which High and Late Medieval chancelleries managed forms of proof, once these had been produced and preserved – namely, the cartulary and

---

[4] See Schulte, Mostert, and van Renswoude, *Strategies.*

the emissions register. These genres consisted of book-form representations of charters – in the hands of recipients and issuers, respectively – that in the daily routine of chancelleries paralleled and increasingly substituted for actual charters (often preserved by their recipients in treasuries apart from their chancelleries).[5]

The third section turns to the means that emerged in High Medieval chancelleries for accessing the knowledge inscribed in such books, which drew directly from the worlds of theology and law at universities. Drawing on recent work by medievalists, I argue that Scholastic erudition provided several essential "little tools of knowledge," such as lists, tables, and indexes, that chancellery officials adapted to organize the books they were producing.[6] Since cartularies and emissions registers had different features and served different needs than Bible commentaries or the *Summa Theologica* of St. Thomas of Aquinas, a brief discussion considers how Scholastic tools had to be modified to serve the intentions of record-keepers – a discussion that will continue throughout this book.

The importance of such little tools was emphasized in a lively volume of essays edited by Peter Becker and William Clark. Drawing primarily on recent work in the history of science, Becker and Clark highlight the significance of a "regime of diagrams, charts, lists, and above all tables" that they see emerging in the eighteenth century as the foundation for a specific regime of knowledge and power.[7] They claim that attention to such little tools can take us beyond the general issue of how bureaucracies transform societies by also helping us understand the constitution of both bureaucratic political authority and academic rhetorical authority as these emerged during the Enlightenment. I extend the term chronologically by paying close attention to the variety of similar little tools that were honed and deployed in the political chancelleries of early modern Europe. Doing so is important because the historiographical approaches of the last century have generally placed such phenomena in the background, considering them useful for source criticism but not themselves part of the epistemic substance of actual sources or of historical knowledge.[8]

Chapter 4 subsequently presents a specific case that illustrates vividly how a focus on proof shaped book-form records management around

---

[5] Another genre of record book, the notarial register, is discussed through its role in the evolving European legal system; see also Nussdorfer, *Brokers*.

[6] But see Kosto, "Statim invenire ante," who questions the sequence from learned to administrative tools.

[7] Becker and Clark, "Preface," in *Little Tools*, 11–12.

[8] This approach resonates with recent research in the German school of *Wissensgeschichte*. See Brendecke, Friedrich, and Friedrich, "Information."

1500 – namely, the chancellery of the kings of Portugal from the middle of the reign of Afonso V to the reign of João III, or from approximately 1460 to 1550. This case study also provides a first demonstration of my assertion that through the fifteenth and sixteenth centuries, chancellery *practice* revolved primarily around books, not separate charters (even though sealed charters retained special symbolic and legal status).[9] At the center of my investigation are two book-form products: (1) the series of retrospective regnal registers produced in the 1460s, known as the "reformed *Chancelarias*," which reproduced a selection of important acts issued by previous Portuguese kings; and (2) the *Leitura Nova* registers ordered by Manuel I and produced between 1504 and 1552, which expanded and glorified on the Afonsine project into beautiful illuminated parchment registers.

Proof, Records, and Documents from the Roman Tradition to Late Medieval Practice

Probative documents and records accumulated in pre-modern Western Europe according to practices that reach back to Late Antiquity and the Roman system of registering legal testimonials through a government official, the *tabellio*. Although the idea of licensed scribes who could authenticate documents survived the Roman collapse and evolved into the European office of the notary, both notaries in particular and the production of documents in general became separated from direct lordship or dominion. As Cornelia Vismann argues, the resulting lack of systematic record-keeping guaranteed by rulers fundamentally shifted the way that documents functioned in politics and in society more broadly.[10] The High Middle Ages up to the 1300s were *par excellence* the age of the "instrument" – the self-authenticating and independently circulating memorial of a legally binding act, often in the form of a signed or sealed charter or diploma. Writing remained a vital technology for establishing facts for law and politics – as expressed in the phrase *ad perpetuam rei memoriam* found on many charters – but the burden of authenticating the resulting inscribed objects moved from rulers and their officers to the document itself, and to the communities empowered to interpret it in social context.[11]

---

[9] Administrative codices have seen only limited scholarship until recently. See Kloosterhuis, "Mittelalterliche Amtsbücher."

[10] Vismann, *Files*, especially chapter 3.

[11] How and when various forms of instruments might serve as evidence, or even proof, is a complex question; see Koziol, *The Politics*, 24–25, and Heidecker, "30 June 1047," 85–94. A review of current literature appears in Morsel, "En Guise."

References to the Roman past nevertheless continued to shape expectations and practices of record-keeping long after formal Roman authority had collapsed. Given this cultural background, the Western recovery of the Roman law codes in the High Middle Ages created a new set of conditions under which documents could be deployed in courts and in political conflicts.[12] Formalized by generations of legal thinkers, and by the early modern period gathered into extensive compendia such as Giuseppe Mascardi's *Conclusiones Probationum omnium*, neo-Roman law around 1500 provided detailed guidelines for how a court should view witness testimony, documents, and various other sources of evidence in deciding what had been proved by the parties.[13]

The Roman law that dominated the thinking of Late Medieval and early modern jurists discussed both proofs ("De Probationibus," Codex, Book IV, Title 19) and instruments ("De fide instrumentorum," Codex Book VI, Title 21; Digest, Chapter XXII, Title 4; in daily practice, Novels XLIX 2, 2).[14] The relevant titles provided guidance about the weight that should be accorded to documents produced by the parties to a suit, and on how to cope with document losses owing to fire and other contingencies, but contained few general principles for establishing (or rejecting) any particular document's veracity as evidence. Far more influential on practice was the Code's enshrinement of the functions of the late Roman *tabelliones*, who became models for medieval and early modern notaries. The *tabellio* was a late Roman government official possessing the authority to receive, authenticate, and keep records of public or private agreements in a public archive, the *tabularium*.[15] Documents later produced from a *tabularium* during litigation before a public court enjoyed special authority as evidence, called *publica fides* ("public faith").[16] Such documents, known as *instrumenta authentica* or *instrumenta publica*, were still open to challenge in court, like all evidence, but the party challenging them bore the burden of proving that they were flawed. This tradition thus gave public archives a prominent role in

---

[12] Herzog, *A Short History*, provides a comprehensive narrative of Roman law and its reinvention in medieval Europe. For an archival science perspective, see Duranti, "Archives."

[13] Mascardi, *Conclusiones Probationum*.

[14] A seventeenth-century edition of Justinian with extensive commentary in *Corpus Iuris Civilis*, edited by Godefroy; on instruments, see 2: cols. 277–83.

[15] Literature about the Roman archives is scarce. An introduction can be found in Posner, *Archives*; see also Demougin, *La mémoire*.

[16] The titles of the *Corpus Iuris* on "De Fide Instrumentorum" dealt largely with situations where records from a public *tabellio* were *not* available.

public and private litigation – a legacy that profoundly shaped European understandings of what documents and archives were for.[17]

The collapse of Roman administration in Europe and the diffusion of political authority that occurred between the sixth and eleventh centuries largely undermined the operation of this system of public authentication, but left in place the vocabulary and the concepts, ready to be reintegrated into legal practice as new institutions took form. The Latin Church, moreover, continued to sustain archives that claimed public faith for their contents, while kings continued to issue diplomas, erratically, whose signets and formulation built on the Roman tradition as imagined by the actors involved.[18] Particularly in Italy, the civil notarial tradition never faded entirely, and was quickly revived in the eleventh century by urban authorities interested in ensuring that contracts could be enforced and property defended.[19] Elsewhere in Europe, however, the recipients of documents (who were not generally public authorities in the Roman sense) became the primary preservers of legal proofs in their own repositories, a practice that can be seen emerging as early as the sixth century among monasteries that sought privileges and legal protection from territorial rulers. In essence, the Western European tradition of recipients' archives, along with the cartularies they generated and the issuers' registers that began appearing in the High Middle Ages, helped substitute for the absent public archives of the Roman system.[20]

When Roman law texts began reinfusing European legal practice after 1200, the dissonances between public archives (episcopal, princely, or notarial) and the private accumulations of anyone who preserved documents had to be worked out in a process that differed substantially from region to region. Jurists and intellectuals from the thirteenth century onward eagerly set to work on this project of harmonization – part of a larger project of adapting the recovered Roman law to the very different circumstances of medieval Europe.[21] They produced increasingly refined scholarly treatises on various aspects of the law and legal procedure, along with a growing genre of practical handbooks that sought to bridge

---

[17] In the formulation of medieval canon law thinkers, a proof was characterized as a "*probatio probata* if the proof was derived from a public instrument, but as *probatio probanda* in case the instrument was a private writing" (Willett, *The Probative Value*, 2).

[18] Koziol, *The Politics*, especially 17–62 on both practice and historiography.

[19] Nussdorfer provides a lucid and comprehensive discussion of the function of notaries in Rome from the High Middle Ages onward in *Brokers*. See also Keller and Behrmann, *Kommunales Schriftgut*.

[20] On records, administration, and repositories in the early Middle Ages, see Brown et al., *Documentary Culture*.

[21] On the later reception of the Roman law in the various national traditions, see Strauss, *Law*, and Kelley, *The Foundations*.

the considerable gap between neo-Roman principles and actual practice. This always involved complex layering of Roman law – the *ius commune* – with the various ethnic laws resting on statutes and law codes with Germanic roots, and with fluid customary law, not to mention with the equally dynamic canon law of the Church.[22]

In this process, the authority of *tabelliones* and the public faith possessed by records kept in a public archive transferred first to European notaries, and then – albeit incompletely – to the chancelleries and archives of the relatively autonomous lords, churches, and communes spread across Europe. As Mascardi put it in his 1587 compilation, "Those documents are universally called public instruments or public writings, or authentic, which are believed by the law *or by particular custom* without further support" (my emphasis).[23] In contrast, "As for those writings called private ... it must be said these are those not made by a public person, and they do not have authority per se, unless acknowledged by one's adversaries."[24] Denis Godefroy, an important late-sixteenth-century commentator on Justinian from northern Europe, explained that a "public instrument is one written by a public hand, that is the hand of a public notary, namely by the hand of a *tabellio*, and published in a public form," thus explicitly assimilating early modern notaries to the Roman *tabellio*.[25] By the sixteenth century, simply coming from a public archive in itself conveyed authority upon documents. As Godefroy put it in his commentary on Justinian, "Documents produced out of public archives provide public testimony," thereby expanding a concept that rested on particular Roman conditions to early modern polities and their archives more generally.[26] Even though the nature of archives had changed fundamentally since Antiquity, these commentaries show that the vocabulary of public faith in public instruments remained potent throughout the early modern period.

Although Roman law theories gave public repositories a central role, few political actors before 1100 actually possessed permanent chancelleries that could record their acts or register those made by other parties, even in Italy. North of the Alps, this remained the case into the thirteenth and even the fourteenth century.[27] Instead, any available scribe (usually a cleric) could be

---

[22] On canon law, see Willett, *The Probative Value*, 29–41. On documentary practice in customary and written law, see Teuscher, *Lords' Rights*, and Lepsius and Wetzstein, *Als die Welt*.

[23] Mascardi, *Conclusiones Probationum*, 19, §73.

[24] Mascardi, *Conclusiones Probationum*, 19, §79.   [25] Godefroy, *Praxis civilis*, 1539.

[26] *Corpus Iuris*, edited by Godefroy, Book 2, cols. 277–83; Book 2, col. 281, §20, De comparatione litterarum (in commentary). See also Willett, *The Probative Value*, 31.

[27] A lucid narrative of the emergence of specialized chancelleries in the German lands and their activities appears in Patze, "Die Herrschaftspraxis."

called upon to produce a probative document, which gained its authenticity from the signatures of witnesses or the seals of prominent individuals, who thus testified to their presence at the act. Perhaps the most revealing example of the autonomous authority of documents appears in the chirograph, in which the scribe inscribed two copies of a text memorializing an agreement between parties on a single parchment, then divided the parchment by cutting or tearing in such a way that the two versions could be matched up along the division to establish their authenticity.[28] Documents in the possession of the parties themselves proved that an agreement had been enacted, and preserved the details of its terms into the future.

The forms and uses of charters as they evolved from the central Middle Ages to the sixteenth century were tightly bound to the way that political power operated in this period, particularly through what one might call a political economy of privilege. Although Christian and Roman political theory granted nearly unlimited authority to kings and to the Roman emperor (whoever he might be), in practice medieval rulers at all levels delegated much of their formal authority to others (de facto acknowledging their lack of power) through the form of privileges.[29] Privileges (which above all legitimated control over property) circulated not only through grants made to gain political support (in transactions traditionally called feudal), but also as gifts, through purchase, and in the form of leases. Charters, in turn, attested to specific transfers of privilege, and therefore generally took a fundamentally hierarchical form, with the grantor acting as the superior, ultimately authorized by God's arrangement of the entire human political world. The transfer of privilege was a ceremonial and reciprocal act, in which deference and recognition on the part of the recipients confirmed the superiority of the grantor, as witnessed by the grantor's peers.[30] High Medieval charters memorialized this moment of emprivilegment – in both its practical and ceremonial dimensions – by listing high-status witnesses who could testify to the act, should a dispute arise later on (though this left open the question of how to gain authentic knowledge of a deed if all the witnesses had died).[31]

---

[28] Clanchy, *From Memory*, 87–88.

[29] The logic and practice of power in medieval Europe remain an abiding question for scholars that is beyond this chapter's scope.

[30] Writing was sometimes added to the physical parchment only after the collective act of issuance: Kos, "Carte sine litteris," 97–100. Similarly, Brun, *Schrift und politisches Handeln*, shows that Emperor Sigimund issued privileges that contained no information (since they vaguely confirmed all previous privileges) but did materially represent the relationship that was claimed to exist between issuer and recipient.

[31] See Nussdorfer, *Brokers*, especially chapter 1; Nicolaj, "*Originale, authenticum, publicum*," 12, notes that in Late Antique practice, documents in a public repository enjoyed perpetual authenticity, thus obviating this issue.

Another form of authentication, which became more common later in the Middle Ages, relied on the seal of the grantor or, if the grantor lacked a seal, that of a witness present at the act who did bear a seal. Papal bulls, to take the paradigmatic example, gained their name from the *bulla,* the papal lead seal attached to them that demonstrated their provenance from the pope himself.

In southern Europe, the practice of recording contracts and other legal acts by notaries grew rapidly after circa 1100. Particularly for contracts between relative equals, the notary's record might circulate among the parties in extracts they kept, but was authenticated only by its representation in a register kept by the notary (notably, in a codex), which provided a reliable and inexpensive way to authenticate what had been enacted or agreed. In contrast to the Roman *tabellio,* the notary was not directly an officer of the state, but rather was licensed by a privilege from the Church or from a ruler. Italian cities soon demanded that notaries' registers revert to the city upon each notary's death, thus creating a public record over time of property transfers, inheritances, and other contractual matters.[32] Significantly, notaries' registers in Italian towns long remained open to the scrutiny of any interested individual. In important respects, practices of authentication began to diverge south and north of the Alps after 1100, with sealed documents playing a much greater role farther north, whereas the notarial register gained a predominant position, including in the business of governance, farther south.

Two critical features link the various ways that legal and political actors used documents as proofs well into the High Middle Ages. First, document production was neither necessarily carried out nor guaranteed by any public authority. Although rulers claimed to be responsible for providing justice and protecting their subjects, they did not on the whole do so by tracking transfers of property and privilege through records that they themselves maintained. Second, as a direct consequence, most probative records rested in the hands of recipients, rather than in the hands of rulers or grantors of privilege, and gained authenticity primarily from features built into the document itself, rather than from a relationship to records in public hands. Elsewhere, records authenticated by a notary's register represented a novel hybrid of private and public authenticity. Adjudication of disputes – at once both a political and a legal matter in a system for which the idea of public authority was so diffuse – took place in courts provided by rulers (or operating under privileges

---

[32] See especially Keller and Behrmann, *Kommunales Schriftgut;* Nussdorfer, *Brokers,* who cites extensive literature; and Schulte, "Notarial Documents."

issued by a ruler), but relied on the production by the parties of witnesses or of self-authenticating documents that testified to their claims.[33]

As royal and other forms of political authority became more effective and more bureaucratized after about 1200, this documentary regime came to be supplemented by new practices by which rulers and their chancelleries became primary issuers as well as guarantors and preservers of documents. These developments, part of the broader High Medieval renaissance that gave many European institutions new and often durable shapes, resulted in various mixed regimes of record-keeping. The self-authenticating charter or the extract from a notarial register remained a vital form of testimony throughout the early modern period, but increasingly resided side by side with other genres of documentation. Equally important was the overall trend toward increased use of written records in other spheres. This trend, while not continuous, meant that far more records existed and circulated in later periods than had been the case earlier – a process that accelerated even further as paper became a cheap and widely available medium for record-keeping in the fifteenth century.[34]

Archival practice from the tenth to fifteenth centuries always showed a close connection to the way records operated in public life. Early in the period, it was often the document-as-object (what Cornelia Vismann too disparagingly terms "trinkets made by hand of precious materials") that provided effective testimony.[35] Users placed great importance on documents' authenticating and representational features: The presence (or absence) and prestige of issuers and signatories, the attachment of seals, and the impressiveness of script and layout all lent documents weight in courts both political and juridical, often in ways only obliquely captured by the formal text recording an act.[36] Preserving and protecting these documentary objects was a vital concern for their possessors, who

---

[33] As emphasized in recent medieval scholarship, the distinction here is not between oral and literate legal culture, but rather regarding how documents could be deployed. See Koziol, *The Politics*; Teuscher, *Lords' Rights*.

[34] On Italian practices in the High and Late Middle Ages, see Guidi, "The Florentine Archives"; de Vivo, Guidi, and Silvestri, *Archivi e archivisti*; and Lazzarini, "Records."

[35] Vismann, *Files*, 72. In addition to the famous swords and clods of earth in repositories described by Clanchy, *From Memory*, 35–43, see also Teuscher, "Kompilation und Mündlichkeit."

[36] Recent research emphasizes that the text of a document never conveyed more than *part* of its meaning. See, for example, Koziol, *The Politics*, 9–15, who shows how an important event could be highlighted in a charter "because of the pointed absence of any reference to it," and where a person is identified as an enemy "precisely because he is not mentioned where he should have been."

sometimes used the Roman term *archivum* to designate the treasuries where they stored their charters and diplomas among other preciosities. Often kept in the sacristy of a local church or in another location safe from fire and theft, and locked into chests with multiple locks, charters needed to be not accessible except to authorized parties. They routinely shared space in the treasury, alongside saints' relics, swords with important histories, flags captured from rival rulers, and the sacral objects used in performing religious services. Monasteries (which gained lands through gifts from nobles and laypeople) were among the first to establish such treasuries, with cities eventually following suit. By comparison, the nobility, who were often itinerant and less concerned about sustaining their authority through documents, were less likely to memorialize important acts in writing, and more likely to lose such writings in the course of travel, inheritance disputes, or popular rebellions.[37]

Despite the emphasis that medieval politics and medieval archivality continued to place on the document-as-object, the texts inscribed on documents always possessed an important role as well. Because texts helped identify the actors and witnesses present at (or absent from) the granting of privileges, and because they described the privileges granted and the terms accompanying the grant, various users continued to have recourse to the texts, including monastic chroniclers recording the history and possessions of their houses and royal propagandists asserting their masters' glory.[38] Moreover, as rulers and cities professionalized their law courts, and as writing surged as a tool of governance and control more broadly in the twelfth century, more and more possessors and issuers of privileges began creating new tools that could mobilize the traces of acts of issuance found in charters. Before the period at the core of this book, a prior series of transformations had already moved European documentary practice decisively beyond the basic methods sketched (far too simply) up to this point in this chapter.[39] It was the emergence of these new practices, which took place primarily through the medial form of the codex or book, that set the stage for later developments.

---

[37] Monasteries under family control often housed noble documents. Stowasser, "Das Archiv," especially 15–17 on the Babenberger at Klosterneuberg and the Habsburgs at Lilienfeld up to 1299; Potin, "Entre trésor sacré." On flags in archives, see Schmid, "Fahnengeschichten."

[38] A recent example of close analysis is found in Gorecki, *Text and the World*.

[39] The fact that the sealed self-authenticating charter nevertheless remained at the center of scholarly interest for so long is itself worthy of reflection. See Kuchenbuch and Kleine, *Textus*; Morsel, "En Guise d'Introduction"; Vismann, *Files*, 74.

Cartularies and Registers: Managing Records in Books in the High Middle Ages

Organizing records of important deeds and acts became more difficult as their number increased after the twelfth century, and by the later Middle Ages, all but the smallest accumulations required *aides-memoires* to assist their users.[40] Two medieval genres of codex emerged to help guide the possessors of documents: the cartulary and the emissions register. Each came to play a major role in documentary practice across Europe, with rapid increases in production in the eleventh century for cartularies and the later twelfth century for registers.[41] Cartularies grew, in part, out of recipients keeping their charters in a treasury or *archivum*, carefully locked and guarded, but also relatively inaccessible and thus unknown. Similarly, those who issued privileges to others – originally, emperors, kings, and popes, but later many more authorities – understood that they needed a record of their acts for future consultation, and very early on, turned to book-form registers to fulfill this goal. In later periods, chancellery books took on many other configurations, most of which drew on the compiling and organizing technologies already found in cartularies and registers.

No matter the contents, records gathered in books could be provided with metadata to aid finding information. I use the term "metadata" broadly here, rather than technically, to signify inscribed signs that were about the document where they appeared, rather than being directly about the acts to which the document pertained. Ranging from underlining and rubrication to complicated codes and pointers, such metadata were inscribed primarily to allow faster access to specific documents within larger collections, and will be discussed at length in this book. Metadata in this sense constitute "information about information."[42] In the later fifteenth and sixteenth centuries, the growing volume and complexity of stored records also led to the differentiation of multiple storage spaces, which could then be described in systematic inventories and classifications, which also mostly took codex form.

---

[40] Pope Innocent III produced some 300 surviving letters per year around 1300, whereas Pope Boniface VIII a hundred years later produced about 50,000 letters per year; Clanchy, *From Memory*, 60–61. On "information overload," see Rosenberg, "Introduction."

[41] The literature on medieval cartularies and chancellery registers is vast. For an overview, see Kosto and Winroth, *Charters*; Silagi, *Landesherrliche Kanzleien*; and Tessier, "L'enregistrement." On books more broadly, see Meier, Hüpper, and Keller, *Der Codex*.

[42] On archival metadata in general, see Williams, "Diplomatic Attitudes." Williams distinguishes between extrinsic and intrinsic metadata, or metadata of the system (referring to electronic systems, but applicable more generally) and metadata of the records.

A widely expressed goal of creating chancellery books was to make records findable: As an Innsbruck ordinance put it in 1523, all records should be "registered and kept in the chancellery, so that one may actually know what was at any time received, discussed and issued."[43] Fortunately, secretaries' need for access to bodies of records in their repositories shared much with scholars' interest in managing the information they found in the Bible, the Church Fathers, or in the Classics, which eased the movement of methods from the scholarly to the administrative sphere, as will be discussed in the following section.[44]

My use of the terms "cartulary" and "emissions register" here is ideal-typical and simplifies the wide range of applications that each term found at the time. A *cartulary* reproduced in book form a selection of documentary testimonies about an institution's privileges and other key moments, whose originals usually remained in its *archivum*. Cartularies responded to multiple memorializing impulses, among which legal deployment of the texts of foundational charters was only one. The term *emissions register* refers to a book-form record of the instruments issued by a single ruler or chancellery, normally as self-authenticating charters given to multiple recipients over time. Those who issued charters recognized the difficulty of knowing what they and their predecessors had actually given away, and adopted various practices of registration, either as textual copies or in more schematic ways, that typically led to register books in protocol form.[45] Both of these chancellery tools therefore responded to various parties' desire to mobilize records in sustaining the institutions they headed. In essence, they represented concrete manifestations of the medieval expansion of "governance on the basis of knowledge" (to borrow Brian Stock's Weberian formulation).[46]

A note of caution is important: While functional imperatives – above all, the "ease of finding" expressed in an increasing number of sources – help explain the emergence of the cartulary and the register, they surely did not provide the only incentives, nor should we assume that the only goal of producing such tools was administrative convenience. In particular, monasteries began producing cartularies very early in the career of European bureaucracy, and in ways closely connected to other practices of memorializing the past. Early cartularies included monastic records

---

[43] TLA Innsbruck, Ober-Österreichische Regierung, Kopialbücher, "An der Fürstlichen Durchlaucht," vol. 2: The document reports on efforts to ensure that all matters processed by the Innsbruck administration were findable.

[44] I owe this insight to Teuscher, "Document Collections."

[45] Charlemagne had already expressed the concern that "nobody... was able to keep track of the missives and directives that had been issued"; Vismann, *Files*, 72.

[46] Stock, "Schriftgebrauch."

from ritual as well as political contexts, and covered both privileges and spiritual material such as brotherhood lists and calendars of Masses for past members and friends of the abbey.[47]

Several logical and functional differences separate the complementary genres of cartulary and register.[48] Cartularies (as I use the term) were books that reproduced (or transmediated) charters, diplomas, and other documentary instruments in an institution's possession. *Recipients* of documents created cartularies, which they used to address the logistics of mobilizing documents-as-objects and to provide their owners with working texts that could have both forensic and informational value. Cartularies exist from as early as the eighth century and continued to be produced – including in print – as late as the seventeenth century. Monastic scribes produced the vast majority of surviving early examples, since monasteries depended on gifts and privileges for their institutional autonomy and material well-being, and were already sites of literacy and book production for spiritual reasons. The format and content of cartularies varied considerably, with chronicles, narrative reports, spiritual texts, and various other materials appearing alongside charters and diplomas on their pages.[49] Despite this variability, a few features give the genre clear definition. First, the records found on the pages of a cartulary reproduced in some form what were separate, typically loose documents with diverse origins. Second, the originals had typically been issued by multiple authorities, and were now held in a single institution's *archivum*. Third, each document, however represented, occupied contiguous space on the cartulary's pages.

Cartularies reproduced only some features of probative objects from the treasury – primarily, the words inscribed on them[50] – so as to allow those objects to be deployed more effectively in diverse contexts. They also inherently contained some metadata, since they represented records while simultaneously *pointing to* authoritative memorial objects stored elsewhere in some way. Scribes often added additional metadata, such as rubrics or mise-en-page clues, to the locational metadata that established links between precious originals and textualized copies. Locational identifiers included iconic signs appearing on both cartulary pages and

---

[47] A good overview of the issues is found in Bouchard, "Monastic Cartularies."

[48] Genicot, *Les Actes Publics*, 48, establishes the logical distinction that I follow; much of the specialized literature uses "cartulary" for any codex containing relatively complete representations (typically called "copies") of charters, and "registers" for records made synchronously with the emission of a charter.

[49] See, for example, Tock, "Les Textes Non Diplomatiques."

[50] Surprisingly, visual representation of seals is a late and quite scattered phenomenon in cartularies; Bedos-Rezak, "Towards an Archaeology," 59.

marked documents,[51] various systems of letters and numbers,[52] and mapping systems like the one described in a sixteenth century urban cartulary from Lucerne:

... in every case, the charters that lie in one box are written down one after the other, and the names of the boxes in the chancery are the same as the titles contained in this book, so that one can find the documents more easily.[53]

Inevitably, cartularies not only reproduced, but also *substituted* texts in books for the precious original objects, with important consequences: By presenting copied texts in place of meaning-laden objects, cartularies transformed not only the texts available to chancelleries and magistrates, but also the mediality of political information itself.[54] Even though the loose charter and the cartulary page contained records of the same act, the change in medial configuration had major consequences for how the new record and document, which was significantly different from the locked-up original, might be accessed and deployed.[55]

In emissions registers, issuers of privileges, too, preserved their access to records of their acts by creating informational duplicates of the charters they issued; these duplicates went into books kept in their chancelleries.[56] The papacy itself, despite some major lacunae, never abandoned the practice of registering the issuance of various documents, including privileges, thereby providing the Church and all of Latin Christendom with an important model of document management.[57] Ambitious monarchs – notably Frederick II in Sicily, who was able to draw on models from the Byzantine and Islamic worlds in his rivalry with the papacy – also had every interest in recording and preserving knowledge about the

---

[51] See Teuscher, "Document Collections," for examples.

[52] For example, the *Habsburg Urbar* in Baden designated locations as "a, b, und c" and marked the individual documents accordingly; Stowasser, "Das Archiv," 37–38.

[53] StALU, COD 1515, fol. 4r.; see Head, "Mirroring Governance," and Anton Gössi, "Archivordnungen."

[54] Bouchard, "Monastic Cartularies," 31–32, notes that "if a cartulary's original purpose was to create an orderly sense of what the monastery actually owned and how the monks had acquired it, supplementing rather than replacing their collection of original charters, then its purpose was modified once it existed. It quickly became in essence a substitute for the archival documents from which it had been copied." On the discursive and performative dimensions of the charter as testimony, see Bedos-Rezak, "Toward an Archaeology," 58–60.

[55] This transformation also illustrates the inherently recursive nature of metadata, which by necessity are also *data*.

[56] The term *register* was used throughout the Middle Ages and early modern period for a wide variety of codices that recorded knowledge. See Patze, "Herrschaftspraxis."

[57] No papal registers survive from the late ninth century until the mid-eleventh century. Registration began again under Alexander II in conscious imitation of Late Antique precedents. Blumenthal, "Päpstliche Urkunden," 11.

privileges they issued.[58] The key definitional criterion for an emissions register is that it recorded the issuance of documents, a characteristic that distinguished it from a cartulary, which documented documents' receipt. Indeed, entry of a charter into a register was often an explicit part of the process of approval and issuance.[59] Registers were similar to cartularies, however, in that they contained representations of a series of charters, one after another in protocol form. In this way, charters, cartularies, and registers all testified to acts of granting privileges (or other acts of an empowered actor or institution) and belonged to a single intermedial system for representing legal and ceremonial acts that thrived after 1100.

Most scholarship has treated both cartularies and registers as containing *copies* in some sense, reserving the term "original" for the circulating document with its physical and textual signs of authenticity. Such a perspective corresponds to the position taken in Jean Mabillon's enormously influential *De re diplomatica* of 1681, but recent research suggests that this view of originals and copies corresponds poorly to medieval views about the way that documents could authorize testimony.[60] From a strictly legal perspective, Giorgio Costamagna's careful examination of jurists' handbooks from Genoa shows that the key distinction in medieval legal practice was not between originals and copies, but rather between authentic and inauthentic records.[61] Making a comparable point in a broader theoretical context, Brigitte Bedos-Rezak argues that not documents, but rather the acts they referred to, were the focal point of interest for medieval documentary practices, so that "in that sense, every surviving document reporting such events may best be understood as a copy."[62] This helps explain why "medieval scribes, ... those who undertook the actual work of reproduction, seem not to have been so

---

[58] Most discussions of emissions registers assume that rulers' interest in knowing which privileges they had granted to others provided the key motivation for registration. Ernst Pitz suggests a radical revision of this view in "Diplom und Registereintrag," arguing that the creation of registers freed royal judges and the authors of statutes from local common laws; he illustrates his provocative hypothesis with material from twelfth-century England.

[59] In some cases, acts approved by a ruler were recorded in a register, but a loose charter was expedited (that is, inscribed and transferred to the recipient) only if the recipient was willing to pay for it. In other cases, the emitted charter seems to have been produced first, and only reproduced (often in summary form) in a register later. Metadata in registers, especially the marks known as *Vermerke* in German, encoded notes about the process. See Spangenberg, "Die Kanzleivermerke."

[60] The persistence of this view is critiqued by Geary, "Entre gestion," 13. For copies, the old view is discussed Morelle, "De l'original à la copie."

[61] Costamagna, "I concetti." See also Nicolaj, "*Originale, authenticum, publicum.*"

[62] Bedos-Rezak, "Towards an Archaeology," 43. For a theorized approach to archival documents and representation, see Yeo, "Concepts of Record (1)," and Yakel, "Archival Representation."

concerned with unique and authentic originals in the same sense that Mabillon was," since their products in cartularies enjoyed authenticity even without the probative features of circulating instruments, such as seals or signatures. Moreover, practices of authentication were unstable and changed over time, producing a situation in which "a given diplomatic text belonged to an intertextual system, and was probably not understood as a discrete instance of discourse in isolation from the archive which contained it."[63] Finally, we must remember that authentication was a social practice, in which social and political considerations, such as a notary's personal status and social network, could outweigh formal aspects of particular documents.[64]

A key difference between registers and cartularies was that the two genres operated in different information environments and had different logical relationships to circulating single-leaf records; in consequence, producing information out of a register raised different challenges than did locating charters in an *archivum*. Registers came from chancelleries and were procedurally connected with the production of circulating charters, whereas cartularies were retrospective products of an inward gaze in smaller record-keeping environments, above all monasteries. These differences meant that registers typically accumulated more abundant metadata than cartularies, as medievalists have long recognized.[65] In addition, the large number of entries in registers and scribes' tendency to abbreviate charter texts, sometimes down to effectively tabular form, also encouraged the creation of metadata internal to the register itself.[66]

Joachim Wild's careful comparative study of fourteenth-century Bavarian monastic registers provides a vivid demonstration of how the increasing degree of abstraction in Late Medieval emissions registers encouraged the use of cross-reference and abbreviation, highlighting in the process the important distinction between texts and information in chancellery practice. The registers in question recorded land leases to the monasteries' peasants. When Bavarian courts after 1300 began demanding written evidence for disputes involving leases longer than a year, tenants began demanding that their landlords issue them charters

---

[63] Bedos-Rezak, "Towards an Archaeology," 59.

[64] Petra Schulte explores this issue with illuminating case studies in *Scripturae Publica*.

[65] See, for example, Bier, *Das Urkundenwesen*, 22.

[66] Wild, *Beiträge*, 5–8. Bier, *Das Urkundenwesen*, 21, argues the point more generally for Brandenburg in the fourteenth century: "[Wir finden] in den amtlich geführten Kanzleiregistern ein ganzes System verschiedener Formen der Wiedergabe der Urkunden."

recording the terms of their leases.[67] The monasteries did so, and their abbots and scribes registered the charters in new books, generally in tabular and protocol form. Charters were registered in successive, similar blocks of space in a pre-bound register book and were entered in approximate chronological order. In the earliest registers from the 1320s and 1330s, the entire text of each charter was reproduced in full in the register, presumably before the charter itself was issued to the recipient. Soon, however, the monasteries' scribes stopped copying highly standardized sections of charters, such as the *intitulatio* and *corroboratio*, replacing them with a simple "etc." In addition, metadata could lighten the scribal burden through entries like one for the reissue of a charter in 1339, which simply said, "according to the terms written above on folio 115."[68] Further abbreviations followed, and by the fifteenth century, many of the registers simply listed the significant variables for each lease – the lessee's name, the property description, the length in years, and any nonstandard terms – in tabular form without any effort reproduce the charter's text.[69] Even though the textual form of the entries had changed radically, their information content (provided the reader was properly informed) had not.

Chancellery Books and Scholastic Knowledge Tools

My key claim for the rest of this chapter is that when we look at how chancelleries managed the growing flow and accumulation of probative records in the fifteenth and sixteenth centuries, technologies of the book played a central role in their strategies and output. Manuscript codices – with cartularies and registers serving as paradigmatic forms – were tightly connected with the ongoing production, circulation, and preservation of loose documents, but they have received little attention in early modern research, especially with regard to archival practices. Moreover, because codices rather than loose documents were in the forefront of chancellery experts' practice, as I will show, evolving technologies of the book found ready entry into chancelleries, and provided secretaries and registrars with the "little tools" they needed to gain control over their rapidly growing collections. Just as medieval governance rested on an

---

[67] While Wild mentions Bavarian law, it is notable that the Council of Lavour in 1368 also established that all contracts for leases on land required the production of a legal instrument in two copies, one to be held by each part. See Willett, *The Probative Value*, 36.

[68] Wild, *Beiträge*, 13.

[69] Wild, *Beiträge*, 6–10. Between 1331 and 1415, various monasteries produced registers that took the step "zur völligen Aufgabe des Urkundenformulars."

intertextual and intermedial system of reference involving documents and texts, as Bedos-Rezak argues, so did early modern governance – but the systems of reference (which included, as one important component, systems of archiving) changed in fundamental ways in response to the changing genres, purposes, and volume of written records.

Over the last generation, a group of extraordinary scholars has analyzed the manuscript books of the Middle Ages to discern how medieval scribes composed and wrote, and how they responded to their readers' changing uses of written material in theological, legal, and erudite contexts. Brian Stock, Mary Carruthers, and others have probed the mental and social practices that lay behind reading and writing practices, while Malcolm Parkes, Richard Rouse, Mary Rouse, Paul Saenger, and Brigitte Bedos-Rezak have looked into the distinct and identifiable functions that books had, embedded in the specific social and cultural milieu of the medieval university or court, and have probed the work of those who compiled, organized, and produced the books that educated Europeans made use of from the eleventh to the fifteenth centuries.[70] As medieval thinkers' use of certain stock phrases demonstrates, they were deeply concerned about *finding* information, among other things – a concern they expressed in phrases such as *facilitas inveniendi, statim invenire,* and *folia librorum quaerere.*[71] High Medieval book producers addressed this concern by putting great efforts into refining books and the metadata they contained, and advertised the tools they offered to readers that would enable them to find the information they sought in a particular book. The larger cultural question of why Europeans turned to books as information-access tools in these ways, and what consequences this had for erudition, literature, and politics, is beyond the scope of my discussion here, but remains a lively and provocative field of study that is far from exhausted.

Here, two facts are critical: (1) Powerful tools for managing information in codices emerged first in the realms of theology and law, in close connection with the appearance of the first universities in Europe; and (2) these tools also appeared, but in substantially adapted forms, in the offices of governance when chancellery staffs began deploying them a century or so later.[72] I will concentrate on the most important codical

---

[70] See, for example, the forthright discussion of utility in Rouse and Rouse, *Preachers,* 40–42.

[71] Appearing, respectively, in Zedelmaier, *"Facilitas inveniendi"*; Rouse and Rouse, *"Statim Invenire"*; and Parkes, *"Folia."*

[72] Kosto, *"'Statim invenire ante,'"* argues that administrative codices may have preceded, rather than depended on, the twelfth-century Scholastic revolution in knowledge management.

finding tools that emerged with the rise of Scholastic erudition, and then turn to the forms they took when they started appearing in Late Medieval chancellery practice. Adaptations of these tools to the needs of chancelleries were flexible and heterogeneous, and continued throughout the early modern period across Europe, as will be demonstrated by case studies throughout the book.

The tools for managing information in codices that emerged out of the Scholastic milieu can be separated into several elements:

- Ways to mark discrete pieces of information in a text (*distinctiones*) and to locate those markers (loci)
- Ways to organize writing on pages (*mise-en-page*) through the size and color of text, through the division of the page into different spaces, and so forth, so as to make scanning and browsing more effective
- Ways to organize entire codices (*mise-en-livre*) through such elements as running heads, foliation, division into books and chapters, and tabs, all of which made access to a specific locus easier
- Ways to organize and especially to connect ideas to loci and other textual markers through compact finding aids such as indexes and tables

Scholastic practice involved a series of choices (conscious or unconscious) about each of these elements, starting with the Late Antique evolution across most of the Mediterranean, during which the codex superseded other medial forms such as the tablet or scroll (something that had largely taken place long before the period discussed here).[73] Once the codex became the key way to gather longer or multiple texts into a single medial unit, a whole series of configurational choices emerged about how to organize each volume. Should leaves, openings, or pages be numbered? Which conventions should regulate margins, internal divisions, the placement of metadata, and so forth? For each of these, the outcomes that became common in Western Europe stand next to alternatives that can in some cases be found in other literary traditions around the globe.

Scribes in the later Middle Ages and early modern period thus used numerous "little tools" associated with alphabetic script and the forms of the leaf, the quire, and the codex. These tools, while certainly significant in their consequences, generally remained constant for the purposes of

---

[73] An introduction to early techniques for organizing the codex can be found in Grafton and Williams, *Christianity*. We should not assume that techniques were lost simply because we do not see them in common use during a particular era. See Raible, *Die Semiotik*.

this study. With some exceptions, such as the English exchequer, chancelleries used sheets, quires, and books in their operations, which they stored in bags, boxes, and chests. Texts might be recorded in scripts of different size, weight, and color, but they almost all relied on the Latin alphabet, and by the 1100s, virtually all texts were inscribed with spaces between words and with the use of (often erratic) interpunctuation.[74] These forms both enabled and constrained what could be done with manuscript documents in ways that changed only slowly between the 1300s and the 1700s. As a consequence, we can speak of the European manuscript codex as a relatively stable medial form over these centuries. The introduction of first block-type and then movable-type printing in Europe over the course of the 1400s affected both reading habits and practices of erudition, but the changes involved penetrated only slowly into chancelleries and archives. Ultimately, changes in pedagogy and in the circulation of knowledge initiated by print culture did transform the training and horizons of secretaries and registrators, so they help explain the changes that mark the endpoint of this study in the late seventeenth and eighteenth centuries.[75] For the crucial period from 1400 to 1700, however, we can treat the underlying "little tools" of alphabet, page, and book as largely constant.

The most fundamental requirement for managing long texts inscribed in a consistent medium is that the texts be divided into smaller units according to some scheme. Long strings of alphabetical characters must be separated into smaller units, often according to a hierarchy of subdivisions (e.g., book, chapter, verse, word). Such divisions may reflect features of the content or features of the medium (or both). For example, a larger work may be divided into multiple codices or books that represent physical units; a book may be divided into chapters that reflect divisions of content and into leaves whose margins, header, and main body again reflect medial divisions. Both the Classical civilizations of the Mediterranean and Christian Late Antiquity possessed very long texts divided into "books." These originally corresponded to a single scroll, which was a material unit of relatively fixed length, but became textual rather than medial units when multiple "books" were transcribed into a single codex. Further division into chapters set by the author or a subsequent editor or scribe was much less consistent.[76] This system was

---

[74] On the former, see the ambitious study by Saenger, *Space between Words*; on the latter, see Parkes, *Pause and Effect*.

[75] See Goeing, *Storing*, for a close analysis directly connecting Humanist knowledge practices with institutional record-keeping in sixteenth-century Zurich.

[76] Parkes, "The Influence," especially 51–52. See also Dames, "The Chapter."

applied to Christian texts as well, with both parts of the Bible divided into books and chapters (although Christian Bible chapters did not become standardized until the thirteenth century, and verses until the sixteenth century[77]).

When the scroll was the primary medium for storing longer texts, subdivision into medial units smaller than the single scroll faced challenges in how to identify specific passages within a single long stretch of papyrus. With the advent of the codex, which consisted of discrete leaves, the theoretical possibility of page- or leaf-number references emerged, although these remained rare in practice for learned works before the High Middle Ages. Not only was a workable content-based system of books and chapters already in place, but each exemplar of a text inscribed in multiple manuscript codices typically displayed different pagination. This meant that page-number (or folio-number or opening-number) references were of limited utility, whereas book and chapter references remained valid.[78] For this reason, content-based rather than medium-based subdivisions generally remained the norm from the triumph of the codex until the advent of print, at least for any text that was frequently reproduced. A great wave of content-based division and subdivision of older literature took place during the High Middle Ages, providing increasingly standard divisions, while newly produced works had books and chapters from the outset.

The intense study of texts that characterized erudition at the new universities of the twelfth century produced further divisions, known as *distinctiones,* and introduced more precise text locations, known as loci. The original use of *distinctiones* was to provide the "various figurative or symbolic meanings of a noun found in the scriptures, illustrating each meaning with a scriptural passage."[79] Collections of such *distinctiones,* soon organized alphabetically, began to circulate before 1200, followed by complete concordances to the words found in the Bible, the first of which appeared in 1239.[80] Similar divisions and concordances appeared for other canonical long texts, including the Roman law books of Justinian and the works of Aristotle and Augustine. Major theological works, such as Peter Lombard's *Sentences,* were soon organized into *distinctiones* as well.

---

[77] See Lowe, "The Medieval History," 2; Moore, "The Vulgate Chapters."

[78] On the prehistory and early history of page numbers and foliation, see Saenger, "The Impact," especially 254–71.

[79] Rouse and Rouse, *Preachers,* 7ff, provide a lucid chronology of "little tools" in this period. See also Parkes, *"Folia."*

[80] Rouse and Rouse, "Concordances."

To work effectively, the establishment of content divisions (whether at the level of books and chapters or at the level of the single word, as for concordances) required a metadata framework that allowed the reader to move from a reference to the textual locus.[81] Alphabetization provided one way to organize concordances, with the concordance then providing references to the books and perhaps to chapters and verses in the Bible where the desired word was located. Other techniques helped make it possible to quickly find a specific locus within a long text, such as by using the layout or *mise-en-page* of the codex to give features that oriented the user. In the lucid formulation of the Richard and Mary Rouse,

> one cannot help but appreciate the benefits of [certain changes in the layout of the book and the page]: the material has been consciously arranged so as to help the user quickly find the section and the passage for which he is searching. Signposts such as running headlines, marginal letters of the alphabet designating individual extracts, marginal notation of the authors who are cited, rubrics dividing the subjects and paragraph marks distinguishing the extracts one from another, and a table of chapters all assist in this purpose. Color, size of letter and spacing are all effectively used to distinguish visually one part of the text from another and to help the user find his place.[82]

As the strongly utilitarian tone of this summary suggests, High Medieval scribes and book producers took identifiable pains to make their products usable – or at least, as Simon Teuscher notes, to give them the appearance of being usable.[83] They also took pains in other respects, depending on who had commissioned a codex and what its audience might be, making books impressive, beautiful, distracting, or otherwise suited to their audiences. On the whole, however, these latter qualities had less attraction for the fifteenth-century chancellery officials who adopted the new book technologies to organize their collections and document management – though with some intriguing exceptions. Notably, chancellery secretaries eagerly seized on the utilitarian elements

---

[81] As noted vividly by Leonardi, "Premessa," vi–ix, such referential forms of reading remained vigorously contested by Humanist-style erudition. On the logic of reference, see Blair, *Too Much to Know*.

[82] Rouse and Rouse, *Preachers,* 27. On various *mise-en-page* techniques, see Martin and Vezin, *Mise en page.* Many of the techniques that flourished anew in the twelfth century had been known much earlier. See, for example, Raible, *Die Semiotik,* who reproduces (p. 7) a first-century CE inscription, noting that "bis auf die Interpunktion im heutigen Sinn ... wird hier im 'Layout' das vorweggenommen, was in der 'normalen' Entwicklung der lateinischen Schrift erst etwa ein Jahrtausend später zur Norm wird."

[83] Teuscher, "Document Collections," 216–17, describes a textual compilation whose index and *mise-en-page* gave the appearance of organization that was, in fact, absent. He speculates, "This is one of several manuscripts where learnedness in part seems to be feigned, probably in order to impress potential readers and, maybe more importantly, buyers."

highlighted in this section to make registers and inventories easier to use, adapting and improving them as they proceeded.

In the use of one mundane but extremely powerful tool, chancellery officials soon went beyond of the producers of erudite or literary works: folio numbers marking the individual leaves of a codex. Registers and cartularies seem to have been among the earliest genre of book to regularly apply foliation (that is, having a number placed on each leaf of the main body of the volume), and to use these numbers for internal reference.[84] Important distinctions between a chancellery book and a work of scholarship or literature favored this development. First, the quintessential learned book in the Middle Ages reproduced and commented on a canonical text of some kind such as the Bible, the works of a Church Father, or Roman law. Readers who wanted to refer to a specific passage could not rely on the foliation of the particular copy they were using, since they knew that other readers – their interlocutors – would be looking at differently foliated exemplars (given the technologies of reproducing manuscript books). Instead, authors referred to books and chapters, or to keywords that were rubricated in their copy, which they could expect would be present in other copies. Additionally, the sphere of references in learned books was wide, extending not only to other copies of the same book, but also to other books themselves lacking foliation. The sophisticated tools of distinction and layout used by Scholastic learning were well adapted to exactly such circumstances.

In contrast, a register or cartulary usually existed only in a single exemplar that contained many separate documents that were often highly repetitive. Moreover, the sphere of reference relevant to chancellery officials was often *internal* to the volume or to a series of codices: They needed to find a specific charter that related to another, recorded on a particular page. Meanwhile, the contents of the unique chancellery book naturally lacked any standardized subdivisions such as books and chapters. Under such circumstances, foliation provided an effective way to link references to texts, and we therefore find foliation being used even in highly parochial works such as the monastic registers studied by Wild, with their references "to the terms written above on folio 115."[85] Foliation appeared early in registers because it worked, particularly when joined with layout features such as headers, spacing between entries,

---

[84] Saenger, "The Impact," 254–56, describes cartularies as the first genre in which we find "foliation used for reference purposes" (in the Farfa *Liber largitorius* before 1132), and notes that "medieval inter-volume folio cross references were extremely rare, and then usually between volumes within a scholar's private library *or within a series of familial or institutional registers*" (emphasis mine).

[85] Wild, *Beiträge*, 13.

marginal references, and other techniques of *mise-en-page* drawn from the Scholastic tradition.

Another category of reference tools of great importance consisted of tables of contents (variously designed) and indexes. Indexes and tables of contents are quintessential metadata, in one sense: They are *about* information found in a book or pile of documents, and help a user find and make use of the material to which they refer. The term "index" itself suggests pointing as the distinctive feature of such tools. We can distinguish different types of tables and indexes in both Scholastic practice and in Late Medieval and early modern chancelleries according to their internal logic, although contemporary terminology was applied loosely with various intermediate examples. For example, an encyclopedia can be viewed either as a series of keywords with brief references that lead to other, more comprehensive texts – thus, a kind of index – or as an independently compiled text that may itself possess an index and a table of contents.[86] Organized reference products also were texts, and as such, could themselves become the subject of metadata: There were, as we shall see, indexes to inventories, and so forth.[87] Nevertheless, the key logical feature of such finding aids is that they operate predominantly as tools to gain access to *other* texts through reference, rather than as freestanding texts in themselves. Tables and indexes are also inherently reductive; that is, finding aids generally contain less text as well as less information than the corpus to which they refer (again, with potential exceptions[88]).

Malcolm Parkes's review of medieval indexes (taking the term broadly) divides the tools used by Scholastic erudition "to facilitate both the study of a text and the location of information within it" into two logical categories: *hypertexts* ("material essential to understanding a text, which followed the order of the text") and tools that provided "*independent access* to information."[89] In the first group, he places glosses, marginal commentaries, and other elements of what scholars today call apparatus, as well as tables of contents. All such tools are characterized by the fact that the organization of the interpretive tool or finding aid *mirrors* the organization of the texts it is about. Glosses and footnotes do so, in part, by appearing on the same leaf as the primary text and being tied to that

---

[86] The subtle gradients between "text" and "index" or "data" and "metadata" are also explored in Blair, *Too Much to Know*.

[87] Weijers, "Les index."

[88] A concordance that located and defined every single word in the underlying text could be very much longer than the text itself, yet still serve as a reference and finding tool, because it was organized alphabetically.

[89] Parkes, "*Folia*."

text by various systems of numbers, pointers, or inscribed lines. End-notes and tables of contents do not appear on the same page as their referents, but still reproduce the organizational structure of the main text in their internal order. Tables laying out the contents of a codex emerged quite early in both intellectual and administrative contexts. Systematic tables of contents mirrored the full structure of the main text, book by book or hierarchically arranged, with each book broken down into chapters. Analytical tables of contents selectively represented the book's contents, picking out those elements worthy of mention, such as a list of all the personal names that appeared, in order of their appearance. Scholastic intellectuals were inventive in creating sophisticated analytical tables to assist in the use of larger works, and their work circulated widely in the university settings where chancellery specialists often gained their educations.

Parkes's second category – tools that provide independent access to information[90] (which I call indexes) – works in a fundamentally different way: first by establishing worthwhile loci (or *lemmata* or keywords) within a text, which might be underlined, written larger, or inked in color so as to make it easier to find them; and then, crucially, creating a *second* textual space in which the same *lemmata* are placed in sequence according to a different formal principle, together with a pointer to each *lemma*'s location in the main text. The most familiar type of index is alphabetical: Keywords or names are first identified in the text under consideration, and then separately reproduced in alphabetical order, forming the index per se, where they are linked to page numbers. Looked at this way, it is clear why alphabetical indexes and page numbers go well together. Alphabetization provides a simple formal principle for ordering the *lemmata* in the index, while page numbers provide a method for connecting alphabetized *lemmata* to specific loci in the text. However, this was not the combination found in most Scholastic indexes, because most theological, legal, and literary books in the Middle Ages were not foliated. Instead, the Scholastic alphabetical indexes provided pointers to books and chapters. To provide closer references, indexers developed clever additional tools, such as divisions of chapters, pages, or openings into seven sections marked by letters (most commonly a–g) in a system

---

[90] Parkes's formulation is not entirely felicitous. The key point here is that pointers to information in a text (consisting of a *lemma* and a locus) are inscribed as a separate text *organized according to a separate and transparent principle*. That is, instead of mirroring the organizational structure of the main text, an index orders a set of referential terms – the *lemmata* or keywords – according to a second principle that is independent of the structure of the main text (e.g., the sequence of letters in the alphabet).

developed in Paris before 1300,[91] or the system of five-line numbered blocs developed by the Franciscans at Oxford around 1250.[92]

Alphabetization, although known, was not the most common indexing principle used in Scholastic books. Rather, the *lemmata* appeared in the index, often in a sequence that reflected the order of the world as conceived by medieval thinkers. For example, they might be ordered by the spiritual status of what they named: Those referring to the Trinity, to the Virgin, or to Christian virtues might be placed before those naming earthly referents. Indexes to books about language ordered *lemmata* by parts of speech, while other Scholastic finding aids used the tree or the human hand to provide a formal ordering principle for *lemmata*.[93] Another ordering principle – rare in Scholastic works, but natural for chancellery codices – was chronological: An index could reference *lemmata* or entries in chronological order of the emission date of the charters in question, for example. Administrative inquests might use topographical indexing, which arranged *lemmata* in accord with locations on a map. Thus, while the underlying logical definition of the index may be clear, and rests on the index's ability to provide access to loci independently of a text's internal organization, the details of its implementation could vary widely.

Alphabetization itself was far from straightforward, particularly in a world where scribal production was slow and the materials, especially parchment, quite expensive.[94] Today we can alphabetize long lists perfectly with a click of the mouse, but considerable labor and costs arise when humans do the same work manually. Indexers must choose how many letters of keywords to use in sorting the keywords. Most premodern indexes used only the first letter to alphabetize the index terms, even though scribes recognized the possibility of multiletter indexing, which appeared from the twelfth century onward where it provided a decisive advantage (such as in very long indexes).[95] Rather, the imperative to use parchment and scribal labor frugally clashed with the more complex process needed to alphabetize by more letters. Typically, a scribe laid out his alphabet on the pages of the index *before* adding any entries, creating the spaces where words beginning with each letter would be recorded. Scribes soon gained a reasonable sense of how much space to allocate for each letter of the alphabet. Alphabetizing by two or more

---

[91] Rouse and Rouse, *Preachers*, 33–35, attribute such seven-fold subdivisions to the Dominicans in the thirteenth century.

[92] Parkes, "*Folia*," 37.   [93] Parkes, "*Folia*," 33–35.

[94] On the history of alphabetization, see Brincken, "Tabula Alphabetica"; Daly, *Contributions to a History*; and Zedelmaier, "*Facilitas*."

[95] The range of possibilities sketched in Parkes, "*Folia*," 39–40, extended up to four-letter (*abcd*) systems.

letters required a larger number of smaller spaces, however (more than five hundred 2-letter spaces for a 23-letter alphabet in theory, though fewer in practice, and thousands of potential 3-letter spaces), increasing the likelihood that the scribes would guess wrong in their initial allocation of space in the index. If the index provided too little space for a particular letter combination, entries would have to squeeze or pour over into another letter's space; even worse, if the layout provided too much space, precious parchment would remain blank. Various systems of interim drafts, slips, or cards to organize the *lemmata* before inscribing the final version on parchment were themselves time and material intensive. Even in the 1690s, the guardian of the Torre do Tombo archive in Lisbon apologized for not providing "the true rigor of two-letter indexing" in a newly created three-volume index to a series of registers because the labor involved would have slowed the entire project.[96]

The lack of standardized orthography posed another challenge, especially for chancellery indexes, which by the fifteenth century mostly worked with vernacular languages. This problem was particularly thorny for German, where several initial consonants were virtually interchangeable. In response, chancelleries modified the alphabet used in alphabetization. For example, in Innsbruck, by the mid-fifteenth century "b" and "p" were indexed under one heading, as were "f" and "v." Another set of complex choices involved specifying *lemmata*, even when loci worthy of indexing had been identified. Should persons be listed by the first letter of their given names or their family names? Should place names appear by the first letter of the toponym, or the first letter of the geographical category involved (town, village, castle)? Different chancelleries and scribes responded in different ways, revealing that the answers to such questions were not obvious, and this diversity provides us with clues about what scribes in a particular context found most important. Lorenz Fries in Würzburg in the early sixteenth century chose to place a large number of indexed treaties under "v" (for *Vertrag*) with no further sorting, yet his comprehensive index, the *Hohe Registratur*, remained in heavy use for two centuries.[97] Likewise, Lisbon scribes in 1519 indexed all recipients of court housing stipends who were noble under "d" (for "Dom"), perhaps reflecting the desire to separate these recipients from non-nobles.[98] We should not assume, in any event, that the scribes involved were simply unaware of the solutions we might favor today.

---

[96] The guarda-mor's phrase is "o rigor verdadeiramente de abecedario com segundas letras"; cited in Azevedo and Baião, *O Arquivo*, 46.
[97] The *Hohe Registratur* is discussed at length in Chapter 8.
[98] ANTT, Nucleo Antigo 140.

Conclusion

Early modern record-keepers after 1400 operated on a complex terrain defined by medieval assumptions about the information worthy of preservation and the forms and methods available for doing so. In terms of content, neo-Roman law and its elaboration after 1100 laid down fundamental genres of documents – above all, the legal *instrumentum* in the form of a charter or diploma – and sophisticated criteria for authenticity, both material (e.g., seals, subscriptions, notary marks) and institutional (e.g., princely and papal authority, notaries). Although reality was often more complex than the rules worked out by jurists, early modern archives nevertheless incorporated such rules into their fabric in innumerable ways. Meanwhile, the remarkable elaboration and refinement of book technologies emerging from medieval scholarship provided a powerful set of tools that enhanced several key medial forms – above all, the manuscript book. Chapter 4 uses a case study of the sophisticated registers produced at Portugal's royal court after the mid-fifteenth century to place the elements sketched in this chapter into specific historical context.

4   A Late Medieval Chancellery and Its Books
Lisbon, 1460–1560

Introduction

To anchor the sweeping discussion provided in Chapter 3, we turn to a first specific example of written political records management around 1500, concentrating on the nexus between a dedicated chancellery and the medium of the codex and its associated tools. The royal chancellery in Lisbon possesses some important conjunctural features that make it a good candidate for such an examination. Significantly, the chancellery undertook repeated, serious efforts to reform how it preserved and organized the most important royal records, and it backed its enterprises with considerable resources from rulers with the means, at least temporarily, to invest in such reforms. Portuguese royal councils, subjects, and chancellery specialists themselves all felt that previous practices left important documents inaccessible and unmanageable – a perception that rested on real lapses in record-keeping during the early fifteenth century. As in much of Europe, the advent of the later Middle Ages had seriously disrupted earlier practices from the twelfth and thirteenth centuries, so that the Portuguese royal chancellery faced genuine challenges in regaining control over both the flow of current documents and its accumulations of older material. Novel applications of existing tools of medieval knowledge management, deployed in new configurations of codices and metadata, characterized the chancellery's response.

On the illuminated frontispieces found in a series of fine parchment volumes in the Torre do Tombo archive in Lisbon, a long mandate from King Manuel I (r. 1494–1521) appears that ends with the following command:

> And so that one may find the necessary things for those who may need them, with greater certainty and less labor, we order that [you] organize the aforementioned Tombo and its writs with great diligence. And after they have been organized and harmonized, we order that those that appear that they might be necessary at some time be newly copied and written truly.[1]

---

[1] Illuminated inscription and royal order appearing on the title page of many volumes of the *Leitura Nova* of the royal Portuguese chancellery (ANTT *Leitura Nova* [henceforth *LN*]).

With these words, the king initiated an extraordinary archival project. Known then and now as the *Leitura Nova* ("new reading"), it generated some 60 volumes of 200–300 parchment leaves each, before lack of money in the 1550s forestalled its continuation.[2] The *Leitura Nova* represented the high point of a century of intensifying chancellery organization and the production of new chancellery books in Lisbon, which also included newly copied chronicles and new legislative compilations – all in addition to continued production of regular emissions registers. A half-century before King Manuel commissioned the *Leitura Nova,* a more modest but structurally similar project to rescue the increasingly illegible and deteriorating registers of Portugal's fourteenth- and early fifteenth-century monarchs had begun during the reign of Afonso V (r. 1438–1481). The *Leitura*'s extensive illuminations and the careful tables of contents in each volume, however, set its volumes apart from the products of the 1460s and from most other chancellery books appearing across Europe at this time. The project and its antecedents are revealing because of their particular combination of administrative conservatism and material sumptuousness, two characteristics that had strong correlates in Portuguese royal politics and culture.

The newly elevated kings of Portugal began issuing formal instruments immediately after they began using the royal title in 1139, and began creating registers to record their emitted charters from the 1220s onward, though the surviving registers are heterogeneous in form and extremely uneven in their coverage.[3] By the fifteenth century, registration of emitted charters (mostly privileges and appointments to office) had become routinized: Royal deeds and writs were registered after being approved, probably on quires of ten to twelve leaves, which were then bound to produce annual volumes.[4] Inventories from the early sixteenth century confirm the presence of such annual registers, though subsequent rebindings – especially after the chancellery archive was seriously damaged in the Lisbon earthquake of 1755 – have disrupted the preservation

---

The translation here is based on a transcription by Pedro Pinto from *LN* 4 (Além Douro 4). The same text from a different volume (*LN* 9 [*Odiana* 1]) appears in Deswarte, *Les Enluminures,* 230–32.

[2] On the series' end, see the report written in 1583 by Cristovão da Benavente. Dinis, "Relatório," especially 154–55.

[3] Some documents survive from the chancellery of D. Afonso Henriques (r. 1139–1185), and the first intact ledgers date to late in the reign of Afonso II (r. 1211–1223). On medieval registers before D. Afonso V, see Costa, "La Chancellerie Royale," 143–69; Costa, "A Chancelaria Real"; and Freitas, "The Royal Chancellery."

[4] During the reign of Afonso V, charters were registered after the expedited document was drafted, with a delay that could run from days to a few years. See Da Silva Durão, "1471."

and ordering of the quires.[5] Similar registration practices continued through the reign of Afonso V, and then accelerated substantially under his son João II (r. 1481–1494). João's chancellery continued to use parchment for both documents and registers (in contrast to the paper registers found in much of Europe), but at an increasing rate, which correlated with the emergence of a typical "new monarchy." Whereas Afonso V across his long reign issued an average of 2.7 acts per day that required registration, João II's chancellery registered 2,000–3,000 royal acts per year.[6] The chancellery further intensified its records production during the reign of Manuel, as part of his reforms in the name of royal patronage and control; indeed, by the reign of João III, four separate scribes managed registration, specializing in different kinds of records.[7] Portugal thus fits into the Western European trajectory characterized by an explosive growth in document production by governments in the years around 1500. In contrast, the consistency of preservation and the stability of the royal archive, located in the Torre do Tombo of the royal castle since the reign of Dinis (r. 1279–1325), distinguished Portugal from the archival chaos and dispersion that the neighboring kingdom of Castile and other monarchies experienced during the relentless wars of the mid-fifteenth century.

Portugal experienced its own tumults in this period, however. The royal house was frequently divided by alliances to different factions of a powerful upper nobility whose members, like the Dukes of Bragança and Viseu, were not just closely related to the royal house but nearly its equal in revenue and military strength. The Crown did enjoy an unusually central position in the governance of the realm, reinforced through its Crusading history and increasing incorporation of the powerful military orders into the Crown's administration. After a dynastic interregnum in 1383–1385, the new house of Avis drew on consistent support from a Cortes representing the clergy, towns, and lower nobility. The Avis kings followed an expansionist policy toward the outer world that generated only strife within Iberia, where Portuguese projects to gain the Castilian crown again and again ended in failure, but that succeeded down the African coast and into the Atlantic beyond the imagination of its first proponents. Portugal's growing overseas empire not only brought the monarchy enormous new revenues, but also increased the influence of Lisbon compared to the rest of peninsular Portugal.[8]

---

[5] *Chancelaria* refers both to the office and to the registers it produced. See Freitas, "Chancelarias Régias," and Costa, "A Chancelaria Real," on the surviving volumes, their structure, and their provenance.

[6] Freitas, "Chancelarias Régias," 147.   [7] Dinis, "Relatório," 153–154.

[8] For a general overview through 1450, see Marques, *Portugal na Crise.*

The monarchy's success in making the royal court the hub for all political matters, despite the retention of a strongly seigniorial social order, was sealed when João II had the Duke of Braganza tried and executed for treason in 1483, then personally assassinated the Duke of Viseu (his cousin, brother-in-law, and brother of his future heir Manuel I) in 1484. In the judgment of Antonio José Saraiva, the Portuguese state of the sixteenth century presented the appearance of modernity in its external affairs, and especially in its commercial enterprises, while resting on the persistence of an archaic social order internally that was characterized by seigniorial property relations and a steady increase in church property, much of it managed through family entails and chapel endowments for the benefits of aristocratic lineages.[9] These circumstances found a strong echo in internal record-keeping practices as well, which concentrated on structures of privilege and royal grant when dealing with Portugal itself. The records of Portugal's overseas enterprises have their own history apart from the records of the royal administration analyzed here.[10]

Reforming Record-Keeping in the 1460s: The New *Chancelarias* of Afonso V

Afonso V, after a turbulent regency, governed largely with and through the great houses, represented among others by his uncles Afonso and Henry (the "Navigator"). Nevertheless, he helped establish the legal foundations for royal supremacy, which gained weight when they were codified in the *Ordenações Afonsinas* of 1446, a law code whose division into books, titles, and chapters reveals the growing influence of Roman law and Scholastic practices in Portugal.[11] Despite Afonso's own lack of interest in administrative matters – he spent much of his reign scheming to gain the Castilian crown – his officials in the chancellery initiated major mid-reign changes in how documents were managed. Considerable evidence suggests that this first reform of the chancellery in Portugal, beginning in 1459, responded in part to popular pressure from the towns represented at the Cortes. According to the introduction to one of the new chancellery books discussed later in this chapter, the third estate complained in 1459 about the difficulty of confirming legal titles issued by the Crown. In response:

---

[9] Quoted in Dias, *Portugal do Renascimento*, 349.
[10] Most early records of Portuguese maritime imperialism were stored in the Casa da India in Lisbon, which was entirely destroyed in the 1755 Lisbon earthquake.
[11] Freitas, "Tradição legal."

among the many things [the king] did to improve matters and in favor of his loyal people, because it emerged that in his tower of records there were many books of registers from past kings, where his subjects encountered great costs without advantage in looking for various matters that affected them, on account of the great prolixity of the writing contained in the aforementioned registers, he ordered that … those matters whose substance was suitable for perpetual memory should be copied.[12]

While we need not take at face value this justification for the project of creating new registers that ensued, the very fact that the project took place indicates that Afonso's chancellery had both the interest and the resources to invest in preserving past royal acts, in addition to recording the activity of its own king. As Judite A. Gonçalves de Freitas concludes, "all the evidence indicates an organized and disciplined chancellery, with routines and defined procedures," though one also vulnerable to the "fragilities of medieval central administration."[13] This description also applies to many fifteenth- and sixteenth-century chancelleries across Europe as they began carrying out projects to reorganize the material accumulated in their vaults.

Under the supervision of the head of the chancellery, the *guarda-mor* (chief secretary) Gomes Eanes de Zurara, who was also the official royal chronicler, the scribe (*escrivão*) Fernando de Elvas created at least eight volumes that registered selected acts from the reigns of Pedro I, Fernando, João I, and Duarte, covering the period from the 1360s to the 1430s.[14] Although the original emissions registers (*Chancelarias*) of these kings (referred to as the "primitive registers"[15]) were the primary source for these compilations, some evidence indicates that Zurara and Elvas also drew on loose documents in compiling these new volumes.[16] The primitive registers contained both full-text and abbreviated entries, depending on the date, genre, importance, and production sequences of the acts that were being registered; by comparison, in the new codices, which were designed for future use, the proportion of summary entries rose to more than 70 percent.[17] A wide variety of royal acts were chosen

---

[12] *Chancelarias Portuguesas: D. Duarte*, 1:9.   [13] Freitas, "Chancelarias Régias," 146.

[14] See Costa, "A Chancelaria Real," 98–101. In the older literature, Zurara is found as Azurara.

[15] The term "primitive" is introduced by Freitas, "Chancelarias Régias."

[16] Personal communications from Saul Gomes and Pedro Pinto, January 2012. See also Freire, "A Chancelaria."

[17] This material is analyzed in depth in Freitas, "Chancelarias Régias": Based on comparisons between primitive and later version of the *Chancelarias* of Duarte, and on the primitive registers of Afonso V, she concludes that 34 percent of entries took summary form; in the reformed registers, this share rose to about 72 percent.

for permanent memory, leaving out primarily those, such as appointments to office, that expired with the lifetime of the recipient.[18]

The production of new selective and retrospective registers for past reigns, in parallel with new primitive emissions registers for the current reign, allows comparisons between how Afonso's officers approached these different tasks. Formally, the content of the two series of codices was similar, since each represented in register form the king's acts. However, the new series consisted of a *retrospective* reproduction of material from existing registers and documents, clearly setting it apart from the running registers. In some respects, the selection of material undertaken while making the new registers resembles the process of archival appraisal in modern archival theory – in particular, the emphasis on "lasting value" as a criterion. Nevertheless, the preservation of the primitive registers and the lack of systematic differentiation between the different types of *Chancelerias* suggest that we should be cautious about applying modern terminology in this situation. The differing contexts and production that distinguished the two series of registers also led to differing features in the two series, even though both made extensive use of familiar technologies of book production, and even though both lacked systematic indices, tables, or other supplementary finding aids.

As a sample register page from the 1450s (Figure 4.1) shows, the primitive registers privileged text over decoration, and economy over elegance. The pages were divided into clear block entries whose modest initial capitals helped highlight the beginning of each new document. Marginal notes provided diverse metadata, such as notaries' marks, cancellation marks, and keywords giving the names of individuals for whom a privilege was issued. The leaves had folio numbers; the date of foliation is not certain but may be contemporary, since some notes in the new reformed registers of the 1460s referred to folio numbers in older registers.[19] Abbreviation was common, and the scribes used space on the page economically, with narrow margins and adaptations to the edges of uneven parchment leaves. The hands varied from entry to entry in these volumes, since different royal scribes made entries as individual charters were drafted or emitted. Entries appeared in approximate chronological order, though a delay in the recipients' payment for the issuance of a writ could lead to substantial dislocations in sequence, sometimes for months.[20] The entire series of primitive registers from Afonso

---

[18] This criterion is repeated by Cristovão de Benavente. See Dinis, "Relatório," 154.

[19] See Freitas, "Chancelarias Régias," 142, for an example of such a reference.

[20] See Freitas, "Chancelarias Régias," 145, on the construction of these codices out of serially produced quires that were later bound.

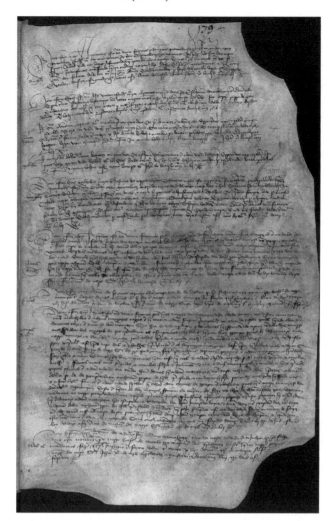

Figure 4.1 Sample page from the primitive *Chancelaria* of King Afonso V (r. 1438–1481), vol. 13, from 1456. This leaf and the quire it is part of represent a contemporary product made in tandem with the issuing of royal writs and charters. Note the irregular parchment and summary entries. Chanceleria de D. Afonso V, vol. 13, signature: Torre do Tombo, Lisbon, PT/TT/CHR/I/0013 (slide 1).

Image provided by the Torre do Tombo (ANTT), Lisbon, and reproduced by permission.

V's reign – today consisting of 38 volumes – had no contemporary finding aids beyond the reference marks, the *mise-en-page*, and the underlying chronological order of the entries.[21]

The reformed *Chancelarias* for past kings created in the early 1460s also employed late medieval book technologies, but with different goals and thus a different appearance (Figure 4.2). The text was laid out in two columns, and each entry began with a large and elaborately decorated red or bicolored capital, along with a summary in red ink of the record's details and keywords. In their formality and richness of execution, these codices resembled contemporary Humanist scholarly works more than registers. As in the primitive registers, the reformed registers' leaves were foliated, and marginal notes appeared on many pages. Chronological order – a key feature of the primitive registers– was present only irregularly in the new *Chancelarias*, however, and entries did not appear in groups corresponding to the geographical divisions of the kingdom.[22] Most likely, the sequence of documents in these codices resulted from the order in which Zurara and Elvas encountered and reviewed the material under consideration, though only detailed study can confirm this supposition. In light of these codices' elaboration, the absence of either an index or any tables of contents is surprising. These tools were common in the fifteenth century, and there is no reason to believe that Zurara and Elvas were unacquainted with them. Finally, we may note the generous margins and elegant script that Elvas employed in making these new *Chancelarias*. The consistency and care of the hand, the quality of the parchment, and the use of decoration all sharply distinguish this volume and its mates from the primitive registers for King Afonso's own charters that the same chancellery was producing at exactly the same time.

Before exploring possible explanations for these differences, let us turn to the *Leitura Nova* volumes that the chancellery began working on in 1504, since they share and extend the differences from everyday registers already visible in the reformed *Chancelarias* made under Afonso V.

The *Leitura Nova*

In the years between 1460 and 1504, the Portuguese crown became considerably richer, it successfully asserted its monopoly as the arbiter for all major political actions and patronage, and its agents greatly increased the rate at which they produced records of royal decisions.

---

[21] The original bindings were lost, and the material was put in disarray in 1755.

[22] Freitas, "Chancelarias Régias," 139, referring to the single new volume dedicated to Duarte.

Figure 4.2 The first page of the reformed *Chancelaria* of King Fernando (r. 1367–1383), produced in 1463 by Fernando de Elvas. On f. 200 of the codex, the signature "Fernandus Elbensis scripsit, anno Domini Mª CCCC° LX° tertio" appears (Costa, "A Chancelaria Real," p. 100). Chancelaria de D. Fernando, vol. 1, signature: Torre do Tombo, Lisbon, PT/TT/CHR/F/001/0001 (slide 9).

Image provided by the Torre do Tombo (ANTT), Lisbon, and reproduced by permission.

These features reinforced and reflected one another: New resources allowed the Crown to demonstrate its largesse through *merces,* such as appointing subjects to various lucrative offices, and by granting *doações* and *privilegios* to its nobles and ecclesiastical institutions. João II and Manuel I also energetically used their powers of pardon and legitimation to bind the nobility to the Crown. Both these acts themselves and the fact that the Crown carefully recorded them – down to the monthly provision of housing allowances to young *fidalgos* and upwardly mobile subjects' sons at court[23] – reinforced the centrality of royal power. Manuel I's decision to expand on Afonso's reformed *Chancelarias*, and to create a permanent, authorized, and truly splendid compilation – a book-form *archivum* of royal deeds – in the *Leitura Nova* thus reflected political reality as well as the monarch's ambitions and self-regard. It paralleled major projects to produce new codified statutes, to revise Portugal's municipal charters, and to recopy the chronicles of past reigns into lavishly illuminated parchment codices – all steps that manifested royal authority in action during Portugal's past and present.[24]

The *Leitura Nova* soon became a new core of the royal archive, still known as the *Torre do Tombo* owing to its location in Lisbon's royal castle. By the later Middle Ages in Portugal, the term *tombo* had come to mean the register that circumscribed and legitimated a patrimonial estate consisting of lands, rights over churches and chapels, and other privileged possessions, most notably an estate in the form of a *morgadio* or hereditary trust (known in English as an entail). *Morgadios* and the parallel chapel endowments were of enormous importance to the Portuguese nobility from the fourteenth through the nineteenth centuries, since they allowed property to stay together through the vicissitudes of inheritance and family disputes. Thus, the Torre do Tombo was simultaneously both a site for the Crown to celebrate its own authority and generosity and the place where Portugal's aristocratic families could defend their family's most important resources. In creating an accessible "new reading," a *Leitura Nova,* of the vital privileges that founded the material wealth of the high nobility, Manuel ensured that the Crown would remain the pivotal arbiter of Portugal's landed elite. No matter how catastrophic the state of the Crown in other ways, the *Leitura Nova* made it the centerpoint of noble legitimacy through its power to inform, review, and approve the *tombos* of the entire ruling class.[25]

We know about the *Leitura Nova* not only from the volumes themselves, all of which have survived, but also from several reports by scribes in the Torre do Tombo that mention these books in the context of the entire institution's contents and organization. The first two reports, dating from 1526 and 1532, respectively, are by Tomé Lopes, a senior secretary who helped carried out the production of the *Leitura Nova* from

---

[23] ANTT Nucleo Antigo 140, from 1519.

[24] For the administrative reforms of the period, see Dias, *Portugal do Renascimento*.

[25] Rosa, *O morgadio em Portugal*; Rosa and Head, *Rethinking the Archive*.

1510 into the 1530s.[26] After a period of quiescence in the 1530s and 1540s, the appointment of the distinguished humanist Damião da Goís as head of the *Leitura Nova* and as royal chronicler to João III briefly revived the project, while the report of Cristovão de Benavente from 1583 gives us an early retrospective view.[27] Taken together, this documentation provides an unusually well-rounded picture of a distinctive and impressive early sixteenth-century record-making enterprise that went well beyond the efforts of Afonso V's chancellery while staying focused on the probative imperative of validating privileges and supporting royal authority.

The *Leitura Nova* consists of 61 (in some counts, 60) volumes, organized according to a comprehensive scheme and founded on an explicit mandate. A description of the scheme is copied into the first volumes that were completed, under the heading "Ordinance on how this and other volumes are placed and on the manner one should take in the search for writings." As the heading suggests, making sure that important records could be found was a central concern of the *Leitura* from its outset.[28] The mandate by which the king set the project in motion appears on the illuminated frontispieces bearing the royal arms, which are found in 28 of the completed volumes (Figure 4.3).[29] As cited earlier, Manuel's mandate describes the series' intentions in clear language that links the representation of royal power to the utility of "greater certainty and less labor" in locating important records of past royal action. As Sylvie Deswarte argues in her astute analysis of the illuminated frontispieces: "[Each frontispiece] is above all a framing of the royal edict, of the prologue in which the king presents himself as the promulgator of the enterprise of the *Leitura Nova*. It thus constitutes a presentation of the royal person through the medium of his heraldic signs and his emblem."[30] The first imperative of the entire series was, therefore, to assure proof through the material representation of royal acts, authenticated by the direct command and participation of the current monarch. It is thus entirely consistent that along with the *licenciado* who reviewed the copies against the original records, Manuel I personally signed the

---

[26] Lopes's reports are published in Pessanha, "Uma Rehabilitação."

[27] Benavente's report, with a biographical study and additional documents, appears in Dinis, "Relatorio."

[28] Transcribed from *LN* volume 17 (Estremadura 1, whose text was signed on September 11, 1504) in Deswarte, *Les Enluminures*, 233–35.

[29] All 28 of Manuel's title pages are reproduced in the Appendix of Deswarte, *Les Enluminures*. Another 15 volumes contain illuminated title pages attributing the volumes to João III but without any text. Illuminated cartularies – much less registers – are rare. See Stirnemann, "L'Illustration du Cartulaire."

[30] Deswarte, *Les Enluminures*, 53.

Figure 4.3 Illuminated title page from *Leitura Nova*. The title pages of the *Leitura Nova* volumes included elaborate illumination that varied from volume to volume, but always reproduced the royal decree commanding the series' production. The illuminations on the title page of *Místicos*, vol. 3, include a scribe at work (lower center). Leitura Nova vol. 32, Livro 3 de Místicos, signature: PT/TT/LN/0032 (slide 2).

Image provided by the Torre do Tombo (ANTT), Lisbon, and reproduced by permission.

first three volumes to be completed.[31] The king further affirmed his personal support for the enterprise in a letter granting *merces* to the production team in January 1517, and added an item to his testament of April 1517 that ordered his successor to continue the "reform of the Torre do Tombo," noting that "the work that has been begun and that is done there seems to me to be a very advantageous matter."[32]

The project continued throughout the reign of João III (r. 1521–1557), albeit at a considerably slower pace. In 1526, Tomé Lopes reported to the king on "the nature of the things in this Tombo that your father, the King (whom God preserve) ordered to be copied and kept in the books that were made," after having had some difficulty in reporting on previous kings' decisions.[33] Lopes listed the primitive chancellery registers for earlier kings (with one volume per year) and the *Leitura Nova* as it stood at that point: "37 volumes of books of 300 leaves each, with their tables made with four *titulos* in each one, all written and finished."[34] Damião de Góis, appointed *guarda-mor* in the early 1550s, briefly revived the project after a period of inactivity. His chronicle, published in 1566, noted that this was an "extensive work, and of great weight, that could not be completed in [Manuel's] time, nor in that of King João III his son," and stated that there were still many items to record.[35]

The process of making the *Leitura Nova* also left considerable traces in older records, which help us understand how records were selected for inclusion by the chancellery staff.[36] Annotations on the cover of some older registers indicated that they had been reviewed for material worthy of inclusion in the *Leitura Nova*. On the first leaf of the (current) volume 20 of the primitive registers of Afonso V, for example, the phrase "Looked at for the *comarcas* and reconciled" appears in a sixteenth-century hand.[37] Elsewhere, short red summaries appear squeezed in between or sometimes over register entries, along with red (and then crossed-out) volume designations corresponding to the *Leitura*, a scribe's

---

[31] Manuel's signature appears in *LN* volumes 9, 17, and 30, completed and signed on September 11 and 12, 1504. Deswarte, *Les Enluminures,* Appendix V.

[32] The letter of January 13, 1517, in Deswarte, *Les Enluminures,* Appendix VIII; his testament in Appendix IX.

[33] Pessanha, "Uma Rehabilitação," 288.   [34] Pessanha, "Uma Rehabilitação," 289.

[35] Cited in Deswarte, *Les Enluminures,* 33.

[36] ANTT Gavetas XIX, Maço 4, Doc. 4, is evidently a preparatory notebook for the *Leitura Nova* into which some documents were copied, sometimes with notarial certification, before being recopied into the actual parchment volumes. I thank Pedro Pinto for bringing this volume to my attention and explaining its function.

[37] ANTT CHR/I/20, with entries mostly for 1439–1440. On the recto of the second leaf: "visto pellas Comarcas & concertado." The note cannot date to the reformed *Chancelarias* of the 1460s, because that series contained no volume for Afonso's own acts.

Figure 4.4 Detail from a primitive register of Afonso V, ca. 1440, showing the working annotations added during the production of the *Leitura Nova*. The original text in light brown ink, shown here as medium gray. The dark annotation *esc^ipta* ("escripta") and the initials in the left margin indicate that copying was completed. To the left of *esc^ipta* is a crossed-out annotation in red ink (here darker gray) indicating the destination series, Além Douro. To the right of *esc^ipta*, another red-ink annotation provides keywords about the entry's content. Chancelaria de D. Afonso V, vol. 20, signature: PT/TT/CHR/I/0020 (slide 17).

Image provided by the Torre do Tombo (ANTT), Lisbon, and reproduced by permission.

mark and the note "esc^ipta" (*escripta*), indicating that they had been transcribed (Figure 4.4). Elsewhere in the registers, the comment "Escusado" appears next to items not to be copied.

All in all, the Lisbon chancellery left behind many signs of a systematic procedure of selection and indexing during the production of the *Leitura Nova*.[38] After the earlier *Chancelarias* and the loose documents in the *gavetas* (storage drawers in the Torre) had been reviewed for inclusion, the project continued to incorporate selected acts of Manuel and João III during their reigns, in parallel with the ongoing production of regular *Chancelarias*.[39]

King Manuel's close personal attention to the *Leitura Nova* corresponds to a primary difference that distinguishes this series from reformed *Chancelarias* of Afonso V – namely, the great efforts that Manuel's chancellery took to authenticate each volume and each individual leaf. These efforts reflected legal practice that privileged authentic records, while putting less weight on whether a record was an original or a copy.[40] Specific features of the *Leitura Nova* proved that the records on its pages

---

[38] See Pessanha, "Uma Rehabilitação," 288. The personnel and procedure are described further in Deswarte, *Les Enluminures*, 33–40.

[39] On loose material, see Lopes's 1526 report in Pessanha, "Uma Rehabilitação," 289–90. The distribution of material in Manuel's primitive *chancelarias* suggests that attention to these mundane products might have declined when the *Leitura Nova* commenced. See Portugal, "Mapa dos anos."

[40] Discussed in Chapter 3; see Nicolaj, "*Originale, authenticum, publicum*."

Figure 4.5 Detail from typical leaf from the *Leitura Nova* (Além Douro 1, fol. cvi[v]) showing the form of notarial authentication used across the bottom of the two columns. The page here is signed by the clerk and notary Gabrielus (Gabriel Gil). Leitura Nova vol. 1, Livro 1 de Além-Douro, signature: PT/TT/LN/0001 (slide 250).
Image provided by the Torre do Tombo (ANTT), Lisbon, and reproduced by permission.

were authentic public instruments (Figure 4.5). We should not overlook the performative elements that contributed to this assertion, including the use of illumination and decoration, the perfection of the parchment and layout, and the rich bindings that the volumes originally possessed, with the royal arms carved into the covers.[41] More concretely, several features of the *mise-en-page* and *mise-en-livre* also directly established the entries' reliability.

Notably, at the bottom of nearly every page of the *Leitura Nova*, across several thousand leaves, the supervising *escrivão* of the chancellery added his notarial signet, carefully placed to prevent new lines of text from being added in either column. Such notarial signatures not only confirmed the absence of tampering, but also gave the entries public faith (*publica fides*) according to notarial practice. Moreover, the supervising scribe added an entry on the last inscribed page of most volumes both confirming his inspection of the contents and naming explicitly the total number of leaves.[42]

Each *Leitura Nova* volume was a selective register taking the form of a copybook; it preserved for the king's use authentic records of the lasting privileges that he and his predecessors had issued. The scope of the project, its opulence, and the fact that it was conceived as an ongoing project that would continue as long as the kings of Portugal kept issuing legal acts requiring perpetual memory, however, all distinguish the

---

[41] Dinis, "Relatório," 154.

[42] Interestingly, the same practice appears in the primitive *Chancelaria* of Manuel. Mabillion, *De re*, 237, mentions registers with notaries' signs on every page and final signature as enjoying full authenticity.

Leitura Nova from almost all other sixteenth-century copybooks. Indeed, many indications suggest that for its creators, the collection constituted an *archivum* in itself, a treasury of authentic records attested by notarial signatures and by the visual royal presence on the illuminated frontispieces. Whereas sixteenth-century theory and practice elsewhere had begun differentiating the *archivum* of original charters from the books kept in chancelleries, and eventually from information management registries, the Lisbon chancellery chose to create an *archivum*-in-codices to record and guarantee the monarchy's acts. In this respect, the *Leitura Nova* stands as a high point of the medieval tradition of preserving authentic records to fulfill a probative imperative. Elsewhere in Europe, the dynamics of increasing paper flow and complex domains pushed developments in quite different directions, as we will see.

Finding Proofs in the *Leitura Nova*

As Manuel's founding mandate indicated in its evocation of greater certainty and less labor, proof did not by itself exhaust the *Leitura Nova*'s significance. Indeed, the king's order to organize the Torre do Tombo before commencing the work, along with the simultaneous drafting of a guide to the overall structure of the *Leitura*, shows that efficiency in *finding* proofs was another explicit goal of the entire project. This second goal gained its most visible expression in the extensive analytical tables of contents found at the beginning of each volume of the *Leitura*. We now turn briefly to the systematic structure of the entire project – the order of the *archivum*, so to speak – and then in more detail to the finding aids designed to fulfill the king's commands.

The *Leitura Nova*'s authors divided the textual space of its 60 volumes into two major sections, with a different ordering principle for each: One part was ordered geographically, and the other was oriented to political actors and their actions.[43] In all, forty-seven of the sixty volumes corresponded to the territorial divisions of the Portuguese royal administration, the *comarcas*. When Manuel's chancellery started the project, Portugal consisted of six *comarcas,* which the *Leitura Nova* combined into four series: Além-Douro, Beira, Odiana, and Estremadura. A fifth division for Ilhas was added in 1550.[44] The division of Portuguese space thus was

---

[43] On the Torre do Tombo overall, see Ribeiro, "Como seria a estutura."

[44] Além-Douro included Minho and Trás-os-Montes, as noted in the "Hordenança" for using the collection, while Odiana included Entre-Tejo-e-Odiana and Algarve, though the latter was formally a separate kingdom. See Dias, *Portugal do Renascimento*, 726, for a map. The *Foraes Novos* (volumes 43–47 today) and *Inquirições* (current volumes 48–52)

mapped onto the division of the codices in the *Leitura Nova*. Approximate chronological order provided a secondary principle, since new books were added to each of the four geographical categories when a volume became full.

The second category of organization (which includes volumes 30–42 and 53–60 of the *Leitura* as shelved today) included volumes oriented toward specific actions on the part of the king. These included *Místicos*, *Extras*, *Reis*, *Diritos Reaes*, *Mestrados*, *Padroados*, *Legitimações*, *Doações del Rey*, and *Privilegios*. The *Místicos* were a large catch-all category of acts in six volumes that included the affairs of "the queens, infantes, dukes, etc., and of others already named but whose affairs have to do with more than one comarca," although the "Hordenança" also observed that "this will cause confusion to some in the search for their affairs, which is to be avoided."[45] The other categories were clearer, including royal relations with the church and the military orders, as well as royal legitimations (crucial to the nobility) and other acts of royal grace.

For practical use, an important feature setting the *Leitura Nova* apart from the reformed *Chancelarias* of the 1460s was that each volume of the *Leitura* possessed multiple, carefully organized analytical tables describing its contents. These tables were keyed closely to the genre of material that each volume contained, and were thus different in the geographical and the thematic volumes. Most of the volumes pertaining to the *comarcas* had three (or occasionally four) separate tables: The first listed individuals named in the volume's entries, the second identified towns and places, and the third pointed to ecclesiastical institutions. The finding aids in the *Leitura Nova* are notable for the beauty of their execution, with fine calligraphy spread generously across many pages of expensive parchment with illuminated headings and large rubricated introductions (Figures 4.6 and 4.7). As in the main entries and illuminations, the Lisbon chancellery went to great lengths in the "titulos" (tables of contents) to produce an *archivum* for the ages.

Despite their material ostentation, the finding aids in the *Leitura Nova* were technically quite simple tables. For example, they did not alphabetize the individual entries. In most of them, individuals, places, or ecclesiastical institutions appear in the same order as in the actual volume,

---

are also subdivided geographically, although with different groupings and divisions than the main series. Benavente (Dinis, "Relatório," 155) also mentions "outros liuros nesta forma, em que estam as cousas que tocam alemmar, a saber, Affrica, Guinee, Brasil, Ilhas e Jndia," but aside from the one volume of Ilhas, these seem not in fact to have been part of the *Leitura Nova*.

[45] Cited here after Deswartes, *Les Enluminures*, 234, considering various possible sources of confusion in finding records.

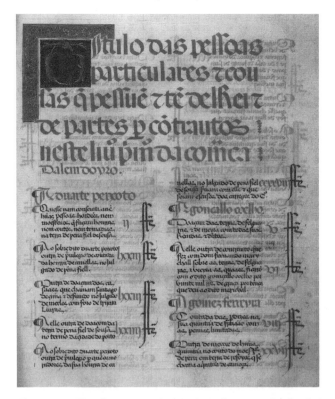

Figure 4.6 The first page of an index of persons in the *Leitura Nova* (Além-Douro, 1), displaying an illuminated capital and red intitulation, and illustrating the generous margins and elegant script that the scribes employed. This page also relies on a complex reference scheme as discussed below. Leitura Nova vol. 1, Livro 1 de Além-Douro, signature: PT/TT/LN/0001 (slide 7).

Image provided by the Torre do Tombo (ANTT), Lisbon, and reproduced by permission.

meaning that in each table, the sequence of folio numbers increases steadily (as in Figure 4.7). In a few early volumes, a more complex way of organizing the tables appeared, one akin to concordances, which demonstrates the diligence and creativity of the scribes involved. Rather than simply listing the *lemmata* in the order that they appeared in the codex, some tables grouped the entries for each person in the order they appeared, one after another, under a larger red heading giving the name, before moving to the next person (as seen in Figure 4.6). Consequently, page numbers increased within each person's entries, then restarted for

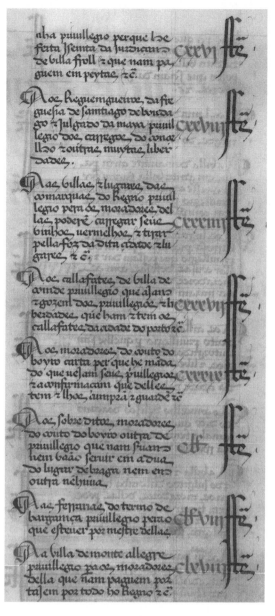

Figure 4.7 A column from the body of the table of places in *Leitura Nova*, Além-Douro, vol. 1. The layout illustrates the linear arrangement found in most of the *Leitura*'s tables, in which folio numbers rise sequentially (here from cxxvi to clxviii, with numerals in red ink in the original). This table thus mirrors in its spatial organization the position of each referenced locus in the codex, rather than being alphabetized or otherwise ordered differently from the entries themselves, as in an index. Leitura Nova vol. 1, Livro 1 de Além-Douro, signature: PT/TT/LN/0001 (slide 27).

Image provided by the Torre do Tombo (ANTT), Lisbon, and reproduced by permission.

the next person. Producing such an index would have been more labor intensive than simply listing *lemmata* in sequence of appearance (as in Figure 4.7), which may explain why only a few tables take this approach. Ultimately, simply listing *lemmata* in the order of their appearance in the main text (which could lead to multiple entries for a single *lemma*) remained the predominant way that the *Leitura*'s scribes operated.

Conclusive evidence shows that the royal chancellery was familiar with alphabetization at this time, even though it was not used in the *Leitura*. A parchment index to names in another chancellery volume was arranged alphabetically in 1519, after the first *Leitura* volumes were completed.[46] The index in question, on twenty-one parchment leaves in two quires, lists alphabetically the names of all recipients of *moradias* (housing allowances at the royal court). These individuals were registered in a separate very large codex (which is lost). Although not nearly as careful in its execution as the *Leitura* – there are numerous corrections and additions, and entries are squeezed onto some pages – this index confirms that alphabetized book indexes were a recognized technique in the Lisbon chancelleries of the early to mid-sixteenth century.

The lack of alphabetization in the *Leitura Nova's* tables was noted critically by later chancellery staff, along with the lack of a single comprehensive index to the entire series. In 1632, the current head of the Torre do Tombo, Manuel Jacome Bravo, complained that most volumes of the *Chancelaria* (that is, the collection of royal registers, including the primitive registers, the reformed registers made during Afonso V's reign, and the *Leitura Nova*) lacked indexes, asserting that "for these 403 volumes it is necessary to make alphabets, and to copy those same alphabets into one or two volumes, through which one could search what is registered in the books with little loss of time." Bravo (incorrectly) described the *Leitura Nova* as having alphabetized volume indexes, but nevertheless complained that

these books are very large and heavy, and it is necessary to pull them down off the shelves where they rest every time that it is necessary to look for something; this is to the harm of the bindings with the result that they are now in very poor condition.[47]

Only at the end of the seventeenth century did the chancellery produce an alphabetical index to the whole *Leitura Nova,* and that only by one letter.

---

[46] ANTT Nucleo Antigo 140. On its cover, it is labeled in large script of the sixteenth century as "Liuro dos caualleiros de 1519." On the first leaf of the main body, the index is dated to "ano de mil etc. b^c Xbiiijs [?]," although the last section is blotted.

[47] Both citations are reported in Azevedo and Baião, *O Arquivo*, 44. The full document can be found in Rau, *A Tôrre do Tombo*.

A final aspect of the *Leitura Nova* deserves emphasis: its conception as an *ongoing* project to preserve selected acts of the monarchs of Portugal in a permanent form. As was the case under Afonso V during the production of the much more readable reformed *Chancelarias* of former monarchs, the production and registration of royal writs and charters in primitive *Chancelarias* continued in the royal chancellery of Manuel I and João III, in parallel with the reinscription of registered acts into the *Leitura Nova*. But acts of Manuel and even of João III also appear in the *Leitura,* showing that the series was not limited to the retrospective reinscription of previous registers, as Zurara's 1460 volumes had been. The 1583 report of Cristovão de Benavente (who had worked in the chancellery since the late 1550s) makes it clear that for him, the *Leitura Nova* was suspended, not terminated: "But this *Leitura* has been interrupted, because no money has been given for it for many years."[48] Explicit concern for future record accumulation was an important aspect of early modern European archivality that grew in importance throughout the period.

Conclusion

The Torre do Tombo of the Portuguese monarchy, and particular the extraordinary *Leitura Nova* produced by the royal chancellery during the first half of the sixteenth century, represented a high point of Late Medieval record-keeping technology. This technology put great emphasis on the authenticated traces of a ruler's past acts of privilege and patronage. The form of its most impressive archival product in Portugal, the *Leitura Nova*, created for the monarchy's own future use, embodied the priorities and cultural practices of Late Medieval archivality while also reflecting the Portuguese monarchy's construction as a highly centralized patronage organization. For royal acts of lasting importance, both symbolic and juridical authentication remained essential. Careful transcription after detailed review ensured that only truly significant records gained entry into this canon through a "new reading." These records gained authenticity through their formality of layout (already present in the reformed *Chancelarias* of Afonso), which was then heightened by illumination and by the meticulous notarial confirmations found on every page of the *Leitura Nova*.

As the reformed *Chancelarias* created under Afonso V demonstrate, the first impulse behind the reform of the Portuguese chancellery and its

---

[48] Dinis, "Relatorio," 155.

records from the 1460s to the 1550s was to *preserve* authentic records in proper form, not to ease the finding of such material (even though it was the third estate's complaints about the difficulty of using the existing registers that justified Zurara's enterprise). Zurara apparently perceived no need to produce finding aids at all for his "reformed" volumes. When Manuel I added ease of use to his chancellery's obligations, the secretaries responded with the elegant tables of materials found in the volumes of the *Leitura Nova,* but did not adopt alphabetization. What mattered, it seems, was *representing* the individuals, towns, and ecclesiastical institutions that received the king's grace – placing them in the tables, as in the body of the *Leitura* – more than *listing* them in disaggregated and abstract alphabetical form. Manuel's *Leitura Nova* thus took place next to his newly issued legal code and his equally sumptuous recopying of old royal chronicles in creating a parchment machine for the legitimation and glorification of the Portuguese monarchy and its nobility.

The financial stresses that the Portuguese crown faced under João III and under Sebastian, as the fruits of colonial empire withered under Spanish, Dutch, and French pressure in parallel with a general economic slowdown across continental Europe, undermined both the representative and the routine operations of recording royal acts in books. The administrative friction and royal neglect that Portugal experienced under Habsburg rule after 1580 only exacerbated these problems, so that by the early seventeenth century, complaints about the dysfunction of the Torre do Tombo grew louder.[49] These were amplified, no doubt, because archives increasingly functioned in European polities not only as treasuries of authentic deeds, but also as dynamic potential sources of political information. The Portuguese crown sought to manage its legitimating proofs through a comprehensive and authorized archive-in-a-book, but found the project ultimately unsustainable. Other chancelleries after 1400 responded both to the growing mass of unordered older material and the growing official interest in information as well as proofs with very different strategies, which the following chapters will analyze.

---

[49] See especially Rau, *A Tôrre do Tombo.*

5 Keeping and Organizing Information from the Middle Ages to the Sixteenth Century

Introduction

Early modern chancellery officials, like those in the Middle Ages, continued to imagine their repositories as being an *archivum* of authentic documents that could help defend the privileges and liberties of the institutions they served. In the words of Georg Aebbtlin in 1669, "the *archivum* is the first corpus of a registry, and on account of its value and worthiness the most precious and distinguished, from which the other ... corpora originate, and on which they should build."[1] Yet close examination of how various chancelleries actually handled the records in their possession, including the ones gathered in the treasury archives intended for legitimating charters, reveals a more complex picture. The records in the hands of political authorities during the High Middle Ages consisted of heterogeneous materials whose value rested on many different characteristics. Proofs and privileges certainly constituted one key element within rulers' repositories, but so did tax rolls, protocol books, chronicles, briefs and verdicts from past legal conflicts, correspondence with neighboring and distant powers, marriage alliances and wills, and all sorts of other material. As the volume of records produced internally and received from outside swelled even further in the fifteenth century – a development accelerated by the increasing availability and use of paper – what was conceptualized as a single repository of stored proofs began to differentiate into multiple assemblages held in various storage spaces, under the control of different agents, and used in different ways.[2]

Such assemblages expanded as scribes created written records for many purposes, and chancelleries preserved them for many uses beyond *ad perpetuam rei memoriam* – or for no apparent reason at all. Although the resulting piles, strings, quires, and codices consisting of parchment

---

[1] Aebbtlin, *Anführung*, 14.
[2] Explored first in Pitz, *Schrift- und Aktenwesen*; see Head, "Configuring European Archives."

and paper documents may not have enjoyed the prestige of sealed charters, they nevertheless made vital contributions to practices of records management as these evolved throughout the period. By the seventeenth century, as Aebbtlin recognized, such material had generated multiple archival corpora, each with its own imperatives and challenges. In Chapters 3 and 4, we analyzed charters, deeds, writs, notarial records, and other instruments falling under the broad heading of the probative imperative. In this chapter, we turn to much more heterogeneous category of informational records to probe their later medieval trajectories, and to see how these shaped the way information for future use was recorded and stored.

Political information is a category that extends far beyond the written forms that circulate in some societies.[3] The discussion here, however, concentrates on records containing such information that were gathered by the agents of European rulers and their institutions, that were inscribed or received in their chancelleries, and that found a place in their accumulations of written material.[4] Even for this restricted sphere, the question of how Late Medieval and early modern governments collected and deployed information is complex, and is currently spurring innovative studies in a wide variety of contexts.[5]

The information that appears in records is relational, medial, and profoundly dependent on the context of records' production, use, and storage. Information can be recorded during processes of communication either orally or through the medium of writing; it can accumulate on paper during processes of administration and adjudication in the form of summaries, excerpts, lists, and tables; or it may be the product of conscious reflection on the part of various agents, ranging from rulers and magistrates to administrators and clerks.[6] These characteristics also make it clear that no simple distinction can be drawn between probative and informational records. Probative records have always conveyed information in various medial forms – as texts, but also through seals, illumination, *mise-en-page,* and other ways – just as those who sought information in archives often looked at both probative and nonprobative records during their searches. Nevertheless, there is a real and important

---

[3] Zins, "Conceptual Approaches," reviews definitions of the term "information" beyond Claude Shannon's mathematical-entropic definition.

[4] Brendecke, Friedrich, and Friedrich, "Information."

[5] On the broader issues, see Brendecke, *Imperium und Empirie*; Burke, *Social History*; Soll, *The Information Master;* and de Vivo, *Information and Communication*. Much of the relevant medieval work was cited in Chapter 3; see also Fianu and Guth, *Écrit et Pouvoir.*

[6] On oral communication as a target of record-keeping, see de Vivo, "Archives of Speech."

difference between these two ways of looking at records (as proofs or as information), captured in their orientation toward future time. As discussed previously, records that enjoyed the capacity to prove past acts "for perpetual memory" played a pivotal conceptual role in medieval record-keeping.[7] In contrast, this chapter addresses records that pertained (at least in the minds of those who produced those records) to a shorter futurity, and in turn remained supporting players, at most, in conscious reflection about record-keeping. As James Given argues, "Most medieval administrative documents, like tax lists and instructions to officials, were intended to be used only at the time at which they were composed. Once they had been used, they had little further function."[8]

In fact, nonprobative records presented chancelleries with multiple uncertainties because their future relevance (which might justify their preservation and organization) was not fixed. In consequence, no simple rule – keep or discard – could ever apply to them.[9] Medieval administrators were quite aware that any record *might* in the future serve a currently unanticipated need. The inquisition records discussed in this chapter amply illustrate this point, which helps explain the care that inquisitorial scribes used in tabulating depositions in their registers: They knew that previous testimony could help illuminate future witnesses' statements, and in fact used past records systematically to do exactly this during their investigations. Thus, the contrast is not between culturally anchored perpetuity for probative records and fleetingness for everything else, but rather between imagined fixity and uncertain duration. Future uses could always be imagined, but were also subject to imponderable future circumstances. This may help explain why, increasingly, nonprobative material survived, creating facts on the ground (or in basements, vaults, and attics) that later archive keepers had to face.

The goals that medieval regimes pursued in producing and collecting informational records nevertheless remained rather narrow. Chancellors and scribes after 1200 mostly recorded information that – not surprisingly – was closely connected to the proofs of authoritative acts that they had always preserved. One very old category consisted of recording the

---

[7] The importance of records' orientation to different future times at the time of their making is explored by Morsel, "En Guise d'Introduction."

[8] Given, *Inquisition*, 33. Proofs, too, could be separated into those of permanent value and those whose object expired, as seen in statements made by the compilors of the *Leitura Nova*. This observation, built on but going beyond Clanchy's reflections (*From Memory*, 154–72), leaves open the question why such material was so often preserved.

[9] Modern archivists characterize this issue under the theory of appraisal, which Fiorella Foscarini describes as "a crucial demand and a major intellectual challenge" ("Archival Appraisal," 107).

law, for example. Capitularies preserved royal and imperial edicts and the laws adopted by various polities and, therefore, are one of the oldest forms of informational records in Europe.[10] Landed possessions and sources of income were also concerns of authorities at all levels from very early on. Thus, rent rolls, land-books, and the like were widely produced, the most famous early exemplar of which is Domesday Book. Such documents dovetailed or overlapped in various fluid ways with the charters that demonstrated possessors' rights to what they owned, or what they had granted to others.

Information gathering could also grow out of the administration of justice. Almost the only judicial records preserved from the Early and High Middle Ages were instruments of judgment; these found their way into registers and cartularies because they served as testimony about past acts of judges and courts. When first clerical and then secular officers became more active in investigating and prosecuting crimes, rather than merely judging the cases brought to them, they began producing informational records – depositions, inquest reports, and procedural records – that were not themselves probative.[11] In particular, the Latin Church's aggressive campaigns against the crime of heresy after the eleventh century stimulated changes in the volume and sophistication of investigative records, while also providing an important forum for deploying the Scholastic book tools. Investigative practices and the related methods that monastic orders developed for visitations of their houses included new ways to collect and organize information about the world – techniques that anticipated those later found in political chancelleries of the fourteenth and fifteenth centuries.[12]

In addition to these specific areas of political action, another feature of later medieval governance was the growing importance of written communication among political actors, which generated the broad category of "letters." As medieval political units increased in scale and in intensity of dominion, written records began to flow between sedentary chancelleries, the often peripatetic rulers, and their provincial and local agents. In addition, the emergence of formal diplomacy in the fifteenth century

---

[10] Establishing the law and making it known to subjects was a key area in Classical as well as medieval systems of record-keeping; see Sickinger, *Public Records*. On the dissemination of the law, see Johanek, "Methodisches zur Verbreitung," 88–101. Tracking the decrees of the city government was a major spur to archival innovation in Florence after the fourteenth century, as described by Tanzini, "Pratiche guidizarie."

[11] The traditional view, expressed in terms of the laws of evidence and proof, is found in Caenegem, "Methods of Proof," especially 94–95. Newer views can be found in Fianu and Guth, *Écrit et Pouvoir*, with a particular focus on England; Teuscher, *Lords' Rights*; and Lazzarini, "Records."

[12] Glénisson, "Les enquêtes administratives," especially 17–25.

created a new category of writers, including envoys and ambassadors, and large new genres of correspondence.[13] Entire families of textual genres – requests for information, reports, letters of instruction, petitions, and explanations of actions – emerged that both enabled and constrained administrative communication. Ranging from the highly formulaic to the idiosyncratic, such documents supported the exercise of power for all but the smallest domains, albeit always together with face-to-face interaction, symbolic acts, or the many other ways in which political actors conveyed their intentions to one another.[14]

Finally, we must recognize that while information-gathering efforts and intensified communication after 1300 generated more chancellery records (as well as many records that did not end up in chancelleries), these activities and their products were more subject to friction and instability compared to the charters, cartularies, and registers discussed in Chapter 3.[15] In comparison to the formality of the typical probative instrument, heresy investigations or inquests into status and revenue were complex, entangled in local particularity, and conditioned by long and often poorly documented sequences of past actions (many of them invisible to rulers and the law). The stripped-down version of reality found in a typical charter served specific legal, political, and symbolic functions. In contrast, the more heterogeneous information about human experience and action found in nonprobative records needed to be more comprehensive to make sense at all, both when made and when used.[16] Yet scribes could at best capture only a fraction of the social context, the cultural expectations, and the unavoidable particularity of each case. This selectivity highlights how recording and using written information raised different issues than did proofs, and resulted in different genres of records and more fluid patterns of reuse, misuse, or disuse. The heterogeneous mass of informational records, which increasingly occupied separate storage spaces in fifteenth- and sixteenth-century regimes, therefore provided opportunities for creativity and change.

Despite the distinctions sketched in the preceding discussion, one important feature united the management of both probative and informational records in major political chancelleries around 1500: the codex as a vital component in secretaries' toolkits. We have already seen how codices with their metadata became essential tools for managing charters.

---

[13] For diplomatic correspondence, see Senatore, *"Uno mundo de carta,"* and de Vivo, *Information and Communication.*

[14] Traditional archival science provides detailed typologies of records. See Papritz, *Archivwissenschaft,* I: 167–253.

[15] What is *not* archived is also an important question. See Thomas et al., *The Silence.*

[16] This idea is developed further in Head, "Empire at Home."

A high point of this development was the expansive *archivum*-in-books that the Portuguese royal chancellery created in the *Leitura Nova* of the sixteenth century. This chapter argues that books became equally important for handling nonprobative information. Letters, reports, and ad hoc documents may have circulated and accumulated on their own, but chancelleries and their secretaries again turned to the codex to collate, order, and manage the growing floods of documents and the information they contained. The Innsbruck chancellery around 1500 discussed in Chapter 6 provides a case parallel to Lisbon, since it, too, comprised an enormous effort to meet rulers' expectations by producing codices rich in metadata.

The following discussion focuses on two historical situations that illustrate with particular clarity how chancelleries accumulated and managed informational records up to 1500: judicial inquiries, using the Inquisition against the Cathars as a key model; and administrative communication within regimes, using Habsburg Innsbruck as an exemplary case. Chapter 6 explores a particularly revealing system for managing information through codices, by offering a detailed analysis of the Innsbruck copybooks of the early 1500s. Comparable efforts to activate information potentially embedded in loose documents through inventories and systematically organized repositories – from the Trésor des Chartes in fourteenth-century Paris to the finding aid created for the Prince-Bishops of Würzburg in the sixteenth century – are the focus of Chapters 7 and 8.

Visitation and Inquisition in the Genealogy of Information Management

As European rulers built up bureaucracies in the twelfth and thirteenth centuries, one legacy from Late Antiquity and the central Middle Ages they confronted was their responsibility to guarantee justice. As long as the ruler's duty lay primarily in rendering final judgment or in confirming settlements that parties reached before him, however, the few judicial documents that were produced fell squarely into the category of deeds to be memorialized.[17] Later, when European monarchs and the communal regimes began actively prosecuting crimes, judicial records – unsurprisingly – multiplied alongside other genres in their chancelleries. Prosecution of wrongdoers on the part of the authorities generated distinctive

---

[17] For the developments in France, see, for example, Baldwin, *The Government*, 37–38, who notes that the royal court rarely produced documents under Louis VII (r. 1137–1180) and Philip II (r. 1180–1223).

records, many of which were informational rather than probative in nature. The evolution of Europe's various legal systems is a vast topic whose many dimensions cannot be addressed here.[18] One particular thread of the larger story, however, offers evidence of particular interest for a study of recorded information: the inquisitorial methods that emerged after the 1180s as part of the Latin Church's efforts to suppress religious dissidents, particularly the Cathars in southern France and northern Italy.[19]

The Dominicans charged with investigating heresy in Languedoc were not the first churchmen to systematically seek out religious deviants. Bishops had long been charged with suppressing individual heretics in their sees, and they started carrying out investigations and trials to this end around the year 1000.[20] More systematically, monastic visitations, during which outside inspectors reviewed the life and piety of a religious order's members, extended back to the central Middle Ages, but accelerated greatly with the rise of the Cluniac and especially the Cistercian orders after 1100. The 1119 *Carta Caritatis* that founded the Cistercians mandated annual visitations of each individual house of the order. These visitations served as "an instrument of control, communication, and correction," in Jörg Oberste's assessment – functions markedly similar to what papal inquisitions sought to achieve in the communities of Languedoc a century later.[21] By the mid-twelfth century, Cistercian procedures for visitation had been formalized in the rule of "De forma visitationis," which is found among the records of many abbeys from that time.

Through the twelfth century, however, common practice limited what a visitor could record in written form, since the reestablishment of harmony was the primary goal, rather than gathering testimony.[22] It was only around 1200 that visitations began including obligatory written reports – in synchrony with the Church's growing concern over heresy, and with movement toward greater formality in all sorts of legal procedures, which culminated in the IV Lateran Council of 1215. In 1190, for example, the Cistercian general chapter began requiring a written report

---

[18] Herzog, *A Short History.*

[19] The literature on visitations and inquisitions is vast. Most important in shaping my understanding are Given, *Inquisition;* Lambert, *Medieval Heresy;* La Roi Ladurie, *Montaillou;* Moore, *The Formation;* and Peters, *Inquisition;* Peters, *Heresy and Authority.* The collection edited by Bruschi and Biller, *Texts,* is particularly valuable.

[20] Moore, *The Origins of European Dissent.*

[21] Oberste, "Normierung," especially 316. Oberste also systematically analyzes the documents resulting from monastic visitations in *Die Dokumente.*

[22] Oberste, "Normierung," 320; on the limitations on written records, see Oberste, *Die Dokumente,* 34.

from each visitation that recorded the number of monks, novices, and servants, and described each convent's resources and debts. In 1250, the Dominican order established the general principle that "what the visitor can plainly and fully observe, if it relates to his mission, should be written down."[23]

The records produced by such visitations were not proofs, but rather provided the general chapter or an order's head with *information* about the state of individual houses, which could be used to decide on action toward that house or on policies for the order. The emergence of written visitation reports explains the first part of James Given's conclusion:

> In fashioning their techniques for manipulating the objects of their inquiries, the inquisitors took few steps that can be regarded as completely innovative, but the way in which they incorporated existing techniques of rule into a peculiarly coherent and effective engine of repression is possibly without parallel in medieval Europe.[24]

Inquisitors in the Languedoc used recorded information far beyond what orders or bishops were doing at the time, anchoring the inquisition's importance for the history of record-keeping as well as the history of repression and discipline.

Well into the fourteenth century, the papacy, Church authorities in southern France, and secular rulers headed by the kings of France carried out a systematic campaign against the Cathar religion in Languedoc. In an 1184 bull, *Ad Abolendam,* the Church criminalized specific movements that the papacy deemed heretical, including the Cathars, and sought to mobilize and coordinate episcopal investigations and censures with secular prosecution. The 1208 murder of the papal legate Pierre de Castelnau in Toulouse, after years of demanding more aggressive secular prosecution of Cathars, led to a declaration of Crusade in the Languedoc, and eventually to a French royal expedition that pursued political advantage while supporting Catholic orthodoxy in the south of France. Open military conflict continued until 1229. It was not until 1244, however, that the last military stronghold of the Cathars, Montségúr, was captured, and the large number of Cathar clergy taking refuge in the castle executed.

Warfare may have destroyed the publicly visible Cathar movement, but the Church – in particular, the Dominican order founded in 1216 – remained deeply concerned that Cathars continued to practice their

---

[23] Oberste, "Normierung," 321; the quotation is from the order's master, Humbert of Romans.
[24] Given, *Inquisition*, 24.

religion underground. Additionally, past experience revealed that the local bishops lacked the means or motivation to carry out rigorous inquiries when sympathetic nobles and burghers helped protect a movement. To ensure more systematic investigation, the papacy after 1200 began establishing special tribunals under papal license to investigate anyone suspected of heretical beliefs or practices. While seeking primarily to persuade or pressure those whom it investigated into repenting, these tribunals also had license to hand over the recalcitrant and the relapsed for punishment, including execution, by secular authorities.

These tribunals, which we now refer to as the papal inquisition or just "the Inquisition," operated intensively in Languedoc for more than a century, and developed chillingly effective techniques for locating possible Cathars, for persuading them to inform on their fellows, and for creating social and economic pressure for religious conformity. Whatever the religious impact of the Inquisition, it is certain that record-keeping was central to the institution's success. Both the papacy and the Dominican order sought effective prosecution of those persons whom they deemed heretics, but without creating out-of-control reigns of terror as had happened when some early papal inquisitors had begun investigations without limits on their coercive power.[25] Keeping tight control from above on inquisitorial procedure became an important part of the Inquisition's structure, since rogue inquisitors could bring the Church into disrepute and hinder the search for heretics. In consequence, a number of experienced inquisitors created manuals that recorded both the many documents establishing inquisitorial panels and the most effective practices they had developed. These manuals, which circulated throughout Europe, had a lasting influence on later judicial and political procedures.[26]

The inquisitors charged with eradicating Catharism from Languedoc kept extensive written records inscribed in codices, which are normally called inquisition registers. Only a small fraction of these registers survive. Specifically, only four registers remain, a pittance compared to the nineteen registers and fifty-six other books in the archives of the Carcassonne inquisition alone – now all lost – that are documented by an inventory of the seventeenth century, or the sixteen registers probably held at Toulouse.[27] Each register was bursting with information, including names, narrative depositions, descriptions of family ties, feuds, and

---

[25] The most notorious was the reign of terror instigated by Conrad of Marburg in the Rhineland in the 1230s, which ended with his assassination. See Peters, *Inquisition.*

[26] See Trusen, "Vom Inquisitionsverfahren," especially 435–450.

[27] Given, *Inquisition,* 27–28. On the theoretical issues that these registers raise, see Arnold, "Inquisition, Texts and Discourse."

other aspects of daily life, along with rich metadata contained in the register's organization and in marginalia, indexes, and tables of contents. Just the single surviving register from Toulouse mentions 5,518 individuals cited before the inquisitors who were in charge of the investigations in the city. Significantly, the surviving registers also contain many traces confirming that the inquisitors reviewed individuals' previous testimony and sentences and looked for depositions given by others to find information about the individuals who were testifying.[28]

To succeed in finding information among so much material, the inquisitors deployed state-of-the-art metadata. Since individual heretics were the Inquisition's key targets, the names of suspects and witnesses were the first kind of information to be indexed or otherwise organized. For example:

At the beginning of the register containing the records of the trials conducted at Albi in 1299 and 1300 by Nicholas d'Abbeville, inquisitor of Carcassonne, and Bishop Bernard de Castanet, we find a table listing the names of individuals implicated in heresy by the testimony recorded in the register. This table is arranged according to the names of the individuals who gave depositions ... The name of each deponent is followed by a list, arranged by place of residence, of those mentioned in that individual's testimony. The table contains 583 names.[29]

The collation of names this way – akin to the *distinctiones* in preaching manuals or the details of concordances – enabled inquisitors to arrange follow-up interrogations at a later date, and may have eased their efforts to understand the network of Cathars in a given region, since it stripped away the details of interrogations to leave nothing but linked names.

Spatial ordering was another key method used by the scribes creating these registers. They could group depositions by place or create topographical tables that were part of more elaborate systems for finding individual depositions. In the 1240s Toulouse manuscript (which, it should be noted, reproduced testimony gathered using different media), depositions were grouped by the village where each was taken. To some extent, the perambulation of itinerant inquisitors would have produced such an ordering, since they often interrogated many witnesses from one location on a single day. Even so, the fact that testimony was collated and recopied into the register suggests that the inquisitors chose to organize testimonies by place.[30] Bernard Gui's register of sentences from the early

---

[28] Given, *Inquisition*, 39–40, gives examples of inquisitors confronting suspects with their own previous testimony, as well as reading testimony given by others that implicated the suspect; the number of 5,518 individuals is given on p. 39.

[29] Given, *Inquisition*, 41.   [30] Given, *Inquisition*, 35.

1300s has an alphabetized initial table of places (*Nomina locorum secundum ordinem alphabeticum*), then a chronological list of all the sentencings (*sermones*) that Bernard carried out (mirroring the chronological sequence of the actual entries, which also subdivided the crimes and sentences imposed in a standard order), and finally a list of individual names grouped by places of residence in alphabetical order.[31]

With these three finding aids, a user could locate individuals of interest either by scanning names or by looking under the toponym, either of which provided folio references to loci in the main text. Knowing a sentencing date would lead to the correct *sermo* by the folio numbers provided in the table of *sermones*. Marginal notes throughout Gui's register refer to relevant testimony in other registers by giving the name of the book or the name of the inquisitor involved. Other marginalia (including in the tables) provide updates on cases or flag potentially useful information by providing the names of further suspects.[32]

Abundant evidence from the registers themselves confirms that inquisitors really did find suspects' previous depositions and use relevant depositions from other witnesses to pressure suspects to confess and repent. Additionally, the fear that inquisitorial registers inspired in suspects and the general population, including the frequent accusations that these reports were replete with falsehoods, reveals that those outside the inquisition recognized the power of the information in the inquisitors' books.[33] When they could, individuals under suspicion stole or bought records that they feared might implicate them. Indeed, in Carcassonne in the 1280s, a complex plot to steal and burn the local Inquisition's registers was foiled only because the local inquisitor, Jean Galand, had taken the key to the locked chest containing them with him to Toulouse.[34]

The fact that various inquisitors also composed manuals for their brethren and for posterity highlights not only the importance of the legal procedures developed during the search for heretics in the Languedoc, but also the growing interest in systematic inquiry and its associated record-keeping, which became attractive to various actors in Late Medieval Europe. Like the increasing formality of monastic and episcopal visitations, inquisitorial manuals were one aspect of a general shift in European legal culture toward the collection of evidence according to written rules. The manuals themselves are critical sources because they

---

[31] Gui's *Liber Sententiarum* published in Pales-Gobilliard, *Le livre*; my description relies primarily on Given.

[32] Given, *Inquisition*, 28–42.

[33] Bruschi and Biller, *Texts*, 6; Arnold, "Inquisition, Texts and Discourse," 64; Given, *Inquisition*, 42–44.

[34] Given, "The Inquisitors," 349.

reveal the priorities and the methods that various inquisitors developed in the practice of suppressing heresy. They also transmitted both methods and cultural attitudes to other spheres, especially since the senior clerics who had access to them in the fourteenth and fifteenth centuries also served both the Church and European monarchs in other capacities, where they could apply the insights they had gained from reading these manuals.[35]

The most famous and widely circulated of the inquisitors' manuals came from the pen of Nicolau Eymerich, a Catalan Dominican who served, among other capacities, as Inquisitor General of the Kingdom of Aragon in the 1350s and 1360s.[36] Eymerich's *Directorium Inquisitorum* contained extensive reference material, including excerpts from various theological and legal treatises, but its third section provided specific guidance for each phase of an inquisitional tribunal's work. Along with instructions on how to announce an investigation, how to negotiate with secular rulers, and how to interrogate suspects, Eymerich discussed document creation and authentication, including the use of notaries.[37] Although Eymerich did not go into detail about the creation and use of registers – little tools of knowledge are often taken for granted – he did describe the *aides-memoires* that inquisitors should keep as they listened to witnesses:

If delators are so numerous that it would be impossible to hear each of their depositions judiciously, the inquisitor should write down in a little book foreseen for this purpose – one for each diocese – what and whom they denounce, their names, and the names of other witnesses they produce, together with the name of the town or village where these live.[38]

After giving this instruction, the manual continued with model entries that laid out the informational structure of these little books:

Diocese of X: So-and-so, born in ____, living in ____, with the profession of _____, denounced so-and-so, living on ___ street, practicing the occupation of _____, for having claimed (for example) that the body of Christ was not really present in the sacrament of the altar.
    To ask: So-and-so, living at _____, on _____ street, with the profession of _____; and so-and-so.[39]

---

[35] Glénisson, "Les enquêtes." More recently, Brendecke, *Imperium und Empirie*, 46, argues that the culture of observation and reporting pioneered by inquisitors was important for later developments in European politics (notably in the Spanish Empire and its overseas possessions).

[36] The following discussion rests primarily on the abridged edition published in French: Eymerich and Peña, *Le manuel*. See also Given, *Inquisition*, 44–50.

[37] Eymerich and Peña, *Le manuel*, 111–12.   [38] Eymerich and Peña, *Le manuel*, 151.

[39] Eymerich and Peña, *Le manuel*, 152.

The kind of detailed guidance found in this manual paralleled the evolving chancellery formularies and guides to the *ars dictaminis* appearing across Europe in the thirteenth century, in that it gave officials precise guidance about how to render information useful in written form.[40] Equally telling is Eymerich's passing remark that such books should be "foreseen for this purpose," which captures the forethought that lay behind even simple information-gathering tools.

The careful record-keeping practiced by the papal inquisitions represented only one example of a broad trend toward more production and preservation of documents that accelerated after 1200. Moreover, inquisitorial procedures in general – that is, those resting on trials *per inquisitionem* – shifted the focus of providing justice from negotiation to investigation, thereby spurring administrative inquests as well.[41] Driven by the desire to uncover the Cathars hiding among the Christian population of southern France, the Church began sending inquisitors with broad investigative powers who could try known heretics while simultaneously gathering information, which was captured in sophisticated codices. Not just the Cathars, but all residents in a town under inquisition were obliged to report everything they knew to the inquisitors, who carefully noted potential leads among the mass of information they received and tracked connections with metadata in their registers. In this way, each inquisition institutionalized information within a rigorously hierarchical context and modified existing techniques for tracking knowledge in books to make this information available through time. The resulting registers gave the inquisitors a powerful tool for breaking through the networks of kinship and friendship that had allowed Cathars to continue practicing their religion after 1244, and led to the eventual extinction of Catharism altogether.[42]

To sum up: Trials *per inquisitionem* appeared first in the Latin Church, but the relative effectiveness of inquisitorial courts helped encourage the spread of inquisitorial procedure into secular courts after the thirteenth century, in tandem with the revival of neo-Roman law across Europe.[43] Inquisitorial documentary practices spread as well, albeit with considerable limitations, since the inquisitors diligently recorded their own practices, advising which tools for information gathering worked best for

---

[40] The *ars dictaminis* have long been associated with Renaissance learning; see, for example, Baron, "Leonardo Bruni." Analysis of their administrative dimension is found in Brown, *Bartolomeo Scala*.

[41] The argument here follows Brendecke, *Imperium und Empirie*, 46–51.

[42] See Trusen, "Vom Inquisitionsverfahren" about the connections between inquisition procedures and later trials of heretics and witches.

[43] For Germany, see Strauss, *Law*; for France, see Kelley, *The Foundations*.

witnesses of various kinds. The manuals they produced enabled secular officials to design their own information-gathering systems, which in turn resulted in rapidly growing stocks of depositions, registers, reports, and other records. As we will see, dealing with these accumulations, as well as with the growing body of records resulting from administrative communication, challenged chancellery officials across Europe in the fifteenth and sixteenth centuries.

Governance, Information and Documents in Late Medieval Chancelleries

As the discussion so far has made clear, writing became used with greater intensity in a growing number of contexts from the twelfth century onward across the European subcontinent. Among the many contexts involved, political organization and the management of public affairs (however those may have been defined at particular times and places) are the most important for understanding the plethora of repositories and eventually archives that such record-keeping produced.[44] While the intensification of governance on the basis of information was far from being a simple matter of steady increase, chancelleries and their equivalents clearly produced, kept, and used more written material as the High and Late Middle Ages continued.[45] The causes, course, and significance of intensified uses of writing have been key questions for medievalists over the last two generations, and extend far beyond the scope of this study. Even the study of writing in politics, which is not limited to the growth of administration through written records, is a vast topic that can only be sketched tangentially as we concentrate on early modern archival practices. Systematic record-keeping and the accumulation of archives have widely been viewed as both "an unavoidable consequence of modern states' operation and as an essential means through which administrative states emerged" in Europe.[46] Moreover, although the medieval administrative state was *constituted* to a very significant extent through the records that it produced and kept, it must also be *studied* through those very records, insofar as they have survived – a factor introducing an irreducible element of recursivity to every analysis.

---

[44] Official records are only part of what Hagen Keller defines as *pragmatische Schriftlichkeit* ("pragmatic uses of writing"). See Keller, "Vom 'heiligen Buch' zur Buchführung."

[45] On this growth, see Brendecke, "Papierfluten." For an important note of caution about assuming the papers that we see in official repositories represent a full picture of political life, see Brendecke, "*Arca, Archivillo, Archive.*"

[46] Rodríguez de Diego, "Significado," 186.

Given this book's particular interest in the evolution of record-keeping practices, the following discussion focuses on three political loci that gave rise to durable practices of record-keeping, practices that continued to be used and recombined in endless ways throughout the Late Medieval and early modern periods: the monastery, the princely chancellery, and the town government. A key contribution of Europe's monasteries to European archivality had been the cartulary and related forms of preserving core documents for later use. The analysis in this chapter focuses on princely chancelleries by looking at one paradigmatic case – namely, the French king's government based in Paris, and its abrupt shift toward using written records during the reign of Philip II Augustus (r. 1179–1223), as described in John Baldwin's magisterial study. Cities were equally significant for the Late Medieval transformation of record-keeping, and a substantial literature considers Italian cities in particular.[47] Here, I will concentrate on developments in three German cases – Cologne, Nuremberg, and Lübeck in the later Middle Ages – as they appear in the equally magisterial analysis of Ernst Pitz.[48] As we will see, urban protocols not only intensified record-keeping in general, but also produced early forms of document registry.

In John Baldwin's account of the "quantum leap in the development of the Capetian monarchy" under King Philip II Augustus, changes in record-keeping play an important role. This dramatic leap led to new forms of governance, but also enables the historian to see more comprehensively how that governance worked. As Baldwin notes:

The state of documentation privileges the historian of Philip's reign over those of previous French monarchs ... Philip's administration both generated and preserved evidence sufficient to provide clear outlines of the great transformations that took place in his government ... The records were not merely testimonies to Philip's achievements but also direct products of his government.[49]

In particular, three signal events early in Philip's reign created strong incentives for more extensive record-making and record-keeping. The first was the king's participation in the Third Crusade from 1189 to 1192, which led to his absence from the realm; the second was the loss of the

---

[47] See most recently de Vivo, Guidi, and Silvestri, *Archivi e archivisti*; Lazzarini, "Records."
[48] Pitz, *Schrift- und Aktenwesen.*
[49] Baldwin, *The Government*, xix. He further refines his perspective on p. 394: "This evidence is not merely passive and innocent testimony to the past but also the direct product of the institutions under study, and our sources must be viewed in interaction with the administrative organs that generated them."

Crown's existing fiscal records and charters to Richard the Lionhearted of England at the battle of Freteval in 1194; and the third was Philip's acquisitions of new domains, the most important of which was Normandy, which possessed a relatively sophisticated chancellery and arsenal of record-keeping practices.[50] Together, these events spurred the creation of a new royal chancellery that would henceforth be sedentary in Paris, rather than following the king, and which would begin recording both important information and its own acts in book-form registers beginning in 1204 (although as Elizabeth Hallam and Judith Everard note, systematic registration of emitted charters began only in 1304, a century later).[51]

Once the king's clerks had begun writing records in books, they soon commenced innovating how they did so. The first register launched in 1204, Register A, began with a large amount of material copied into it at once; in subsequent years, material was added bit by bit until the entire register was "recopied under an improved organization. Once again additions were inserted through the register until it, too, became unwieldy and required recopying."[52] Clerks repeatedly added more material than they had planned, and created extra space in registers by adding quires at the beginning or the end, or by adding material anywhere space was available. Eventually, the chancellery developed a first, and then a second, system of sections within these registers, which required thought about which categories ought to be established. Register E, from the 1220s, included eighteen sections; before it was created, the records found in the older Register C were annotated "as to whether the document was to be, or had been, recopied and to what section it should be assigned."[53] Within these volumes, charters made up only about half of the pages, next to a "great profusion of other kinds of information."[54] In subsequent years and reigns, the chancellery created ever more records in diverse forms, enhanced by royal acquisitions of additional domains and their records. As we will see in Chapter 7, the resulting mass of material eventually gave rise to sophisticated inventorying efforts in the late fourteenth century.

---

[50] Baldwin, *The Government*, 405.

[51] Baldwin, *The Government*, 410, notes, the French royal "archives contain only 28 original pieces from the entire preceding history of the French monarchy." For registration under the Capetians, see Hallam and Everard, *Capetian France*, 2nd ed., 316. There are no registers from earlier Capetian reigns. On the absence of evidence for Carolingian registers, see McKitterick, *Charlemagne*, 46.

[52] Baldwin, *The Government*, 412–13.   [53] Baldwin, *The Government*, 413–14.

[54] Baldwin, *The Government*, 415.

The point here is not that royal record-keeping in France was particularly advanced, or that it served as a model for other regions. Indeed, the opposite was the case: French clerks clearly adopted practices that can be seen earlier in Normandy and England. Rather, what we see in Paris is how even a limited decision to begin preserving records in a systematic way generated incentives that accelerated the production and preservation of papers, as well as means of organizing them. Record-making and record-keeping, at least in the cultural context of the High and Late Middle Ages, were in and of themselves incentives to more record-making and more record-keeping. Strong positive feedback loops seem to have existed, with the result that repositories generally kept growing after this era (despite the occasional destruction of repositories through the vicissitudes of war, plague, or political chaos). As Peter Brun demonstrates vividly for early fifteenth-century Switzerland – otherwise not a hotspot for record-keeping – those who already used written records expected to preserve the memory of new official acts by means of more written records.[55] "Texts generate more texts" is an important principle that set the stage for ever more complex ways to preserve and organize documents in the course of governance in Late Medieval Europe.

As Brun's study also suggests, the use of writing was not at all evenly distributed across different forms of political organization in the later Middle Ages. Only the largest noble polities north of the Alps, such as the crowns of England and France, were in a position to begin systematically generating and keeping written records before about 1300. Around the Mediterranean, where Roman legacies were more tenacious, central records begin to take shape slightly earlier, and were in full swing by the late twelfth century.[56] The papal registers became continuous – after sporadic earlier practices going back into Late Antiquity – with the registers of Innocent III, which began in 1198.[57] In Catalonia, substantial numbers of lay charters were archived starting in the tenth century, so that there were enough records in the comital archive in Barcelona by the twelfth century to require systematic reorganization before being drawn upon to draft a *Liber feudorum maior* in 1193.[58] One later site that illuminates a variety of developments with particular clarity is the Habsburg administrative center of Innsbruck, which will provide several case studies as we proceed.

---

[55] Brun, *Schrift*.
[56] For a broad overview of the issues, see Pitz, "Diplom und Registereintrag," 101–108.
[57] Hageneder and Haidacher, *Die Register Innozenz III*.
[58] Kosto, *Making Agreements*, 17.

The Innsbruck Chancelleries from the High Middle Ages to the Sixteenth Century

Understanding record-keeping and its evolution in Innsbruck requires a more detailed examination of the processes of administrative evolution that took place as the county of Tirol developed into the administrative center for the complex of western territories belonging to the Habsburg dynasty, known as *Ober- und Vorderösterreich*. Both geographic distribution and the structure of the domains managed from Innsbruck after 1400 gave administrators strong incentives not only to collect proofs and the kind of passive information – lists, rent rolls, and the like – that rulers everywhere were gathering at the time, but also to organize more systematically all communication about the complex issues raised by a composite county whose rulers were often located in other far-flung territories.[59] It also seems quite probable that the Tirol's orientation toward Italy helped encourage the emergence of sophisticated administrative codices for the scrutiny of fiscal accounts and the registration of charters there in the 1200s.[60] The chancelleries in Innsbruck therefore offer multiple important perspectives on the history of archives. The background and discussion here pertain to the entire history of this strikingly well-preserved early modern archival system.

The later medieval history of the Tirol can be divided into two parts, each of which was vital for the practices that emerged there between the thirteenth and seventeenth centuries. In the first, the Counts of Tirol, based primarily south of the Brenner Pass and some fifty miles north of the Italian city of Trent, aggressively built a domain that included not only the Alpine valleys around their home but also control over the sees of Bressanone (Brixen) and Trent, the county of Görz, and extensive territories in the Friulian territories of Udine and Trieste and to the east in Carinthia. The German-speaking counts ruled over many Rhaeto-Romance and Italian speakers, and their administrative practices drew on both Italian and Germanic practices. During the long reign of Count Meinhard II from the Görzian line (r. 1257–1295), the comital chancellery introduced systematic fiscal records, while the registration of outgoing deeds is firmly documented by 1308. Meinhard's seizure of various jurisdictions from the Bishoprics of Trent and Bressanone

---

[59] On composite monarchies, see, for example, Elliott, "A Europe of Composite Monarchies."

[60] My analysis rests on Heuberger, "Das Urkunden- und Kanzleiwesen," and Riedmann, "Die Rechnungsbücher." For the fifteenth century, see also Stowasser, "Die österreichischen Kanzleibücher." Essential throughout are Stolz, "Archiv- und Registraturwesen"; Stolz, *Geschichte und Bestände*; Haidacher, "Das Schriftgut"; and Beimrohr, *Das Tiroler Landesarchiv*.

probably encouraged administrative innovation, just as the conquest of Normandy inspired Philip Augustus's secretaries to initiate the use of registers and similar tools in France.[61]

As elsewhere, the consolidation of political power and the development of systematic administration included the production of codices that allowed the counts' officers to track what mattered most for comital power. The first such codices to emerge in the Tirol were books (known as *Raitbücher*) that documented the annual rendering of accounts of the local fiscal officers responsible for collecting and disbursing funds. A continuous series of these codices from 1288 to the 1360s contained the annual reports, presented before the count's fiscal chamber, of the amounts collected and spent on the counts' behalf by individual officers. The entries were ordered by date of the accounting, and gave the location and the witnesses present; in many cases, the scribe also recorded the date of the same officer's previous accounting – a piece of metadata that allowed easy comparison of fiscal performance from year to year.[62] The first section in each entry listed the revenue from various sources and subofficers in the territory involved, which the chamber then totaled, together with any balance remaining from the previous year's accounting. A second section listed expenses (often with a reference such as "commanded by a letter from the lord"[63]), leading to a total of revenue and expenses and a new balance for transfer to the following year. The officer also received a charter recording this balance, although the emission of such charters left no record in the *Raitbücher* themselves; those books recorded information, not proofs. Some volumes had a contemporary table summarizing each account rendered, with each accounting numbered in Arabic numerals (in contrast to the Roman numerals used for the actual sums). The physical form of the books varied considerably, and they have since experienced the usual travails of displacement and rebinding, but the consistency of their contents is impressive.

Careful research by Richard Heuberger and others has established that from the outset, secretaries in the chancellery participated in producing these codices.[64] This is significant because it provided a pathway for

---

[61] The narrative history of the Tirol appears in Baum, *Sigmund*.

[62] The discussion here follows Riedmann, "Die Rechnungsbücher." Some volumes are published in Haidacher, *Die älteren Tiroler Rechnungsbücher*. On the fifteenth-century Raitbücher, see Wiesflecker, "Die 'oberösterreichischen' Kammerraitbücher."

[63] The phrase in Latin is "per litteras domini"; in a few cases, the relevant letters were bound into the codex. See Riedmann, "Die Rechnungsbücher," 318.

[64] Heuberger, "Urkunden- und Kanzleiwesen," 98–117, tracks the chancellery's involvement in the production of the Raitbücher from 1288 onward. In 1288, the counts already employed eight scribes.

record-keeping techniques to circulate among different offices, including the council, the chamber, and the chancellery. In the Tyrolean case, the most important habit to appear in these books (which continued to provide a key ordering principle in both chamber and chancellery for centuries) was the strict observation of chronological order in making entries. Whether this was a conscious choice from the outset or whether it emerged simply because accountings happened one after another, it became an ordering principle for other Innsbruck records series, too (which elsewhere were *not* necessarily kept in chronological order).

Within a generation of the earliest *Raitbücher*, the Tyrolean secretaries were also producing serial registers for the charters and deeds issued by the counts.[65] The chancellery launched each register volume by creating and binding a quarto-sized paper codex, reserving the first few leaves for a table of entries. Unless special circumstances intervened, the main entries followed in exact chronological order, and contained, at least in the early volumes, the full text of the expedited instrument. Notably, the table of contents and entries were updated simultaneously; in some cases, it even seems that the scribes entered a charter in the table of contents *before* placing the text in the main body of the register: Metadata and data were reciprocally linked in the formation of these codices.[66] Heuberger argues that the text found in the register also generally preceded the production of emitted charters, as shown by numerous contemporary corrections and by close examination of the registers' marginal metadata (*Vermerke*), which provides clues about the process by which both charters and register were created.[67] Clearly, the Tyrolean chancellery and chamber participated fully in the general European tendency to begin collecting and managing records – both probative and nonprobative – in books during the thirteenth and fourteenth centuries.

The second major phase in the medieval Tyrolean chancellery's operations followed the Habsburg family's accession to the county of Tirol in 1363,[68] especially after the territory's chancellery migrated to the more

---

[65] Heuberger, "Urkunden- und Kanzleiwesen," 265–270, doubts that any chancellery-based series of registers existed before 1308, although individual comital officers may have possessed personal registers akin to the notarial registers in use across Italy. See Heuberger', 329–46 for the full range of surviving chancellery books from 1253 to 1335.

[66] Heuberger, "Urkunden- und Kanzleiwesen," 272.

[67] Heuberger, "Urkunden- und Kanzleiwesen," 279–300, including a meticulous analysis of one exemplar's creation. He debates whether these volumes should be called "registers" or "concept-books" (*Konzeptbücher*), only to conclude sensibly (300) that this is a question of use, not of form.

[68] The county of Görz followed only in 1500.

conveniently located town of Innsbruck in 1420.[69] This move was a belated response to the administrative division of the Habsburg lands among first two lines (in 1379) and then three (from 1404), and the familial conglomeration of the county with a variety of further territories reaching as far as Alsace and Switzerland to the west.[70] In addition to being subjected to the frequently bitter rivalries between the competing Habsburg branches, the entire western Habsburg zone faced intense territorial threats from the Dukes of Burgundy and Bavaria, and not least from the Swiss Confederation, which seized some of the family's oldest possessions in the Aargau in 1415. Uncertainty over which Habsburg archduke should administer the western zone continued into the 1420s, but by the 1430s, and especially after the election of Albrecht II as King of the Germans in 1438, the position of the Tyrolean line of Habsburg archdukes became more secure. The unstable period from 1363 to the 1430s disrupted regular record-keeping, however, and left major gaps in the surviving documentation.

The return to stability of the 1430s was accompanied both by a general economic upturn as the worst ravages of the Black Death began easing, and by the discovery and increasing exploitation of the Tirol's rich silver mines, much to the benefit of the Tyrolean line. By the time Archduke Sigmund (known as *der Münzreiche*, "rich in coin") came of age in 1446, after a typically disruptive struggle against his uncle and regent, Emperor Frederick III, the conditions were ripe for a revival and reform of the administration of the Austrian western lands from their emerging center in Innsbruck.[71] The first phase of this expansion took place during the reign of Sigmund (which neatly overlaps the reign of Afonso V in Portugal and the commencement of the reformed *Chancelarias*), but the full development took place only after Maximilian I had reunited the separate Habsburg lines by deposing Sigmund in 1490. From the late 1490s to the late 1520s, the records collected and managed by Innsbruck's administration – now organized into territorial, court, and Imperial chancelleries – steadily developed into an intensive book-based information management system suited to the complex conglomerate of territories, rights, and revenues these chancelleries oversaw.

---

[69] See Stolz, *Geschichte und Bestände*, especially 5–11 for the shifting domainal/territorial ambit of the Innsbruck chancellery and archive.

[70] Baum, *Sigmund*, 39.

[71] On the bitter struggles during the regency, during much of which the Tirol and its elites were in rebellion, see Baum, *Sigmund*, 63–82.

During the reign of Archduke Sigmund, his officers undertook only modest efforts to change inherited practices, despite the resources they enjoyed. A new series of *Raitbücher* (account books) created specifically for the archducal court began in 1454, eventually superseding the older territorial series. Around 1460, the chancellery began keeping drafts or copies of outgoing letters and instructions, most likely preserved in loose form until they were bound into codices around 1523 as part of the new system of copybooks organized by Ferdinand I.[72] Sigmund also expanded a complex of buildings first purchased by his father Archduke Frederick IV as his residence and center of governance in Innsbruck, including space for the chancellery and the *archivum*, which later moved into new vaults known as the *Schatzgewölbe* to form the *Schatzarchiv* (the treasure archive) during Maximilian's further expansion of the Innsbruck administration. Nevertheless, much of Sigmund's reign was taken up with intensive maneuvering among the Swiss Confederation, the Dukes of Bavaria, and his Habsburg cousins, which eventually led to his abdication under pressure in 1490. It was during the reign of Maximilian – a ruler who, like Manuel I in Portugal, regularly intervened in the administration of his realms – that the Innsbruck chancellery truly expanded.[73]

Maximilian's personality had something to do with the evolution of record-keeping in Innsbruck, owing not only to his "personal attention to an endless amount of paperwork," but also to his "many schemes, always impatient, always in a hurry, generally over-ambitious."[74] It was the structure of the realms with which Maximilian's officers had to cope, however, that made the management of information and specifically of communication the center of his secretaries' efforts after 1498.[75]

---

[72] These Kammerkopialbücher are described in Beimrohr, *Das Tiroler Landesarchiv*, 81. See Wiesflecker, "Die 'oberösterreichischen' Kammerraitbücher," 7–8, for a discussion of the forms found before 1515. Haidacher, "Das Schriftgut," 205, concludes that renewal had already begun under Sigmund.

[73] During Maximilian's reign (as archduke, 1490–1519; as king of the Romans, 1486–1519; and as emperor, 1493–1519), he issued multiple ordinances establishing the offices needed to administer his multiple reigns. See Fellner and Kretschmayr, *Die Österreichische Zentralverwaltung*, Section I, Vol. 1, especially 1–28; in biographical terms, see Benecke, *Maximilian I*, especially chapter 12. The individuals active in Sigmund's and Maximilian's court are exhaustively analyzed in Noflatscher, *Räte und Herrscher*.

[74] Benecke, *Maximilian I*, 123.

[75] Maximilian's personal court fell under the German *Hofkanzlei*. The administration of Ober- und Vorderösterreich – that is, the county of Tyrol and the Habsburg possessions under Innsbruck's administration – fell to the *Landeskanzlei*. The operation of the empire supposedly flowed through the *Reichskanzlei* nominally headed by the *Reichserzkanzler* (Imperial Archchancellor), the Archbishop-Elector of Mainz. See Fellner and Kretschmayer, *Die österreichische Zentralverwaltung*, 139–50; Walther, "Kanzleiordnungen," 351; and Bauer, "Das Register- und Konzeptwesen," 247–79.

Maximilian became king of the Romans (and thus heir to the imperial throne) in 1486, seized control of the archduchy in Tirol from his cousin Sigmund in 1490, and inherited the imperial title from his father Frederick III in 1493. From his imperial accession until 1502, he engaged in a complex series of negotiations with his chief rival at the imperial Diet, the Archbishop of Mainz, over the reform of the entire empire's constitutional and fiscal arrangements, spiced by a war with the Swiss in 1499 and near-bankruptcy on his part from 1500 to 1502. Not only was Maximilian himself largely itinerant during this period of his reign, but his senior advisors and bureaucrats often served as negotiators and ambassadors themselves, and were thus often absent from the actual secretariats.

Keeping track of so many moving pieces while simultaneously maximizing Maximilian's flow of revenue and troops from the Habsburg domains, not to mention adjusting the organization of the emperor's own court to the changing imperial institutions that emerged after the Imperial Reform of 1495, required constant communication among the parties involved. From early in his reign, Maximilian and his chief advisors designated Innsbruck as the record-keeping nerve center that would link his various enterprises, not least because the Tyrolean silver revenue managed through the territorial administration there provided the main collateral for Maximilian's extensive and highly leveraged borrowing from the Fugger bank in Augsburg. In 1507, Maximilian complained that he had sent agents to "review various of our old letters and registers, but this has apparently not taken place yet: therefore we advise you with emphasis to leave them undisturbed in this pursuit."[76] A few years later, engaged with the papacy during the Italian Wars, Maximilian demanded that "you should open the chests where those same [papal bulls about appointment to the bishoprics of Trent, Bressanone, Gurck, and Seckau] lie, which our secretary Andreas Teübler will indicate to you, find and examine the same bulls, and promptly let them be copied." In addition, all the bulls were to be registered anew, and the three keys to the chests where they lay were to be given to specific officers he named.[77]

Even if Maximilian had been more consistent in his planning, steadier in his oversight, and less quixotic in his goals, the turbulent later years of his reign, disturbed by war and hampered by the constant shortage of funds, would have been a difficult time to carry out large and systematic

[76] TLA, Archivsachen I 2 (sealed letter of 13 January 1507).
[77] TLA, Archivsachen, I 2 (sealed letter of 30 July 1509).

reforms of the Habsburg chancelleries and their procedures. Nevertheless, major milestones did occur during this reign, and current practice in the key centers – Innsbruck, Vienna, and Graz – became important preconditions for the radical changes that began under Maximilian's successor in the German Habsburg lands, his grandson Ferdinand I (who reigned as Archduke of Austria under his brother, Emperor Charles V, beginning in 1521). It is to one of the earliest and most impressive products of Ferdinand's reign in Innsbruck that we now turn.

6   Information Management in Early Modern Innsbruck, 1490–1530

Introduction

Following the accession of Archduke Ferdinand I as regent of the Habsburg Austrian lands, his western territorial chancellery in Innsbruck inaugurated a sophisticated system of interlocking copybooks in 1523. These copybooks represent a striking comparison to the contemporaneous *Leitura Nova* in Lisbon, in that they focused on the effective tracking of information just as much as the *Leitura* concentrated on proofs and royal patronage. One purpose of the Innsbruck copybooks was to connect the *Regiment* – the chancellor and staff of councilors delegated by the archduke to manage all routine administration of the Habsburg lands dependent on Innsbruck – with Ferdinand himself. Ferdinand remained a peripatetic ruler in constant motion not only between his own centers of Innsbruck, Vienna, Graz, and (after 1526) Prague, but also throughout the Holy Roman Empire, where he often represented his brother.[1] Ferdinand's regular absence from Innsbruck was in itself nothing new: Although his grandfather Maximilian I had been fond of the city, he, too, had spent much of his reign moving through the empire and Habsburg lands in nearly constant perambulation.

Ferdinand's establishment of new regional administrations (known as *Regimenten*) in several regions, under his close personal supervision while able to act in his name on a wide variety of political, judicial, and fiscal matters, generated demands for record-keeping that could connect these new officers with their archduke, on the one hand, and with the local administrations of the many diverse territories under their supervision, on the other hand.[2] The information-tracking tools described here therefore

---

[1] For a broad overview of Austrian archival history, see Hochedlinger, *Österreichische Archivgeschichte*. Fichtner, *Ferdinand I,* chapter 5, discusses Ferdinand's career and administrative provisions.

[2] Haidacher, "Das Schriftgut," 208. The establishment of *Regierungen* or *Regimenten* is analyzed in detail in Rosenthal, *Die Behördenorganisation,* especially 43–50 and 99–121. See also Starzer, *Beiträge,* on Lower Austria.

exemplify how Western European rulers at all scales in this period sought to mobilize record-making and record-keeping as flexible tools of knowledge and power – as extensions of individual and institutional memory about a wide variety of concerns, one might say. They also exemplify how the proliferation of written material in various social spheres itself spurred even more writing, as discussed previously. While conveying information as well as proving acts and contracts had always been among the fundamental uses of writing and reading, these new tools reveal both new expectations on the part of rulers around 1500 and inventive responses from the growing staff employed to fulfill these expectations.

The Innsbruck *Hofkanzlei* (archducal chancellery) chose a familiar medial form – the codex – in creating its new information management system. Their work drew liberally on earlier configurations found in Innsbruck, such as the chronologically organized *Raitbücher* and registers. Secretaries recast older techniques to create comprehensive records series that gave the chancellery easy access to its correspondence with the archduke, with the Tyrolean regional chancellery, with the other territories in its ambit, and with litigants whose cases had reached the chancellor. In the same years, a parallel set of practices was launched in Vienna, about which considerably less is known today because of the loss of those records.[3] One of the advantages of concentrating on the Innsbruck case is the superb preservation of multiple series of copybooks, document bundles, and index volumes from throughout the early modern period, which allows us to see the approaches taken at various times.

The complex responsibilities that Innsbruck gained under Maximilian made it one hub in a widespread Habsburg administrative network. This shaped the way that the Innsbruck chancellery invented new record-keeping tools that allowed Ferdinand, his advisors, and the chancellery's own staff to keep track of people, money, and royal commands.[4] In contrast to the Lisbon royal chancellery, which created a codical *archivum* that both manifested and recorded royal patronage and majesty, the Innsbruck chancellery created an *informational* repository, in the form of serial copybooks provided with alphabetical indexes that reproduced incoming and outgoing documents in a wide variety of genres. As

[3] The Vienna chancellery ordinance of 1526 required new record books, called *Gedenkbuch* or a *Gedächtnisbuch*, along with the preservation of the underlying documents in bundles; see Stolz, "Archiv- und Registraturwesen," 105–6. These materials do not survive except for records pertaining to Tirol that were transferred there in 1565; see Beimrohr, *Tiroler Landesarchiv*, 84.

[4] The more traditional functions of tracking proofs and feudal obligations by the territorial chancellery – a separate institution – continued; see Beimrohr, *Tiroler Landesarchiv*, 60, 76. See also Walther, "Kanzleiordnungen," 343.

had been the case in Lisbon, the push of creativity in Innsbruck also led to the introduction of other new tools, including inventories of old documents and eventually a serial records registry (see Chapters 8 and 12, respectively, for case studies). Nevertheless, the chancellery copybooks established in 1523 must be the first stop in understanding the Innsbruck system.

Copying correspondence was not in itself new, of course, especially in urban settings. Florence began keeping copies of its outgoing political correspondence in 1395, for example, while the Milanese chancellery of Francesco Sforza systematized and expanded its missive books in the 1460s.[5] Bern began copying incoming letters shortly after 1400, and outgoing letters after 1442.[6] When the resources of a major monarchy became available for such enterprises, however, recognized methods could expand into novel comprehensive systems of records, whether oriented to probative documents (*Leitura Nova*) or, as in Innsbruck, to the administration of a complex composite empire.

The system that emerged in Innsbruck relied not only on techniques already circulating among cities and regimes across Europe, but also on a series of specific organizational reforms instituted by Ferdinand and his advisors. These have received considerable attention, since the new chancellery ordinances (*Hofordnungen, Kanzleiordnungen*) of this period went far beyond earlier exemplars and proved to have extraordinarily long-lived effects.[7] The production of explicit ordinances regulating the appointment of senior officers and chancellery staff while also defining their duties, payment, and working conditions is itself a symptom of growing formalism and increasing reliance on written documents. To put it another way, such ordinances showed that not only the secretaries and scribes in the chancellery and the lawyers sitting in the back rows of royal councils, but also rulers themselves accepted that recorded information was vital for their status and power. The chancellery ordinance issued by Archduke Ferdinand for his court chancellery (*Hofkanzlei*) in 1526 went into considerable detail about the kinds of books the various secretaries should maintain. His secretary for Upper Austria (including Tirol), for example,

[5] An overview of Italian innovations, especially for diplomatic correspondence, can be found in Senatore, *"Uno mundo,"* especially 85–88; and for Venice, in de Vivo, "Ordering the Archive."
[6] StABE, Deutsche Missivenbücher (A III), available online.
[7] Fellner and Kretschmayr, *Die Österreichische Zentralverwaltung,* who also publish most of the main ordinances in 2:2; Walther, "Kanzleiordnungen"; and Rosenthal, *Die Behördenorganisation.* See also Tennant, *The Habsburg Chancellery,* for a philological approach and on the training of Maximilian's secretaries.

should take care that he shall maintain three memory books about all the above named matters that are his responsibility to complete, in which he should daily write down the decisions of the council (*ratschleg*) and also as needed the verbal answers or decisions, which were given to the parties but for which no letters were issued; item, he shall keep and preserve in an orderly way all supplications, missives or other similar writings, also completed or registered copies, so that one may easily and quickly find them when one has need of them.[8]

Naturally, the archduke did not personally compose the detailed instructions found here, which were issued in his name. Still, as Maximilian's own example showed (as did that of his grand-nephew Philip II of Spain), rulers were eager to approve increasingly detailed guides regulating those who managed their records and would, they hoped, provide them with information "easily and quickly." These ordinances created the essential preconditions for the emergence of the Innsbruck copybook system and other Habsburg chancellery archives, even if they failed to spell out the details; indeed, those details emerged only over a generation of experimentation and adaptation.

The key innovation of the Innsbruck system was not simply the institution of copybooks or "memory books" by certain officers, or even the separation of books into series that organized written material pertaining to different substantive areas of princely interest. Rather, the most salient development was the creation of an information system that *linked* circulating documents (both from outside and within the administrative system) to specific series of copybooks, using chronological order as a key structural principle while providing the copybooks with well-designed indexes to allow effective searching. Various pieces of the system can be traced back to outgoing missives copied for retention after 1460 or to the fiscal management system of the medieval chancellery, but the fully developed system emerged only in 1523, when Ferdinand took charge of affairs in Innsbruck. The following discussion focuses on the state of affairs in 1523, with occasional references backward and forward as needed.

Copying a Flow of Records: Innsbruck Innovations in 1523

Let us begin by looking at a paradigmatic exemplar of an Innsbruck copybook, the first produced in one new series originating in 1523. This volume, which belongs to the series *Von der Furstlichen Durchlaucht* ("From his Princely Highness"), covers incoming correspondence from

---

[8] Fellner and Kretschmayaer, *Die Österreichische Zentralverwaltung*, 1(2): 93.

Archduke Ferdinand for the years 1523–1526.[9] Like most of the copy-books discussed here, this large and sturdy paper volume of more than 500 precisely cut leaves was rebound, probably in the seventeenth or early eighteenth century, in white leather with metal clasps. A few early volumes filed with this series that were not rebound are wrapped in a heavy parchment wrapper with leather ties, which probably represents the original binding of the entire series.[10] A number of clues indicate that the volume was first bound only after most of the writing work had been done. Most importantly, the index to the volume, which takes up the first forty-four leaves, is on visibly different paper that was originally larger than the main body of the volume and was cut to match when it was bound.[11] The index has a separate title page:

Tables [*Tablatur*] about
The Book "From his Princely Highness"
1523
1524
1525
1526
First Volume

The format and title of the index, as well as various internal details, all confirm that each index was produced only after a volume's pages were full.[12] It is thus conceivable that the index was at first kept separately from the volume, and only bound in later. We might imagine senior secretaries keeping the indexes at their desk, while leaving the actual bulky volumes somewhere else in the chancellery – except that the relatively good preservation of this index, and the fact that few or no indexes have been lost, makes this unlikely. The differences in format between index and volume reflect their separate production, but the two segments were then most likely bound together immediately, once complete.

---

[9] TLA Innsbruck, Ober-österreichische Regierung, Kopialbücher, Von der Fürstlichen Durchlaucht, vol. 2. The first volumes in each series belonging to this system display considerable variety, becoming more homogeneous by the 1530s.

[10] Such a binding appears on TLA Ober-Österreichische Regierung, Kopialbücher, Von der Fürstlichen Durchlaucht, Vol. 1, which predates the new series, and for loose documents bound in the early sixteenth century as the Ältere Kopialbücher (Beimrohr, *Das Tiroler Landesarchiv*, 71), suggesting that this was standard for codices assembled in the early 1500s.

[11] The paper used for the indexes often varies from the main volume in size and (when visible) watermarks.

[12] Notably, most indexes throughout the series are in a consistent hand and ductus, suggesting that each was made in a relatively short time. For the volume discussed here, the title page lists all four years it covers in the same hand, meaning that the scribe who created the index knew at the outset what period it covered.

The main body of this copybook is divided into several sections. The entire volume has folio numbers in Arabic numerals at the upper right-hand corner of each recto leaf. A small number of original documents with a clearly different page format are bound into the volume, but these are not foliated, suggesting that the folio numbers were put on the pages before the volume was bound – and indeed, probably before anything was copied onto its pages.[13] In approximately the first 140 folios, large blocks of entries appear primarily in two hands. After this, more hands appear, often varying from entry to entry. This suggests that a backlog of material was copied into this volume at one time (as one might expect in the first volume of a new series); afterward, shorter entries were made on a regular basis. Entries range from a few lines to multiple pages in length, and generally average about four to five entries per page. With some 467 leaves appearing in the document's main body, a rough calculation suggests some 2,000 entries were made in the entire volume over four years, or one to two per day, on average.

As the series title "From his Princely Highness" suggests, the main entries included instructions, correspondence, and other communications from Archduke Ferdinand and the staff in immediate attendance on him, wherever he was, that had been sent to the administrative council in Innsbruck (*Regiment*). Despite the title, a number of letters back to Ferdinand were also copied into the book, particularly if they were responses to something he had said in a previous letter. A parallel series of nearly identical copybooks, entitled *An der fürstlichen Durchlaucht* ("To his Princely Highness"), contains most of the correspondence that the Innsbruck council and administration sent to Ferdinand. Thus, these two series, taken together, capture an extended dialogue about many different subjects between the prince and his servants (or, to be exact, between the prince's immediate officers in attendance on him in person, and his officers situated in one of his permanent administrative centers).[14] Among many other subjects, one finds a number of documents about the operation of the chancellery itself, showing that administrative reform and effective record-keeping were on the minds of those working for Ferdinand. One of the first entries includes approval to hire an additional registrator in Innsbruck, for example. In addition, in 1524,

---

[13] Blocks of foliated but blank pages are good evidence for foliation before entries began. In TLA Ober-Österreichische Regierung, Kopialbücher, An die fürstliche Durchlaucht [ADFD], Bd. 3, 1525–1526, the foliator inadvertently jumped by 100 while entering the folio numbers – an error that was left uncorrected: The index simply has no entries for the missing leaves 131–230.

[14] To carry out the same functions in Vienna, somewhat different methods were used. See Stolz, "Archiv- und Registraturwesen," 105–106.

the Innsbruck administration responded to the prince's request to send the registrator Wilhelm Putsch to Vienna, since "he knows better than anyone how to give instruction about how to preserve your Princely Highness's sovereignty and privileges out of such registries."[15]

To make the large number of entries in this and similar volumes accessible, the scribes first applied various *mise-en-livre* and *mise-en-page* techniques. A fundamental principle – broken now and then, but not in way that disrupted the system's larger coherence – was the separation of incoming from outgoing correspondence. Another key practice principle remained the chronological order of entry. Although minor deviations appear, mostly when multiple entries occurred in a single hand and ink, chronological order of entry was the norm, which made it possible to browse for specific items if a chancellery official knew when the matter had been under discussion. In addition, some of the volumes, particularly early on, had page breaks or large headings to identify months within each year.[16]

Within this basic framework, the *mise-en-page* in these volumes supported easy finding. Entries took block form in a single column, with clear spaces between them, and with the sender or recipient and the date given at the beginning or end of each entry. To further facilitate browsing, the scribe gave each entry a bold heading in larger script, and highlighted individual words – most often the names of the persons, towns, or domains involved – inside the entries by using large script and thicker strokes. These highlighted keywords stand out strongly from the flowing script of the body text, and can be scanned very quickly, allowing a user to leaf through the book (already oriented by the series designation and the date) to find individual entries. Headings and in-text keywords were regularly augmented by additional keywords in the margin, which appear to have been entered during the indexing process. In effect, two professional scribes had a chance to review each entry and provide a heading, text keywords, and marginal keywords to characterize the entry for future searches.

We can learn a little about the style and predilections of the different scribes by looking at how they formatted their headings and marginal

---

[15] Von der fürstlichen Durchlaucht, Vol. 2, fol. 46[v] and fol. 157[r], respectively.

[16] For example, TLA, Ober-Österreichischen Regierungs-Kopialbücher, Von der Fürstlichen Durchlaucht, Vol. 1, 1521–1523, and slightly differently in Vol. 2, where each month starts on a new page, sometimes after several blank pages (suggesting that the original working format of the copybook consisted of preformed quires for each month). After 1523, entire volumes appear to have been created and foliated before entries began.

keywords. In our sample volume, for example, one scribe favored terse headings consisting simply of names separated by periods:

Stielingen. Costentz. Aidgnossen (fol. 142^r)
Stühlingen. Constance. The Swiss

In contrast, another scribe gave narrative headings:

Neu Confirmacion und lehenbr[iefe] auf der Camer zu registrieren [fol. 46^v]
New confirmations and letters of enfeoffment are to be registered in the treasury
Der Fürstin eergelt von der Steuer (fol. 59^r)
Her Highness's dower, from the tax.
Wildprettschiesser zu Ymbst, Lanndegg (fol. 84^r)
Hunters in Imbst and Landegg

Some entries could be quite cryptic, as with the slightly weary heading:

Lang instruction Trienndt anfenncklich die Regierung betreffent
Long instructions on Trent, initially concerning administration[17]

It seems that the scribes had some leeway about keywords, but quickly fell into familiar patterns and developed fixed terms for particular matters. In this sense, the keywords found in these copybooks are forerunners of the specialized rubrics that were part of the more complex post-1564 registry of the archducal court, discussed in Chapter 12. Significantly, however, the surviving keywords clearly did not belong to any systematic catalog of pertinences, like a modern authority file like the Library of Congress subject headings: They grew out of the texts in an inductive way as they were copied, rather than providing a preset grid for labeling the contents.

The use of keywords fed directly into the indexing process. Each volume in the extensive range of copybooks beginning in the early 1520s had a separate index, which provided direct access to some (but by no means all) of the highlighted terms in the individual entries. These indexes made the entire enterprise viable by providing quick access to items that seemed important at the time of each volume's compilation and indexing – judgments that likely remained valid for some years, when recourse to these records was most likely to occur. The Innsbruck indexes show considerable variation in some features, and considerable variations in the skill of the clerks making them, but share a few structural qualities that contributed to their effectiveness. Most important among these shared features were two simple organizational approaches that helped the indexers make choices about keywords and their alphabetization.

---

[17] All from TLA, Ober-Österreichischen Regierungs-Kopialbücher, Von der Fürstlichen Durchlaucht, Vol. 1, 1521–1523.

Anyone who has worked with early modern indexes, particularly of manuscripts, knows that headword choice and alphabetization were far from obvious to those charged with making indexes. Alphabetization of entries by their first letter only was the norm, most loci received only a single index entry, and the headword (*lemma*) chosen for alphabetization was not always what one might expect.[18] Even Florence's powerful Medici family alphabetized its ledgers by only one letter, generally used individuals' first names to place entries (lots of Giovannis and Giuseppes!), and sometimes indexed phrases by words such as "Una."[19] In Lisbon, as we have seen, a list of names was alphabetized around 1518 by first name, except for nobles, who were all put under "D" (for "Dom") without further distinction. Early modern German orthography raised special challenges, since the letters B and P, C and K, and F and V were largely interchangeable, and no standardized dictionary assigned words among these possibilities. Books could be "Buecher" or "Pücher" depending on the scribe, or even in the products of the same scribe on the same day.[20]

The indexes to the Innsbruck copybooks (as well as to other products of the Innsbruck chancellery, most notably the Putsch inventories discussed in Chapter 8) resolved many of these challenges with two organizational tools. The first tool, found almost universally in Innsbruck alphabetization from the early sixteenth century, was to list headwords according to a scheme that employed two columns rather than one. The first column contained qualifying terms about the lemma, such as "castle," "village," "family," and so on. The primary index term appeared in the second column – in most cases, a family name or toponym – and provided the sole basis for alphabetization. The illustration in Figure 6.1, taken from one of the Vienna Putsch inventories, shows this practice clearly, even in a dense and complicated index with little attention to textual aesthetics. In this example, which includes items alphabetized under the multiletter combinations "leu" and "lie," various supplementary terms – including "Perch zu" ("mountain at," a reference to mines), "Vngelt zu" ("revenue from"), "von" (designating a noble

---

[18] General discussion appears in Daly, *Contributions*. Zedelmaier, *"Facilitas inveniendi,"* points out that scholarly indexers were ahead of administrative ones throughout most of the early modern period. Pointing to Pappias's *Elementarum doctrinae erudimentum* of 1053 with abc (three-letter) alphabetization, Daly notes that "earlier collections may be more perfectly alphabetized while fifteenth century collections are still observing only first-letter order" (71–72).

[19] Daly, *Contributions*, 82; the same applies to the Barbarigo ledgers from the 1440s to 1480s.

[20] Tennant, *The Habsburg Chancellery*, dismisses the hypothesis that Maximilian's chancellery sought to standardize chancellery orthography.

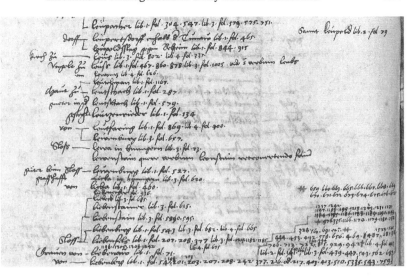

Figure 6.1 Alphabetization in an inventory made by Wilhelm Putsch in Vienna in the 1530s. Modifiers are to the left of the main column, in which each entry begins with a headword referring to the name of a place, person, or office. Alphabetization is by the first three letters. On the upper right, one additional headword is added. On the lower right, one can see how Putsch added additional entries for headwords in multiple rounds, after the initial list of headwords had been composed. (This same page is reproduced in Stowasser, *Das Archiv*, p. 47.) Original: HHStA Vienna, Repertorien Alter AB 332/2 (Alt AB 25), p. 196.

Image provided by the Haus-, Hof- und Staatsarchiv, Vienna, and reproduced by permission.

family), "Sloß" ("castle") and "Graffschaftt" ("county") – appear in the first column. Alphabetization, however, follows the place name or patronym in the second column, which naturally brought together related entries in the same area of the index, and prevented the family "von Liebenberg" from appearing under "v" while the castle of Lieben-berg appeared under "s" (for "Schloss"). Rather, both appear together near the bottom of the illustration, under "lie." Entries within a letter combination were not alphabetized further. In all cases, the referenced loci are given after the alphabetized keyword ("Lib 3 fol 615").[21]

---

[21] The fact that the folio numbers recorded after headwords are almost always in ascending order strongly suggests that this index was made after the entries into the main text were complete.

The same technique is used, though using only the first letter of each keyword, in the Innsbruck administrative copybooks. In most cases, the pages of the index are laid out into two or three clear columns, with qualifiers in the first column (sometimes right justified), the alphabetized keyword in the second column, and the folios referenced in the third column or appended to the keywords, as in Figure 6.1. Small differences of *mise-en-page* do appear from volume to volume and from scribe to scribe, however. Some scribes used horizontal lines or a series of dots to connect qualifiers to keywords to folio numbers, whereas others spaced and justified them differently to keep the connections clear. The same system appeared in volumes drafted in the fiscal chamber (which used a different page layout and alphabet, but still followed the same three-column *mise-en-page*.)[22]

In the copybook indexes, a considerable number of abstract keywords appear, along with family names and toponyms. Indexers sometimes also used toponyms as qualifiers rather than headwords, suggesting the action or institution involved was more important than its location:

Salzbürgischen.........**Aufrüerer**
Salzburg...................Rebels
Tyrolischer.............**Ausschuß**
Tyrolean..................Delegation[23]

Where confusion was possible, multiple entries also occurred:

Vertrag zwischen Hungern und....**Beheim**....fol. 345/355/365
Treaty between Hungary and..........Bohemia
Vertrag zwischen......................**Hungern und Beheim**...fol. 345/355/364
Treaty between...........................Hungary and Bohemia[24]

The indexes did not index every keyword from the main body of these volumes, however. Whereas the number of keywords found in the headings, texts, and margins of the main volumes was quite large, only the most important items or keywords found their way into the index, suggesting that the secretaries expected browsing as well as index searching to be important for future users of these books.

To ease the process of searching for terms, the indexers also modified the alphabet they used. The letters most likely to cause difficulty were

---

[22] See the note inserted inside the cover of TLA Ober-Österreichische Regierung, Kopialbücher, An der Fürstlichen Durchlaucht, Bd. 1 (1519–1521) by modern archivist Heinz Noflatscher, noting the volume's provenance from the chamber and use of its indexing system.

[23] Both from the index to TLA Ober-Österreichische Regierung, Kopialbücher, An die fürstliche Durchlaucht, Bd. 3, 1525–1526.

[24] These examples are from An die fürstliche Durchlaucht, Bd. 3, 1525–1526.

simply grouped together. Most often, B/P, C/K, D/T, F/V, and I/J each formed a single grouping for index entries, in each case ordered by the first letter, alphabetically, in the group. Thus "Pücher" as well as "Buecher" would appear under "B," and so forth. Most of the indexes lacked an "X," and "Y" was also often omitted or combined with "I" and "J"; "Q" appeared in some indexes, but not in others, apparently at the discretion of the scribe involved.[25] The copybooks produced in the fiscal chamber, in contrast, used nearly full alphabets well into the 1520s.[26]

Another Innsbruck technique, found in one volume of the series *Causae Domini* from 1530 to 1531 as well as in the inventory indexes created by Wilhelm Putsch (Chapter 8), required the indexer to subdivide each letter of the alphabet into two-, three-, or even four-letter subheadings (as seen in Figure 6.1, with "leu-" followed by "lie-"). In a large index, this expedient practice balanced the desire to alphabetize by more than one letter of the keyword against the more complicated process that full alphabetization would require. In the *Causae Domini* volume, such letter combinations were pre-inscribed on the forty-six leaves of the index.[27] Unfortunately, the scribe's diligence was largely in vain, since many of the approximately 230 resulting letter-combinations, entered at a rate of approximately five per page of the index, have no entries at all. The various approaches to alphabetization and indexing in Innsbruck make it clear that secretaries and scribes were experimenting as they adapted older techniques to the new demands they faced.

Copybooks As a System within the Innsbruck *Regiment*

The individual volumes of Innsbruck chancellery copybooks were impressive demonstrations of secretarial skill, but their interactions as part of a larger system were even more important. A comprehensive system of copybook series commenced in 1523, which tracked queries, decisions, and instructions traveling into and out of the archducal chancellery. The system as a whole allowed the chancellery to function as a communicative hub.

---

[25] The distinction between Latin and German secretaries might affect whether "Q" appeared. On the secretarial staff in sixteenth-century Innsbruck, see Stolz, *Archiv- und Registraturwesen*, 85–86; Noflatscher, *Räte*.

[26] See, for example, TLA Ober-Österreichische Kammer, Kopialbücher. Geschäft von Hof. Bd 5 (1498), and TLA Ober-Österreichische Kammer, Kopialbücher. Geschäft von Hof. Bd 88 (1523–1524).

[27] TLA Ober-Österreichische Regierung, Kopialbücher, Causa Domini, Bd. 3, at the end of the volume on paper with a different watermark from the main body.

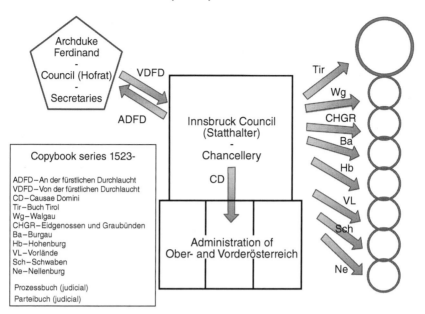

Figure 6.2 Schematic representation of the Innsbruck *Regierung* and the copybook series created after 1523 for administrative communication. The array of boxes in the center represents the main offices that together constituted the *Regierung*. Arrows indicate the primary direction of flow of the correspondence captured in the copybook series. One pathway for correspondence led to or from the Habsburg princes and the officers in their personal entourages (pentagon); other copied correspondence was sent out to regional administrators under Innsbruck's authority (circles).

One axis of communication ran from Innsbruck to Archduke (and later King and Emperor) Ferdinand I, wherever he might be, tracking exchanges on a variety of topics in two parallel series of volumes, "To his Princely Highness" (labeled ADFD in Figure 6.2) and "From his Princely Highness" (VDFD in Figure 6.2).[28] A third series launched in 1523, *Causae Domini* (CD), contained copies of the correspondence – instructions, mandates, responses to supplications and queries, payment orders, and so forth – that ran from the *Regierung* (the governing council, their secretaries, and the chancellery) to other central administrative offices, in particular to the fiscal chamber. An additional eight series of

[28] What happened to the documents copied into the copybooks varied. See the discussion later in this chapter, and Haidacher, "Das Schriftsgut," 208–209.

copybooks, all launched in the same year 1523, recorded the outgoing correspondence from the *Regierung* to the regional subdivisions under the Innsbruck administration's purview: Tirol, Walgau, Burgau, Hohenburg, Schwaben, Eidgenossen-Graubünden, Vorlände, and Nellenburg.[29]

In parallel with these eleven new series of copybooks in 1523, a major change took place in the tracking of important judicial cases before the Tyrolean council (as embodiment of the usually absent archduke): Instead of loose bundles of draft documents on judicial affairs, kept in parchment binders, the chancellery began producing formal paper copybooks (*Prozeßbücher*), including indexes, that closely resembled the administrative copybooks in the other series created at this time. The chancellery also launched a new series of books entitled *Parteibücher*, which recorded correspondence sent to litigants in civil cases.

One final, specifically archival element completed this system, although it is not possible to establish with certainty exactly when it began. In addition to copying large amounts of incoming and outgoing correspondence into multiple series of standardized codices, the chancelleries in Innsbruck at some point began preserving the originals of incoming documents and the drafts of outgoing documents – that is, the same documents whose contents were also copied into the copybooks. Whenever such preservation did begin in Innsbruck – certainly by the 1560s – the deposition of loose documents mirrored the structure of the copybooks, with the originals or drafts corresponding to a particular copybook stacked in the same order as the entries in the copybook – something that happened naturally because both receipt/production and copying took place in chronological order. The earliest evidence of intentional accumulation of draft documents for certain outgoing correspondence dates back to 1460, in the form of a collection of such material that was, tellingly, bound into codices around 1523.[30] By the 1560s at the latest, the chancellery bundled loose documents from selected chancelleries into monthly stacks that corresponded to the index volumes produced at the same time, following a procedure earlier visible in Vienna. These two dates – the binding of loose documents no later than 1523, and the practice of ordered preservation of loose documents in 1564 – provide *termini post* and *ante quam* for the ordered storage – that is, for the archiving in a modern sense – of the originals of incoming

---

[29] The entire system is reviewed in Beimrohr, *Tiroler Landesarchiv*, 71–73. The volumes on "Eidgenossen-Graubünden" reflect lasting Habsburg claims, or at least memories, of the domains the family had lost to the confederations to their west. Additional series commenced after major acquisitions, such as Constance (beginning in 1550).

[30] TLA, Ober-Österreichische Regierung, Ältere Kopialbücher. The dates covered are 1460–1523. Beimrohr, *Tiroler Landesarchiv*, 71.

documents copied into the copybooks, as well as drafts of outgoing documents. Despite uncertainty on this one point, the Innsbruck copybooks reveal a conscious and intelligent dedication to managing information for the future and created a framework that made the simultaneous and integrated preservation of loose documents possible, even if we cannot date the beginning of such practices in Innsbruck with precision.[31]

Conclusion

Close investigation of late medieval records organization, with particular attention to two specific cases from Lisbon and from Innsbruck, leads to several conclusions. The first is that the medium of the codex provided the essential tools that medieval and early modern chancelleries used to develop new ways to manage both documents (as physical objects) and records and their meaning (which emerged from the deployment of documentary objects and the signs they bore). For charters and instruments, as well as for the inquests, correspondence, reports, and similar documentary genres that constituted a growing part of the flow of political records from the thirteenth century onward, organization and access depended primarily on books held in chancelleries. Both the *archivum* as treasury of probative objects and the chancellery repository as a store of information operated, in significant ways, through the medium of the manuscript book.

My second conclusion reflects the distinction between probative objects and informational records, between the *archivum* and the archive, or between the treasury and the chancellery. Although the two conceptual models represent ideal types that were just coming into focus during the later Middle Ages, and which only later supported the concept of an archival threshold, the two possible modes of deploying records reflect tendencies found in both medieval and early modern chancelleries. The apotheosis of the *archivum* appeared in the remarkable *Leitura Nova* created in Lisbon after 1500. During the same period, a systematic effort to capture the flow of records-as-information in books appeared in the Innsbruck copybook system launched in 1523.

---

[31] Discussed in Beimrohr, *Tiroler Landesarchiv*, 70, and Haidacher, "Das Schriftgut," 208–209, although I am not persuaded by their arguments for early preservation followed by "transmission loss." The history of de-acquisition in pre-modern archives remains largely unstudied. Many losses, no doubt, were attributable to friction and entropy; others were likely due to war, fire, disasters, or conscious culling. See Esch, "Überlieferungs-Chance."

Of course, neither system captured everything that was taking place or being recorded in the respective chancelleries, nor does this analysis address every kind of work that accumulated documents could perform around 1500. Even so, the growing flow of information in various media and the steady accumulation of both books and documents recording past actions and information themselves became a critical challenge to administrative repositories by the later fifteenth century. The relentless increase in accumulated records – whatever their repositories and form – along with princes' conviction that these accumulations contained potentially valuable proofs and knowledge, created incentives to establish order and create finding tools. How chancelleries responded to such accumulations, to the implicit understandings embodied in them, and to the available approaches and tools is the topic of the next part of this book.

Part II

The Challenges of Accumulation (1400–)

Although in possession of sophisticated medial tools for making, keeping, and using records, European chancelleries by the mid-fifteenth century began to be overwhelmed by a new challenge: the explosive growth in records they and others produced, accompanied by growing expectations from rulers that a well-managed chancellery could provide information to support their political ambitions and to help defend them against ambitious rivals. Secretaries responded by drawing on the technologies they already possessed – with the codex at the forefront – to create new configurations of pages, books, and indexes that could manage the growing masses of parchment and paper in their care. The clerks responsible for registering emitted instruments expanded their roles, becoming *registrators* responsible for managing extensive flows of correspondence, reports, and other genres of records. Simultaneously, the relatively simple spaces of the medieval *archivum* began experiencing divisions into functionally separate subdivisions that served different purposes. Treasuries of charters lost various other materials, chancelleries began accumulating both current documents and tools for finding older ones, and new spaces emerged to hold other documents – an important step in the emergence of modern archives.

The fundamental medial forms available remained stable through this transformation (even as other textual spheres responded to movable type printing). Quills, ink, and paper; leaves, quires, and books; and sacks, strings, and boxes remained key medial configurations, although the practices for using them evolved according to the availability of resources and the creativity of the responsible actors. In the absence of consistent models, different chancelleries responded differently, leading to a wide diversity of knowledge architectures across the continent. Chapters 8 and 10 address multiple cases in which archival staff sought to bring order to the material they had, or to design better ways to keep and track future documents they anticipated receiving.

To enrich our understanding of these cases, Chapters 7 and 9 distinguish between two major approaches to accumulated records – inventorization and classification, respectively. At its simplest, an inventory or index to an accumulation of material described what was where in whatever order that had resulted from various processes of accumulation (even if it was in no good order at all). After reviewing some ways that material and spaces could be materially described and connected, Chapter 7 turns to the work of Paris archivist Gérard de Montaigu in the 1370s. Montaigu created an inventory to French royal documents that used many of the techniques we will find right through 1700. He worked directly with the royal court's secretaries, and utility of the record-keeping system for the court's needs was a core goal of his work, as it was for all the inventory-makers we will study.

In Chapter 9, we turn to the diverse efforts to structure records repositories according to the subject of the documents involved. Organization by content – what modern archivists call pertinence – seemed obvious to many chancellery staff, and they developed increasingly sophisticated ways to execute schemes of this kind, which are further explored in Chapter 10's case studies from Switzerland. Notably, every system of organization by content reflected the political imagination of its designers: Organizing records remained a fundamentally political act, intended to improve the capacity of the emerging states that secretaries and chancellors served.

7 The Accumulation of Records and the Evolution of Inventories

Introduction

By the mid-fifteenth century, officials in many European polities possessed techniques for managing both proofs and information in support of the rulers they served. Many of these techniques rested on the use of the codex, whose emergence out of European learned culture meant that such techniques were widely shared and relatively consistent across Europe, though they could be applied in different ways. Cartularies recording received charters, emissions registers for privileges that had been issued, copybooks for letters and correspondence, and informational registers with tables of contents or chronological, topographical, or alphabetical indexes were well-established and effective tools found in most major chancelleries by 1500. Indeed, as in Lisbon and Innsbruck, the chancellery book seemed poised to dominate official records and their management, backed up by treasuries of carefully preserved but rarely consulted probative documents in an *archivum*.

Ultimately, however, the intensification of governance that accelerated at the end of the Middle Ages, accompanied as it was by rapid growth in the volume of records produced and preserved, created pressures that superseded codex-based methods for managing information.[1] Responding to the growing masses of documents dumped into chests, rooms, and vaults, and to the proliferation of often haphazardly created chancellery books, as well as to intensifying demands for records about past governmental decisions, chancelleries began creating new tools for managing large numbers of informational objects. These new strategies included comprehensive archival inventories, systems of classification, and later the transaction-oriented registry.

---

[1] The literature on Late Medieval and early modern governance in Europe is enormous. The model of "intensification" has been particularly influential in the German lands; see Moraw, *Von offener Verfassung*. Foundational work includes Giddens, *Nation-State*, and Mann, *The Sources of Social Power*, Vol. 1.

This chapter concentrates on the comprehensive archival inventories that became much more common after 1500. Such inventories represented a key step in the emergence of the modern archive (viewed as an ordered repository containing heterogeneous records with potential future value), as distinct from the medieval *archivum* or from the collections of muddled registers in many Late Medieval chancelleries. Both free-standing inventories and systematic registries linked information *about* records to the spaces where those records were preserved in new and increasingly abstract ways. This allowed for the separation of working chancelleries from their archives, encouraged new methods of dividing and articulating the spaces and physical containers that accumulations of documents necessarily occupied, and required innovations in metadata to connect the various parts.

Although many earlier finding aids provided antecedents, archival inventories as a distinct genre of chancellery document emerged surprisingly late in the Middle Ages.[2] The processes that led to their formation and elaboration, the systems of organization they adopted, and their implications for further changes in records management will occupy the next four chapters, forming a core section of this book. The suite of High and Late Medieval methods revolving around the codex discussed in the previous four chapters provided a vital substrate for these developments, but a burst of heterogeneous recombinations of older techniques across Europe opened up new approaches by the end of the sixteenth century.[3] In each chapter that follows, we will analyze the limitations as well as the potential of the methods under consideration so as to better understand the institutional machinery that undergirded larger developments and the institutional cultures that enabled them.[4] The evolution of one narrow slice of sources – namely, the inventories and comparable tools that began appearing in chancelleries after the later Middle Ages, and that became a major preoccupation around 1500 – helps reveal the larger knowledge cultures behind early modern chancelleries and early modern states.

What is an inventory? Modern archival science is both helpful and problematic in approaching this question. In classic twentieth-century

---

[2] Bautier, "La phase cruciale," 141, locates the first systematic inventories to the mid-fourteenth century.

[3] Brendecke, *Imperium,* provides a penetrating analysis of this development.

[4] My assumption that institutional culture is both a precondition and a product of changes in governance rests on Giddens's notion of structuration. As Giddens puts it, "Information storage is central to the role of 'authoritative resources' in the structuring of social systems spanning larger ranges of space and time than tribal cultures" (*The Nation-State and Violence,* 2).

archival science, inventories are a relatively insignificant subset of the larger category of finding aids, which in turn relate to two core areas of archival management – namely, arrangement and description. Until the 1980s revolution in archival science, arrangement and description were understood, in turn, as deriving fundamentally from two core principles: (1) that archives are in their very nature sites of custody (with the associated idea of an archival threshold) and (2) that provenance and original order provide the best way to physically and conceptually organize material within an archive.[5] Under these assumptions, description (including the creation of various finding aids) is secondary to arrangement, and takes place primarily retrospectively, once material has crossed the archival threshold.[6]

While the analytical clarity of this set of definitions is useful, almost none of the assumptions involved apply to Late Medieval and early modern record-keeping practice. Except for a limited *archivum*, records rarely crossed an explicit archival threshold, and the creation of finding aids was not necessarily retrospective. Instead, early modern chancelleries created descriptions at various times for the records they possessed (or were making), and felt free to rearrange materials not only to make them more accessible, but also to move them out of the way, to keep them safe (which might include packing up documents helter-skelter during periods of military threat), or for other reasons. In short, traditional archival theory assumes conditions that developed historically, and indeed in significant ways as a result of the scribal work being analyzed here; in consequence, modern terminology fits poorly in trying to understand what was happening from the fifteenth to seventeenth centuries.[7]

Recent archive theory has broken from older assumptions in ways that are promising for its application to materials beyond the narrow ambit of the modern state archives that conditioned classical twentieth-century models. Developing first in Australia, efforts to conceive of "post-custodial" archival practice (which does not assume that material has

---

[5] See Chapter 2 for further definition of these terms.

[6] Yeo, "Continuing Debates," 168f.

[7] Framing description in this way leads to overspecialized definitions of finding aids. Frederick Miller, *Arranging*, 93, distinguishes between "creator-supplied finding aids" and "inventories," and gives the latter a strikingly narrow definition – "descriptions of all the series identified with a record group" – which is hardly usable in thinking about premodern repositories. The definition is improved by Kathleen Roe, *Arranging*, 86: "a representation of, and/or a means of access to, archival material made or received by a repository in the course of establishing administrative or intellectual control over the archival material." Similar narrowness of view appears in much German discussion, albeit with stronger theoretical framing; see, for example, Papritz, *Archivwissenschaft*, 3:178.

crossed an archival threshold and been frozen according to its provenance), and subsequently to develop theories for addressing the "records continuum" (which place archival accumulations in a much larger context of records that are created, circulate, change meaning, and accumulate in diverse ways) offer new ways to look at old materials. These approaches are more open to the complexity of early modern materials, and to the heterogeneous ways that secretaries, registrators, and archivists sought to make them visible and legible. The potential for future interdisciplinary conversations connecting historical material and recent archival theory is great, although records continuum theory is not an explicit element in the work presented here.[8]

Since archival science terminology is in flux, I rely instead on a logical definition of inventories that grew inductively out of comparative research: An inventory is a complex record, embodied in a document, that is created for the purpose of finding many other records by making their location possible to determine.[9] Inventories therefore necessarily contain metadata (in the broad sense of "data about other data"), since they describe and refer to members of a corpus of records and tell how to locate them. Indeed, in one sense, an inventory consists entirely of metadata about original materials located elsewhere. This corresponds to early modern practice, since most inventory-makers, as we will see, made inventories to find other records, rather than creating them to provide either proof or information about the world themselves. Yet the reality is more complex: There is a gray zone between a cartulary or copybook, on the one hand, which *represents* documents in storage; and a detailed inventory, on the other hand, which *points to* them.

In practice, inventories could and did come to substitute in certain ways for the records they purported to make findable. Even so, examination of chancellery practices shows that inventories formed a distinct genre of records, almost always created internally within chancelleries and recognized as an important part of their work. Inventories in this sense already existed in the thirteenth and fourteenth centuries. Indeed, lists corresponding to accumulations of records are a phenomenon that emerged in tandem with the preservation of records in the first place, and can be found among ancient Mesopotamian tablets as well as in every documented system of records since.[10] In a broad sense, then, inventories are nearly as old as written documents, whose propensity to

---

[8] Current continuum concepts are discussed in McKemmish, "Recordkeeping."

[9] This approach is consonant with Roe's definition of a finding aid as "a representation" (see note 7), but adds historically specific elements.

[10] Goody, *The Power*, especially chapter 8.

accumulate created circumstances in which tools for finding them – *facilitas inveniendi,* as medieval authors put it – emerged.

For the purposes of this chapter, a more focused definition of the inventory as a particular genre of chancellery or archival records is useful, since it can help identify early modern and modern inventories and distinguish them from alternative approaches to ordering and finding material. An early modern archival inventory united several features:

- An inventory was a *record* that linked record-bearing objects stored in articulated spaces to descriptive entries, thus making the objects' existence and location knowable.

- An inventory was a free-standing and self-contained *document* (in early modern Europe, usually in quire or codex form).

- To do its intended work, an inventory was *separate from and placed apart from* the material it described.

- An inventory required a *method* (an algorithm) for finding particular objects within the space(s) under its purview: therefore, the arrangement of entries in an inventory had to be either homologous in some recognizable way to the objects it recorded or rely on an indexical system to link entries to documents.

As this description suggests, archival inventories shared important features, both structurally and genealogically, with the tables of contents and indexes to codices that began appearing in the High Middle Ages.[11] Moreover, the categories could be blurred in multiple ways – for example, when an analytical table to a series of codices occupied a quire or codex of its own, or when an inventory mixed pointers to documents in a storeroom with references to records in codices. Various other intermediate forms also appear. The fact that most of the inventories discussed here drew directly on techniques for making tables and indexes that the chancelleries involved were already using for their chancellery books adds to the weight of the parallels between book organization and collection organization, as we will see in the work that Wilhelm Putsch did for the Habsburgs.

Nevertheless, important differences separate archival inventories from book indexes and tables. Most significantly, the space of a codex is far simpler to manage than the complex, often heterogeneous spaces of the repositories that early modern inventories had to address. The effectiveness of High Medieval book technologies depended directly on the highly

---

[11] Early modern chancelleries used various names for inventories, including *register, catalog,* and *repertory*; the word *inventory* was often used for a list of possessions made at someone's death or in related circumstances.

ordered space of the codex, consisting of homogeneous pages in a fixed order marked by foliation or page numbers. Foliation – common in administrative codices long before it appeared in learned works – was generally sufficient to connect the loci identified in codex metadata to the actual records, and was the method most commonly used in administrative registers of various kinds.[12]

Records in early modern chancelleries, in contrast, accumulated in multiple spaces and could be grouped by diverse methods (Figure 7.1). In addition to piles, cubbies, and boxes, loose documents might be strung together on strings ("files"), placed in sacks, or wrapped in parchment or paper while still in the chancellery, while books might be stacked horizontally, shelved vertically, or boxed. Even when established in fixed rooms, chancelleries typically ran out of space in their immediate quarters at some point. As a result, many inventories had to take account of various ad hoc accumulations distributed among spaces separate from the formal *archivum* that most administrations also possessed in a sacristy, tower, or other safe and symbolically central space. Not only nearby rooms, but attics, basements, and other quarters might house masses of paper, books, and parchment. During a major reorganization of official document collections in Zurich undertaken in 1646, for example, the city's chief secretary, Johann Heinrich Waser, vividly summarized his current predicament:

In both of the city's chanceries, and also in the council chamber, everything overfilled; item, also another chamber, next to the finance office, is also full of documents; likewise, the old boxes in the *Fraumünster* are also overfilled, with many more boxes piled up next to them outside of the corpora.[13]

Similar complaints about the challenges of "swimming in a world of paper" or dealing with "an ocean of letters and of registers confused as by a storm" were common from the late Middle Ages onward across Europe.[14]

Faced with complex spaces and with a plethora of material, chancellery officers attempted in various ways to cope (though they often failed, or at best gained only partial insight into the totality of their accumulated records). This chapter compares early modern inventories, ranging from simple lists to large multivolume collections, with two detailed case studies from the early sixteenth century then being presented in

---

[12] Saenger, "Benito Arias Montana."

[13] Waser, *Index Archivorum generalis*, StAZH, Kataloge 11, n.p.

[14] The first description comes from Milan in the 1460s, cited by Dover from F. Senatore, '*Uno mundo,*' 25. The second description comes from Gérard de Montaigu, organizer of the Trésor des Chartes in the mid-fourteenth century, cited in Delaborde, *Étude,* cxi.

Figure 7.1 A notary in his office handing deeds to a man with a youth looking on. This painting shows documents stored in a variety of ways: loose documents in piles, in cubbyholes, in sacks, or pinned together, along with codices shelved horizontally and vertically. Job Adriaensz Berckheyde (1630–1693), Haarlem, dated 1672.

Source: *A Notary in His Office 1672,* The Picture Art Collection, Alamy Stock Photo. (Thanks to Heather Wolfe and Peter Stallybrass for bringing this painting to my attention.)

Chapter 8. The inventories in question eventually transcended the narrower category of "inventory" altogether, as we will see in the case of Würzburg. Sixteenth-century inventories are most suited to investigating three questions: How did chancelleries articulate and label their storage spaces to enable access to particular documentary objects, which techniques of listing and describing records were available to officials, and how were the accumulations they described actually arranged (since inventories provide a kind of snapshot of a particular corpus at the moment of inventorization)?

Chapters 9 and 10 then turn to systems of classification, seeking to elucidate various content-based approaches that early modern chancellery officials deployed as an alternative to extensive inventorization as they sought to mobilize the material accumulating in their repositories. Classification schemes in early modern archives were embodied in the arrangement of the material, and became most visible during major reorganizations when archivists faced many decisions about changing such arrangements. Effective classification as a basis for arranging documents also offered the possibility of managing large numbers of records without indexing or inventories, as we shall see.

Differentiating Spaces in Repositories: Architecture, Labels, and Signatures

Early modern inventories sought to make the records that a chancellery possessed both findable and usable.[15] Inventories were, in essence, internal documents, rarely intended for circulation to audiences beyond the chancellery staff and the officials and rulers these served. Documents and the records they bore played multiple roles in early modern governance and political culture, including ceremonial performances, representational discourses, and memorialization, as well as giving textual information during legal and policy disputes. Inventories could provide for all such uses; in consequence, they were among the most functionally oriented products of chancellery officials' labor. As defined here, inventories connected *descriptions* of records with the specific *locations* in space where the documents embodying those records were kept. Thus, before discussing various cases, we must first consider how spaces – both physical and conceptual – shaped the production of archival inventories.

The fact that documents occupied space in the world was a crucial precondition for creating inventories. Chancellery officials rarely treated

---

[15] This section expands on ideas published in Head, "Spaces in the Archive."

space as an abstract Euclidean field, instead identifying spaces through concrete terminology relating to the architecture of buildings or the features of document containers. Even for measurements of extent, pre-modern archivists typically counted containers, in contrast to modern archives for which measures such as cubic feet or running meters of shelving provide a primary metric. For example, plans to move material about the Indies from Simancas to the new Archivo General de Indios in Seville in the 1780s reckoned the amount of material by bundles (*legajos*), boxes (*cajones*), and horse-loads, rather than using abstract measures.[16] The spaces that archivists and officers managed were, as a rule, divided in hierarchical ways, articulated first by architectural features of the available rooms; then by the physical containers in use such as cases, boxes, and sacks; and finally by the groupings that secretaries created within containers using binding, string, wrappers, or other methods.[17]

Most early modern inventories, in turn, relied on the concrete features of particular spaces in identifying the location of specific records. To start with, many repositories were named after the buildings or rooms they occupied, including the Torre do Tombo in Lisbon (which retained its name based on a bastion of the royal castle after moving out of the actual tower involved), the entire fortress of Simancas outside Valladolid, and the *Schatzgewölbe* (treasury vaults, named after the basement spaces reserved for old documents) of Innsbruck. A typical entry appearing in a 1630 inventory to the Simancas collections shows in more detail how architecture, container descriptions, and labels could be combined to specify the physical space that documents occupied:

In Case A [in the] room called *Patronazgo Real Antiguo* there is another [box] of walnut bearing the royal arms and a label that says Oaths and Suits of homage, in which are located the following documents and papers …[18]

In effect, the description of a named room, a labeled case, and a box specified by both its material and various labels gave *directions* for getting to specific locations – homologs to the loci used in codices – which could then be listed in inventories.

Sometimes, in addition to names and labels, literal pathways appeared in inventories, making it clear how an inventory's description of a locus in the archive's space functioned as an algorithm for obtaining a record:

---

[16] AGI Indiferente General, Legajos 1852, 1853, 1854A and B, and 1855.
[17] A theoretical discussion appears in Papritz, *Archivwissenschaft*, 3:227–31.
[18] AGS, Inventorios Antiguos 2–2, "Estado," fol. 1ʳ.

"Go to such a room, look in such a piece of furniture, and you will find such documents." For example, an inventory to the papers of the Estates of Holland from 1677 explained that certain books could be found in

the first room above the gallery by which one goes from the assembly room of their High Puissances to the assembly room of the Chamber of Holland, in that same room, in a case, upon which is posted the letter E.[19]

As in the previous example, the clerk here relied on architectural clues (including some that were not themselves part of the repository) that provided guidance on how to go to where the desired documents were stored. A guide to Swiss confederal records stored in Baden (Aargau) in 1794 still relied on this technique, even though the archive also possessed a detailed inventory. When Daniel Rudolf von Jenner of Bern handed the office of *Landschreiber* (chief scribe) to Salomon Rahn of Zurich in 1794, he drafted a short users' guide for his successor that used architectural and directional terms to locate documents through directions such as "evening side, 2nd cabinet, lower shelf."[20]

Another feature of many pre-modern finding aids was the presence of clear correspondences between the spatial disposition of documents and their representation in the finding aid, which could help in getting from one to the other. In some cases, such correspondences may have resulted from the process by which the inventory was created, since an obvious way to make an inventory of any kind was to move through the space of the repository in a serial fashion, describing the contents and labels of containers for documents one after the other. As a result, documents that were adjacent in the repository's space would often be adjacent in the finding aid as well. The resulting inventories *mirrored* the arrangement of spatial loci in the repository, which allowed for more effective movement from entry to locus.[21] Such homologies appeared in registers all across Europe by 1300 and began to be evoked specifically as a resource for users in many cases. In Lucerne, for example, town secretary Gabriel Zurgilgen wrote in the introduction to a new chancellery register created in 1534:

[19] NLNA 1.01.08 Inv 12673.
[20] ZBZ, Handschriftenabteilung, Familienarchive, Rahn 1302. The horizontal directions are given as *Abendseite* (west), *Mittagsseite* (south), and *Morgenseite* (east); vertical positions include lowest, second, third, fourth, and upper cabinet (*Gestell*), as well as an attic with its own cabinets.
[21] Such homologies were by no means necessary. An example of non-mirroring fourteenth-century copybooks from Würzburg in Scherzer, "Die Anfänge," 39. Discontinuities in repository space, which were common, could also disrupt this tendency.

[I]n every case, the charters that lie in one box are written down one after the other, and the names of the boxes in the chancery are the same as the titles contained in this book, so that one can find the documents more easily.[22]

The 60 chancery boxes stored in the city's repository in the inaccessible *Wasserturm* in the middle of the Reuss river now mapped directly to the pages of Zurgilgen's register, with loci named by letters and non-alphanumeric signs to help orient the user in both.[23]

Most systems for creating loci in repositories also relied on labels attached to containers, along with spatial descriptions or descriptions of the containers themselves. Labels could consist of abstract signs – "Case A," "a case, upon which is posted the letter E" – or could refer to substantive categories, as in a contemporary image showing Würzburg archival cabinets (Figure 7.2), which used labels such as "Privilegiorum" and "Bepst Freiheit" (papal privileges). The Würzburg illustration appears in a remarkable oversight of archival spaces composed in Würzburg by Lorenz Fries in the 1520s, at the beginning of his lifelong project to consolidate the Bishop of Würzburg's records under a single comprehensive system (discussed later). Although his primary product was a complex inventory-index, the *Hohe Registratur*, early in his efforts Fries created or commissioned a series of watercolor drawings that showed the cases built into the bishop's document storage room in the castle across the river from his chancery.[24] Each of the five watercolors shows one of the cases in the castle repository, including such features as the doorway visible in Figure 7.2. In the drawing, the cases are labeled and the rows of drawers numbered, designations that likely appeared on the cases themselves. Such labels made it easier to link spaces in the repository to an inventory that described documents. The author of an inventory could describe a document's location by specifying the label(s) of the container involved, rather than having to compose algorithmic pathways such as those found in the Netherlands inventory cited earlier.

Labels on containers, whether abstract (A, B, C, ...) or descriptive, could therefore function as record locators. Indeed, many historical archives in the twenty-first century still rely on combinations of pre-modern labels and modern record series to create the unique locators that a researcher must provide to obtain access. For example, a collection

---

[22] StALU, COD 1515, "Register der Brieffen in der Cantzly," fol. 4ʳ.
[23] The evolution of archival inventories in Lucerne is discussed in Gössi, "Archivordnungen," and Head, "Mirroring Governance."
[24] Fries's own work took him far beyond the methods he described in his initial oversight, and is discussed at length in the next chapter. See Heiler, *Die Würzburger Bischofschronik*, especially 67–83, 103–15.

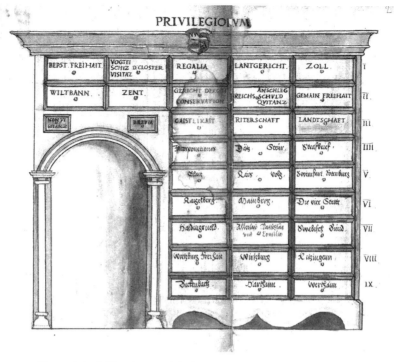

Figure 7.2 A Würzburg archival case with architectonic features, as shown in a watercolor made for Lorenz Fries after 1520. The title at the top indicates that this case primarily contained privileges. Each drawer carries a label for the domain or theme that it provides a space for. Such configurations of named cases or armoires and labeled boxes were common across Europe. Staatsarchiv Würzburg, Manuskript 43, f. 2ʳ.

Image provided by the Staatsarchiv Würzburg, and reproduced by permission.

of copybooks including diplomatic correspondence and other diverse material from early modern Bern still carry the signature *Unnütze Papiere* (useless papers), because they had been labeled and stored under this name in the eighteenth century.[25]

If labels were part of a system, however, they could lend the space of the repository additional texture. In effect, applying labels to containers and spaces added dimensions for description beyond locational terms relating to features of the repository's space. Such additional dimensions

---

[25] StABE online, showing the collection's place in the larger tectonics of the modern archive.

could be constituted in many ways, including conventional sequences such as letters of the alphabet or numbers, substantive sequences such as Europe's political hierarchy or the structure of the domainal space involved, or serial sequences such as chronological order. Finding the "case upon which is posted the letter E" gave the officer looking for documents a good idea where the cases posted with D and F were likely to be located; it also enabled the creation of an inventory in which records or documents could be listed in corresponding order, starting with those in box or case A and so forth. Similarly, knowing that a particular case was designated "Privilegiorum" gave a searcher some sense of the records likely to appear in the individual boxes, making it easier to search for particular material (including material not inventoried).

In this way, systematic labeling could go beyond the one-to-one relationship between a label for a container and an inventory entry, thereby creating the possibility of systematic correspondences between the space of the inventory on the page and the space of the archive itself. Of course, not all early labeling of either repository spaces or inventory categories took this opportunity. For example, Simon Teuscher describes the diverse labels found on documents and in the corresponding registers or inventories in fifteenth-century Lausanne, which included pictograms of various kinds (a goat, *la chèvre*, for a document relating to a Jaques Chevrot, or a wine pitcher and goblet for one pertaining to Michel Tavernet). Such labels, as he notes,

identified charters without integrating them into a model of political order, nor relating them systematically to one another. The system could also not bring the charters into any kind of established sequence: the goat has its logical place neither before nor after the tavern.[26]

Over the course of the fifteenth century and especially the sixteenth century, the benefits of establishing complex correspondences between repository space and inventory space became widely recognized, to judge from the ways – extremely diverse in detail and structural logic, but all drawing on the possibilities inherent in structuring repositories' spaces – that various chancellery officials made use of such correspondences in the cases discussed next.[27]

---

[26] Teuscher, "Document Collections," 215.

[27] In *Archivwissenschaft*, 3: 227–31, Johannes Papritz argues that an evolutionary genealogy links early descriptions of locations in repositories ("the sack by the chimney") and the later development of more abstract identifiers such as letters and numbers, and finally the emergence of full archival signatures in the modern sense.

An Ordered Treasury: Creating the Trésor des Chartes in Paris, 1200–1400

The accumulated records of the French medieval Crown, which came to be situated in special rooms attached to the Sainte-Chapelle in Paris and known as the *Trésor des Chartes* (a term first documented in 1334), provide a particularly revealing introduction to Late Medieval and early modern inventories.[28] Practically speaking, we know more about this corpus's development than for most comparable accumulations north of the Alps during the same period, since unusually good documentation about its early growth and its highly systematic inventorization by Gérard de Montaigu in the 1370s survives. The Trésor's relatively early closure and fossilization in the fifteenth century also preserved its Late Medieval organization and finding aids better than is generally the case, leaving intact important evidence about its early organization. The ebb and flow of registers and inventories produced for the Trésor also confirm the importance of surrounding political conditions and of the individuals responsible for preserving material as it gathered.[29]

Of particular value is the remarkably detailed preface that Gérard de Montaigu drafted for his third inventory to the collection, composed in 1372. The preface vividly highlights the choices that he and other guardians of the collection faced, and makes it clear that many of the challenges that confronted archival reorganization projects around Europe in the following two centuries had already been recognized by the late fourteenth century, as had many of the possible solutions to them. The Trésor's history also demonstrates that the intensification of archivality that accompanied the emergence of European states, though significant for those states' operations, did not involve new medial forms or new ways of thinking about records, but rather reconfigured existing techniques in creative and relatively effective ways. Not until development of full-fledged registries well after 1500 – something that itself grew out of Late Medieval precedents – can we say that a new technology of files was at work.[30] For the period between 1400 and 1600, Montaigu's preface thus frames the possibilities and the limits that chancellery officers across

---

[28] On the dating of the term, see Delaborde, *Étude*, xxiii. The literature on the Trésor des Chartes is extensive. Yann Potin's dissertation, "La mise en archives du Trésor des Chartes (XIIIe–XIXe siècle)," has not been published, though I draw on the helpful summary published online at http://theses.enc.sorbonne.fr/2007/potin.

[29] A recent essay by Guyotjeannin and Potin, "La Fabrique," provides an important supplement and corrective to the classic work published throughout the nineteenth century and culminating in the critical studies of Henri-Françoise Delaborde.

[30] This break is recognized by both Bautier, "La phase cruciale," and Visman, *Files*.

Europe during these years confronted in dealing with masses of both probative and informational records.

The French Crown established a sedentary chancellery in Paris in the late 1190s, which almost immediately began producing heterogeneous chancellery books (*registres*) as well as other documents. Indeed, one reason that King Philip II founded this new chancellery was the loss of most of his older registers and documents to the English at the Battle of Freteval in 1194. Over the following decades, his officers refined their working collections, which were kept primarily in codex form. Their chancellery books contained copies of many items also kept in their original form, such as papal bulls and charters issued by others, along with records of charters issued by the king. The royal register thus always had a connection to the royal *archivum* containing originals, although we know little about the *archivum*'s location and condition around 1200 beyond the fact that it resided in the royal palace.[31]

During the long reign of Louis IX, multiple registers, document lists, and other repertories accumulated, often produced in synchrony with important turning points in his reign. For example, the king's departure on a Crusade in 1248 triggered important changes in the chancellery to prepare for his absence, while his subsequent departure in 1269 coincided with the production of two detailed registers of royal record holdings, prepared in connection with his planned absence from the kingdom.[32] One such register, the *Rubrice litterarum repositarum in almariis domini regis* ("Highlights of the letters deposited in the chests of the lord king"), contained summaries of documents pertaining to the royal domains. The *Rubrice*, which was organized as a table of contents, generally corresponds to one particular register, the *Registre Velutum*, but also refers to more documents than actually appear in the underlying register. In regard to the *Rubrice* and *Registre Velutum*, Delaborde observes that "the documents were copied according to the sequence in which they were materially disposed in the archive."[33] The *Rubrice* therefore served as a proto-inventory to the *archivum*, he argues, as well as a table of contents to the heterogeneous copybook that reproduced some particularly important records. Here, Delaborde follows the assumption that originals always remained the focal point of chancellery interest and use. However, if we follow more recent research and assume that secretaries worked primarily with the records copied in the register, rather than with the loose copies preserved in chests or sacks, then the evolution of the

---

[31] Delaborde, *Étude*, xxii.

[32] On the two registers of 1269 and 1270, see Delaborde, *Étude*, xx–xxi.

[33] Delaborde, *Étude*, xiii–xvii. For the quotation, xx–xxi.

system might well have run in the other direction. Tables of contents to registers, such as the *Rubrice,* may have operated as de facto inventories to the homologously organized *archivum.* In any event, the overlaps among repository, register, and index described here illustrate how codex finding technologies could flow over into archival finding technologies.[34] Such chancellery registers and extracts, combining aspects of a copybook and an inventory, remained common throughout the early modern period across Europe.

At the beginning of Louis IX's reign, the king's document hoard possessed neither a dedicated space nor officials dedicated to its preservation. Located in the palace, it was the responsibility of the corps of clerks (all clerics, in this era) who served the royal household and undertook diverse tasks involving written correspondence and documents, depending on the king's needs.[35] Only with the construction of the Sainte-Chapelle between 1239 and 1248 did the *archivum* receive a permanent home in the new church's multilevel sacristy, built primarily to safely house Louis's collection of holy relics, but also the site of his treasury of records.[36] Much of the space reserved for documents was occupied by material from the Chambre des Comptes. Nevertheless, one section, the future Trésor des Chartes, became the final home not only for the king's *archivum* of charters (which gave the collection its name), but also "many rolls, writings, compositions, trials, investigations, inquests and other things both from the parts of Gaul and from Occitania."[37] This collection gained its own dedicated keyholder in the early 1300s, although the production of new repertories making the collections' contents accessible to the chancellery remained extremely sporadic during the difficult years of the fourteenth century.

The appointment of Gérard de Montaigu as warden of the Trésor in 1370 by a king determined to rebuild his damaged kingdom finally provided a custodian with the time and resources necessary to carry out systematic organization of the accumulated material. Montaigu's description of the state in which he found the Trésor – "an ocean of

---

[34] The second register pertained to a large collection of documents about Languedoc, which the crown had acquired during Louis's reign, again extracted and copied in a sequence that apparently mirrored its arrangement in the repository (Delaborde, *Étude,* xxi).

[35] Delaborde, *Étude,* xxi–xxiii.

[36] On the multiple resonances of the *archivum* in the sacristy, see Potin, "Archives en sacristie," which explores a wide range of discursive, liturgical, and symbolic dimensions that the placement conveyed.

[37] The description of genres is from Gérard de Montaigu (1372), from the preface to his third inventory. The preface has been published a number of times; I rely on Delaborde, "Les Inventaires du Trésor," here 566.

letters and of registers confused as by a storm" – may belong to a long tradition of archivists' statements bemoaning the chaos they faced (and justifying the salaries and expenses they incurred), but the sporadic and inconsistent nature of the finding aids and registers surviving from before his tenure suggests that he truly faced considerable challenges upon taking office. As warden, Montaigu served as custodian of a royal treasury whose contents remained of interest to the king and his servants. Such treasuries undergirded what Yann Potin describes as a "Christian economy of value," in which objects, including documents, enabled a "regime of loyalties that structured royal power."[38] Indeed, Potin points out that the king's jewels in the Sainte-Chapelle treasury also received an inventory in 1380, a luxurious register whose 3,900 entries far outnumbered those in Montaigu's inventory to the Trésor des Chartes.[39]

Montaigu's responsibilities included ensuring the safety and honorable treatment of treasured documents, while he also had to deliver specific records that the king or his advisors might demand. Spurred both by his prince's commands and his own sense of mission, Montaigu spent the first eighteen months of his tenure carrying out a comprehensive and remarkably thoughtful reorganization of the Trésor's records, as documented by an evolving series of inventories. His first concise listing of material dates to immediately after his appointment, and a second version with signs of revision to a few months later. Montaigu completed the third version of his inventory in 1372. The new inventory explicitly superseded all earlier repertories and finding aids, as Montaigu states:

With this inventory, therefore, and with no other that is found in this treasury, you must press on: for all of the ones by other earlier custodians of this Treasury or by me, have been irrevocably changed.[40]

This statement indicates that Montaigu's process of reorganization had proceeded sufficiently to render the older inventories useless.

Before looking at the arrangements that Montaigu describes in his remarkable preface, its rhetorical construction deserves notice. Written in straightforward, lucid Latin, much of his text is in the first person (when describing Montaigu's actions) or the second person (when addressed to a reader seeking particular items). Throughout, the vocabulary is suffused with terms relating to finding and ordering. Many common expressions

---

[38] Potin, "Entre trésor," 47.

[39] Potin, "Entre trésor," 52. Although distributed among multiple locations, the jewels were "lointainement associés aux trésors du nouveau Temple qu'est la Sainte-Chapelle." In that treasury, the Trésor des Chartes "manifest une forme d'accumulation, centrée sur l'organisation de la mémoire du royaume" (55).

[40] Delaborde, "Les Inventaires," 564.

appear that explicitly highlight the value of finding records (discussed in Chapter 2), such as *facilitas inveniendi* and *statim inveniet*, as do verbs for finding (*reperire, invenire*), along with words for ordering, marking, and placing (*ordo* and *ordinare, signare, reponere*). Aside from one paragraph in which Montaigu describes the disorder he initially encountered and excuses, extravagantly, all past custodians for the Trésor's condition, both the tone and the vocabulary are relentlessly practical. Throughout, Montaigu provides guidance to potential users and admonitions to future custodians – for example, to reshelve material after it has been removed, and to maintain the chronological sequence of register volumes as they arrive from later kings. The Trésor as a whole may have served multiple functions among the king's possessions, but Montaigu's inventory focuses primarily on the practical problem of finding specific records, and on the ongoing challenge of keeping records findable over time.

The choices that Montaigu made during the creation of his inventory, as described in his own preface, revolved around three major issues: how to describe and articulate the Trésor's space, how to arrange documents in that space, and how to organize an inventory that effectively described the records and their arrangement. His responses to these issues were interlinked, of course, but decisions on one did not predetermine decisions on the others, as we will see. The very first choice that Montaigu faced, once he had decided to rearrange the documents and to make a new inventory, was what the primary unit of arrangement and description would be. The existing Trésor had a number of armoires or cases, as well as numerous *scrinia* or boxes (conventionally known as *layettes* in the Francophone literature) of diverse sizes and shapes. The room that the collection occupied had several windows and doors, which had provided reference points in earlier registers, and was part of a larger sacred space defined by the Sainte-Chapelle itself. Among all of these available ways to contour space, Montaigu's preface immediately identifies the box as the basic unit of organization for documents: "in this treasury there are three hundred and ten little cases or boxes or chests."[41] Later in the preface, he identifies "very many books, including as many registers as others containing diverse material confused without any order whatsoever"[42] as the second major category of items to be ordered. In Montaigu's inventory, and in all subsequent organizations of the Trésor, boxes and books provided the basic units of organization and finding and, therefore, were the key loci cataloged in the Trésor's inventories – a pattern found in many other early modern archives as well.

[41] Delaborde, "Les Inventaires," 564.   [42] Delaborde, "Les Inventaires," 565.

Montaigu's choice of primary units in the Trésor's space was vital for the production of a clear and systematic inventory, but did not exclude further ways to articulate the space of the repository, on both smaller and larger scales. The boxes found their place in the existing armoires, while the books were placed "in the lower little chests." Strikingly, Montaigu chose to place the numbered boxes in the chests primarily "according to their length and width ... all of them rotated and shifted to whichever location I found suitable according to the subject matter and the disposition of the places."[43] By including Euclidean measures of extent as well as the content of boxes in choosing their placement, Montaigu treated space in an unusually abstract way, compared to many other similar projects. The early date of his reorganization and inventory emphasize that developments in the same direction over the following two centuries did not rest on some new *mentalité* more open to rigorous abstraction, but rather on the particular circumstances that different authors of inventories faced. Notably, Montaigu's choice also meant that simple browsing in the repository on the part of chancellery officials could no longer be an effective way to locate material on a particular subject, since the boxes, although each still dedicated to particular matters, were not necessarily placed into the armoires in a sequence that reflected their content. Compare the situation in Würzburg illustrated in Figure 7.2: There, a chancellery secretary could visit the tower storage rooms and quickly locate a particular area of interest simply by observing the labels of the cases and their individual drawers, without ever consulting an inventory. In Paris, in contrast, only inventories (or the practical knowledge of the Trésor's officers) could provide oversight or a guide to where documents on various topics were located within the Trésor.

Montaigu's spatial orientations were relentlessly practical. He described material as located "in the lower chest opposite the door" or in "the middle chest to the left of the entry door." Ease of finding was Montaigu's key concern, overriding symbolic orientation, even though the collection was located in the king's chapel and sacral treasury. Some books that Montaigu found entirely useless had previously been stored "on top of the big case," while money was kept in wedge-shaped boxes "beneath the big cases facing away from the door, behind the boxes for Flanders."[44] Montaigu's decision to locate boxes primarily by their size

---

[43] Delaborde, "Les Inventaires," 567. Thus, as Delaborde notes (*Étude*, cxxvii), "Sans d'occuper aucunement de leur contenu, Montaigu les [boîtes] fit ranger dans des armoires de manière à perdre le moins de place possible."

[44] All citations from Delaborde, "Les Inventaires," 566–65.

did not relieve him of the obligation to provide users with usable algorithms for finding particular material.

Finally, Montaigu anticipated subdividing the space of the individual boxes, though in 1372 this remained largely a future project. After concluding that his current inventory was "general, and not particular," he continued:

> Now, however, it would be fitting, and I am beginning to view each item in order, one by one, and at length conceiving of the materials and letters to be ordered and marked, and in particular, composing a particular *repertorium* so that it would be possible to find at once and promptly whatever letter was sought by a particular person, whether in a box or in a book, so as to say that it was the second, the third, or the fourth ...[45]

Only for papal bulls and letters from England did such detailed inventories exist already, he noted. In this passage, we see the author of the Trésor des Chartes imagining a comprehensive inventory that identified the locus of every single record *within* the boxes and books that provided the primary structure of his collection. Neither the methods nor the ambition to create comprehensive inventories were lacking in the later Middle Ages, even if few actual inventories before 1700 approached the kind of precision that Montaigu imagined in his preface.

Montaigu's multilevel division of space raised the question how to label the various containers in the Trésor. At the largest level, as we have seen, Montaigu turned to the doors and windows of the storeroom as reference points. By contrast, for boxes and books, he chose to number each type of container serially by location after he had rearranged them, replacing an earlier system that had labeled the boxes with combinations of letters. His full argument for numbering boxes is worth repeating; the boxes were

> signed by number, as first, second, third, fourth, etc., and not by letters and combinations of letters, as had been done (although imperfectly) by some of my predecessors; because these had a shortcoming, on account of the confusion and the difficulty or indeed impossibility of finding them, since to find a box labeled with CB or GH, it was necessary to search around the entire treasury.[46]

In contrast, the "infallible continuity of numbers"[47] ensured that boxes could always be easily identified, and easily returned to their correct spots. Each box, as the inventory's introduction made clear, was marked with a serial number. Since boxes would not be necessarily visible inside

[45] Delaborde, "Les Inventaires," 567.   [46] Delaborde, "Les Inventaires," 564.
[47] Delaborde, "Les Inventaires," 564. The armoires had no labels of their own, but were identified primarily by the numbers or contents of the boxes stored within them.

the armoires, Montaigu also attached a label to each armoire revealing "which are the boxes within it, in this form: From such a box up to such a box." By looking at these labels, Montaigu informed his readers, "you can find the box more easily."[48]

Up to this point, Montaigu's treatment of his boxes and cases had been relatively indifferent to the content of any box: Boxes could go into the cases in whatever way used the space most efficiently and were simply numbered serially. Since many boxes contained documents that all pertained to a single subject, however, Montaigu shaped his system to allow users to make use of this fact: "important and noteworthy boxes are by no means labeled only with numbers, but also with added notes such as *Delphinatus, Flandria, Navarre* and similarly, as you can see."[49] Numerical and substantive labels could easily coexist, as they did in repositories all over Europe.

Having laid out how the Trésor's space was divided and labeled, and having described how documents were placed in this space by box and armoire, Montaigu's preface then addresses the organization of the inventory that gave access to the documents in their boxes:

This inventory proceeds by alphabetical order; for there is no name of a prince nor sobriquet for a country or city, that does not begin with some letter of the alphabet, and it is thus impossible to fail to find the one you want whenever you look.[50]

In addition to the alphabet's universal applicability, Montaigu faced another structural conundrum that helps explain his decision to create an alphabetical index. A finding aid can either *mirror* the arrangement of the material it accesses or *index* it. When Montaigu rearranged some boxes of the Trésor according to their sizes and shapes, however, he removed any justification for an inventory that mirrored the collection, since the boxes' locations no longer had a necessary relationship to their contents. Had he drafted his inventory box by box, as earlier registers of the Trésor had done, the result would have jumbled substantive themes on his inventory's pages. Such a jumble would have required its own index to be usable; indeed, other inventories, such as Wilhelm Putsch's, required exactly such indexes. Montaigu astutely skipped the middle step and went straight to indexing the boxes. Over a century later, Lorenz Fries in Würzburg made exactly the same decision, albeit for slightly different reasons.

---

[48] Delaborde, "Les Inventaires," 564.   [49] Delaborde, "Les Inventaires," 564–65.
[50] Delaborde, "Les Inventaires," 565.

Reorganizing a corpus of documents and the records they bear requires multiple choices, as does making an inventory to any collection, with or without reorganization.[51] The comparative study of inventories reveals the range of choices available in a region or during a particular period, which provides clues both to the *mentalité* and the textual technologies available to specific scribes and secretaries. Gérard de Montaigu's work in the 1370s sets the stage for further comparisons because of its relatively early date and good preservation. Additionally, his articulate and detailed preface to his 1372 inventory is priceless. Montaigu's thinking was by no means trapped in concrete categories: he was able to think of archival space in terms of lengths and widths as easily as he thought of it in terms of territories or persons. He was also flexible in deploying labeling schemes, making use of numerical designations as well as labels in identifying a container's contents. Finally, he clearly understood that his new inventory could not simply mirror his rearrangement of the boxes; instead, he adopted the textual technology of alphabetization as the key ordering principle in building an effective index to the collection. Each of these choices retraced possibilities explored extensively in books in the context of *mise-en-page* and particularly *mise-en-livre*.[52] Other archivists in the next two centuries would draw on these possibilities as well, recombining abstract and concrete, arbitrary and substantive, and mirroring and indexing in different configurations. The following chapters turn to a closer examination of two major examples of such work after 1500.

---

[51] Such choices look fundamentally different to an archivist working within the paradigm of provenance and to the pre-modern archivists studied here.

[52] Cf. in particular Parkes, "The Influence."

8 Early Modern Inventories
Habsburg Austria and Würzburg

Introduction

The challenges that confronted Gérard de Montaigu in the 1370s accelerated over the following century, since the wider availability of paper enabled an increased pace of record production in all forms. In addition, chancelleries confronted growing expectations that not only received charters and information about emitted charters should be preserved, but also a wide variety of other records. Yet this was also an era when much of Europe was torn by devastating wars – the Hundred Years' War and associated civil wars that disrupted England and France, the struggles over a "middle kingdom" in Burgundy, and the dynastic struggles between the Luxemburg dynasty and the Habsburgs in Germany and Bohemia – which led to major breakdowns in record-keeping. The combination of burgeoning masses of paper and frequent disruptions transformed the record-keeping landscape and saw the appearance of urban centers, especially in Italy, as a leading source for new practices.[1] In Germany, as shown brilliantly by Ernst Pitz, the *Stadtbuch* found in many urban communes – a codex used to record decisions about all sorts of matters – began to spawn multiple series of record books in the late fourteenth and fifteenth centuries that documented everything from new citizens to trash collection.[2] As the political scene stabilized across much of Europe in the late fifteenth century, princes and kings (or rather, their secretaries and chancellery servants) began rebuilding their record collections as well. The resources available to a dynastic family like the Habsburgs allowed their chancelleries to launch ambitious programs for making their records safe, known, and accessible, such as the Innsbruck copybook series described in Chapter 6.

---

[1] Comparative analysis and documents for Italy appear in de Vivo et al., *Fonti per la storia*. On Milan, see Senatore, *'Uno mundo'*; for Venice, see de Vivo, *Information*, and de Vivo, "Ordering the Archive." Other cases are discussed in Keller and Behrmann, *Kommunales Schriftgut*.

[2] Pitz, *Schrift- und Aktenwesen*.

Drawing on tools like those we have already seen in action in Paris, secretaries like Wilhelm Putsch began creating inventories of older stored records on a scale never before seen. Two such cases are discussed in detail in this chapter, each of which demonstrates both the capacity of early sixteenth-century chancelleries to create or acquire, retain, and manage many documents, and the challenges that organizing the resulting accumulations posed.

Mirroring and Indexing in the Austrian Inventories of Wilhelm Putsch, 1520–1545

The reign of Emperor Maximilian I (1486–1519) coincided with rapidly intensifying use of written communication by the Habsburg imperial administration, which was distributed between Innsbruck, Vienna, and other urban centers. Under Maximilian's oversight, his chancellors drafted increasingly detailed chancellery ordinances, while a sophisticated system of copybooks reached full fruition in Innsbruck after 1523 under the rule of Maximilian's grandson Ferdinand I. Similar developments were under way in Vienna and elsewhere in the Habsburg lands.[3] By the 1520s, the various chancelleries involved had learned how to move information to and from the ruler via letters from the various regional centers, while also tracking royal orders and council decisions in a way that allowed for future reference. Despite its shortcomings, the document production and management regime of the Austrian Habsburgs was by 1520 was one of the most systematic in Europe.

Successful innovation in these areas did nothing to address the state of the Habsburgs' holdings of older material – and in the 1510s, that state was abysmal. A commission was established in 1512 to bring some order to Vienna repositories, but collapsed after the government learned that its secretary, Lukas Breitschwert, had been selling documents to Habsburg rivals such as the Bishop of Trent.[4] In Innsbruck, Maximilian's enthusiasm for constantly changing schemes caused as much confusion as improvement, although he did order the allocation in 1501 of a new fire-proof space, the *Schatzgewölbe* (treasure vault) in the Innsbruck castle, for storing old records. In 1508, a case with boxes (*ain Truhen mit Tatlen*) was built in this space and some copies of valuable documents were produced to send to Vienna. By 1527, when Wilhelm Putsch began

---

[3] An introduction to Habsburg documentation practices is found in Pauser, Scheutz, and Winkelbauer, *Quellenkunde*. Still particularly valuable is Stowasser, "Das Archiv," especially 28ff. A brief overview is found in Hochedlinger, *Österreichische Archivgeschichte*, 29–34.

[4] See especially Stowasser, "Das Archiv," 29–30 from a Viennese perspective.

the project of making a comprehensive inventory, the *Schatzgewölbe* contained 5 cases or armoires and some 227 numbered boxes. These containers held about 30,000 items, including sealed charters, files, reports, and petitions, along with a modest number of codices.[5]

Putsch's career as a creator of inventories was remarkable: Over some fifty years of service to the Habsburgs lasting until 1551, he created three comprehensive inventories for major collections of material. The first, in which he worked out his methods, described the archive of the Counts of Görz, which the Habsburgs inherited in 1500. The second cataloged the Innsbruck *Schatzgewölbe*, while the third provided the first systematic inventory of the Habsburgs' documentary holdings in Vienna, also called a *Schatzgewölbe*.[6] Putsch entered Habsburg service around 1500, and he is documented in 1504 as a scribe in the Innsbruck chancellery. By 1515, he had gained the title of *Registrator*, indicating he had specialized in document management: In Late Medieval archives, registrators took primary responsibility for maintaining the various chancellery books that tracked issued charters and other documents of interest.[7] Responsibility for document repositories often accompanied these duties. The internally oriented tasks that registrators undertook made them, in effect, proto-archivists, as Putsch's case shows. From the early 1520s, Putsch's services were in demand in Vienna as well as in Innsbruck, and he moved between the two centers for the rest of his life.[8]

Traces of Putsch's work are found throughout the Innsbruck corpus from his era, but the major projects discussed here began only in the 1520s. Thus, they represented an additional aspect of the major changes

---

[5] Stolz, "Archiv- und Registraturwesen," 87–94. Stolz maintains that Putsch reorganized as well as inventorized this repository, although the haphazard placement of materials and the persistence of 50 uncataloged boxes suggests that any reorganization was limited in scope.

[6] Stowasser, "Das Archiv"; Stolz, "Archiv- und Registraturwesen," 89–95; Kögl, "Die Bedeutung"; Hochedlinger, *Österreichische Archivgeschichte*, 29–30. The Görz inventory is TLA *Repertorium* 10; the Innsbruck inventory is TLA *Repertorium* B368-B373. In Vienna, the autograph volumes (as well as one copy replacing a lost volume) carry the signature HHStA AB 332.

[7] Du Cange's glossary of medieval Latin shows the term *registrator* in use by 1325, at first as a synonym for notary or scribe. Soon, however, the term took on the meaning of a specialist in scribal technology, as in a 1425 Roman reference that distinguishes the scribal responsibility from the notarial role: "public abbreviator, writer, and registrator, and apostolic notary by imperial authority." See Du Cange, *Glossarium*, "Registrator."

[8] While the literature attributes Putsch's request to retire in 1526 to deafness and declining eyesight, an Innsbruck council report in March 1526 emphasizes pay. Putsch apparently refused to continue carrying out two jobs – the position of secretary that he was filling temporarily, as well as registrator – unless his salary was raised. When the council offered him the salary of his predecessor as secretary, "hat Er doch solchs stracks abegeslagen." TLA Regierungskopialbuch ADFD, vol. 3, ff. 237v – 238r.

in record-keeping that began with Ferdinand I's appointment as regent for the region.[9] By this time, Putsch was already familiar with several repositories in lower Austria, including Vienna and the *archivum* of charters still at Wiener Neuburg, as well as with various satellite collections that Ferdinand's administration sent him to in 1525.[10] His efforts to establish order in the various archives, including at Wallsee in Lower Austria and for Görz, whose papers were in Innsbruck, still represented ad hoc efforts to illuminate these lesser accumulations, but the grand inventories for the dynasty's two most important repositories, the Vienna and Innsbruck *Schatzgewölbe*, that Putsch launched in 1527 were part of an ambitious project to finally gain control over this material.[11]

Putsch's first comprehensive inventory was made for the archives of the County of Görz. The Habsburgs were the heirs of their Görz cousins, meaning that when the last member of the Görz line died early in 1500, the Görzian archive fell to the Innsbruck chancellery. Nothing happened with this material after the Habsburgs took control of it until around 1515, when Putsch followed an imperial command of 1508 to extract copies of its most important charters.[12] This process, Christoph Haidacher speculates, may have required him to rearrange the Görz material stowed in the *Schatzgewölbe*, which in turn may have led him or his superiors to consider creating a full inventory. The result – begun not before 1515 and substantially complete by late 1525 – was a single large volume of nearly 2,000 pages that systematically described the 7,000 to 8,000 documents the archive contained.[13]

Like every inventory, Putsch's inventory of the Görz documents rested on specific choices, which we later see refined for the larger inventories in the Innsbruck and Vienna *Schatzgewölbe*. We cannot say how much of the underlying collection's structure depended on the organizational choices of its Görzer custodians, and how much we can attribute to the Innsbruck chancellery and to Putsch himself. Putsch's inventory does link many of the listed documents to numbered boxes (*Lädl*), but in the absence of older inventories, these boxes' dates remain uncertain. The new inventory remained rather haphazard as well: The final product clearly gathered together material from separate phases and includes

---

[9] Fichtner, *Ferdinand I*, especially chapter 5.
[10] See Stowasser, "Das Archiv," 33; Kögl, "Die Bedeutung," noting that Putsch had traveled extensively on the Habsburgs' behalf early in his career.
[11] The critical Hofkanzleiordnung of 1526 is described in Fellner and Kretschmayr, *Die Österreichische Zentralverwaltung*, 2:91–96.
[12] Haidacher, "Auf den Spuren." Thanks to Dr. Haidacher for sharing a prepublication manuscript of this article.
[13] TLA, Repertorium 10.

draft versions for some sections of the collection. After a brief description of its basic organization, the analysis here will focus on Putsch's specific choices about how to create an inventory.

Whatever the backstory, Putsch clearly encountered material that was already loosely grouped into various categories by means of the boxes and armoires, although none of the ordering principles in use, including chronology, was comprehensively applied.[14] Because it recorded documents in a box-by-box and case-by-case manner, Putsch's inventory ended up mirroring this disposition of the material in its own internal organization. Such mirroring was a decisive feature of all of Putsch's work, as it was in many other contemporary products. A 1422 Habsburg inventory made in the Aargau (originally from the 1380s) explicitly laid out the mirroring principle:

> In this book, all the documents that our lordship of Austria has in the fortress at Baden are marked under a.b.c. … And a document one finds marked with an a lies in the box that has an a on it, and the letters one finds listed under b one finds also in the box that has b on it, and so as under a.b.c. on and on and marked with the other signs that are found afterwards, in the same way.[15]

Early modern archivists understood the usefulness of such homology, in which the structure of the inventory corresponded to the structure of the underlying collection. In Putsch's Görz inventory, a leaf bound into the middle of the inventory (around p. 80) laid out such this structure in a table listing 53 subjects, which appear to fall into six main groupings:

- Görzian fiefs (3 categories)
- Alliances and contracts with other princes (1 category with subdivisions)
- Administration of rights, domains, and subjects (18 categories)
- Administrative districts, one by one (13 categories)
- Material about relations with other domains (17 categories)
- Useless matters (1 category)[16]

This ordering reflects a certain content-oriented logic (or pertinence, in archival science terms), but was neither systematic nor comprehensive.

Since Putsch's inventory for the Görz material mirrored the order of the documents it cataloged, he also created an alphabetical index to the inventory, using the sophisticated indexing methods available in

---

[14] TLA, Repertorium 10, confirmed by Haidacher, "Auf den Spuren."

[15] Cited in Stowasser, "Das Archiv," 37–38. Stowasser notes (n. 2) that in addition to letters, signs representing a cross, a lily, a woman's head, the Austrian coat-of-arms, a pick, a gallows, a shoe, and a crown appeared.

[16] The grouping is my own, and is not found in the source, which is a simple list. TLA Repertorium 10, n.p. after p. 80.

Innsbruck. In light of the relatively haphazard arrangement of the Gör-zian material in the *Schatzgewölbe* and inventory, only an index could deliver the ease of finding that Putsch was charged with providing. The index was made separately from the main volume, as is evident from the slightly smaller paper on which it is drafted; only later was it bound into the inventory volume (whose current binding does not date from earlier than 1555).[17] Putsch used 48 leaves of paper for his index, on which he first inscribed two- or three-letter combinations in alphabetical order before beginning to enter references to documents in the inventory. Like other Innsbruck indexes from this period, Putsch's entries consisted of three columns, with qualifiers preceding an alphabetical headword, and page numbers (labeled "fol."!) following them on each line. Additionally, as was the case for the Innsbruck copybook indexes from the same years, Putsch experimented with indexing details at the level of *mise-en-page,* though these experiments had little consequence for later indexes.[18] While laying out the Görz index, Putsch also had to estimate how much space to leave between the three-letter stubs, but his guesses often turned out to have been wrong. Some combinations, such as "Gam-," turned out to be unnecessary, since no entries beginning with these letters existed. Others, in contrast, became too crowded, forcing Putsch to add a second column (see, for example, "Bi/Pi" and "Pf"), or even add blocks of entries all over the relevant page (see "Pet/Bet" and "Per/Ber"). Rather than reformatting the entire index to adjust for his incorrect original assumptions, Putsch fit things as best as he could without restarting. Formality in the *mise-en-page* was a low priority, leading to a drab and messy product compared to the calligraphic indices in the *Leitura Nova,* for example – but a much more effective finding aid.[19]

Putsch's larger projects to inventorize the Innsbruck and then the Vienna *Schatzgewölbe* began in the mid-1520s, about the time when he was finishing the Görz inventory. We know he traveled repeatedly between Vienna and Innsbruck from 1525 to 1529, and then worked primarily in Innsbruck until the completion of his major inventory of the *Schatzgewölbe* there. Once the Innsbruck project was complete, around

---

[17] This conclusion is reinforced by the visible wear and patina on the outside surfaces of the quire containing the index, indicating that it was not only made separately, but also kept separately from the main body of the inventory for some time. Haidacher, "Auf den Spuren," confirms that Putsch made the index as well as the inventory.

[18] Notably, he entered headwords differently in relation to the pre-inscribed stubs than in later indexes.

[19] The Görz inventory remained a useful tool for decades, at least until large numbers of documents (carefully marked) were removed to Vienna. See Haidacher, "Auf den Spuren."

1540, Putsch moved to Vienna to complete his inventory for the collection there. Each inventory consisted of a multivolume listing of documents, as well as a separate one-volume index to the inventory. The fact that Putsch's indexes refer not to the *Schatzgewölbe* themselves, but rather to codex pages in the inventories, sets it apart, formally, from indexes such as Montaigu's to the Trésor des Chartes, in which index entries referred directly to loci in the repository.

Given the lack of earlier inventories for either *Schatzgewölbe*, it is difficult to say how much rearrangement of the material Putsch undertook in Innsbruck and Vienna. On the one hand, the fact that he specified the construction of a number of new cases for the Vienna *Schatzgewölbe* in 1526 suggests that he planned substantial changes in the hoard's storage arrangements[20]; on the other hand, scattered references suggest that much of the material was already in boxes (*Laden, Scateln*) by the end of the fifteenth century.[21] While Otto Stolz speculates that Putsch was responsible for a new arrangement of the material in the boxes, first by subject matter, and then chronologically, Otto Stowasser is more cautious, arguing that Putsch's work did not bring about "a significantly new division and arrangement, [but rather] extended and deepened the order ... already found in the Tirol inventory of 1484." In any event, the subject categories of the *Schatzgewölbe* boxes were entirely conventional, and similar to those found in other contemporary archives.[22]

The key feature and power of Putsch's inventories lay in their comprehensive indexing of a large and diverse corpus of material, an approach that resonated with the system of copybooks emerging in Innsbruck during the same era. The Innsbruck inventory identified individual documents according to genre, including "letter, receipt, verdict, authorization, permission, compromise, assignment, contract, missive, instrument, authenticated copy (*Vidimus*), ratification" and more.[23] The Vienna version followed the same basic structure and had a similar range of content, although its execution was "in many ways deeper and the division into groups more rigorous."[24] Putsch's finding aids gained power because, like the Trésor des Chartes, each Habsburg *Schatzgewölbe* contained much

---

[20] TLA Hofkanzlei, Regierungskopialbuch Von der fürstlichen Durchlaucht, v. 2, f. 461ʳ, 22 December 1526. Discussed in Stolz, "Archiv- und Registraturwesen," 90.

[21] Stowasser, "Das Archiv," 41–42, discusses the earlier inventories that Putsch had before him, most of which do not survive.

[22] Stolz, "Archiv- und Registraturwesen," 94; Stowasser, "Das Archiv," 43.

[23] Stolz, "Archiv- und Registraturwesen," 93; see also Kögl, "Die Bedeutung," 201, who notes that many fiscal documents are included in the Vienna inventory.

[24] Stowasser, "Das Archiv," 45.

more than a traditional *archivum,* even if it borrowed the old terminology of "treasury" (*Trésor, Schatz*) as a title for the entire corpus. Nevertheless, Putsch's inventories were not comprehensive guides to the Habsburg monarchy's documents. A great deal of material, including the various chancellery books and copybooks that he and his colleagues were perfecting at the very same time, remained outside the *Schatzarchiv,* as did the loose documents supporting them.

Among the finding aids Putsch created, the mirroring between physical space and inventory space was most systematic in his Innsbruck inventory, where both the arrangement of boxes and the layout of the inventory were layered and hierarchical in close parallel.[25] In both Innsbruck and Vienna, the space in the vaults was arranged by furniture consisting of cases (*Kasten*) and boxes (*Laden*); as in Paris, the boxes were numbered sequentially, with 227 in Innsbruck and 151 in Vienna.[26] Into these labeled spaces, documents were distributed according to a varying number of major categories. Some categories occupied several boxes, whereas others shared a box with other categories, depending on the extent of the material involved.[27] In Innsbruck, the correspondence among categories, the arrangement of text in the inventory volumes, and the arrangement of boxes holding the actual documents were mediated by the armoires in the *Schatzgewölbe:* the five volumes of the inventory corresponded exactly with the five armoires holding boxes with documents, which also corresponded (albeit imperfectly) with five main categories of document. This one-to-one homology was emphasized by the use of color in the inventories' bindings, as Putsch laid out on the first page of his index volume:

Table of contents for the five books, in which are summarily registered the documents and writings of the house of Austria, which lie in Innsbruck in the upper document vaults behind the women's chamber in five armoires [*cästen*]; and each armoire has its own particular book: namely for the first armoire, the first book bound in black; for the second armoire, the second book bound in white; for the third armoire, the third book bound in red; for the fourth armoire,

---

[25] The following discussion rests on examination of TLA Repertorium B368 (index) and TLA Repertorien B369–73 (inventory), which are Putsch's original volumes for Innsbruck; a later sixteenth-century copy also exists (see Stolz, "Archiv- und Registraturwesen," 91, 100–102), as well as a later copy now in Vienna. In Vienna, I consulted HHStA Repertorien AB 25 [with additional signature Repertorien Alt AB 332–4 (index) and Alt AB 332/1–3 (inventory)]. An additional volume, which would be volume 4 of AB 332, is missing entirely (see Bittner, *Gesamtinventar,* 1:226–30). Stowasser refers to this Vienna set as Putsch A in his notes; it is mainly in Putsch's own hand.

[26] Vienna: Stowasser, "Das Archiv," 45.   [27] Beimrohr, *Das Tiroler Landesarchiv,* 26.

the fourth book bound in yellow; and for the fifth armoire, the fifth book bound in green, and every leaf of these five aforementioned books has two numbers, one on each side.[28]

At the bottom of the oversight table of categories, an additional note created a second level of correspondence:

Note: The red numbers in the margins of the five books mean the numbers of the boxes of the five cases in the vault, in which the same documents lie, and these boxes are in all 227.[29]

A third level of correspondence between individual documents and individual entries rested on the chronological order – generally consistent, though with many minor deviations – that both shared.

The armoires in Innsbruck possessed broad substantive coherence, in that each covered a definable range of matters. The first armoire, cataloged in the first volume of the inventory, contained formally probative material, on the whole, beginning with the all-important *Lehensbriefe* that established the network of feudal grants and privileges that structured aristocratic dominion in Austria. Charters appointing princely officers and recording debts and their payment also appeared in this section of the collection. The second armoire and volume began with the privileges granted by the Habsburgs to communities and corporations, along with treaties and contracts, material pertaining to the family's regalia, and other matters related to Habsburg dominion over others. In the third armoire and volume, each territory under Innsbruck's control had its own box or boxes, while the fourth armoire and volume included material about the Habsburgs' imperial role and relations with other sovereigns and with ecclesiastical institutions. Finally, the fifth armoire and its corresponding inventory volume contained material about relations with non-noble neighbors and former subjects, notably the Swiss, and with individuals through petitions and lawsuits.

The consistency of homologies from collection to inventory, sustained by the parallel articulation of the repository's space and the inventory's pages, allows us to understand the inventory and index in Innsbruck as a mechanism for connecting a system of substantive categories to a system of spaces in a way that facilitated – rather than blocked – searches. Physical spaces were represented by separate codices or their sections, by color-coding and numbering of the volumes and cases, and by serial

---

[28] TLA, Rep B 368, first, unpaginated leaf. Internal evidence suggests that this title page was added to the volume after it was otherwise complete. Cited from Stolz, "Archiv- und Registraturwesen," 91–92.

[29] TLA Rep B 368, fol. vi^v. Also cited in Stolz, "Archiv- und Registraturwesen," 92.

numbering of boxes within the cases. Onto this articulated terrain, Putsch mapped conceptual spaces based on content or pertinence by dividing the armoires into a sequence of containers (consisting of part of one box, a whole box, or several boxes) of appropriate sizes that corresponded to both general and more particular categories.[30] Within individual categories and boxes, another ordering principle – chronology – provided further order, completing the hierarchy downward to the level of the individual document.

The mirroring between repository and inventories in Innsbruck and in Vienna was heightened and made visible through a series of textual and *mise-en-page* technologies that Putsch deployed. These connected the individual documents, the inventory, and the index by means of identifiable signs, such as dates and keywords. In Innsbruck, for example, Putsch and his assistants added three notes to the dorsal side of each document they inventoried: One listed the keywords under which it would be indexed, the second gave the year, and the third identified the number of the box in which it was stored. Later, the volume and page of the inventory that recorded a document were added as well. Even viewed in isolation, therefore, each actual document contained multiple pointers to its box and chronological position within it (which also corresponded to its location in the inventory), as well as to the index that made it findable.[31] In Vienna, Putsch inscribed the keywords, date, and category (but not box) to which the document belonged on the dorsal side.[32] The *mise-en-page* of the inventories supported the same correspondences. In the left margin of each document's summary in the inventory, Putsch copied the most important keywords for easy browsing. The box numbers, where given – somewhat irregularly in the first Innsbruck volume, B369 – are written with colored ink and placed in the left margin. The right margin is reserved for the years each document covers: This was necessary because, although the overall arrangement was roughly chronological, many disparities occurred, such that quick access to the year of each document was also helpful for browsing.

---

[30] These categories were complex and diverse, involving genres of document, types of royal/archducal actions, political and spiritual hierarchies, and the historical disposition of domainal territories. Such features, which were in themselves unremarkable in the *Schatzgewölbe* Putsch was inventorying, are not discussed further here; the issues of classification that they involve are taken up in Chapter 9.

[31] The system is described in Stolz, "Archiv- und Registraturwesen," 93–94.

[32] Stowasser, "Das Archiv," 44–46, provides examples of the inventory entry and dorsal marks in figures 1 and 2, respectively. Stowasser emphasizes (especially 46, n1) that these novel "Rückvermerke" were far more useful archivally than the medieval ones previously used, and for the Vienna *Schatzgewölbe*, are almost all in Putsch's own hand.

In Vienna, the *Schatzgewölbe* that Putsch encountered held documents in 19 cases (marked with letters from A to T) and 151 boxes (labeled with serial numbers from 1 to 149, with some duplication). The larger number of cases seems to dissuaded him from simply matching the volumes of his inventory to the cases as he had in Innsbruck, nor was he able to group the material substantively into distinct inventory volumes. Instead, Putsch chose to detach the sequence of boxes from the sequence of subjects in the inventory volumes. This allowed him to group *topics*, rather than boxes, in the inventory, while also grouping *material* to fit the available spaces in the repository. In this way, Putsch's Vienna scheme broke with the systematic mirroring between repository and inventory that the Innsbruck system displayed, and more closely resembled Montaigu's approach in fourteenth-century Paris, although it went further in providing a content-oriented way to search the material.

Putsch's approach in Vienna made his inventory more logical in its divisions, since these no longer needed to correspond to the repository's space. The first volume (cases A–F, boxes 1–45) contained probative material, starting with precious charters and continuing with various material contained in formal *Briefe*; this volume did maintain full mirroring between repository and inventory. Volume 2 (cases F and G, with additions from L and P, or boxes 47–48, 81–88, 115–120, and 150–151) was devoted primarily to ecclesiastical material, together with two fairly intact collections from inheritances in Görz and Niederwallsee. The physical space that this material occupied was much less extensive than the space devoted to the material inventoried in volume 1, but Putsch allocated an abundance of inventory space to provide a much more finely articulated division of ecclesiastical institutions, with separate categories for the church's central institutions, for Austrian bishoprics, and for a long list of individual monasteries. The inventory listed these in their order of importance, not by the order of the cases and boxes in which the relevant material was stored. Volume three (cases H, J, K, M, N, and O, and boxes 57–80 and 89–111) contained all material about relations with external powers, starting with the empire and ending with a detailed list of noble lineages, and largely followed the order of the box numbers. Finally, volume 4 (cases P–T, and boxes 113–114, 121–128, and 130–149) dealt with the administration of Lower Austria in particular.[33]

By occasionally disregarding the distribution of documents in the Vienna repository, Putsch was able to produce a more coherent set of inventory volumes in his second try, one that could be searched by

---

[33] All divisions are cited on the basis of the extensive table in Stowasser, "Das Archiv," 48–54, reviewed by examination of HHStA Repertorien AB 322/1.

category as well as by its alphabetical index. We do not know whether the larger number of cases in Vienna freed him to consider this approach, or whether his experience with the Innsbruck inventory, which included considerable material placed in ways that did not correspond to Putsch's larger content-oriented plan, led him to modify the strict mirroring he had followed in Innsbruck.

Further examination of Putsch's work reveals that his understanding of the Habsburgs' stored documents reached outward to encompass the Habsburg domains as a whole, suggesting an imagined or virtual "complete archive" for all these lands and the Habsburgs' dominion over them. The charge that Putsch received when he arrived back in Vienna in May 1527 – after the reluctant Innsbruck administration had finally released him – reveals the larger ambitions of this project. According to a memorandum recorded in January 1527, the purpose of his labors was to ensure "that such letters should be allocated and transferred to each of our administrations, which they serve with their contents, as necessity requires, [so that] they may be found and used."[34] Emperor Maximilian had already imagined a coordinated network of archives for his domains, as had the Imperial Arch-chancellors in Mainz, who sought to create an empire-wide virtual archive under their control in 1495, but these earlier efforts had achieved only limited success. Under Ferdinand I, Putsch played a vital role in bringing a similarly ambitious project much closer to reality.[35] He traveled back and forth between Innsbruck and Vienna, supervising the transfer of material between them, and scouted additional collections both in Lower and Upper Austria. He also supervised a steady flow of documents inward from various other repositories, most significantly from Wiener Neustadt to Vienna. Finally, he played an instrumental role in creating parallel inventories and indexes for the central collections, whose usefulness was heightened by having a copy of each inventory sent to the other repository.[36] Through these efforts, both archival centers and their repositories became parts of a larger imaginary collection whose two

---

[34] Cited from the Hofkammerarchiv Vienna, Niederösterreichisches Gedenkbuch I, 28, f. 38, in Stowasser, "Das Archiv," 37.

[35] The weakly institutionalized archive of the Holy Roman Empire was the responsibility of the Archbishop of Mainz as Arch-chancellor of the Empire, but existed as records haphazardly distributed among Mainz, Vienna, and Prague, mingled with local records. See Fellner and Kretschmayr, Die Österreichische Zentralverwaltung, 26f, with an edition of the 1498 Reichshofskanzleiordnung appearing at 48–50.

[36] One volume of a sixteenth-century copy of the Innsbruck inventory survives in Vienna as HHStA Repertorien Alt AB 351. See Bittner, Gesamtinventar, 1:227. A 1604 report on the Innsbruck archives reports the presence of "Vier Puecher darinn die Niederösterreichische Schatzregistratur … registriert zufinden seindt." Cited in Stolz, "Archiv- und Registraturwesen," 102.

inventories mirrored the spatial separation of the two *Schatzgewölbe*. In the words of the most profound analyst of Putsch's work, the Vienna inventory "forms a conscious ideal entity together with the [Innsbruck inventory], so that only the two taken together represent the entire contents of the old archive of the Dukes of Austria."[37]

Putsch's massive inventories in Vienna and Innsbruck were powerful tools for ordering older records and making them accessible, and represent an important component of the broader program of record-keeping and records management that the Habsburgs undertook in the early sixteenth century. These inventories' effectiveness was only amplified by the fact that each included a sophisticated alphabetical index. In each case, the index, although referring to people and places found in the inventoried records, was very clearly an index to the inventory *books*: The references for each headword gave a volume and page (labeled "fol."), rather than a case and box in the repository, as had Montaigu's inventory to the Trésor des Chartes. As a consequence, a user could not locate documents by using the index alone, though he did learn more about the document in the inventory's summary description.[38] Instead, the description in the inventory allowed the user decide whether the effort of extracting the original record from the repository was worth undertaking, while the locational information that the inventory provided made such retrieval possible. In contrast to the information that cartularies or registers provided, inventories were useful as part of a coordinated *system* that arranged documents in a comprehensive way by linking chancellery offices to repositories located somewhere else.

Putsch drew on his experience with the Görz inventory as he built the indexes to the Innsbruck and Vienna inventories, using the sophisticated methods already in use in the Innsbruck chancellery, including multiple-letter stubs, systematic combined alphabets, and careful distinction of headwords from qualifiers. The most noticeable feature of the indexes for the two *Schatzgewölbe* inventories, however, is their sheer extent. The approximately 3,000 documents inventoried on the 1,872 pages of the Görz inventory generated an index of 48 well-filled leaves. The two index volumes that Putsch prepared for Innsbruck and Vienna each comprise a full volume of around 1,000 pages that indexed some 30,000 documents.[39] Despite his growing experience with indexing, however, Putsch still frequently misjudged the space necessary for various alphabetical

---

[37] Stowasser, "Das Archiv," 43.

[38] Stowasser, in particular, lauds Putsch for the high quality of his summaries or *Regesten*, in "Das Archiv," 44 (with a figure showing examples).

[39] I have not found an estimate of the number of items inventoried in the Vienna Putsch inventory, but the number of boxes is comparable to the Innsbruck collection. See Stolz, "Archiv- und Registraturwesen," 92.

combinations in the index, leading him to use various expedients, such as separator lines or vacant space on a previous or subsequent page, to fit in entries after the primary space was full.

Several details in the Innsbruck and Vienna indexes give clues about how and when they were made from the underlying inventory volumes. The bulk of the entries under any given letter combination are in a single hand and refer to steadily increasing volume and page numbers in the inventory (remembering that the index referred to the inventory, not to the documents). This pattern demonstrates that the indexes were created by going through the inventory volumes in a single pass, page by page, entering headwords and pointers into the predefined alphabetized spaces of the index. Only later additions (recognizable by differing hands and ink) are out of sequence, whether because an inventory entry received an index entry later on, or because additional documents were added to the collections, and afterward to the corresponding inventories and indexes.

Putsch's inventories and indexes provide an excellent case for considering an important question about early modern archival inventories: To what extent were they direct continuations of older book technologies, and where did the differences between the pages of a book and the space of an archival repository require changes or adaptations? On the whole, Putsch seems to have relied extensively on the methods that the Innsbruck chancellery was already using in the early sixteenth century to organize its chancellery books. This is perhaps most clearly visible in his choice to structure the alphabetical indexes for each of his major inventories as indexes to a book or books, rather than as indexes to a collection of documents. This choice certainly made his indexes easier to produce, since the work could be done as a final phase of the project, taking place entirely in the chancellery on the basis of the inventory volumes. During the prior stage of creating the inventory volumes, headwords had already been selected and put in the margin of the inventory (as well as on the back of the documents), so that consultation in the vaults would only rarely be needed to complete the index. Additionally, the simplicity of the inventory volumes' space – just a volume number and page number provided a full and very compact pointer – allowed for considerable density in the index. In contrast, specifying the loci where actual documents resided would have required at least three designators (armoire, box, and date) and would still have depended on further guides to the locations of the armoires and boxes in the larger architecture of the Innsbruck and Vienna courts.[40]

---

[40] Later examples of such box maps exist in Innsbruck, such as TLA Archivsachen I, Karton 1, 7: "Verzeichnisse des Schatzarchivs," which includes a gridded table

Putsch seems to have left no written reflections about his methods and choices, as had Montaigu. His successor in Vienna, Johann Schwein-hämbl, did leave a brief report dated in 1547 that summarized the history of the system that Putsch had established, and that reflected the challenges of maintaining it. Schweinhämbl began, very helpfully, by confirming that the chancellery now possessed four "registraturpüecher" as well as an index that had been newly made "about the treasure letters (*schaczbrief*), in the order in which they now lie."[41] He then explained that the material had twice been moved to avoid the threat of Turkish capture, after which steps were undertaken to establish a clearer order and make them easier to move. New armoires holding eight exchangeable boxes had each been labeled according the alphabet, while the boxes again received numbers. Schweinhämbl's main concern was to ensure that future additions to the *Schatzarchiv* should be entered properly in both inventory and index:

And when a document needs to be entered, the person in charge should actually look at the categories of the four books, [to decide] under which category and in which volume the same document should be properly entered and laid in the correct box ... ; and every time from now on when a document enters this ordering system, the person should also remember, as soon as he has entered the contents, that he also put it into the index under the right letter, so that it may be found in the future again, since one wants to depend mostly on the index.[42]

These comments confirm the tight integration of repository, inventory, and index that Putsch had sought, and which his successors thought it important to sustain.

Schweinhämbl also expressed concerns about tracking borrowed documents and ensuring the proper indexing of new documents, highlighting a characteristic that distinguished archival from codical information management: Documents in archives were movable objects that could travel about in ways that pages in a book did not. This movability proved damaging to the Vienna Putsch inventory not long after its completion. After a renewed division of territories among separate Habsburg lines in 1564, large numbers of documents were displaced from Vienna to Prague and Graz and Innsbruck. The task of tracking all such movements was beyond the limited staff of the Vienna *Schatzregistratur*, who were left with an inventory pointing to all sorts of documents that no

---

showing box locations; and TLA Archivsachen I, Karton 2, 1, 39–42, with a detailed table cross-referencing Putsch's original boxes to a later arrangement in the seventeenth century.

[41] The document is published in full in Stowasser, "Das Archiv," 61–62, here 61.
[42] Ibid., 61.

longer resided there. The Vienna Putsch inventory consequently fell out of use.[43] In contrast, in Innsbruck, which lost less material in this transition, the Putsch inventory remained the primary finding aid to the older material right through the nineteenth century. This longevity suggests that Putsch's adaptation of the summary table, detailed analytical table, and alphabetical index – all technologies perfected first inside of codices – were adequate to the information needs of one of Europe's most important ruling families and the state they were building in Austria.

Lorenz Fries and the Heterogeneous Records of the Prince-Bishops of Würzburg

The man who reorganized the secular archives of the prince-bishops of Würzburg and created a durable finding aid for accessing them was nearly an exact contemporary of Putsch. Lorenz Fries also confronted the records of a dynamic administration responsible for heterogeneous territories, though Würzburg was significantly smaller and simpler to apprehend than the vast range of the Habsburg domains. From 1520 until his death in 1550, Fries labored among the prince-bishops' holdings of records in document and codex form, ultimately designing and executing a series of interlocking finding tools that provided unusually effective access to this diverse material. Like Putsch, Fries spent his career in forming books out of older material and launching new copybooks, in reorganizing the storage of both loose documents and codices, and in generating metadata in many forms – ranging from simple lists for boxes of documents to his *Hohe Registratur,* an encyclopedic three-volume guide and index to important information (which was ultimately completed by his successor, just as had been the case for Putsch's final inventory in Vienna).[44] In addition, Fries was a historian of major events befalling the prince-bishopric, including the German Peasants' War in 1525, and produced a Humanist-influenced *Chronicle of the Bishops of Würzburg* that eventually became a standard work on the principality's origins.[45]

Würzburg lies in southeastern Germany; historically part of Franconia, it had long-standing ties to Bavaria and Austria that intensified in the early modern period. The forms of record-keeping and archiving that

---

[43] Bittner, *Gesamtinventar,* 1:*13.

[44] Fries's work has been reexamined most recently in Fuchs et al., *Lorenz Fries.*

[45] The former was published in pieces in the late nineteenth and early twentieth centuries; a consolidated edition appeared as Schäffler and Henner, *Die Geschichte des Bauernkrieges,* 2 volumes. The latter was published as Grosch, *Chronik der Bischöfe.* See also Heiler, *Die Würzburger Bischofschronik.*

developed there during the thirteenth and fourteenth centuries were unremarkable, and generally followed the pattern that can be seen farther south in Innsbruck and across the emerging German princely states of the era. In the fifteenth century, Würzburg suffered serious disruptions, as did most European domains, but the breakdown of princely record-keeping seems to have been particularly acute under the leadership of a series of spendthrift and incompetent bishops who alienated most of the see's income and lost political ground to their cathedral chapter. Recovery also followed a pattern typical for German principalities, beginning under the reforming bishop Rudolf II von Scherenberg, who reigned from 1466 to 1495. The reorganization of the prince-bishopric's chancellery begun under Rudolf II and accelerated under his successors also followed typical patterns, concentrating first on the regularization of charter issuance, then on the recovery of lost or forgotten charters and the creation of chancellery books to record important decisions by category. A growing staff of university-trained secretaries managed these tasks.[46]

Lorenz Fries joined the bishopric's secular administration in 1520 after university studies in Leipzig, Wittenberg, and Vienna, during which he earned an MA.[47] His initial appointment as *secretarius* immediately placed him among the higher ranks of the princely chancellery, a status confirmed by his official appointment as princely councilor in 1525. His work on the prince-bishops' trove of records is documented by the extensive marginal comments that he added throughout the corpus surviving from his lifetime. Fries's reading and annotation served both his historical researches and his increasingly ambitious projects for a comprehensive guide to the useful knowledge that the records contained. Both tasks were made more difficult by the chaos he encountered among the records he examined, and by their physical dispersion in three urban repositories (the chancellery itself and two sets of vaults in the city) along with a vault in the Marienberg castle across the river from the city – not to mention the separation between the bishop's records and those held by the cathedral chapter, which possessed most of the older charters documenting the see's privileges.[48]

Although the organizational tools and practices available in Würzburg resembled those found in Innsbruck and elsewhere, the system that Fries

---

[46] On archival practice in Würzburg before 1520, see Frenz, "Kanzlei," and Scherzer, "Die Anfänge der Archive."

[47] A brief biography appears in Schäffler, "Die 'hohe Registratur,'" especially 4–6.

[48] The degree of disorder is suggested by Frenz, "Kanzlei," 142–43, who describes how the collection "geriet in Unordnung" in the mid-fifteenth century, so that Fries encountered outright "Archivchaos" at the beginning of his tenure.

and his successor Johann Schetzler built using these tools was distinctive, and indeed extraordinarily ambitious in its approach to mobilizing archival knowledge. What Fries created in the multivolume *Hohe Registratur* and in the finding lists, indexes, and other tools distributed among the entire heterogeneous collection was an interlocking system that went considerably beyond the inventories we have examined so far. It seems plausible that the size of the Würzburg administration – big enough to employ trained and ambitious professionals, but small enough to avoid division into multiple, parallel chancelleries such as those found in Innsbruck and Vienna – made possible the unusual degree of integration found in Fries's and Schetzler's work.

The earliest phase of Fries's lifelong effort to create a usable archive took place in the Marienberg, where a large vaulted room contained five cases full of loose documents, in addition to various odds and ends left after Fries had cleaned the space up. It seems likely that Fries substantially reorganized this collection, and he may well have arranged for the construction of the cases, although the basic organizational structure of this *archivum* appears to predate his work among these records.[49] Thanks to his labors, by about 1530 Fries was able to produce a clear guide to the Marienberg documents that provided both visual images of cases, drawers, and their labels (such as the one depicted in Figure 7.2) as well as an overview that he described as a "common register, arranged alphabetically, about the abovementioned cases, and what rests in each box, with indication of the box's number and row."[50] In addition, as documented in this common register, he prepared summary alphabetical indexes, kept with the boxes, that allowed access to the more important documents in each box. For the armoire labeled *Proprietatis*, for example, Fries wrote, "one finds in each drawer a particular leaf or quire, also arranged according to ABC, showing what sort of charters are contained within."[51] These box indexes, which seem to represent the first phase of Fries's work, remained useful for at least forty years, since their presence was still noted in the 1550s (though all are now lost). In addition, Fries produced, and Schetzler amended, an overall alphabetical guide to the

---

[49] Frenz, "Kanzlei," 143, attributes the actual cases to Fries; Schäffler, "Die Urkunden und Archivalbände," especially 148, and Heiler, *Die Würzburger Bischofschronik*, 72, note clear evidence of continuity from the pre-Fries to post-Fries organization of the material in the Marienberg vault.

[50] The register's title is found in the version copied into the *Hohe Registratur* and published in Schäffler, "Die Urkunden," 150. A very clean manuscript in Fries's own hand of the entire description, including hand-colored drawings of five cases, survives as StAWü Manuskript 43. On the various copies, see Schäffler, "Die Urkunden," 143–44.

[51] Cited from the published version in Schäffler, "Die Urkunden," 149.

Marienberg collection that provided the locations (by case and row) where documents pertaining to various topics or lordly actions could be located. This overview index was subsequently updated and bound into the more comprehensive *Hohe Registratur*.[52]

During the same years, the Würzburg chancellery undertook the formation of various chancellery books that brought together relevant records on specific topics, which came to be known as the *Libri diversarum formarum*. The prince-bishop also possessed issuance registers for previous bishops' charters, along with fief books going back to the fourteenth century.[53] A wave of rebinding or recopying of older material as well as the launch of many new series left the Würzburg chancellery with some 349 books in 61 series by mid-century. We can identify one turning point in these developments as the appointment of chancellor Marsilius Preuninger in 1525, whose charter of appointment made him responsible for "all of our fiscal books [*Salbucher*], such as Contracts, Servants, Border Conflicts [*Gebrechen*], fiefs, and all of our chancellery books and writings," and ordered him to register all important documents in the future.[54] The *Libri* represented a key operational resource for the chancellery and they saw far more intensive use than the loose charters stacked in the Marienberg castle; consequently, they became the focus of Fries's project for a comprehensive finding system.[55]

In addition to the overview of charters bound into the beginning of the *Hohe Registratur*, Fries copied in an overview of the chancellery books.[56] This guide did not index individuals or places, but instead tracked the series of volumes and their subject matter, which consisted of various types of lordly action on the part of the prince-bishops. The entries named each series, described the number of volumes and their bindings, and gave the period each volume covered. In addition, Fries discussed the function and importance of each series, often including notes about the series' history and development. For the important series of office books (*Ambtsbücher*), Fries observed:

---

[52] This version is published in Schäffler, "Die Urkunden," 148–57. It indexes lemmata for *categories* of action or person, and the spaces linked to them, rather than documents.

[53] The various series of volumes, and the reign when each began, are laid out in Schäffler, "Die Urkunden," 24 (as corrected by Frenz, "Kanzlei"). Only a few series predate 1500.

[54] Frenz, "Kanzlei," 145.

[55] Traces survive of efforts after 1525 to protocol all outgoing correspondence in StaWü Standbuch 1010, "Register der außgangenen Miss. Ao. 1523 usque 1529." The registration of letters begins late in 1524, but continues only until 1528. See Petersen, "Die Hohe Registratur des Lorenz Fries."

[56] The guide to chancellery books, in Schetzer's hand, appears in Schäffler, "Die Urkunden," 28–52.

The older bishops did not use separate books for this; rather their officers were appointed in the fiscal chamber [*camer*], and thereafter taken under obligation by the chapter (as is still the practice today). Bishop Johann von Grumbach and bishop Rudolf [II] sometimes let the salaries [*Bestallung*] of the officers they had taken on be registered by the chancellery in the *Contractbucher*, but bishops Lorentz von Bibra, Conrad von Thungen, Conrad von Bibra and Melchior have their own particular books for office salaries.[57]

For the extensive category of *Gebrechenbücher* recording boundary disputes, Fries's comments sometimes expanded into essays extending over many pages.

Fries's marginal annotations are abundant across this entire corpus, and many of the volumes have tables or indexes in his hand.[58] This shows that he approached the corpus of chancellery books as he had the drawers and cases on the Marienberg, preparing individual guides to their contents that could then become one foundation for the more comprehensive *Hohe Registratur*, to which we now turn. The *Hohe Registratur* consisted of a comprehensive three-volume alphabetical guide to the bishops' possessions, interests, and responsibilities as secular administrators, with specific pointers to relevant records. Some of these pointers referred to the cases and drawers in the Marienberg, but most referenced pages in the sixty-one series of chancellery books, which reproduced the information needed for most administrative matters involving the principality. Evidence from several phases of the *Registratur*'s production survives to the present, allowing us to gain a good picture of how it was compiled. Notably, a series of preliminary drafts for certain letters of the alphabet (designated the *Entwurf* in older literature) survive from the 1520s, along with a corrected and much expanded autograph set of volumes 1 and 2 (the *Concept*).[59] We know that this "concept" was, in turn, copied into a more luxurious version on parchment (the *Reinschrift*), but these volumes burned in a fire that ravaged the Marienberg in 1572.[60]

Fries worked on the *Hohe Registratur* in alphabetical order, compiling the contents in a letter-by-letter manner.[61] This alphabetical organization is unusual and significant. Instead of assembling his overall finding

---

[57] Schäffler, "Die Urkunden," 28.

[58] Heiler, *Die Wurzbürger Bischofschronik*, 75–76, 79.

[59] Schetzler's necrology states that Fries began his work on the *Hohe Registratur* shortly after the Peasants' War, which means in late 1525 or 1526, whereas Schäffler argues he began even before 1525. No doubt, multiple phases of the larger project proceeded in parallel, as noted in Heiler, *Die Würzburger Bischofschronik*, 109.

[60] The terms *Entwurf*, *Concept*, and *Reinschrift* were introduced by Schäffler in "Die 'hohe Registratur.'"

[61] Schäffler, "Die 'hohe Registratur,'" 8.

aid by moving through the collection in a book-by-book or box-by-box pattern, as had Putsch, Fries, once he had created the lists and tables for various boxes and chancellery books, did his compilation according to headwords. His headwords thus represented a kind of authority file, preselected to refer to places, people, or other topics of princely interest. Once he had completed a rough draft that listed all the matters he wanted to include, Fries began at A again (nearly 16 years later!) with improvements and refinements. The *Hohe Registratur*'s second version (*Concept*) for the letter A states that it was begun on "sabato post Luce evangeliste, die Cordule 1541."[62] The date for the beginning of the work on the letter B has been lost, C came in 1543, and so forth, through the end of volume 1 at K, completed in 1547. Fries did not live to complete volume 2, whose draft is also less coherent than the first. The third volume is entirely Schetzler's work.

The first surviving *Concept* volume provides the best understanding of the systematic nature of Fries's enterprise. The bulk of the volume, alphabetically ordered A–K, consists of entries for places, people, or subjects, preceded by a table of *lemmata* (alphabetical by several letters, with some errors) and the oversights of cases at the Marienberg and of the *Libri* series in the chancellery. The main entries vary considerably in length and detail. Some consist of only a few lines describing some document in relation to a village and giving an abbreviated locational record. For the hamlet of Lower Euerdorf, for example, Fries wrote:

Lower Euerdorf: Concerning the see of Würzburg's privileges there, Conrad von Hutten, then officeholder for the district of Trimberg, at some point carried out an investigation; they [the documents] lie, bound together, at the palace in the chest Contracts under the letter A.[63]

Because it described a bundle of loose documents, this was actually an unusual entry; a large majority of the references were to volumes and folios of the *Libri diversarum formarum*. But it also displayed a key feature of Fries's work: Entries almost always *explained* as well as located documents, as Thomas Heiler notes in his detailed study.[64] In many cases, particularly for important and more abstract headwords, the explanations were expanded into systematic essays running several pages in length.[65]

The *Hohe Registratur* could thus serve multiple functions for the episcopal officers who had access to it. It was, first of all, a finding aid for those in search of documents about specific topics. Someone who

---

[62] Schäffler, "Die 'hohe Registratur,'" 14.   [63] StAWü Standbuch 1011, fol. 158^v.
[64] Heiler, *Die Würzburger Bischofschronik*, 105.
[65] Heiler, *Die Würzburger Bischofschronik*, 108, notes that little material outside the chancellery collection is referenced in such essays.

needed to find documents about a specific village, lord, corporation, or profession could use the alphabetical headwords in the table of contents to locate both a brief introduction to the material and pointers to the relevant records. The summary guides to cases and to book series located after the first volume's table of contents could also guide a clerk who needed to find where a particular genre of records was preserved. Finally, working through the *Hohe Registratur*'s pages allowed browsing for more general information, meaning that the *Hohe Registratur* could serve as a gazetteer or kind of encyclopedia – certainly not its primary task, as some earlier literature suggested, but not insignificant for the training of secretaries and officials. Fries's design allowed later users to benefit from his own extensive reading and searching through the records, perhaps undertaken initially as part of his historical writing as much as his registorial work.

Two other questions about the *Hohe Registratur* are of particular interest: the relationship between these volumes and Fries's work as a chronicler, and the deposition of the *Hohe Registratur*'s final version, rendered on parchment, to the storage rooms on the Marienberg, where it burned in 1572. Each of these aspects offers further clues to how its creator imagined the development of the *Hohe Registratur*, and the uses he and the episcopal administration envisioned for it.

From the beginning of his service in Würzburg, Lorenz Fries served as a chronicler and historian as well as a secretary and functionary. Moreover, the production of the *Hohe Registratur* coincided exactly with Fries's work on the *Chronicle of the Bishops of Würzburg*, with the latter being cited as an authority in a number of entries.[66] Thus, the extensive work on older documents that Fries performed in the 1520s fulfilled his duties as chronicler just as much as his duties as secretary. These resonances make it clear that Fries's responsibility to his lord and employer was not confined to secretarial tasks, but lay in making records *useful* in diverse ways to the prince-bishops, including through the "historically founded defense of the transmitted privileges of 'his' episcopate."[67] Fries's *Chronicle* saw publication only in 1713 (in abridged form), but the parchment original and a lavish 1572 illustrated copy, like many early modern chronicles, remained a resource for the principality's officers that circulated only in manuscript.[68] Fries himself confirmed the

---

[66] Heiler, *Die Würzburger Bischofschronik*, especially 103–115.

[67] Heiler, *Die Würzburger Bischofschronik*, 294.

[68] Approximately 180 manuscript copies survive, many of them modified or updated by the copyists, available at Franconica Online. On fifteenth- and sixteenth-century chronicles in archives, see Schmid, "Die Chronik."

Chronicle's anticipated uses when he informed the bishop: "I also did not arrange and write it for the general reader, but only for your princely grace and my gracious lords of the cathedral chapter."[69] In the *Chronicle*, therefore, we see one part of a coherent but restricted knowledge system, a system that also included the *Hohe Registratur*. In this respect, Fries's Würzburg project shares important similarities with the Portuguese *Leitura Nova* during the reign of King Manuel, which reread not only the royal archive but also the statutes and the chronicles of the kingdom of Portugal in splendid parchment codices.

Understanding Fries's larger knowledge system for Würzburg – comprising the chancellery books, the *Hohe Registratur* itself, the *Chronicle*, and other works – also helps explain why the most complete and splendid copy of the *Hohe Registratur*, on parchment and quite possibly illustrated, resided not in the chancellery but in the Marienberg. If the project's most important purpose had been, as Heiler has suggested, to serve as "a finding aid through the accumulated copies of the episcopal see," Fries and his successor Schetzler would not have stored the best version of the *Registratur* in such an inaccessible location.[70] Additionally, this placement demonstrates that the elaborate "presentation copy" of this archival catalog was not intended for public display. Neither administrative function nor representation aimed at some wider public exhausts the Late Medieval understanding of "the archival image," for which secrecy and sumptuousness could easily go together, and for which even a finding aid to copybooks could simultaneously still be understood as a *treasure* that enhanced the status of a ruler.[71]

Conclusion

The archival products traced in the last two chapters – beginning with the abstract definition of storage space and the systematic approach to inventorization that Gérard de Montaigu exercised in the Trésor des Chartes, then the systematic cataloging of records found in Wilhelm Putsch's Innsbruck and Vienna, and finally the guide to political knowledge represented by Lorenz Fries's *Hohe Registratur* – together help

---

[69] In the manuscript's prologue, cited in Heiler, *Die Würzburger Bischofschronik*, 295.
[70] Heiler, *Die Würzburger Bischofschronik*, 112.
[71] On the subtle relationships between the secrecy of the *archivum*-as-treasury and the public consequences archival preservation, see Ketelaar, "Records Out and Archives In." The term "archival image" first emerged in Ketelaar, "The Archival Image," and inspired Navarro Bonilla's *La imagen* and "El Mundo."

define a major reorientation in European archival culture.[72] Each of these projects participated in the culture of the *archivum*, in which documents that memorialized actions provided the paradigm for most actors' understanding of both why records should be saved or copied and how their management should take place. At the same time, each project responded to the rapidly growing pace at which documents were being produced and used in governance. In consequence, each of these inventories also illustrated and embodied rulers' and chancelleries' growing interest in documents-as-records – specifically, records that could be mobilized and made accessible by means of the technologies already available for organizing information in books. Documents-as-objects remained conceptually important, but records-as-texts – texts that could be reproduced in copybooks, circulated in political contestation, or deployed in relation to other texts – and thus records-as-information were what rulers were demanding of their secretaries by the sixteenth century. By organizing and easing access to multiple relevant records about many matters, early sixteenth-century archivists played a vital part in the textualization of political knowledge that Simon Teuscher has recently described.[73]

By the mid-sixteenth century, Lorenz Fries in his *Hohe Registratur* transcended the treatment of archival space as a homologue of codical space. In contrast to Putsch's catalogs to the Habsburg *Schatzgewölbe*, Fries's work approached privileged information over spaces. To be sure, the *Hohe Registratur* still took the form of a codex, and it provided a guide to knowledge largely arranged in codices. But no longer was the logic of arrangement constrained by the seriality of the book, just as the records involved were no longer limited to memorializing instruments and their proof function. Fries's archive, by the time of his death, was conceptually as well as functionally a knowledge-management system, breaking the bounds of the traditional *archivum*.

---

[72] This juncture was defined by Bautier as that from "[l'époque] des trésors des chartes (XIIᵉ–XVIᵉ siècle)" from that "des archives arsenal de l'autorité (XVIᵉ–début du XIXᵉ siècle)" (Bautier, "La phase cruciale"). A different formulation, from "sakrales Buch" to "Buchführung," appears in Keller, "Vom 'heligen Buch' zur 'Buchführung.'"

[73] Teuscher, *Lord's Rights*, and "Document Collections."

9   Classification
The Architecture of Knowledge and the Placement of Records

Introduction

Early modern secretaries and archivists deployed a variety of scribal tools, many of them first honed in the organization of manuscript books, as they made finding aids of various kinds to help manage the proofs and information that were accumulating, ever more rapidly, in their chancellery offices and storerooms, vaults, and towers. An understanding of these scribal processes and practices is fundamentally necessary before we begin tracing how archival record-keeping evolved and changed after 1500, since that evolution continued to rest on the same basic tools and medial forms – the sealed charter and manuscript letter, the book-form register or inventory, the alphabetical index – that were already widely available around 1400. With a firm grasp of the available tools and forms, we now address how Late Medieval and early modern European efforts to keep and organize records also paid close attention to the *content* of the records involved, especially in determining where to place records within storage spaces. Gathering material together by its content – a practice whose benefits were amplified by scribal and book technologies but did not depend on them – opened the door to an approach to knowledge that is significant not only for old archives, but also in modern information science. That approach, put simply, is classification.

The human capacity to generate abstract categories and to connect categories to one another in groups and classes is fundamental to all knowledge. When done systematically, such processes can be called classification in the widest sense. This term has more specific meanings in information science, which vary somewhat depending on whether one is speaking of libraries or archives. In both environments, the most salient systems of classification have focused on the content of the items being classified as the basis for the categories in use. For a user, it is the classification of a library's books by subject (however that is defined) that makes previously unknown books accessible; the archival term that corresponds to this approach has traditionally been *pertinence*, defined as "a principle of arranging records based on content, without regard for their provenance or original order."[1] Classification in the context of both archives and libraries involves assigning record units such as books, files, or documents to preexisting, substance-oriented categories, and then relying on those categories as the primary basis for accessing the units. For pre-digital material, it generally means placing documents within the space of a repository according to their classification, rather than primarily by source, size, authentication, or some other criterion.[2]

In European archives, classification became a powerful tool when archivists began thinking of their collections as forming a coherent whole, whose overall architecture could be configured to allow for more effective finding and deployment of their contents. Although content could be defined in highly diverse ways, most archivists – with the notable exception of the Austrian registrators – sought to place documents with related content together in the same archival spaces, thereby consciously or unconsciously generating entire archival corpora organized by pertinence. As archivist Christoph Schönbeck in Berlin put it in 1641, the way to cope with disordered masses of administrative material was "diligent reading and scrutiny of all the material, and its methodical placement" in locations defined by a system of subject categories.[3] By linking categories to spaces, and by organizing both categories and spaces according to some overarching logic, whether derived from the outside world or based on the practices of a chancellery, finding records became possible without the creation of inventories or indexes.

This chapter analyzes several classificatory approaches used by premodern European archivists – in particular, the "ideal-topographical" method fully developed in fifteenth-century Savoy – in effort to illuminate how the classification of documents could work either together with or independently from other methods of indexing or inventorying them. Chapter 10 then provides a series of additional case studies, which

---

[1] We do not normally refer to cataloging of books by author, title, size, or some other criterion as classification. The archival definition of *pertinence* is from the Society of American Archivists' online glossary. The same glossary defines *classification* in the archival context as "the organization of materials into categories according to a scheme that identifies, distinguishes, and relates the categories."

[2] Classification does not require, logically, that material be placed in a storage space according to its classification. Thus, whereas American open-stacks libraries shelve books by subject classifications (using the Library of Congress or Dewey Decimal classifications), closed-stacks repositories often shelve books by size.

[3] Schönbeck called for "vleißige durchlesung aller materien und derselben methodica repositione" within the system of classification he was establishing. GStA PK, Sammlung Altfindbücher, M 632, f. 348[v], from 1641. (Thanks to Franziska Mücke for the reference.)

articulate diverse forms of classification and their relationship to changing conceptions of political authority and state practice, especially in the early modern Swiss Confederation from 1500 to 1700.

Some readers may be surprised to learn that during the nineteenth century, classification of archival records by their content was largely eliminated as a principle for arranging archives in Europe. Modern archivists since the 1850s have relied on a different principle for the physical arrangement of records, known as provenance or *respect des fonds*, which allows content-based classification only as a secondary principle for ordering documents within archival space. As the influential Dutch Manual authored by Samuel Muller, Johan A. Feith, and Robert Fruin stated, "It is not the subject of a document but its destination which must determine the place it is to occupy in the archival collection."[4] This does not mean, of course, that recent archivists have ignored content, but rather that they address it as something to be managed primarily through archival description – that is, by indexing and other finding aids. Those responsible for chancellery collections from the fifteenth to nineteenth centuries, in contrast, generally *did* give documents' content a substantial role in structuring their repositories, as the cases we have already examined make evident.[5] Chancellery secretaries and registrators relied on classification at various levels and according to various logical systems either to provide a larger architecture for their ordering schemes or as a way to allocate individual records to particular spaces. Boxes and armoires in chancellery collections were typically defined by the subject matter of the documents they contained, although some might be defined by provenance or genre. Efforts to classify records and to use classification as an ordering principle for entire repositories continued to rely on the codex technologies discussed so far, and often were made visible to archives' users through book-form inventories. Classification represented an additional dimension of organizing, which could make inventories and indexes more systematic by providing an underlying substantive logic.

Most of the evidence on classification cited in this text comes from smaller states and their archives, primarily from Central Europe. When

---

[4] Muller, Frith, and Fruin, *Manual*, §21, 72. See also Papritz, *Archivwissenschaft*, 3:1–26. Extensive discussion appears in Blouin and Rosenberg, *Processing the Past*. The categories of provenance and pertinence remain matters of debate in contemporary archival science.

[5] To cite Schönebeck, praising his own innovations in organizing the archive of the Secret Council in Berlin into carefully defined and delineated spaces according to subject: "Using the old method, I found it unbelievably difficult to place the discarded or scattered pieces found so abundantly in the registry properly and in an appropriate way. With the new method, it will be easy, and I would rather properly position a hundred now than 20 before" (GStA PK, Sammlung Altfindbücher, M 632, f. 348ᵛ).

examining the overall arrangement of repositories, this restriction on size makes it easier to see systematic connections from record to corpus to collection. Additionally, larger polities, with their more voluminous and heterogeneous repositories, were less likely to impose a single comprehensive order on their holdings; if they did, they typically turned to registry, an approach to records management that is discussed in more detail in Chapters 11 and 12. The development of the registry system, which ordered records primarily by their place in the flow of political business, precluded the employment of classification as a primary architectonic principle. The distinction between comprehensive organization by content through classification, on the one hand, and comprehensive organization by the flow of business through registry, on the other hand, represents a growing chasm in archival practice that gained particular significance in the eighteenth century and lay behind the emergence of provenance as a key archiving principle in the nineteenth century.

Lists, Maps, Taxonomies: Classification and Archival Tectonics

The form of classification most familiar today appears in libraries, especially in the subject classification systems favored in the United States. A cataloger allocates every book that comes into a library to standardized subject categories, based on a system such as the Library of Congress or the Dewey Decimal standard, and chooses one subject as the criterion for the book's placement on the shelf, as designated by a subject-oriented call number. The universe of possible subject classifications is sometimes called the authority file, since it simultaneously legitimates and limits a cataloger's choices about how to represent the content of a particular book.[6] Although the arrangement and description of archival records involves different issues and has evolved quite differently, the role of classification in the history of archives does reproduce two key features of library classification: the allocation of documents to preexisting content-based categories, and the placement of documents in the repository's space according to such designations.[7]

---

[6] The Society of American Archivists' online glossary defines an authority file as "A compilation of records that describe the preferred form of headings for use in a catalog, along with cross-references for other forms of headings." If its headings relate to substantive content, an authority file will consist of content categories that cover the range of possible content in a systematic way.

[7] Ironically, the triumph of provenance as the only legitimate principle for archival arrangement has led recent scholars in archival science to vehemently deny that

For classification to provide guidance on where to put documents, it must provide a system of categories with the several important features. First, the system must provide an appropriate category for *every* incoming document (even if that category is *Varia* or "all sorts of records," as in many early modern archives). Second, the system of categories must be relatively transparent to those responsible for filing and finding documents, either because of their own prior knowledge or through the formation of explicit guides (thus, authority files) to the entire system. In early modern archives, classification as a source of archival architecture often rested on an implicit comprehensive map of the relevant world, which could thus comprehend the documents that this world produced. Classification in this mode looked outward at political life and its representations, as well as inward to the repository, and provided a systematic (rather than ad hoc) way to conceive of the relations between the two. It is also tempting to think that the desire to relate masses of records to larger epistemic conceptions of order became more attractive in parallel with the new forms of systematic thinking and formalism that emerged in the Renaissance and particularly in various forms of Baroque erudition, though we have too little direct testimony from archivists to know for sure.[8]

In examining particular archival classification systems, we can examine two aspects of archivists' work in creating them that illuminate their expectations and the concepts on which they relied. First, how did the comprehensive system of categories conceptualize the world? Second, what kind of topology structured the system of categories and the corresponding archival spaces? The first question relates to the substantive foundations of classification, the second to its formal qualities. Both, as we shall see, were subject to incremental as well as transformational change during the early modern period. A great deal of research has investigated similar questions in related spheres, including in library catalogs, museums, and other collections, since historians have looked to classification in various contexts as providing clues to the imaginative and cognitive horizons of actors in the past.[9] While classification in

"methods of arrangement of archives and libraries ever influenced one another"; see Lodolini, "The War," 38. Equally, the purist Prussian promoter of provenance, Heinrich Otto Meisner, sharply distinguishes "bibliothekarisch" organization according to subjects or pertinence from archival approaches based on provenance; see Meisner, *Aktenkunde*, 168.

[8] See Navarro-Bonilla, *La imagen.*

[9] McNeely and Wolverton, *Reinventing*, 20–21, argue for caution, however: "The categorization of knowledge, whether in tables, trees or Dewey decimals, has exerted a fascination among ... scholars far disproportionate to its actual importance."

archives may contribute to this wider goal, the focus here is on a narrower question – namely, the subset of early modern archives for which classification provided the primary organizing principle. This chapter focuses on the substantive dimension of classification, while Chapter 10 addresses the evolving formal structures that emerged in some archives organized by classification.

Early modern archives drew on a number of schemes for classifying accumulated documents, and particular archives routinely applied more than one of these patterns, thus giving the corresponding repositories multiple parallel structures, with different classification schemes for distinct parcels of documents. Most of the cases discussed in this chapter dedicated one grouping to an idealized political–ecclesiastical hierarchy of Europe (and the larger world): Subject categories began with the universal Christian empire with the emperor at its head, and the parallel world of the Latin Church headed by the popes. After emperor and pope, category headings moved systematically through kings, dukes, and counts, and through cardinals, archbishops, and bishops, to various lower ranks and estates. Thus, a model of hierarchy in the world defined a grid of spaces for the documents that resulted from relations and correspondence with each constituent place in the hierarchy.

A second grouping found in many repositories mapped the feudal and territorial domains that the authority making the archive controlled, establishing a series of archival spaces that corresponded to territorial or domainal units according to some logical political sequence (which was usually not alphabetical). Both probative and administrative records relating to each domain (not only as a territory, but also as a bundle of privileges under the authority's control) could then be placed into the repository in a systematic way.

Other groupings and classifications appeared less commonly, with some being tailored to the powers a particular polity exercised and the relations to others that it sustained, and others focusing on material features of the documents to be classified. Ultimately, the result in any particular case was a comprehensive but not necessarily unitary assemblage of classification spaces, in which each conceptual space typically corresponded to a physical and subdivided space for document storage.

The second question – how individual categories related to one another formally within a given classification system – was separate from the question of what the content of the categories was. For the archives discussed in this chapter, for which classification provided a key structural principle, three basic logical forms predominated: the segmented list, the map, and the taxonomy. Choosing list-like, map-like, or taxonomic approaches to classification and record location represented a fundamental decision about the architecture of the resulting repository and the nature of its finding aids. Each option imposed a specific dimensionality onto classification space, and only one dimensionality could be predominant (though the others might appear as subordinate principles). A segmented list placed categories and records in a one-dimensional string; mapping typically relied on correspondences between repository, inventory, and a multidimensional conceptual world; and taxonomy rested on a logic of hierarchical division and subdivision to arrange its comprehensive set of categories. Although the organizational logic in each case was independent of the content of the categories and records (at least in principle), certain elective affinities did emerge, at least for the Central European cases discussed here.

All of the cases discussed in this and the next chapters represented the products of conscious efforts to reorganize a polity's trove of documents so as to make it more useful. This characteristic is important because it allows us to assert that the classifications and logic that define each case derived from considered choices on the part of those carrying out such an effort. Major reorganizations were expensive and risky undertakings (as the eventual failure of a 1698 effort in Lucerne emphasizes), and their progress strongly suggests that their creators consciously sought to take a relatively uniform approach. Renward Cysat's self-conscious experiments around 1600 in arranging and labeling categories, for example, provide rare and illuminating evidence of this fact.

It is equally important to recognize that classification was never the only way in which early modern archivists responded to the challenges they faced. Previous chapters have already analyzed a number of cases, such as the Innsbruck copybooks, in which classificatory approaches were *not* central to secretaries' work, even if gathering of documents by pertinence appeared elsewhere in the same collections. Even where a good deal of subject-oriented sorting did take place, as in the *Leitura Nova* with its volumes dedicated to specific territories, both comprehensive schemes for placing documents and systematic architectures could be lacking. Thus, classification was never a systematic *necessity*. Typically, archives in which classification was deemed less important seem to have had longer traditions of register-keeping and indexing, which responded to many of the same functional needs as classification. It is in such archives that we see the emergence of systematic registry – that is, systems in which documents were placed according to process-based criteria (rather than according to their contents) and then indexed.

The Ubiquity of the Segmented List

Lists of records represent one of the oldest forms of finding aid, found abundantly in ancient, medieval, and early modern archives.[10] Many lists reproduce the arrangement of the things they describe or select from; consequently, divisions in an underlying repository are quite naturally reproduced in lists about those repositories, leading to the formation of segmented lists. Equally, selective lists of any kind can be divided according to the listmaker's intentions and perceptions, leading to topical segmentation even when the list's arrangement does not correspond with the arrangement of the things listed. Lists played an important part in the evolution of codex technologies for ordering information, and they continued to appear throughout the early modern period right up to the present.

The significance of listing as a finding aid in our context is that many small archives in the fifteenth and sixteenth centuries had no finding aids beyond them. Political entities whose *archivum* comprised only a modest number of charters and records experienced little need for more complex tools. Additionally, cartularies represented a kind of "filled" list in which selected documents thought to be important were listed, with or without reproduction of their text, in a sequence that reflected their physical location, their date, their content, or some other criterion.

Lucerne, for which we have fine and continuous series of archival products and practices, provides a good example. The first evidence of an intentional collection of charters dates to 1409, when the city recorded the fact that some charters in an individual's possession were transferred to chests (*Kisten*) belonging to the chancellery. The first inventory of the Lucerne *archivum*, dating to 1433 and drafted by the city's secretary, Egloff Etterlin, consisted of a list of the most important charters, with some of the texts also reproduced, as in a typical cartulary. The charters themselves were by this time preserved in a special treasury, the *Wasserturm*, in the middle of the swiftly flowing Reuss River, where they accumulated in nine boxes and two cabinets, safe from both fire and easy scrutiny.[11] In 1505, the chancellery bound the 1433 inventory-cartulary in a new silver binding (giving it the later designation *Silbernes Buch*), suggesting that it was still in use at that time.

The *Silbernes Buch* did display an impulse to classify the documents it listed, since it segmented its listing of charters into seven categories, with

[10] Goody, *The Power*; Salinero and Lebeau, *Pour faire une histoire*.
[11] Gössi, "Archivordnungen," 3

the listed documents appearing in roughly chronological order in each category.[12] The segmentation and classification were not based on the way the material was placed in the *Wasserturm,* in this case, since the seven categories in the book did not match the nine containers in the tower. Additionally, the *Silbernes Buch* noted that many documents in the *Wasserturm* were not listed in its pages, "since they are of very little use for us."[13] We also know that the chancellery itself contained further documents, including books with the town council minutes, various other serial record books (as were typical in Germanic urban chanceller-ies), and dossiers from meetings with Lucerne's Swiss allies, none of which were inventoried.[14]

Segmented lists of this kind, ranging from single sheets of paper to full cartularies, were common across Europe in the fourteenth and fifteenth centuries, typically taking codex form if they consisted of more than a few leaves. The ad hoc classification embodied in segmentation could be very simple, but insofar as it enabled finding useful material from a repository, it also could be vital to that repository's use. In Etterlin's segmented list, the city magistrates and the commune appeared as an agent in his first category, which included the city's *Geschworenes Brief* and its alliances, but became the object of others' action in the latter categories, which contained imperial and papal privileges given to the city.

As record-making and record-keeping accelerated in the fifteenth cen-tury, chancellery staff began seeking ways both to order their repositories more effectively and to represent those repositories by creating effective inventories, which could be kept in the chancelleries themselves for easy reference. It is in this context that we must view the appearance of a highly innovative and disciplined approach to both tasks in Savoy during a major reorganization that took place in the duchy's archive during the 1440s. In addition to its distinctive features, the Savoy inventories of the 1440s have exercised considerable influence on historical thinking about Late Medieval and early modern archives because they were brilliantly analyzed by Peter Rück in a 1971 study that dubbed their structure "ideal-topographic." Rück not only elucidated with remarkable clarity

---

[12] Gössi, "Archivordnungen," 3–4. The seven subject categories in this classification were very broad: (1) *Geschworene Briefe,* or mutual sworn pacts among the citizens; (2) alliances with other communes (*Bundesbriefe*); (3) mutual citizenship alliances, a more intense form of association with outside entities (*Burgrechte*); (4) matters concerning the city and its council; (5) rural bailiwicks; (6) privileges from popes, cardinals, and bishops; and (7) privileges from emperors, kings, and princes.

[13] Gössi, "Archivordnungen," 5–6.

[14] See Glauser et al., *Das Staatsarchiv Luzern.* Jucker, *Gesandte,* describes the genres of record produced by communication among the Confederates.

the classificatory logic employed in Savoy, but also showed that similar principles profoundly shaped archival management and particularly archival reorganizations well beyond.[15]

Ideal-Topographical Classification: Defining an Approach in Savoy

Like many other Late Medieval domains, the Duchy of Savoy increased its investment in written documentation in the fourteenth century and expanded and intensified its efforts to document its privileges and possessions in writing during the fifteenth century. The long reign of Amadeus VIII (r. 1391–1440) was pivotal in territorial and administrative terms.[16] In the late fourteenth century, an archival treasury with charters and other documents was already separate from another collection of records in book or roll form that included accounts, land records, and protocols of various kinds. The former was described in new administrative statutes issued in 1430 as "our *crota* or archive [*archiva*], in which rest our letters, instruments and investigations."[17] Beginning in 1405, after the Counts of Savoy acquired several new territories, including the county of Geneva, new inventories recorded the contents of sixteen armoires (*armaria*) dedicated to specific territories and containing variable numbers of smaller containers (*cassia, boytae, soffina, sacci*).[18] In this practice, developments in Savoy resembled those in Paris a generation earlier, as well as in many other fifteenth-century principalities. As was the case half a century later in Innsbruck, the acquisition of another new territory – in this case, the principality of Achaia in 1418 – apparently spurred a fresh approach. This innovation is seen in the inventory prepared by the scribe Nicod Festi in 1421, which relied on juristic categories of organization and had three sophisticated tables rather than simply listing the newly acquired material.[19] Each of these early inventories reveals that proto-classification of documents was already taking place in Savoy, with the spiritual and secular hierarchies providing one set of categories, and the counts' domains another. Nevertheless, the ducal

---

[15] Rück, "Die Ordnung"; see also Rück, "Zur Diskussion."

[16] See Andenmatten and Castelnuovo, "Produzione," on these developments. The following summary draws primarily on Rück, "Die Ordnung," 29–38, 48–68.

[17] Rück, "Die Ordnung," 33.

[18] Rück, "Die Ordnung," 52–56. One of the inventory volumes was dedicated to documents from the county of Geneva. Interestingly, the work of creating an inventory between 1405 and 1409 included the removal of materials that did not touch on comital rights, which were labeled as "nullius valoris" and packed into sacks without further description.

[19] Rück, "Die Ordnung," 65–67.

administration was not satisfied with its ability to locate records – not surprising, given the sprawling, legally and historically heterogeneous domains under the dukes' control – and launched a major reorganization of the records held in the administrative center, Chambery, in 1436.

This reorganization provides the paradigmatic case of ideal-topographic classification and inventory as defined by Rück. Rück's detailed analysis of the Savoyard archival inventory of 1441–1445 covered the rearrangement of ducal documents into forty-five well-organized cabinets, described in thirteen volumes known as the Clair-vaux Register.[20] The key principle of ideal-topographic classification lay in a triple homology between the spatial disposition of documents in boxes, the organization of an inventory with a page or section corresponding to each box, and the order of the larger world to which both the documents and the inventory pertained. As Rück explains,

not only the ideal-oriented organization of an archive's contents in an inventory was the goal, but also a physically visible ideal-oriented placement of the material in the archive's space. Mental and material orders were to coincide. The topography of the archival containers was to mirror the ideal plan.[21]

Instituting an ideal-topographical system generally involved a thorough reorganization of stored records: Documents had to be re-sorted and placed into appropriate locations within the "topography of archival containers," which would be mirrored (though not necessarily document by document) in a book-form guide to the repository. Moreover, when carried out systematically, the ideal-topographical approach placed documents in a way that mirrored the political world in which the chancelleries worked. Such mirroring made most documents accessible without detailed inventories, much less indexes: Placing each document in a space that corresponded to a known political category was sufficient to make it locatable.

Ideal-topographical archives and their catalogs built a system of categories – categories drawn from the larger order of nature and society – into the very architecture of their collection. In this sense, they constituted a form of classification, unlike the inventories discussed in Chapter 8. Putsch's inventories, for example, described documents as he

---

[20] The surviving volumes have summary indexes labeled "Repertorium titulorum huius libri," in which the *tituli*, a typically Scholastic term, pertain to armoires and their general contents, not individual boxes. Some also have a list of the "Ville, castra et castellanie baillivatus" to which the volume pertains. The homology between collection and inventory volume in this system made it possible for the *tituli* to refer to both (in contrast to Montaigu in Paris, whose index references pointed to boxes, or to Putch in Innsbruck, whose index references pointed to codex pages). See Rück, "Die Ordnung," 69.

[21] Rück, "Die Ordnung," 101.

found them, whether or not their physical location bore any relation to their contents' place in the larger political scheme of the Habsburg lands. The resulting inventory needed an index to be usable (and would have needed one even if the disposition of the physical documents had not been so haphazard, because no comprehensive system guided their placement). In Paris and Würzburg, too, records in diverse locations were directly indexed, thereby separating the process of finding them from their physical locations. In most cases, a particular document's location had some connection with its contents, but such a relationship was not reliable, nor was it necessary to the operation of the inventories that Montaigu, Putsch, and Fries created. In an ideal-topographical archive like Savoy's, in contrast, classification of each document – that is, defining it as pertaining to a category that was part of the political universe, which in turn determined its physical placement in the repository – was an absolutely central and necessary feature of the entire system's operation.

While building on earlier practices that remain visible in surviving Savoy inventories of the early 1400s, the Clairvaux Register fully implemented ideal-topographical thinking, turning the stored records in the Savoyard administrative center into a coherent and accessible corpus. After the archivists Henri de Clairvaux and Jean d'Avenières had completed their massive rearrangement, the first six cabinets of the ducal archive in Savoy contained boxes for documents pertaining to the pope, archbishops, bishops, abbots, and other clerics, respectively, while the next eight cabinets pertained to the emperors (German and Greek), kings, dauphins, dukes, and cities, in that order.[22] The sequence of cabinets thus reproduced the ideal of the first, second, and third estates in their hierarchical places; subsidiary functional divisions of each position in the hierarchy pertained to the House of Savoy itself, its affiliated dynasties, and external parties.[23]

The demands of territorial administration, according to Rück, led to the simultaneous creation of a second series of containers that reproduced not the hierarchical order of medieval society, but rather the spatial–political order of the territories under Savoy's rule. The unit of territorial space in these cases was the domain or lordship. In the Savoyard archive, cabinets 14 through 22 contained the records of the ruling dynasty (the domainal heart of the system), cabinets 23 through 31 pertained to the core lordships in their domain, and cabinets 32 through 45 contained records about territories of subordinate lords, or where the

---

[22] Rück, "Die Ordnung," 76–83.   [23] Rück, "Die Ordnung," 72.

house of Savoy exercised only partial dominion. As in the first part of the archive, the physical arrangement of documents sought to reproduce the ideal organization of the Savoyard domains, albeit now in territorial rather than hierarchical terms.[24] Significantly, the place for each individual domain depended on the domain's importance and centrality to the ducal house: The domains were not organized chronologically (say, by date of acquisition) nor indexically (say, in alphabetical order). Such a choice to use substance, not form, as the key to classification was integral to ideal-topographical thinking.

Also noteworthy in the Savoy system of classification was the relative flatness of the archival hierarchy. The spiritual–secular hierarchy of Latin Christendom and a series of domains were spread out next to one another: The container pertaining to the emperor was identical to that for lesser rulers, gaining its distinction from its position within the whole. Likewise, each lordship had a parallel space in a horizontal division of containers. The classification used in Savoy did not rely on the subdivision of categories, from more general to most particular; instead, the three-way *matching* of physical with codical and conceptual spaces provided the contours along which containers and inventory pages were organized. Higher-order categorization occurred only implicitly in the side-by-side presence of multiple series of documents, each organized according to a differing substantive political reality as perceived by the clerks in Chambery.[25]

After choosing this form of organization, the Chambery secretaries apparently realized that they needed to provide categories, or at least placement algorithms, for *all* important records destined for their system of boxes, inventory pages, and categories. Consequently, they specifically addressed the question of how to file material pertaining to senders or recipients who did not have their own category in the main collection ("qui titulum per se non habent"). The solution that Clairvaux and d'Avenières chose was to include such material under the kingdom or other larger entity where the lands were located, putting them in the "external" subcategory of papers for the appropriate category. Various further issues also warranted discussion by the archivists, with specific arguments sometimes placed on the title pages of the relevant volume, so that users could gain immediate guidance about both the specific details

[24] Rück, "Die Ordnung," 92–93, notes that such a double ranking by hierarchy and territory had already appeared in cartularies before the 1441–1445 reorganization.

[25] On the absence of formal hierarchy in this type of archival organization, see Gössi, "Archivordnungen," 12, where he uses the phrase "gleichwertige Nebeneinanderstellung der einzelnen Gruppen."

and the larger principles that ensured that all kinds of material could find a suitable place.[26] Likewise, the archivists wrestled with the reality that many documents could reasonably be placed in more than one compartment and category, and were not hesitant to use cross-references to establish a virtual presence for such documents in multiple spaces of the armoires and inventory. In short, the system of categories in Savoy served as a kind of spatial authority file, whose predefined terms provided an architecture for practices that, as Rück notes, "could have served as a foundational structure for a long time, had it not been violently destroyed in 1536."[27]

The inventory-books that were created to make the newly organized archive easier to access carefully mirrored the topography within the armoires to the linear space of the codex. The mirroring was direct and simple: Each section of the inventory represented one box in the archive. Just as the topography of the boxes mirrored the hierarchies and divisions of the outside world, so the inventory mirrored the boxes. Individual documents were not cataloged in detail, and only the most important documents contained in a particular box were listed on the corresponding inventory pages.[28]

Figure 9.1 illustrates the series of mirrorings through which ideal order was projected onto archival and inventory space. These mirrorings – most importantly, the way that the repository conformed to its users' understanding of politics – provided the key that allowed secretaries to place incoming documents and to locate documents relevant to their immediate needs. Concrete political knowledge about how the political cosmos and the domains of the House of Savoy were configured was, therefore, a prerequisite for effective use of the Clairvaux inventory and collection.

Conclusion

Archivists around 1500 faced rigorous demands to provide materials from their collections in multiple forms that could support their rulers'

---

[26] Rück, "Die Ordnung," 73–74. One such justification is cited at length by Rück, concerning lands in one outside territory pertaining to a lord resident in a different outside territory: "And the reason for such placement according to the location of the lands and not by the habitation of their holder is that the lands will never be moved, whereas tenants move very frequently."

[27] Rück, "Die Ordnung," 74.

[28] The inventory volumes had tables at their beginnings, but these listed categories (*tituli*), not documents or persons as did the indexes in the Putsch inventory and the *Leitura Nova*.

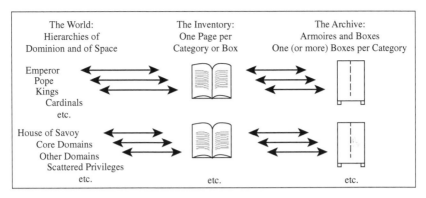

The World:	The Inventory:	The Archive:
Hierarchies of	One Page per	Armoires and Boxes
Dominion and of Space	Category or Box	One (or more) Boxes per Category

Emperor
Pope
Kings
  Cardinals
    etc.

House of Savoy
  Core Domains
    Other Domains
      Scattered Privileges
        etc.

etc.

etc.

Figure 9.1 Schematic representation of the mirroring logic employed in ideal-topographical arrangement and classification. The homologous sequence of categories and spaces in the world, in the inventory, and in the repository made it possible to find records armed only with the right knowledge about the world. The archive represented is the Clairvaux Register of Savoy (1441–1445) as described by Peter Rück in "Die Ordnung."

needs. While possession of authentic original charters or treaties remained the central issue, easy access to the exact texts of diverse documents and the collection and management of other forms of information became equally important. In the German lands in particular, in which endless civil litigation became a major mode of political interaction after the Reformation, archivists faced growing pressure to provide records whose contents made them useful both politically and juridically.[29] Chancellery officials in some states responded by classifying larger corpora of records through increasingly complex systems that placed documents according to the classification of their content, which allowed access without extensive evidence as long as the user understood the logic of the world mapped into the archive. Although modern archival science firmly rejects pertinence as relevant to the (re-)organization of stored records, many early modern archivists took a diametrically opposite position. Not only did they almost universally focus on content in describing their collections, but many also turned to classification as a material ordering approach that could make their archives more accessible by linking individual documents to storage spaces dedicated to

---

[29] The thesis that "Verrechtlichung" of social conflicts was essential to the stability of the Holy Roman Empire after the Peasants' War of 1525 was first articulated by Schulze, "Die veränderte Bedeutung."

relevant subjects. Ensuring the correct placement of documents by content, they were confident, was an excellent way to ensure that future users would be able to find them.

At the same time, the introduction of systematic classification into archives dynamized the process of thinking not only about the security of past charters, but also about the flow of future documents. As seen in the cases in Chapter 10 – which come from across Switzerland – the growing volume of informational documents made and kept by chancelleries, combined with the growing demands for quick and effective delivery of both evidence and information to councils and princes, created incentives to deploy new formal structures that could improve the performance of classification systems. In addition to simple segmented lists (which could embody elementary forms of classification), archivists flexibly deployed ideal-topographical classification that mapped the content of documents against the order of the external world, and eventually turned to complex taxonomies that involved the division and subdivision of categories to provide more precise control over information in documents. Chapter 10 demonstrates how far dynamic forms of pertinence could extend, sometimes testing the capacity of chancelleries and their registrators to fully carry out new models. Ultimately, however, it was the contemporary expansion of registry systems, which emerged in tandem with increasingly bureaucratic governance in other parts of Europe, that supported the vast increase in record-making and record-keeping that continued through the seventeenth and eighteenth centuries, providing the framework for new theoretical approaches to archives in the nineteenth century.

10   The Formal Logic of Classification

Topography and Taxonomy in Swiss Urban Records, 1500–1700

Introduction

Classification of records according to their content offered early modern archivists a powerful approach to arranging both the large amounts of material that were already in their repositories and the even larger amounts they anticipated arriving in the future. An early case of systematic classification in Savoy helped illustrate the difference between merely placing documents that were somehow connected together, on the one hand, and creating a true classification system (keyed to larger understandings of the political world) whose formal logic provided a place for every document from the past and for the future, on the other hand. By adopting or adapting systems of classification, archivists could provide visible structures that reflected the meaning that they understood their documents to bear, and generate new archival tectonics centered on meaning that guided their placement and retrieval of those documents. Such systems decreased the burden of registration and indexing for larger corpora of documents, enabling the limited staff (especially in smaller chancelleries) to cope with the growing streams of new material they produced or received.

The case studies in this chapter all come from a single region, the early modern Swiss Confederation, with most attention being paid to the two major cities of Zurich and Lucerne (centers of the Reformed and Catholic parties within the Confederation, respectively). Probing a politically coherent archival landscape allows for a deeper understanding of how different approaches to classification transformed archival practice across the Confederation through the beginning of the age of modern diplomatics around 1700. In addition, looking at multiple similar cases reveals both the flexibility and the limits of the particular formal logic of organization chosen in each case, thereby giving clues about the incentives for adopting or abandoning particular approaches in each case.

The sophisticated classification practices developed in Savoy during the reorganization of the Chambéry archive and production of the

Clairvaux Register in the 1440s directly affected the evolution of record-keeping in Switzerland, particularly after the Bernese seizure of extensive Savoyard territory in 1536, and may well have influenced Swiss urban archives even before.[1] This influence is seen, among other things, in the introduction of ideal-topographic logic into the urban archives of Bern, Lucerne, and Zurich over the course of the sixteenth century, which contrasted with the growing importance of serial copybooks and eventually full-blown document registries in the Habsburg territories to Switzerland's east. Whether owing to genealogical influence or simply to parallel evolution under similar circumstances, strong elements of ideal-topographic ordering also characterized the reorganization of the Württemberg archives undertaken beginning in the 1530s by Jacob Schreiber and his son, Jacob von Ramingen.[2] The circulation of archival techniques remains an open field for investigation; the discussion here will compare the evolving practices of ideal-topographic organization found in Swiss archives and examine how one city, Lucerne, tried to abandon them in 1698.

Experiment and Innovation in Lucerne's Chancelleries, ca. 1500–1630

Early finding aids in Lucerne before 1500 consisted primarily of segmented lists. By the early sixteenth century, however, signs of ideal-topographic organization began to appear in Lucerne's chancellery collection. In 1534, city secretary Gabriel Zurgilgen in Lucerne laid out the first systematic index to the documents stored in the city's chancellery – that is, to more than the city's *archivum*, though still not to every record that the city possessed (Figure 10.1). The introduction to his *Register der Brieffen in der Cantzley* laid out Zurgilgen's plan, whose reliance on mirroring we have already noted:

… in every case, the charters that lie in one box are written down one after the other, and the names of the boxes in the chancellery are the same as the titles contained in this book, so that one can find the documents more easily.[3]

Although Zurgilgen's rearrangement and the associated inventory were relatively modest in their reach, they display a second key feature of ideal-topographic classification that had been absent from Lucerne's

---

[1] Rück, "Die Ordnung," 12–13, emphasizes this direct connection.
[2] See Chapter 13 on von Ramingen, who published the earliest printed discussions of registry in the 1570s.
[3] StALU COD 1515, f. 4r.

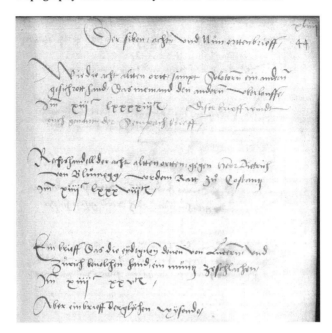

Figure 10.1 Detail from a leaf in the *Register der Brieffen in der Cantzley* ("Register of the Letters in the Chancellery") created by Lucerne city secretary Gabriel Zurgilgen in 1534. Note that the leaf was originally given a Roman numeral (xliiii), then later an Arabic numeral (44), upper right. According to Zurgilgen's explanation, the label on the box in the city's repository in the Wasserturm that corresponded to this leaf would have read: "Der siben, achtt und Nün ortten brieff," following the heading at the top of the page. The first entry has a comment below, "also called the Sempacherbrief," which refers to a key 1393 agreement reached during the formation of the Swiss Confederation. Staatsarchiv Luzern, COD Fach 2, fol. 44ʳ.

Image provided by the Staatsarchiv Luzern and reproduced by permission.

fifteenth-century repository. Each box now contained material pertaining to a single correspondent or subject, and the boxes were ordered according to an ideal topology. A first series – of both boxes and inventory pages – started with charters from and correspondence with first the popes and then the Holy Roman Emperors. The sequence continued with bishops and kings, then smaller clerical principalities and duchies, and then Lucerne's Swiss allies, thereby reproducing the imagined hierarchy of society (as in Savoy). A second series contained documents pertaining to Lucerne's own domains, beginning with privileges from the empire, and then privileges over others, such as local monastic foundations and rural dependencies. Each inventory page was dedicated to a box and listed a few of its important documents. Zurgilgen devised no system of locational or abstract signatures for his boxes, but simply labeled each box with the name of its category—a workable system when only 61 boxes were involved.

Like the Clairvaux Register, Zurgilgen's *Register* in Lucerne mapped its archive, since pages in the *Register* corresponded to boxes in the new storage system, while also systematically reproducing conceptual categories from the larger world in their idealized order. The categories that shaped both the inventory and the physical disposition of documents were either positions in the secular or spiritual hierarchies of which Lucerne was a part, or specific domains in which Lucerne had an interest. The *Register* placed the city on a conceptual terrain as one node with connections upward, downward, or outward to other, essentially similar nodes. The close homologies between Zurgilgen's Lucerne innovations and the logic of the earlier Clairvaux Register supports Rück's hypothesis that the Swiss had learned from their Savoyard counterparts.

Ideal-topographic principles long remained a key to larger-scale classification in many Swiss archives.[4] The principle of double mirroring between collections, inventories, and the ideal world was flexible, and could be adapted to diverse political conditions. Additionally, ideal-topographic approaches to classification could be hybridized with other approaches, absorbing new ideals of order and new modes of thinking. One direction in which such systems could evolve appears in Lucerne after the 1570s. The sixty-one boxes and inventory set up by Zurgilgen remained in use until a new secretary, Renward Cysat, began rearranging them, first as a subordinate in the chancellery and then as town secretary after 1575.[5] In a later reflection, Cysat described the conditions under which he began his work:

I won't say much about the condition of the city archive and chancellery treasury when I began my service, and in what great disarray I found it, though the traces remain today. I had to clean everything up out of the dust and to arrange it into some order, for the eternal convenience of our progeny; yea, I found many lovely parchment charters trodden under foot and crumpled up.[6]

Cysat made extensive changes as he cleaned up, including much sorting and binding of important serial records, which increased the material

[4] The discussion here and following draws on Head, "Knowing."
[5] Gössi, "Archivordnungen," 9–15; Brandstetter, *Renward Cysat.*
[6] StALU COD 440/5, fol. 16v.

available for systematic organization. Cysat's first surviving inventory covered the work he had begun in 1570, and confirmed that the material had been put into the arrangement it described, with a note stating, "Set in this order A° 1577."[7]

Cysat's plan retained the ideal-topographic model, although he rearranged the intertwined hierarchies of Zurgilgen's 1534 *Register* by separating the spiritual from the secular hierarchies, so that each ran from top to bottom separately in the repository and in his inventory's pages. While it is tempting to suggest that this change reflected the growing distinctions between political and spiritual institutions that characterized post-Reformation Europe, Cysat left no comments on why he undertook this step. In any event, each hierarchical position he defined still received its box and page, in order of rank. As we would expect, the first category, "A," contained letters from the pope and his agents; the subsequent boxes, originally labeled "B" and "C," contained material pertaining to ecclesiastical persons in France and Germany, respectively. The secular hierarchy began with box H, which pertained to the Holy Roman Emperors.

After the inventory had been drafted, Cysat continued to experiment. One goal was to find more effective designators for the individual boxes than the descriptive labels that Zurgilgen had created. Cysat's first inventory used an alphabet-based system in which labels ran from A to Z, then from AA to ZZ, and so forth, running in this case to WWWWW.[8] Cysat likely made at least some rearrangements in his boxes' sequence before compiling his first inventory, since the labels do not appear in linear sequence in the inventory. Further adjustments to box labels took place as he was compiling his inventory. Cysat at first copied the box labels in the multiletter format, getting as far as "Iii" on the middle of the third leaf. He then changed approaches, switching to the form "Q4" for the next entry (which also broke sequence from Iii), thereby introducing new kind of alphanumeric representation for the box labels (Figure 10.2). He also went back and adjusted the earlier labels, both in form and in designation: "Gg" became "G1," but "B" became "A1" and "A" became "Z."

Throughout his long career in Lucerne, Cysat kept on tinkering, and even started several new lists describing the archive's content with various new labeling schemes. His reform efforts never resulted in a comprehensive and polished inventory, however, nor were his new signatures

---

[7] StALU Akten 12/112.

[8] StALU Akten 12/112. Cysat labeled some 122 boxes (he used Q and X, but combined J with I). This approach to providing serial labels for all sorts of lists is found in many southwest German chancelleries in the sixteenth century.

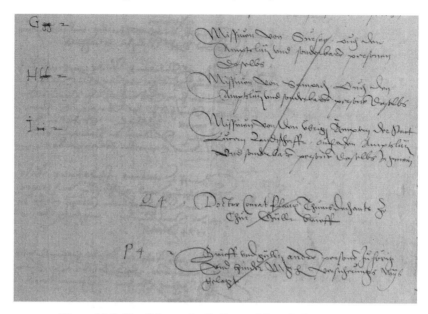

Figure 10.2 Detail from a leaf in Reward Cysat's first complete inventory of his chancellery records in Lucerne, from between 1570 and 1577. The detail shows Cysat's shift from alphabetical to alphanumeric box and category labels. Boxes Ggg (G2), Hhh (H2), and Iii (I2) covered Lucerne's rural dependencies; Q4 and P4 contained financial instruments (*Gültbriefe*) from various individuals. StALU Akten 12/112, opening 3. Provided by the Staatsarchiv Luzern and reproduced by permission.

applied consistently, since we know that many archive boxes in 1698 still used the previous designations.

Cysat's efforts at reform illustrate an impulse toward greater abstraction within the ideal-topographic system that characterized Swiss archival practice in the seventeenth century.[9] His rearrangements of categories also help make visible the system's flexibility, a conclusion confirmed by its many variations among other archives in the region. An ideal-topographic inventory could easily adapt to reflect the political situation of the polity it served, even while retaining the formal logic of mapping correspondences between world and archive. In Cysat's Lucerne, the political world was still conceived in terms of overlapping jurisdictions

---

[9] For comparable efforts to make encyclopedias more systematic in the same period, see Blair, *Too Much to Know*.

and privileges; consequently, his inventory mapped inventory pages and physical documents into homologous, interleaved spaces.

Mapping on Multiple Scales in Zurich, 1646

A generation after Cysat's work in Lucerne, the Zurich archive reached its own crisis of dysfunction, leading to a comprehensive effort that rearranged the central chancellery's document repository, and also placed that repository into relationship with other records in numerous other offices, creating a new, grand oversight of the city's record-keeping landscape.[10] The *Index Archivorum Generalis* to the documents in the Zurich chanceries and archives, which was completed in 1646, represents a sophisticated and fully executed example of ideal-topographic classification.[11] Created by the city secretary (*Stadtschreiber*), later mayor, and historian Johann Heinrich Waser,[12] this substantial manuscript volume's title page immediately announced its broad intentions:

General and complete chancellery register of the city of Zurich, containing notices about all of the documents relating to the city insofar as they are present and are kept in one of the chanceries or in the sacristy.[13]

More than just an inventory to a single repository, Waser's volume gave an overview of the structure and organization of the city's entire documentary machinery. He began by distinguishing twenty-one separate bodies of documents in the city's possession, distributed among various chancelleries and storage areas. The *Index* then described in detail the corpora (categories I–XIII) that Waser controlled in the *Kanzleiarchiv* in the Fraumünster, as they were arranged after the major reorganization that Waser undertook in parallel to the production of the *Index Archivorum Generalis*. When the project was complete, the chancellery archive rested in eight cabinets and 475 boxes according to a refined ideal-topographic arrangement.

Growing confessional tensions within the Swiss Confederation and the uncertain times that Zurich faced as the Thirty Years' War wound to a close encouraged Waser's reorganization, since the chancellery showed

---

[10] Goeing, *Storing*, provides vital insights into the microtechnics of record-keeping in late sixteenth-century Zurich.

[11] The official copy is preserved as Staatsarchiv Zürich [henceforth StAZH] Kataloge 11. Waser made a copy for his family records, as did many compilers of archive guides, now StAZH Msc. L 38.

[12] On Waser, see Domeisen, *Bürgermeister Johann Heinrich Waser*, especially 49–74; Schmid, "Das Hausbuch als literarische Gattung"; and Henny, *Vom Leib*, especially ch. 4.

[13] StAZH Kataloge 11, title page.

itself unable to retrieve useful evidence for either set of negotiations. Additionally, as Waser noted upon his appointment as *Stadtschreiber* in 1633, his predecessor had been too ill to keep the archive in good condition or to introduce Waser properly to the collection, even though he had been working there since 1621. Whatever its origins, the project soon ballooned beyond his expectations, taking until the end of Waser's tenure as *Stadtschreiber* to complete, and eliciting his weary observation that "this, which was only supposed to be an index, has itself become a large book."[14] In his autobiography, Waser described the project as "a nearly endless labor, but most beneficial to the city."[15] Like most contemporary archivists, he also emphasized the sheer volume of documents that he confronted:

In both chanceries and in the council chambers everything is more than filled; item, there was also a room in the town hall next to the accounting office that was full of papers; likewise, the old boxes in the Fraumünster were stuffed, with many boxes stacked on top of one another out of place.[16]

Waser's perceptions reflected both a real increase in documents and his ambition to bring all official documents under the purview of an *Index Generalis* and the parallel *Index Specialis* that he founded.

The classification system that Waser established in the Zurich's key chancellery archive closely followed the principles of ideal-topographic organization as described by Rück. The placement of records in the new boxes and cases depended on a system of categories (*Titul*) and boxes that started with the Holy Roman Emperor and worked its way down the secular hierarchy, followed by a similar tour through the spiritual hierarchy. Thus, the first two boxes in the first cabinet (Section I, Cabinet A, *Trucken* 1–2[17]) "contain all sorts of items from the Roman Emperors and Kings, and also from their embassies."[18] *Trucke* 3 is unexpected, however. In the inventory, under the heading "Third box and *Titul*" the reader finds an entry for "Turkish Emperors from the year [blank] to the year [blank]"! Waser did not comment on why he created a box for the Ottoman sultans (which contained very few documents), but their status as successors of the Byzantine and thus Roman emperors seems the most likely reason.

---

[14] StAZH Kataloge 11, i.

[15] StAZH Msc. A 133, ("De vita sua" Vol. II), 332–33. Thanks to Barbara Schmid for this reference.

[16] StAZh Kataloge 11, vi. A similar comment in ZBZ Msc. A 133, 333.

[17] *Trucke* can mean drawer or box; here, box seems appropriate. A Zurich archival armoire with boxes survives in the collection of the Swiss National Historical Museum, Inventory #LM 1358.b. See Schwarz, "Zwei gotische Archivschränke aus Zürich."

[18] StAZh Kataloge 11, 1.

Given Waser's respect for the formal status of the Ottomans, his refusal to provide a separate box and title for the king of Spain is surprising. Most other European monarchs, from France and England through Denmark and Poland, found a place in boxes 5 through 17 and on the corresponding inventory pages. To find material about Spain, however, the user had to proceed to box 39, where the inventory indicated he would find:

Milan from 1437 to 1639. Contains the Duchy of Milan and its dependencies in itself, and also what may concern the Kings of Spain as current possessors, or their own lands and embassies (except the Netherlands).[19]

Perhaps Waser's Protestant aversion to Spain prevented him from including the kings of Spain among their monarchical peers, though the fact that most Swiss correspondence with Madrid traveled via Milan might also provide an explanation.

After Waser's first section mapping Europe's political–ecclesiastical landscape, a second part of the inventory and archive recorded documents that pertained to the domains that Zurich ruled. The territories the city shared with other Swiss cantons came first, followed by Zurich's own "inner" lordships. Waser notes that "these are indexed not only *generaliter*, but also *specialiter* more than others, because materials from these places arrive daily."[20] As was typical for classification systems in this period, providing a space for future records was a conscious and important goal in creating the articulated space that we see in Waser's system. A third series of boxes and categories traced the administrative structure of Zurich, followed by a final section dedicated to relations among the Swiss cantons. Zurich's role as a leading member of the Confederation produced a considerable flow of documentation that found its place here. This use of multiple series, along with the overarching classification of the city's holdings into twenty-one major sections (only thirteen of which were held by the central chancellery) suggests that Waser was reaching the limits of ideal-topographic logic.

Waser's *Index Archivorum Generalis* surveyed twenty-one distinct archival corpora, including the 485 central chancellery boxes discussed so far and a large mass of judicial records that "because of their quantity, [because of] the lack of space and time, and because they are not worth the work required, are not placed in boxes like the other documents."[21] In his introduction to the *Index*, Waser explained that a further project was also necessary – namely, his *Index Specialis* – "for the sake of

---

[19] StAZh Kataloge 11, 63.   [20] StAZh Kataloge 11, ii.
[21] StAZH Kataloge 11, folio [iv].

concordances, which can be established and preserved by means of this book; since in the *Index Specialis,* matters that are connected come together, even if they are located in different boxes."[22] A closer look at how the *Index Generalis* and the *Index Specialis* worked together reveals the complexity of organization and the diversity of access that Waser imagined for the city's records, ultimately taking him beyond ideal-topographic formalism.

Both the *Index Generalis* and the *Index Specialis* were hierarchical, but in subtly different ways. Whereas the *Index Generalis* connected hierarchy in the world to a material hierarchy in the archive's space, the *Index Specialis* emphasized a hierarchy of information; in archival science terms, the first guided the arrangement of Zurich's core chancellery collection, while the second provided a description. At the core of the *Index Generalis* lay its orientation toward records as material objects assembled into a hierarchy of bodies. On first glance, the *Index Specialis* or *Grösseren Cantzley-Register* seems to follow the same formal logic, based on an outer world mirrored in the physical arrangement of records in boxes. Closer examination, however, reveals that the *Index Specialis* was ultimately oriented toward information rather than objects.

Waser himself stressed the informational function of the *Index Specialis* on the title page of its first volume: It was, he wrote, "all [intended] for the easier reporting and investigation for future matters regarding our honorable city, and knowledge about such matters, and also particularly for others who are curious or lovers of the city."[23] Functionally, the *Index Specialis* diverges from the *Index Generalis* after the two first sections for various emperors. Starting on page 117, the kings of Europe with whom Zurich had communicated were indexed not in order of their status, but alphabetically, a practice that continued in subsequent sections on Electors, princely houses, and so forth. Even though its highest level preserved the mirroring of worldly hierarchy and material arrangement, the *Index Specialis* below these top-level groups was a finding tool that established "concordances" among information placed in an indexical order. Its cross-references to documents held elsewhere and the more detailed calendaring (*Regesten*) of individual items in the *Index Specialis* also made it into an open-ended information tool for a range of possible users, breaking the formalism of ideal-topographic classification.

---

[22] StAZH Kataloge 11, fol. [vi].   [23] StAZh Kataloge 12, title page.

Ideal-Topographic Variations across the Swiss Confederation

Further Swiss examples demonstrate the durability and flexibility of topographic approaches to classifying stored records. A revealing case appears in the archive of the Three Leagues in Graubünden. Unlike relatively stable cities such as Lucerne and Zurich, the Three Leagues lacked a political center and experienced ongoing turbulence throughout the sixteenth and seventeenth centuries.[24] It is not surprising, therefore, that the Leagues had little in the way of an archive at the beginning of the eighteenth century. Although a stable chancellery (based in the city chancellery of Chur) emerged in the 1560s and attempts to register incoming and outgoing diplomatic correspondence survive from the 1620s, such work ceased after the political crisis of 1637. As Rudolf Jenny observes, "the entire collapse of all state organization" in the following years ensured that the Three Leagues' secretaries became unable to find even the alliances (*Bünde*) upon which the polity was founded. In 1683, when the Bündner wanted to re-swear their alliance oaths from 1525, the Leagues' officials could find neither the original charters of the 1525 treaty nor the charters of its 1544 revision, forcing them to postpone the oath ceremony "because one did not know what ought to be sworn."[25] Only the powerful families who completely dominated politics after 1637 possessed good access to core political documents, thanks to a multivolume set of copies of which several major families possessed some version. These private archives informed office-holders from such families about the political and legal landscape and allowed them to pursue family interests.

Several early calls for better finding tools, the last made in 1732, produced negligible results.[26] In 1760, during negotiations with Austria, the Leagues were once again embarrassed because they could not locate basic documents; as a result, they finally took the initiative to build a new space for an archive, and to commission a new inventory describing such documents as could still be found. The decision was accompanied by demands that all private persons hand over any public

---

[24] On the Three Leagues and the political culture prevalent there, see Simonett and Sablonier, *Handbuch der Bündner Geschichte*, vol. 2.

[25] Jenny, *Das Staatsarchiv Graubünden*, 153–55.

[26] Jenny, *Das Staatsarchiv Graubünden*, 195–204. The motivation for a 1732 indexing effort was the planned *division* among the Three Leagues of documents currently held at Chur, rather than their consolidation.

documents in their possession.[27] At least three copies of the new inventory were completed in 1766.[28]

The Graubünden archive was organized in an ideal-topographic manner, but like the archive and the state it represented, it differed considerably from its counterparts in Zurich and Lucerne (not to mention Savoy).[29] Above all, the new system and its inventory were much less systematic than those found in the Swiss cities. This is hardly surprising, since the Leagues' own political organization differed sharply from early modern expectations. As a confederation of communes, Graubünden fit very poorly into the hierarchical political models of early modern political theory. The Leagues did not form a corporate entity like a city. The individual communes of the Leagues, rather than the Three Leagues as a whole, retained the key documents legitimating their autonomy and privileges, and the Diet delegated the administration of the Leagues' subject territories to individuals from leading families. A corresponding blurriness characterized the classifications found in the 1766 archive and inventory.

Traces of a traditional hierarchical view of the Leagues' place in the political cosmos did remain visible in the inventory, as did some functional divisions of papers. For example, after a blank space for describing the first section of the first cabinet, the second section was reserved for "Letters from Rome," followed by "Letters from Como" (the most important neighboring bishopric for the Three Leagues).[30] Was the first section intended for the emperor? It seems likely, since the rundown of secular authorities continued in the following sections, including the Habsburg archdukes in Innsbruck and the Swiss Confederation. For more distant powers, however, the picture wavered: England came only after Venice, and the Netherlands were placed before a box that contained correspondence with a whole list of lesser sovereigns from Sweden to Sardinia.[31]

The second half of the archive, as in most ideal-topographic systems, used territorial classifications to create an ordered set of spaces, beginning with internal affairs of the Three Leagues as a whole, followed by individual subject territories. Here again, the sequence was very muddled, and more than one section was described as containing simply

---

[27] Jenny, *Das Staatsarchiv Graubünden*, 202–16. The construction project included ten new cabinets made out of walnut, with pear-wood drawers and iron-cased doors.

[28] One copy remains with the archive in Chur (StAGR, Msc. AB IV 9, vols. 2–3), a second may have gone initially to Ilanz, and the third quickly wandered into the possession of the Tscharner family in Chur (StAGR D V/3.249).

[29] The following discussion is based on the Tscharner copy.

[30] StAGR D V/3.249, 1–2.   [31] StAGR D V/3.249, 7–12.

"all sorts of letters."[32] A coherent political picture vanished completely toward the last few cabinets, where letters and charters from various outside powers appeared again, albeit this time lacking any visible order. In a sense, the spatial divisions of this archive and its inventory *accurately* conveyed the uncertain and often confusing political topography of the Bündner state. The system of ideal-topographic organization could adapt to such circumstances without demanding extensive labor that was simply not available in smaller states like Graubünden.[33]

Transcending the Ideal-Topographic System: Taxonomies in Lucerne, 1698

For two centuries, an ideal-topographic system of classification served the city-states of the Swiss Confederation well, adapting to their diverse political horizons and remaining sufficiently effective to allow them to thrive politically. Particularly for smaller chancelleries, ideal-topographic classification allowed secretaries to find important records simply by going to the right *place* in the repository, whereas maintaining detailed inventories was a challenge that few of them could meet. Nevertheless, as record-keeping became more complex, and as the volume of records continued to increase, the limitations of ideal-topographic organization became visible. Waser in Zurich had already pointed one a key limitation of classification in the introduction to his *Index Generalis:*

For in many cases, a single record [*Schreiben*] contains various points about diverse matters, which one cannot however separate, but can place under only one *Titul:* for example, when something pertains to the city of Mulhouse and to the Valtellina, no one interested in the latter matter would look under the *Titul* for Mulhouse, and in the former under the Valtellina.[34]

Classification on the basis of content was effective only when each record pertained to one category, but this was often not the case. As archives grew, and as the informational pressure on record-keepers intensified, indexing therefore became a common step in addition to classification. If documents were routinely indexed, however, the correspondence between spaces and content at the heart of the ideal-topographic system lost its urgency. The index ultimately displaced the map, as began to happen in Zurich after 1646.

---

[32] E.g. StAGR D V/3.249, 29, 32.
[33] Further cases showing the flexibility of this system are described in Head, "Knowing."
[34] StAZH Kataloge 11, fol. [vi].

Changes in the political world provided an additional reason to dispense with ideal-topographic systems and to consider new ways of arranging documents. For the Swiss Confederation, the emerging concept of sovereignty undermined the perception that the Swiss cantons were nodes in the larger imperial–feudal fabric of the Holy Roman Empire, and thus the utility of an ideal-topographic mapping that assumed homology between the political world and the organization of an archive's space.[35] This shift spurred an ambitious but incomplete reorganization of the Lucerne archive undertaken at the end of the seventeenth century. Although that project reflected changing political conceptions, it also shows that new options existed for the formal logic of a classification system. The extraordinary preservation of many intermediate products – down to the slips of paper used to label bundles of documents as they moved – also allows unparalleled insights into how Lucerne's archivists understood the challenges they faced and the means at hand to respond.

The reorganization in Lucerne began in 1698, after the city decided to build a new home for its rapidly growing collection of documents.[36] Chancellor Johann Karl Balthasar rearranged both old and current documents in a way fundamentally different from the previous ideal-topographic system.[37] First, Balthasar separated a large body of documents that he considered historical into an "Old Archive" (*Altes Archiv*) that would be henceforth closed. In contrast, documents relating to ongoing administration entered a *Neues Archiv*, which was designed to grow.[38] Second, the logic of the new archive was no longer topological, but rather taxonomic: Instead of mapping records to conceptual spaces, Balthasar introduced a systematic division and subdivision of categories that allowed each individual document (or even passages within a document) to be both indexed and cross-referenced independently of the document's physical location.[39] Finally, these changes in organizational logic *within* the archive reflected an equally momentous change in the understanding of the Lucerne state. In Balthasar's *Neues Archiv*, the categories and subcategories pertained not to the old feudal hierarchy, but to *actions* that the city might take, starting with *Commercium* and

---

[35] This transition is analyzed in Maissen, *Die Geburt*.

[36] Gössi, "Archivordnungen," 19–20; Glauser et al., *Das Staatsarchiv Luzern*, 24–27.

[37] According to Gössi, Balthasar left no commentary on his plan (Gössi, "Archivordnungen," 20). A fragmentary document from after 1688 suggests that the project was already under way at that point. STALu Akten 12/114, "Registraturfragmente, 17. Jahrhundert." This document clearly describes an *indexing* (rather than an organizing) scheme.

[38] The distinction between the two parts is described in Gössi, "Archivordnungen," 18.

[39] Indexing that included subdivision of categories and cross-referencing could take place in ideal-topographic archives, but only through the creation of *separate* indexes, such as the Zurich *Index Specialis*.

continuing with war, religion, and other administrative concerns. In essence, the new archive mirrored an active state whose foundations were a closed question, but whose activities in various spheres drew on carefully organized documents and correspondence containing information believed important to governance. In this way, the new inventory captured real developments. By the late seventeenth century, the city's oligarchs were the rulers of a territorial state whose sovereignty as part of the Swiss Confederation had been recognized at the Peace of Westphalia.

Balthasar's new taxonomic approach subordinated the physical spaces of document storage to informational loci found in individual documents and indexed systematically in the new inventories. The new archive's thirteen major categories or *Partes* (such as *Commercium*) had logical subdivisions called *Capites*, then *Artickel*, and then *Numeri*. These terms harkened back to Scholastic learning and its means of organizing long texts, but their function was now different: The hierarchy of categories allowed each document to have a unique designator – in effect, a content-related record-locator – that related it to larger spheres of action, from its immediate local context up through various subgroupings to the broad categories of commerce, war, or the church. Moreover, the multiple layers of hierarchy that Balthasar set up allowed any piece of information to get such a designator (in contrast to the signed *boxes* of an ideal-topographic system). Geographic designators and positions in the world's political hierarchy still appeared in this system, but only as subdivisions of action-oriented categories.

For example, in *Pars* 10 (*Eidgenössische Vogteien*), *Numerus* 1 pertained to the Thurgau, while subordinate *Artickel* designated lordships and parishes within the Thurgau in alphabetical order (thus resembling Waser's *Index Specialis*). The resulting multipart signatures provided considerable information about the record they referenced. The formalism of alphabetization further distinguished Balthasar's scheme from an ideal-topographic classification, in which categories and spaces depended on substantive criteria, such as a domain's closeness historically to its ruler.[40] Finally, although documents with the same signatures still accumulated in boxes, the boxes received arbitrary running numbers rather than descriptive labels. Arrangement was no longer homologous with description in Balthasar's scheme. Balthasar foresaw simply adding new boxes to the *Neues Archiv* with sequential numbers as more space was needed, meaning that boxes' contents would have no necessary relation to their physical placement within the archive.[41]

---

[40] Cf. StALU Akten 12/131, "Kanzleiregistratur: Weitere Ordnungsarbeiten."

[41] Gössi, "Archivordnungen," 17–18, stresses this point. In the *Altes Archiv*, previous bundles and boxes seem to have remained largely intact, so that subject-oriented

We are extraordinarily lucky that considerable evidence has survived regarding the process by which Lucerne's new archive grew out of the old. These records document a systematic separation of information *in* documents from information *about* documents (metadata). The creation of Balthasar's new inventory and arrangement, with its increasing distinction of information from paper, resulted in a double workflow, with one channel involving the documents themselves and the other involving the creation of indexes about those documents. The city's collection before 1698 had been classified and filed in an ideal-topographic archive, and also contained many unsorted documents – most likely in piles and bundles strewn around the chancellery office – as well as considerable serial material not considered part of the archive at all, such as council protocols and fiscal records. All came under the purview of the new organization and inventory.

The first step taken in 1698 was the creation of *Truckenregister*, inventories to the existing boxes that listed the documents destined for the *Altes Archiv*.[42] Substantial clumps of documents simply moved into the *Altes Archiv* intact, though some material moved to the *Neues Archiv*. Once papers had been physically sorted for the *Altes Archiv*, Balthasar constructed a new, cross-referenced central finding aid for the material in this corpus. This was necessary because his new categories and subcategories no longer referenced the physical locations of documents. He did so by moving back and forth between the actual documents in boxes, the indexed inventory found in each *Truckenregister*, and the new system of categories. Meanwhile, by 1702, the loose documents from the chancellery, along with documents from the old boxes that were moving to the *Neues Archiv*, had been ordered according to a "rough division" (*Rauwe Division*), which also survives.[43] In theory, cataloging the *Neues Archiv* should have proceeded as with the *Altes Archiv*, with a final division of documents into boxes and the placement of entries in the master index that connected the new categories, the loci established during the *Rauwe Division*, and the physical locations of the documents. Unfortunately, this last step never took place. The boxes in the *Neues Archiv* never received their numbers, so that the corresponding index volumes, although laid out, were useless. A report from 1758, commissioned from the

---

signatures and the physical location of documents tended to correlate, though any *necessary* connection was ruptured.

[42] STALu Akten 12/135.

[43] STALu Akten 12/119 and 12/125. This register evidently caused great difficulty and never was completed, as indicated in an internal report from 1702 (STALu Akten 12/115), which lamented the "harmful aggregation of materials about different matters that has flowed together," and the external report cited below.

professional archivist Gebhard Dubs, described how in the *Neues Archiv,*
"in the *partes* and *numeri,* wildly diverse material is mixed together, even
spiritual matters among political and civil affairs etc." This led him to
believe that

> in the reorganization of the enormous flood of documents, one originally only
> separated them *en gros* [i.e., the *Rauwe Division*], and assigned a single topic or
> [geographic] place to 1, 2, 3 or up to 9 boxes according to the exigencies of the
> documents, and distributed the documents according to their content however
> one could, and so registered them temporarily until time would allow them to be
> investigated in detail, and set in the desired order.[44]

Caught halfway between their older feudal ideal-topographic order and
the new state-oriented taxonomic system, Lucerne's documents became
completely inaccessible.

Conclusion

These last two chapters have explored how the content of records could
become the centerpiece for methods of arranging documents. From an
early and often unreflective tendency to segment lists of documents so as
to group those with related content, more comprehensive systems of
classification emerged as early modern archivists sought to master the
piles of paper accumulating in their offices and storerooms. Some of the
most impressive efforts followed the ideal-topographic techniques that
Peter Rück recognized in fifteenth-century Savoy, which mapped the
placement of records to transparent and seemingly natural features of
the political world, such as the hierarchy that stretched down from
emperors to the common people. As ideal-topographic models lost their
coherence among the burgeoning records produced by multiple offices
by the seventeenth century, taxonomies of categories and subcategories
seemed to provide a better way forward, though the experience of
Lucerne after 1698 shows that the labor involved could easily overwhelm
archival personnel.

All of these systems – from simple segmented lists to complex
taxonomies – conditioned archival arrangement on the principle of
pertinence. Classification, which required thinking ahead about the
entire range of possible documents to be stored in the future, was the
most systematic and forward-looking form of pertinence, and formalized
many practices that took place on an ad hoc basis even where no systematic classification existed. Systematic classification systems therefore

---

[44] STALu Akten 12/137.

share important features with what later became known as the "authority file" – a comprehensive list of categories or types applicable in the description and arrangement of all record units in an archive. Authority files are essential features of modern library and archive organization, but were only implicitly present in early modern archival thinking.

Another notable feature of systematic efforts at classification, such as those we have seen in Savoy, Zurich, and Lucerne, is that they represented an important change in how stored records were seen as relating to the future. Late Antique and Medieval record-keeping was certainly future-oriented, as the phrase *ad perpetuam rei memoriam* suggests, but the future use of records remained narrowly conceived: Records were potential proofs to be drawn "just like weapons" in legal or political contestation in an effort to show, in an imagined future, what had taken place in an authoritative past.[45] As the production and retention of political records expanded and became more systematic after 1400, however, and as rulers increasingly began viewing their troves not only as treasuries and armories but also as sources of knowledge, the way that archival accumulations related to the future changed. Classification of material in an archive made past records accessible according to the archivists' view of their significance, while also forming an ongoing and dynamic representation of a government's concerns, travails, and accomplishments. Rather than a passive collection of defensive tools, the classified archive became a tool for more active governance – hardly surprising in a world in which many rulers invested energetically in gaining more knowledge about, and tighter control over, those subject to them.[46]

Classification shared important goals with a different set of practices that were rapidly developing in early modern archives across Europe, which I define under the term "registry." Like classification systems, registry systems had roots that traced deep into the High Middle Ages – for example, in the registers that the papacy, kings, and other authorities (especially towns) began creating after 1200. Registry systems required secretaries to think about future records as well as those from the past, and to design pathways for inventorying and placing documents in a manner that would allow their recovery for various future needs. Registry systems, like the classification systems described here, created records continua reaching from the distant past to the horizon of the future, and connecting makers, users, and the public in new ways. Ultimately, though, registries and classification were mutually exclusive as ordering

---

[45] Aebbtlin, *Anführung*, 40.
[46] Soll, *The Information Master*, provides a compelling demonstration of this point.

principles, a fact recognized when nineteenth-century archival theorists defined pertinence and provenance as the two conflicting ways to organize an archive. The distinction was far from innocent, moreover: Each approach relied on a distinct epistemology of records and the work that they could do, each implied a separate regime of political knowledge, and each incorporated a distinct (and mutually exclusive) vision of governance. Registry and its implications will be the central question for the remainder of this book.

Part III

Growing Expectations and Innovative Practices (1550–)

By the late sixteenth century, the growing sophistication of the practices by which European polities of various kinds managed records came to be matched by growing ambitions to mobilize the information that rulers were convinced those records contained. King Philip II of Spain stands for a new kind of ruler who preferred writing over personal contact in the management of his vast realms. Philip earned the epithet of *el rey papelero* – the paper king – for his attention to papers as he sought to become "fully informed" about the matters coming before him for decision. In his own time, Philip's goals outstripped his servants' capacity to provide information in an effective way, as Chapter 11's analysis of the establishment and subsequent failure of the Spanish crown's central repository at Simancas will illustrate. Nevertheless, innovation in the management of state papers continued along two primary paths.

First, the functional and practical differentiations – of offices, of storage spaces, and of finding tools – that were seen in the sixteenth-century cases discussed in Part II intensified and bore increasing fruit in new structures. These efforts will be illustrated in Spain, where Philip sought to connect his new archive in Simancas with other royal archives and libraries as a comprehensive knowledge system about nature, his empire and its needs, and history. Second, the existing medial forms experienced ongoing recombination and refinement, leading to increasingly systematic approaches to the preservation of and access to stored records within the fundamental framework of paper, ink, books, bundles, and boxes. While progress was extremely uneven across Europe, certain ad hoc reconfigurations produced systems that eventually demonstrated the capacity to grow beyond Late Medieval approaches.

In seventeenth-century Berlin, as discussed in Chapter 11, the establishment of a new archival repository closely connected to the Electors' Secret Council and its chancellery evolved into a system in which record production in the chancellery and record cataloging in the archive shared approaches and categories. This enabled an easier flow back and forth, empowering the growing Prussian state. In the German lands more generally, similar systems of registry – that is, the systematic tracking of records through the course of their use in decision making and into permanent, accessible repositories – increased the ability of rulers and their councils to deploy recorded information strategically and effectively.

Additional systems of registry that took shape from the Late Middle Ages to the early eighteenth century are examined in detail in Chapter 12. Starting with urban book-form registries, in which the mechanics of creating protocol books inherently organized records by their place in deliberations rather than by their subjects, we will look at how new approaches to journaling and indexing in centers as diverse as Leiden and Innsbruck allowed administrative record-keeping to intensify in tandem with growing political challenges. Registries became a critical tool when the nearly ceaseless warfare that began in 1618 put growing pressure on Europe's states to know their strengths and muster their resources.

This period also saw the first professionalization of archival practices and a growing published literature that addressed both the reasons and the methods for organizing states' repositories. This literature, in parallel with a growing use of records in both political and historical contention, ultimately led to major debates over the authority and authenticity of old records. Part IV will turn to the shifting epistemologies and practices of record-keeping that became visible as a result.

11 Evolving Expectations about Archives, 1540–1650

Introduction

From the fourteenth to the late sixteenth centuries, the officials responsible for producing, receiving, and storing the written records of political entities in Western Europe faced both growing masses of material and growing demands to be able to produce specific records. Chancellery personnel – from the chancellors themselves, who were often high political officials and potent political actors, through various secretaries, registrators, clerks, and messengers – confronted changing expectations about which sorts of records would be available on demand to those whom they served, but were also in a position to withhold such records from subjects, rivals, or outsiders. As the volume of material expanded, the responsibility for various phases of records' life cycle increasingly came to be divided among more specialized offices. In parallel with the core chancellery that supported rulers and their councils, as well as expedited final documentation of their final decisions, registration specialists began working separately, reporting to the main chancellery but possessing their own spaces and responsibilities.[1] Further specialization led to specialized storage facilities – "archives," as they came to be called – that absorbed not only existing document treasuries but also organized administrative records from other chancelleries and registries across a domain or realm. Chancellery staff remained the makers and initial users of most documents that found their way into European archives, but specialized registries and archives increasingly took over the management of the stored records, producing them for rulers or individuals seeking evidence of past privileges, verdicts, and other actions.

Cities, principalities, and kingdoms that had already dedicated significant personnel and funds to the operation of their chancelleries found themselves investing in new offices and storage spaces. Rulers were

---

[1] Friedrich, *The Birth*, 83–99, analyzes early modern archival personnel.

convinced that these investments would help sustain their power by documenting claims against rivals, by supporting demands on subjects, and by enabling effective responses when subjects petitioned for benefits or relief. After the Reformation, particularly in the seventeenth century, governments began allowing historians access to some of their stored records as well, often to produce polemical narratives supported by dossiers of carefully selected documents in support of the ruler's legitimacy, authority, and policies. As chancelleries' work became more specialized and diverse, so did the nature and the perception of the written material they were creating and preserving, which was also becoming more differentiated in fundamental and extremely consequential ways.[2]

Moving forward, one focus will be on the ongoing differentiation of spaces, practices, and perceptions about political records that took place across Europe, especially during the seventeenth century. As we have seen in multiple cases, distinctions had already been emerging between a treasury of privileges and proof-documents, on the one hand, and heterogeneous and capacious collections of informational records, on the other hand. The new ambitions for records management behind these distinctions are characterized by José Luis Rodríguez de Diego, who contrasts the archival project launched in Spain by Charles V in the 1540s, when the Crown's archive in Simancas was first established, with the much more ambitious repository that his son Philip II relaunched in the 1560s:

The fundamental difference between the two was rooted in the limited and constrained conceptualization of the archive held by [Charles], compared to the global and general conceptualization by [Philip]; limited to the care and conservation of the rights "of our crown, patrimony, and patronage" under Charles V, extended to those of "our subjects and vassals" under Philip II; confined to the limited space of a single room in the old fortress of the Enriquez in Simancas by the emperor, but expanded through the construction projects ... by his son. Of the Caroline project, only the care of the documents remains. That of his son was entirely different, and unsurprisingly left that of his father entirely in the background.[3]

This chapter begins by discussing Philip II's systematic agenda for information management in the Simancas archive and in the *Instrucción para el gobierno del Archivo de Simancas* that Philip II and his agents issued in 1588. The surviving inventories (and the lack of more) in Simancas show, however, that the actual archive never fulfilled this agenda. One

---

[2] On differentiation of functions and spaces as a way to understand these developments, see Head, "Configuring European Archives."

[3] Rodríguez de Diego, "Significado."

cause of its shortcomings may be that neither the secretarial practices nor the resources available to the key actor at Simancas, archivist Diego de Ayala, were adequate for his and Philip's ambition to turn the Crown into a "fully informed" political actor. Additionally, Simancas's distance from the councils where Spain's administration actually took place hindered the integration of document use and document preservation envisioned by Philip and his advisers, amplified by Philip's instinct to put the archive's patrimonial functions above its informational ones. Simancas is historically important as the first repository conceived as a comprehensive archive (in the modern sense) for both legitimation *and* administration, but its rapid failure is equally instructive in revealing how difficult the rethinking of archives truly was.

A second, nearly contemporaneous case illustrates a similar situation in which a dynamic and resourceful government – in this case, the administration of Elector Joachim Friedrich of Brandenburg (r. 1598–1608) and his successors – sought to reestablish their failed archive. Their goals included the recovery and preservation of key charters and family documents, but also the management of current and past information in the service of the Electors' Secret Council (*Geheimes Etatsrat*), the Electorate's highest decision-making body. As in Simancas, the key *registrators* of the new institution – particularly Erasmus Langenhein and Christoph Schönbeck – sought to create a storage architecture based primarily on content for the documents they received from the Secret Council's chancellery as well as from other sources. In addition, Schönbeck developed new ways to track and index the flow of records sent to him for storage as an aid to future consultation. Although the resulting archive operated with quite traditional secretarial methods, these registrators' attention to the flow of documents ultimately succeeded in creating a workable registry system that integrated their collection with the chancellery of the Secret Council – a system that remained in active use until 1806, and which still structures the historical archive that remains, now known as the *Geheimes Staatsarchiv – Preüssischer Kulturbesitz.*

Chapter 12 turns to document registry in all its diversity. After a more complete definition, that chapter covers the urban book-form registries of Germany and the Netherlands through the sixteenth century, the serial and chronological *Hofregistratur* that emerged in Habsburg Innsbruck after 1564, and a brief forward-looking discussion of the "transaction-file registry" (*Sachaktenregistratur*) system that evolved out of north German and Dutch antecedents, including the system established in Berlin, during the eighteenth and nineteenth centuries. While all of these cases relied on the medial forms of paper, book, bundle, and armoire, new configurations of these tools, coupled with new decision-making and record-management practices, allowed record-keepers to move beyond the recovery of "proofs of past action" to provide their masters with comprehensive information both about the background for current business and the state of that business as decisions were made and as other parties responded. The evolution of fully differentiated registries and archives simultaneously involved the differentiation of functional offices and designated spaces for the preservation of records, and set the stage for political information management of entirely new kinds in the nineteenth century.

Imagining Information in Imperial Spain: The Simancas Project

A turn toward a comprehensive vision of records as the foundation of political knowledge appeared in Europe when Philip II of Spain and his agents imagined and constructed a new central archive in Simancas beginning in the 1560s. Philip's Simancas project fundamentally transformed the existing fortress and treasury for the Spanish Crown's records that had taken initial shape under his father, Charles I of Spain (generally referred to as Charles V in his role as Holy Roman Emperor), after 1540. A high point in Philip's initiative was the guide for the operation at Simancas drawn up by archivist Diego de Ayala under the close supervision of the king himself in 1588, the *Instrucción para el gobierno del Archivo de Simancas*.[4] This document laid out both broad goals and specific record-keeping practices, including rules for responding to requests for documents and a requirement to maintain a reading room for visitors, separate from the storage areas. The goal was not only to "conserve the [writings] that touch on the patrimony, state, and royal crown of these realms and to its rights of patronage [*patronazgo*],"[5] but also to gather all "information that would be useful for the effective direction of current affairs, and of those affairs which may occur every day."[6]

The Simancas case reveals an unstable interplay between traditional views of the archive-as-treasury and novel hopes for "full information" through the systematic preservation and organization of administrative records.[7] Our picture is unusually clear in this case because the physical separation between the impressive fortress-archive and the offices of

---

[4] Rodríguez de Diego, *Instrucción*.   [5] Rodríguez de Diego, *Instrucción*, 97.
[6] Cited from a royal command (*cedula*) in Rodríguez de Diego, "Estudio," 41.
[7] The changing role of information and "being informed" in sixteenth-century Spain is a core issue in Brendecke, *Imperium*, especially part II.

Philip's government in Madrid, several days' journey away, resulted in extensive written communication about the archive's formation and the considerations that guided Philip, his advisors, and Diego de Ayala in Simancas. The breakdown of order in the Simancas collections by the early seventeenth century, meanwhile, shows that distance from administrative centers, along with conservative secretarial techniques and modest staffing, prevented the Simancas operation from fulfilling Philip's expectations; the collection eventually descended into near chaos, although the core treasury established by Philip's father remained inventoried and available for the rest of the *Ancien Régime*.

The origins of the striking fortress-archive in the village of Simancas date back to the beginning of Charles V's reign. As he discovered after his accession to the throne and the urban *Comunero* rebellion of 1520, the tumultuous recent history of Castile had resulted in the dispersion or destruction of almost all royal documents. After Isabella and Ferdinand consolidated their kingdoms in the 1470s and 1480s, they had found themselves largely without archives, and their modest efforts at restoration had produced few results. Their heir Charles began remedying this sorely felt lack by appointing royal archivists to recover the papers of the recent Castilian kings.[8] Rather than gathering the fruits of this labor in Valladolid or in the emerging center in Madrid, however, in 1540 Charles and his council chose the fortress of Simancas, held by a trusted royal servant and located in the hinterlands of Valladolid, as a safe location to preserve the Crown's most precious records. At first, the material sent to this rural fortress consisted primarily of papal bulls in favor of the monarchy and charters establishing royal control over ecclesiastical and secular properties, along with family wills and marriage contracts. In addition, various bodies of papers seized from former royal officials joined the collection in fits and starts as they were obtained. The core charters were placed into a new secure storage chamber in one of the towers, known as the *Cubo del Patronazgo*, but little further work took place during Charles's reign.

Charles's heir Philip, in contrast, greatly accelerated the movement of documents to the fortress after his accession, and paid close attention to its staffing and organization throughout his reign.[9] Simancas was highly unusual in comparison to the practices in the rest of Europe, since it soon

---

[8] Grebe, *Akten,* provides a comprehensive study of Simancas in the sixteenth century. See also de la Plaza, *Archivo General*; Rodríguez de Diego, "La Formación"; and Rodríguez de Diego, "Archivos del Poder."

[9] On Philip II as the "paperwork king," see Parker, *Philip II*. Special thanks to Professor Parker for sharing additional notes on the new edition of the book.

became a central facility not only for the Crown's treasury of charters and privileges, but also for the documents produced by the growing number of royal councils.[10] Philip learned that this documentary patrimony required skilled management after several of Charles's and his own appointments to supervise the repository largely abandoned the task. In 1561, he appointed Diego de Ayala to reside in Simancas as the repository's archivist, "it being such an important thing and a universal good that these documents have a known location where they are guarded and can be found whenever they are needed."[11] Much of Ayala's work during his first years in Simancas involved organizing the core collection of charters, for which he began preparing inventories and alphabetical indexes. Ayala's organizational scheme was highly spatial, including the placement of the most secret material closest to the chapel as well as the royal bedchamber Philip required to be prepared. The facility's layout demonstrates that Ayala, like his master, still thought about documents primarily in material terms – as objects to be controlled, not as information to be deployed.[12] For the most secret documents, such control even excluded the archivist, since Philip sent certain chests with documents from Madrid without sending the keys, which he retained himself.[13]

Ayala's organization and inventorization of charters and bulls in the *Cubo del Patronazgo* and *Patronato Viejo* followed patterns we have already observed in multiple cases.[14] Like Portugal, Spain already had a strong tradition of registering charters and other documents produced in royal chancelleries, though much of this work had broken down for Castile (though not for Aragon) during the civil disorders of the fifteenth century.[15] Ayala drew on these traditions to inventory the diverse material that had been gathered together, which was divided into boxes by

---

[10] Rodríguez de Diego, "Archivos del Poder," 521.

[11] Rodríguez de Diego, "Archivos del Poder," 528–29; several fragmentary documents in AGS, Inventarios Antiguos, 1, also contain this charge. For a letter documenting Ayala's sending of inventories to Madrid, see AGS ARC 5, 5 (January 1, 1567).

[12] In addition to the *Cubo del Patronazgo* buried in the castle tower, further documents pertaining to the royal patrimony, the *Patronato Viejo*, rested in a special room adjacent to the royal apartment and the chapel, which was separate from the four large storerooms (*pieças*) created for administrative documents. My thanks to Dr. Rodríguez de Diego for his tour of the spaces and explanations of their design.

[13] Noted in a number of receipts from Ayala, such as AGS ARC 34, 6, 2 and 6,3.

[14] A draft of Ayala's inventory to patrimonial proofs appears in AGS Inventorios Antiquas 1, 1 [2]. The final version, sent to Madrid, has been published (Sancho Rayon and de Zabalburu, "Índice").

[15] Diego de Rodríguez, "Estudio," 17–18, n16, cites Ayala: "Para solo el registro de corte se fundan principalmente los archivos" (eferring to AGS *Secretária* ARC 6, 500). On Aragon, see Navarro Bonilla, *Escritura*.

counterparty and subject matter; he then rubricated these new inventories and provided them with alphabetical indexes.[16] He also produced various selective document lists in response to demands to inform the crown of its records in specific areas of interest – for example, privileges concerning the kingdom of Naples.[17] These practices treated the accumulated records as proofs in familiar ways, and made them accessible using existing tools.

By 1568, however, Philip's ambitions had expanded: All documents produced by the Castilian councils were to be deposited in Simancas once they were no longer in use, he decreed, and provided with detailed inventories.[18] Philip personally initiated a building program to create additional storage areas, which continued – although accompanied by frequent pleas from Ayala to Madrid to provide sufficient funds – through the end of the century and into the directorship of Ayala's son in the early seventeenth century. The challenge created by the potentially unlimited administrative material arriving from Madrid was quite different from that posed by the charters in the *cubos*, since the material was heterogeneous in content and complex in organization. A key response by Ayala was literally built into the archive: Remodeling in the 1580s created new rooms, each one designated for the output of specific important councils (Figure 11.1). In effect, Ayala's actions also imposed a rough organization by provenance, since each council's output was kept together (at least in theory) just as the council's own chancellery had ordered it, and separate from other councils' records.

Most of the deliveries to the fortress during Ayala's tenure were already organized into bundles (*legajos*) divided by pertinence and internally organized by chronology.[19] Being of recent production, many of the documents were probably cataloged in registers as well, although it seems quite possible these remained in Madrid.[20] When Madrid requested a copy of a document—and hundreds of such *buscas* are

---

[16] Ayala labeled boxes with numbers and alphabetical labels (a–z, aa–yy), and used these in indexing; AGS Inventorios Antiquas 1, 1 [2].

[17] A full modern list of the surviving sixteenth-century inventories appears in AGS, VAR/ INV 02.

[18] AGS ARC 34, 1, 14 (October 16, 1568). Surviving records from 1567 and 1568 document extensive discussions of the need for inventories as well as reports from Ayala on his progress in creating them.

[19] Grebe, *Akten,* 470–77.

[20] Ayala sought to obtain material together with existing inventories or registers whenever possible. In an undated list from between 1568 and 1583, for example, he insists that materials obtained from former officers and their families be sent with "la remisión de inventarios con los documentos de interés" (AGS ARC 32, 1, 8).

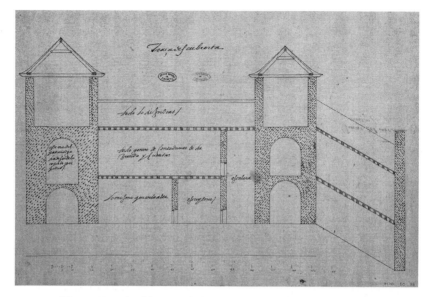

Figure 11.1 Architectural drawing for the expansion of the Simancas archive from 1589, showing the new rooms dedicated to specific council documents. The arched space to the left is labeled for the *patronazgo*; the top floor says *todo lo de Indias*, the second floor *todo genero de Contadurias de Hazienda y Cuentas*, and the bottom floor *Lo messmo quenta alta* and *escriptorio*. Spain: Ministry of Culture: Archivo General de Simancas, MPD, 50, 038.
Image provided by the Archivo General de Simancas; reproduced by permission of the Ministry of Culture.

preserved from the sixteenth century[21] – the request often specified the council, the *legajo* or bundle, and the date, showing that some kind of inventory or register must have remained behind to inform the *buscas*. When a corpus arrived at the fortress, moreover, it likely went into the appropriate room in its existing order. Since Ayala knew where to find each council's documents and could rely on precise *legajo* descriptions for particular items, detailed inventories were never made for these materials.[22] The vast majority of the *buscas* related to private suits, not the crown's own use. Such *buscas* nevertheless required the king's

[21] AGS ARC 60 holds about 450 individual requests for documents from Simancas.

[22] In a report about Simancas drafted August 9, 1780, archivist Pedro de Gallarreta noted that for records of the Council of Indies sent to Simancas in 1658, "los Legajos en que se incluyan estos documentos no se hallaban numerados, y solamente estaban Imbentariados en general, segun el orden con que se colocan" (AGI Indiferente General 1852).

personal signature, demonstrating how Philip envisioned the repository as a site of authentic records for the Spanish nobility and private individuals as well as for the Crown – which allowed the Crown to provide or withhold essential documents depending on the king's own assessment of the parties and issues involved.[23] A surviving collection of more general research reports – often sloppy and barely legible to the modern reader – suggests that the king or his secretaries also sent broad topics of interest to Ayala, asking him to fill them in on what material might be available.[24]

While Ayala struggled to inventorize charters and provide space for administrative documents from the *Consejos* in Madrid and elsewhere, a broader conversation continued about how to organize the king's overall system of knowledge instruments, including royal repositories in Rome, Milan, Barcelona, Cadiz, and Lisbon.[25] The network that the king's advisors imagined included the royal libraries, instrument collections, and other sources of political information, such as the famous interrogatories sent by the Spanish Crown to Spanish parishes and then to American urban administrations. The germ of such ideas, and Philip's fascination with them, appeared in a 1555 memorial from the humanist Juan Páez de Castro to the then-crown prince, suggesting a central knowledge center for the Spanish empire, which was to consist of three rooms or sections.[26] The first room would contain a library of books that could be consulted on all questions; the second room would contain maps and scientific instruments, in particular relating to seafaring and geography, as well as atlases of European cities and provinces; and the third and most secret room would consist of a select archive that would begin with the usual charters, but would also include reports from the Indies and from across Europe.

In the following years, though no single institution carried out Páez de Castro's full agenda, Philip built up the extraordinary library in El Escorial and his core archive in Simancas. The grander agenda also found echoes in Philip's relationship with Simancas, as when the 1588 *Instrucción* reiterated the scheme of three parallel approaches to knowledge in the king's service – though now as three books of extracts and guidance from the archive, rather than as three rooms or separate

---

[23] Rodríguez de Diego and Rodríguez de Diego, "Un archivo."

[24] AGS ARC 61. One document is superscribed with the note: "Ordenancas que se han de buscar."

[25] Rodríguez de Diego, "Estudio," 43–53, raises the question of a "Red de archivos?," to which he answers that such a network could be conceived by the 1560s.

[26] The larger context is described in Brendecke, *Imperium*, 93–96; Grebe, *Akten*, 387–93; and Bouza Alvarez, *Del escribano*, especially ch. 3.

institutions. The first book of charters, the king ordered, should "form a book with the distinctions and clarity that is needed, noting in each chapter in the margins the box or book where each and every one of the documents that is mentioned in this book can be found." A second book – following up on Philip's command in 1568 that Ayala create inventories for each part of the archive – was to summarize all inventories present in Simancas, again giving the volume or box of any documents that were mentioned. Finally, a third book, a "libro de hystoria," was intended to record all of the "curious and memorable things that are or will be in the said archive."[27] This vision of sustaining empire through the superior command of knowledge remained a key aspiration – although perhaps an impossible one – throughout Philip II's long reign.[28] This was an agenda that faced forward to the future, both in the practices it called for and, even more importantly, in the attitude that it embodied.

Nevertheless, the Simancas project ground to a dysfunctional halt within a generation. Ayala was cut off from Madrid, connected only by slow mail and occasional visits, meaning that he could not coordinate his organizational work with the chancelleries, and vice versa.[29] Moreover, the secretarial practices available to Ayala simply could not master the abundance of materials flowing into the fortress with the available staff. By the early 1620s, the authorities in Madrid found Simancas so unresponsive that a formal inspection, a *visita*, was appointed. Although further research is necessary, it seems possible that the relationship between material bundled into *legajos* in Simancas and the original chancellery inventories in Madrid had become unreliable. Antonio Hoyos, who carried out the charge to inspect the archive and reform Simancas's administration, commented on the disorder that reigned: "For I find a thousand matters worthy of remedy, but not easy to be carried out."[30] Indeed, Hoyos apparently decided that the only solution was to create completely new summary inventories for the entire collection at Simancas, and the hasty overviews that he drafted remained the only workable finding tool until 1657.[31] Hoyos's inventories simply listed the *legajos* that he found in each room of the facility and summarized their

[27] Rodríguez de Diego, *Instrucción*, 104–6. Ironically, Páez de Castro himself was soon frustrated by his own inability to access the records in Simancas; see Kagan, *Clio and the Crown*, 103. On use of the collection in litigation, see Brendecke, "'*Arca, Archivillo, Archivo.*'"

[28] See Brendecke, *Imperium*, 94, for an assessment.

[29] Castillo Gómez, "The Culture," 559, notes "certain inefficiency in the functioning of [Spanish royal] archives, particularly at Simancas, due to its distance to the Court."

[30] AGS ARC 7, 1, 9 (August 11, 1629).

[31] The Hoyos inventories, which remained in use into the eighteenth century, are held in AGS Inventarios Antiguos, 2 and 20.

contents. Critically, he included the large corpora of records sent by the Madrid councils, something that Ayala and his son apparently never achieved except at the most summary level.

One last dimension of Simancas's early years deserves mention: the explicit connections to other collections. Starting in the 1560s, Diego de Ayala, at his master's urging, sought to incorporate the best archival practices from other Crown archives, sharing knowledge as part of the interlinked system laid out in Páez de Castro's memorial.[32] The most explicit connection occurred after Philip I visited the Torre do Tombo in Lisbon during his coronation as king of Portugal in 1581. At the king's orders, Cristovão de Benavente wrote a report about the Torre's record-keeping practices, which highlighted the *Leitura Nova* project's approach of creating a permanent book-form record of transactions of lasting value.[33] Ayala responded to Benavente's memorandum point by point in an extended correspondence with the king's secretary Gabriel de Zayas, noting which parts of the Torre do Tombo's practice might be helpful, and which parts did not correspond to the very different circumstances in Simancas. As Diego de Ayala noted, the councils of Castile were organized very differently from those in Portugal "in their dispatches and division of authority over papers and matters of business [*negocios*]."[34] Although Ayala was happy to contemplate volumes of extracts for "matters of perpetual importance" (provided he received the necessary resources to carry such volumes out), focusing his efforts on the production of register copybooks like the *Leitura Nova* would have meant abandoning the great majority of the Simancas material.

It is telling that Philip was especially impressed by the *Leitura Nova*. The surviving record makes repeated references to the "lectura nueva," the main topic of Benavente's report. As the most splendid product of the Portuguese archival tradition, the *Leitura Nova* would have been at the center of the Torre do Tombo's presentation to the new sovereign in 1581.[35] Nevertheless, the *Leitura Nova* was also a profoundly patrimonial and backward-looking enterprise that corresponded to the specific context of Portuguese metropolitan organization. Indeed, the appeal the *Leitura Nova* had for Philip vividly demonstrates the lasting influence of the patrimonial imagination on European record-keeping.

---

[32] The relations between Simancas and other Spanish royal collections are reviewed in Grebe, *Akten*, 393–436.

[33] Rodríguez de Diego, "Estudio," 55–57; Grebe, *Akten*, 418–436. Ayala's comments appear in AGS ARC 34, 1, 1 [2].

[34] AGS ARC 34, 1, 1; Grebe, *Akten*, 424–37.

[35] I am not aware of any detailed record of what Philip saw when he visited the Torre do Tombo, but that he even asked to see the archives of his new kingdom is remarkable.

A similar exchange took place with the archivist of the Spanish embassy in Rome, Juan de Berzosa, who established a collection and inventory there, based on detailed instructions from Madrid, in the early 1560s. Berzosa, too, was ordered to create three books of excerpts for future use: one reproducing privileges from the Holy See to the Crown of Spain; a second recording the presentations of bishoprics, abbacies, and other benefices; and a third recording important historical events. Once Berzosa had completed his inventory and sent it to Madrid, the king ordered it forwarded to Simancas, thereby linking these two repositories.[36]

Thus, Simancas stands at the intersection of divergent approaches to managing stored records. On the one hand, its core consisted of a quintessential treasury of proofs, and its entire architecture and location singled it out as a fortress-treasury that embodied medieval understandings of the value of records. On the other hand, Philip II – more than any other contemporary ruler – and his agents thought systematically about how enhancing their record-keeping could ensure they were armed for both political and juridical contestation within their kingdoms and against their rivals. They clearly envisioned a records management network consisting of multiple, differentiated repositories that kept a wide range of information safe and organized, able to respond to requests for specific documents or with research on important topics. But without an equally ambitious rethinking of his own practices, the king's archivist in the fortress-archive could not meet his king's expectations. The very separation of Simancas from Madrid hindered the kind of innovations that Ayala needed to carry out the mission laid out in the *Instrucción*. In the end, the lack of resources and the divergences between Simancas and the Madrid chancelleries prevented Simancas from fulfilling the broader agenda of creating a fount of political knowledge.

Simancas shows that it was entirely possible in the sixteenth century to conceptualize the possibility of organizing diverse records into a system of repositories. Carrying out the work necessary to establish and maintain such repositories, however, proved far more difficult in a world still dominated by the medial forms of paper and parchment, bundle and book. Success required not only substantial investment in personnel, buildings, and supplies, but also a new orientation that focused not just on precious proofs, but on new tectonics that managed the flow of information through administrative processes as records moved from place to another, and from one medial configuration to another.

---

[36] Grebe, *Akten*, 396, 398. A copy of Ayala's assessment of the inventory (not in his own hand) appears at AGS ARC 5, 42 (1573).

Storage Spaces and Document Tracking in Seventeenth-Century Berlin

On first glance, the Electorate of Brandenburg–Prussia in the first half of the seventeenth century would not appear to be a promising site for major transformations in record-keeping. Like other high noble families in Germany, the Hohenzollerns had begun keeping charters in the Middle Ages, compiling registers and rudimentary inventories first in their home territories in Swabia and Franconia, and then in Brandenburg after their accession to the Electorate in the early fifteenth century. Frequent family squabbles, the Reformation, and the frontier character of much of Brandenburg in northeastern Germany (not to mention the Hohenzollerns' acquisition of the Baltic duchy of Prussia in 1525), however, meant that their record-keeping efforts did not stand out compared to advanced practices such as those in Innsbruck or in Würzburg discussed earlier.[37] Indeed, it was a catastrophic failure of elementary record preservation in 1598 that provided one impulse for the consequential seventeenth-century developments that this chapter addresses. During his accession in that year, Elector Joachim Friedrich discovered that not even his father's will (of considerable significance because of a dispute among Joachim Friedrich's siblings) could be located in Berlin. Dissatisfied, the new Elector appointed Erasmus Langenhein, a secretary who had assisted him when he was administrator of the prince-bishopric of Magdeburg, to reestablish the Electoral archive by organizing the available records and gathering up others that had dispersed to regional depositories or were held by various possessors outside the family.[38]

Langenhein's efforts quickly produced a new collection of charters that were placed into boxes (*Kästlein*) according to pertinence. He also began collecting administrative records from the various offices and chancelleries of the Electorate, including new production as the Elector and his Council reorganized the government. The boxes of proofs found their places on two shelves (*Reposituren*) in a tower of the Elector's castle in Berlin. To provide access to this material, Langenhein also created an

---

[37] Key older works on Brandenburg's early record-keeping include Lewinski, *Die Brandenburgische Kanzlei*; Wagner, *Das Brandenburgische Kanzlei- und Urkundenwesen*; and Arendt, *Die brandenburgische Kanzlei*. A brief modern assessment by Lehmann, "Registraturgeschichtliche und quellenkundliche Aspekte," 13–18, denies any linear connection from the Late Medieval registers to the classic Prussian registry.

[38] The most recent history of the Berlin archives is Klinkenborg, *Geschichte des Geheimen Staatsarchivs*, drafted in the 1920s and updated in Kloosterhuis's careful edition. See also two nineteenth-century works: Raumer "Geschichte," and Cosmar, *Geschichte*. My narrative rests on these works.

inventory in book form, entitled *Registratura archivorum in superiori conclavi turris,* which included summaries of the charters.[39] Like many antecedents, the *Registratura* employed specific physical language in describing its referents:

This inventory includes (1) the 30 boxes in the first shelves (*Repositur*), which are in the back vault closest to the window; (2) then, next, those that are in the same chamber to the left (there are 22 others in between, about which no description occurs here); (3) Pomeranian matters, next to which the aforementioned 30 boxes (*Kästlein*) were collated on this side.[40]

To this point in the archive's development, little that Langenhein undertook went beyond practices already found in Paris in the late fourteenth century, except perhaps the detailed summaries of charters found in the *Registratura.*

Owing to advanced age and growing blindness, Langenhein performed little work on the Electors' administrative documents, but his assistant appointed in 1615, Vice-Registrator Johann Zernitz, took on a parallel project to organize the ruling house's "masses of files" (*Aktenmassen*) on similar principles. Like the charters, documents were divided into broad pertinence categories and placed on shelves, where they were further divided by subject matter into numbered, chronologically ordered bundles called *Konvoluten* (rather than into boxes, like the charters.)[41] The sequence of *Reposituren* for this material started with materials pertaining to the Holy Roman Emperor in Repositur 1 and 2, as one might expect, but soon became quite random, with Hohenzollern territories, neighbors, interlocutors (such as the territorial nobility), and events (such as the Thirty Years' War) following in no particular order.[42] The historian Melle Klinkenborg suspects that Zernitz largely reproduced the order this material already possessed, simply moving files into the new shelves (*Reposituren*) and gathering them into bundles with alphabetic labels (for Repositur 1, Zernitz used A–Qq).[43] Zernitz also created a four-volume alphabetical guide to the material. For the remainder of this collection's history, *Reposituren* and *Konvolute* remained the fundamental divisions, originally as physical spaces, but later as abstract

---

[39] Klinkenborg, *Geschichte des Geheimes Staatsarchiv,* 31–32, characterizes the included material as "Urkunden im weitesten Sinne des Wortes."

[40] Cited from a transcription: Kloosterhuis, "In arduis," 421–22.

[41] The complex history of the GStA-PK's *Reposituren* is given in meticulous detail in Müller and Posner, *Übersicht.*

[42] Kloosterhuis, "Von der Repositurenvielfalt," 48, notes that "hinter der mathematisch logischen Folge steht keine sachlich sinnvolle Anordnung."

[43] Müller and Posner, *Übersicht,* 4.

organizing categories that were frequently renumbered, modified, added, and transformed.[44]

While Langenhein was working, a decision that Elector Johann Sigismund and his Secret Council took in 1613 changed the position of the registry officials and their repository in a critically important way. A new Council ordinance ordered that in addition to managing the substantial archive that Langenhain was assembling, his office should serve as the registry for documents created by the new Secret Council, established in 1605. By decree of the Elector,

> the documents stored in the cabinets of the Secret Council's chancellery should be handed over to the Registrator after a year's time; correspondingly, the Registrator is obliged to be present during Council meetings, for the case that any documents from the archive should be needed.[45]

This arrangement tied the evolving archive tightly to the business of the Council, with the expectation that the material on its shelves would be immediately available when requested by the councilors. Equally, the Council's own chancellery no longer needed to establish an independent system for managing its records beyond their immediate use, because these would be transferred to the archive at the end of the year.[46]

In an era when many European chancelleries were experiencing a differentiation between current repositories closely associated with specific offices, on the one hand, and long-term repositories in vaults or even distant castles, where a minimal staff preserved the records and responded, slowly, to requests for specific material, on the other hand, Brandenburg–Prussia instead blundered its way into an actively managed archive with close ties to administrative business. Christoph Schönbeck, who became registrator in 1639, recognized the significance of this configuration: "The Electoral archive here is not separated from the registry (*Registratur*), as is the case in Cleves, but is rather combined perpetually with it, so that the registrator and the archivist represent one and the same person."[47] In contrast to Simancas, in particular, this arrangement created strong incentives to keep the archive well organized, and further to ensure that whatever approaches it took to organizing

---

[44] Müller and Posner, *Übersicht*, 2 fn1.

[45] Klinkenborg, *Geschichte des Geheimes Staatsarchiv*, 41. Cosmar, *Geschichte*, 16–17, expands rather confusingly on the relationship between chancellery and registrators' office, and registry and archive.

[46] The secret council chancellery eventually did establish a registry, but this operation was small and followed the scheme already established by Zernitz and later Christoph Schönbeck in the archive. See Klinkenborg, *Geschichte des Geheimes Staatsarchiv*, 41; Meisner, *Aktenkunde*, 167–69.

[47] Klinkenborg, *Geschichte des Geheimes Staatsarchiv*, 41 n109.

records corresponded to those used in the production of documents and files in the first place: Chancellery and archive operated as a connected system. The significance of this relationship will become clear as we consider later developments.

These early seventeenth-century developments in Berlin did not at first appear particularly successful. Between the stresses of the Thirty Years' War (during which archival material was repeatedly packed for movement, and in some cases moved and separated to safer locations), and the general impoverishment that the Hohenzollerns' administration faced because of the vast cost of the war and damage to their territorial economy, the Berlin archive of the Secret Council slid toward dysfunction and chaos. In 1628, for example, when the Elector needed the contracts between the Electors and various bishoprics after the Peace of Passau in 1552, the archive could provide no assistance. As the Secret Council reported:

Where such treaties could be found, only God knew! The registry only reached back 30 years, and besides, everything was lying around in disorder, and many valuable items were being eaten by mice. It was no use asking the old registrator [Langenhein] anything, since he was nearly entirely deaf and also blind, on account of his age; meanwhile, the current registrator [Zernitz] could offer nothing more than was found in the inventory, which had nothing to say.[48]

Langenhein died in 1632, and Zernitz in 1639, along with the new vice-registrator Francke, leaving not only a double vacancy but also an archive in a state of the "greatest disarray."[49] The newly appointed registrator, Schönbeck, concurred, stating that upon reviewing the archive's condition, "the confusion was so great, it could scarcely have become worse."[50]

The situation that Schönbeck confronted after 1639 was not promising, nor was he provided with additional staff to help him manage the material in the Electoral archive.[51] His predecessors had left him the material organized (or not) in a typical early seventeenth-century fashion, without either a systematic classification system or extensive finding aids beyond Langenhein's inventory of the charters and Zernitz's rudimentary oversight of the administrative files, the *Akten*. Schönbeck's decision to develop a more systematic "methodus" for approaching the material led to modest but decisive innovations that, together with the waning of

---

[48] Paraphrased in Cosmar, *Geschichte*, 18.

[49] In a 1629 report by Count Adam von Schwarzenberg mentioned in Cosmar, *Geschichte*, 19.

[50] Cited in Klinkenborg, *Geschichte des Geheimes Staatsarchiv*, 45n118.

[51] Schönbeck's background is largely unknown: He was the brother-in-law of one of the Elector's vice-chancellors, and had studied in Frankfurt a. O. and perhaps also in Wittenberg. Surviving documents show that he knew French and Italian along with Latin. See Klinkenborg, *Geschichte des Geheimes Staatsarchiv*, 45–48.

the Thirty Years' War in the 1640s and the Great Elector's eventual support, helped turn the tide of chaos in the Secret Council's archive. During his long career, he created a simple but effective system that remained closely tied, crucially, to the Council's decision making and operations.

Three key changes lay at the heart of Schönbeck's innovations in the management of Electoral administrative records. First, although preserving the terminology of *Reposituren* and *Konvolute*, he effectively virtualized these terms, turning them from mappings of physical storage space into abstract categories and subcategories. In doing so, he also rearranged considerable material and developed new subcategories from the *Konvolute* in an effort to create a classification that reflected the Electoral government's actual operations and priorities. Virtualizing the *Konvolute* also made it possible for each position in the system to expand as needed as new material came in, which had not been the case previously. Second, Schönbeck instituted a set of registers that tracked the annual transfers of material from the Secret Council's chancellery to the archive, the so-called *Publica-Bücher* and *Registratur-Bücher*. By tracking specific bundles of material to their archival location, defined by a *Repositur* and *Konvolut* signature, these books allowed the archivists to respond to future queries from the Council chancellery for specific items. Third, considerable evidence suggests that the structural incentives arising from the relationship between the chancellery and the archive (supported by Schönbeck's conscious efforts) led the chancellery to employ the same classification system implicit in the *Reposituren* and *Konvolute* for its own record-keeping.

Taken together, these developments turned the passive approach that Schönbeck had inherited into a dynamic framework for managing the knowledge in multiple streams – that is, a *Registratur* in German terminology. Schönbeck's system is therefore comparable, though quite differently structured, to those systems emerging from European city governments and from the Habsburg administration of Austria, which employed different methods toward similar ends.

Reposituren *and* Konvolute *as Classification and Authority File*

Schönbeck inherited a repository of files in which labels and finding aids reflected the physical location of materials divided by content. These divisions of content, in turn, reflected the primary business and concerns of the Electoral government. When he looked more closely at the *Konvolute* located on the various shelves (*Reposituren*), however, Schönbeck soon discovered that their arrangement was far from systematic; bundles consisted of only vaguely related material, in many cases, assembled by unknown processes in the chancellery and poorly described in Zernitz's summary inventory. Schönbeck's comments are worth quoting at length: speaking about the *Repositur* supposedly dedicated to "Tolls and Shipping," he wrote:

1. On opening the *Konvolute*, I found many items within that had not been registered [*eingeschrieben*]. If they are not registered, and if different locations are not separated in the *Konvoluten*, how will it then be possible to provide what is requested? 2. Additionally, one finds no order within it, so that the shipping on the Elbe, Oder and Boye [?], item in Lüneburg, Mecklenburg, Hamburg etc. is all laid down in a muddle, and far from methodically [*methodice*], as such an important labor deserves to be carried out... 3. There is no index at all to this material... 4. In Repositur 21–22 for territorial matters about the Mark [Brandenburg], many documents about shipping on the Elbe, Oder and Boye are also found, which still need to be placed here.[52]

Facing such disorder, Schönbeck undertook to transform his system according to the principles listed above.

First, he rearranged the sequence of *Repdevelopituren*, moving some material to new numbers (and presumably, at least at first, to new physical locations), so as to create space for new bodies of material he wanted to interpolate. More significantly, he completely redefined the *Konvolute*: Rather than physical bundles, these now became subcategories within the larger general subject matter of each *Repositur*, which could be flexibly arranged in light of the specific material involved, and whose physical subdivisions – the actual bundles – could be numbered within the larger, virtual *Konvolut*. Schönbeck used existing subdivisions where they made sense, but in many cases – for example, Repositur 7 dedicated to the administration of Prussia – he "by necessity had to claw the rubrics for the administrative offices, positions, cities, etc. out of the files themselves."[53] In effect, Schönbeck created a content-driven, hierarchical classification system for the Elector's files.

The next step was to define a comprehensive system of *Repdevelopituren*, *Konvolute*, and their numbered subdivisions in advance. The new grid of categories Schönbeck developed began with a few general terms, followed by a strictly alphabetical list of substantive categories (called rubrics), which were then numbered.[54] The rubrics were oriented to

---

[52] GStA PK Sammlung Altfindbücher, M 632, ff. 347–48.

[53] Cited indirectly in Klinkenborg, *Geschichte des Geheimes Staatsarchiv*, 52, based on GStA PK, Sammlung Altfindmittel, B 20.

[54] See Cosmar, *Geschichte*, 21–22: "Mit Erlaubnis der Geheimen Raths habe er diese [Convolute] einigermaßen zu ordnen angefangen, nicht nach den Jahren, sondern nach dem Alphabeth mit Bezugnahme auf die Materie."

diverse matters of concern (and thus resembled the heterogeneous terms already found in Zernitz's arrangement, and also in Lorenz Fries's *Hohe Registratur*). Under A and B, for example, the list included "Amtssachen, Adel ..., Angerburg, Bestallungen, Begnadigungen ..., Bernsteinsachen, Brandenburgsche Amts- und Stadtsachen, Balga, Barten, Bartenstein, etc."[55] Institutional actions, domains, particular items (e.g., *Bernstein* [amber]), and groups (*Adel*) all appeared in alphabetical order. The *Konvolut* labels constituted a subject authority file for the entire collection, with suitable options for hard-to-categorize items and new categories.

Once the rubrics within each *Repositur* and *Konvolut* had been defined – that is, once the classification system was complete – placement of incoming new material should be simple, Schönbeck asserted:

> The only trouble will be not to overlook the selection of one or another place exclusively according to the A.B.C., which will be easy... (when they have been first properly defined according to our designed and implemented method), and to place the items and pieces belonging there, as I have begun to do, according to the year.[56]

Within each *Konvolut* and its numbered subdivisions, therefore, Schönbeck imposed chronological order. This approach dovetailed with the policy of annual deliveries from the Secret Council's chancellery, which meant that new material arrived in the year after each file had been closed out (though it required considerable labor in the first twenty years of Schönbeck's tenure to arrange all of the older material). When faced by the *bête noir* of early modern archivists – the fact that single documents often referred to multiple matters – Schönbeck was liberal both with cross-references annotated on the documents and with inserted cross-references on separate leaves (known as *Remissorialzettel*) that pointed to material in other *Konvolute* that also pertained to the matter at hand. When Schönbeck was done, the administrative archive contained 62 *Reposituren* and 6,096 *Konvolute*.[57]

Over the span of a generation, Schönbeck turned a mapping system based on physical locations with an alphabetical inventory into a classification system driven by a flexible system of inductively created categories. In parallel, the main finding aid he created after 1658 to describe the accumulated documents (the *Repertorium*, generally called the "Red Books" because of their binding) consisted of an index to the *categories*, with only minimal description of actual documents.[58] Tellingly, Schönbeck also

---

[55] Cited from Klinkenborg, *Geschichte des Geheimes Staatsarchiv*, 53.
[56] GStA PK Sammlung Altfindbücher, M 632, f. 348.
[57] Klinkenborg, *Geschichte des Geheimes Staatsarchiv*, 56–57.
[58] Klinkenborg, *Geschichte des Geheimes Staatsarchiv*, 55–56.

created a pathway for items that could not be assigned to an existing category when received. The tracking registers (discussed next) had an additional category of *Monatssachen* [monthly matters], allowing material to be categorized as *Generalia*; the documents involved were filed in additional *Konvolute* in strict chronological order.[59]

Tracking Document Flows in the Registratur-Bücher *and* Publica-Bücher

By 1660, Schönbeck's labors had produced a classification system with an overall guide to its categories, in which documents were organized (and frequently cross-referenced) according to a flexible system of subcategories reflecting the administrative paperwork of the Secret Council.[60] His other key challenge was to manage the ongoing inflow of files coming from the council every year. Cosmar's history suggests that such deliveries ground to a halt during the war years (perhaps also influenced by the removal of considerable material to Küstrin, Spandau, and other locations.)[61] Once they resumed, Schönbeck decided very early on to begin tracking such deliveries in two separate series of registers he called the *Registratur-Bücher* (for domestic matters) and the *Publica-Bücher* (for foreign affairs). He appears to have understood that the placement of incoming files (which might well contain multiple records) in the still-emerging system of categories he was developing required considerable judgment, and thus needed to be documented. Tracking registers allowed him to quickly locate material he had received, and would guide later archivists seeking particular case files.[62]

At first, each register operated primarily as a chronological list of acquisitions, with notes about where the material had been placed among the *Reposituren* and *Konvolute*.[63] For interterritorial matters, Schönbeck from the outset provided an alphabetical list of the counterparties found

---

[59] It would be interesting to explore the implications of labels such as *Generalia* in Prussia or *Indiferente General* in Spain as diagnostic signs that classification was emerging as a records management approach.

[60] Details from a current search guide detailing the names of the older finding aids: GSta PK, photocopied guide, "Die 'Alte Reposituren'/Registratur- und Publicabücher," received October 21, 2016. See also Kloosterhuis's note at Klinkenborg, *Geschichte des Geheimes Staatsarchiv*, 54 n133.

[61] Cosmar, *Geschichte*, 21.

[62] Klinkenborg, *Geschichte des Geheimes Staatsarchiv*, 56, concludes that Schönbeck created these reception registers so that every search did not involve an entire *Konvolut* (which might be hundreds of bundles) in the repository, but could rather be focused by date, thereby quickly locating a specific location.

[63] Müller and Posner, *Übersicht*, 2–3; Klinkenborg, *Geschichte des Geheimes Staatsarchiv*, 54.

in each year's arrivals. This approach was well suited to negotiations with other rulers, which necessarily involved well-defined interlocutors. For domestic affairs, however, Schönbeck soon abandoned this approach, instead creating separate series of register books for each main Hohenzollern territory, and then further dividing listings according to rubrics and keywords. Further research is necessary to determine exactly how each series of registers operated, though it is clear from Klinkenborg's description that Schönbeck felt free to be quite selective about the items he chose to list. Less important matters from the Secret Council could be placed into a suitable *Konvolut* without being specifically registered in the relevant *Registraturbuch*.[64] It is not certain whether it was the chancellery or Schönbeck and his staff in the archive who actually recorded the annual transfers in the register volumes. Cosmar, writing in 1835, suggested that the books were produced within the Secret Council's chancellery and transferred together with the actual documents each year. Many of them covered more than one year, however, and Schönbeck also referred to them as "Empfangbücher" (books of receipt), which suggests that they were created from the archive's perspective.[65] The important point is that the chancellery and the archive worked together though this shared resource.

Integration of Document Management and Storage

By creating a system of tracking that drew on the classification system found in the *Reposituren* and *Konvolute,* Schönbeck linked his archive as a living collection to the needs and practices of the Secret Council chancellery. Several clues suggest that strong incentives existed for this linkage to grow and deepen. One telling fact is that Schönbeck early on sought to impose a new requirement on the Secret Council's chancellery – namely, that each file the chancellery created should pertain to only one matter or case (*Materie*). He had struggled with many old files and documents that handled several matters, either by cutting up letters and placing the parts in different *Konvolute,* or by creating *Remissorialzettel.* To avoid this labor, Schönbeck argued that it "would be very useful, and namely, that the matters could be held together very precisely [in the archive], which is otherwise impossible without making extracts when a report discusses three, four or more matters."[66] This development is

---

[64] Klinkenborg, *Geschichte des Geheimes Staatsarchiv,* 56–57.
[65] Cosmar, *Geschichte,* 20n20; the term *Empfangbücher* is used in Müller and Posner, *Übersicht,* 3, and in Klinkenborg, *Geschichte des Geheimes Staatsarchiv,* 56.
[66] Klinkenborg, *Geschichte des Geheimes Staatsarchiv,* 59.

significant for later developments, since it led the chancellery to consider the structure of categories embodied in the *Konvolute* when defining what a "matter" was in the first place.[67] Both parties – chancellery and registry/ archive – faced incentives to attune their understanding of state business and the form in which it was recorded to the needs of the other.

This structural relationship helps provide an explanation why the Prussian system created in the mid-seventeenth century showed the ability to evolve and develop, ultimately leading to highly sophisticated document management resting on case-oriented files of material defined by a systematic classification of political business. German archival science calls such a system a *Sachaktenregistratur,* whose operation required a distinct office, the *Registratur,* placed between chancelleries and archive. The *Sachaktenregistratur,* in turn, spurred later archival theories of provenance, to the degree that the entire vocabulary of German archival science to this day is built around the interaction of registries and archives.

Schönbeck himself did not create a *Sachaktenregistratur.* Only deeper study with a strong comparative dimension will reveal how the Berlin system evolved and identify the sources of innovation within the larger Prussian state system (which included many other chancelleries and repositories, both functionally differentiated within Berlin and territorially differentiated beyond). Understanding the Electorate's evolving system for managing political information can contribute to our understanding of how changing governmental, cultural, and social trends made Hohenzollern Berlin a European center of bureaucratic intensification and paper-based governance.[68]

Conclusion

In both late sixteenth-century Simancas and mid-seventeenth-century Berlin, we see dedicated archivists striving to implement ambitious visions of how the material in their care could support the rulers whom they served. They deployed tools that had taken shape in the later Middle Ages to differentiate their treasuries of older charters and make them more transparent and accessible, on the one hand, and to refine their

---

[67] By the late seventeenth century, the Secret Council's chancellery organized documents into files and encoded them according to the categories used to place them in the archive. See Meisner, *Aktenkunde,* 154–55; on the connection between such practices and the emergence of provenance as a principle, see 167–69.

[68] See Menne, "Confession." Jürgen Kloosterhuis (personal communication, October 21, 2016), suggests that regional archives may have been key sites for innovative practices that only slowly penetrated the larger central repositories in Berlin.

ability to identify and track complex assemblages of records about all sorts of state business in newly formalized administrative registries, on the other hand. Working largely without any formal training or published instruction on how to handle the flood of material they confronted, they responded as best they could, with variable degrees of success. The contrast between a system capable of evolution in Berlin, and one that ossified and failed its creators' ambitions in Simancas, is also striking, especially if we consider that Madrid/Simancas and Berlin relied on essentially identical tools and secretarial practices. Clearly, the physical propinquity of Schönbeck the archivist-registrator and the Secret Council he served was important, and missing for Simancas. Equally critical, the coincidences that brought the Berlin archive into a sustained and living relationship with the Prussian state's most important council helped dynamize the Berlin archive in consequential ways.

As the additional case studies in Chapter 12 reveal, secretaries, registrators, and archivists all over Europe faced a new world of government-through-writing after 1500, which they sought to master by specialization of secretarial functions, differentiation of repositories, and adaptation to new understandings of what stored records were good for. Among these new understandings, the use of records for historical (and usually very partisan) public arguments was slowly becoming more salient, although it still remained limited. In the Holy Roman Empire, new legal languages based on Roman law (or at least thought to be based on Roman law) also transformed the utility of diverse records. Elsewhere, the ambitious political agendas of Europe's rulers put a premium on possessing and controlling old records (as in Louis XIV's France). In the eighteenth century, the possibility of concentrated and effective central archives in service to a ruling family (as in Vienna's Haus-, Hof- und Staatsarchiv, founded in the 1740s) and to the national interest (as in Spain's Archivo de Indias, created in the 1780s) added new dimensions to archival practice. The later sixteenth century and seventeenth century represented a pivotal period for all of these developments, as explored further in the next chapter.

12 Registries
Tracking the Business of Governance

Introduction

New ways of using established text technologies to provide access to political knowledge as part of the business of governance emerged in early modern Europe and reached systematic heights in the German lands after 1700. The general term for such approaches is *registry*, which we can define as (1) administrative structures and practices dedicated to (2) managing circulating documents and the information in them, with (3) the documents organized in ways that privilege the internal processes of the producing actors, and (4) intentionally held accessible to support administrative and political decision making by rulers and their agents.[1] Registry focused record-makers' and record-keepers' attention on the process of making and executing decisions rather than on the specific deeds of authorized actors. An early form of registry appeared in the book-form protocols that European cities began creating in the High Middle Ages; it later flourished in the autonomous cities of the early modern Holy Roman Empire.[2] Elsewhere, the typically Austrian form of *Serienaktenregistratur* (serial-file registry) accompanied the growth of the Habsburg bureaucracy and its new forms of record-keeping in the sixteenth century (whose beginnings were analyzed in Chapter 8). The most intensive version of registry emerged later in the north German and Netherlandish *Sachaktenregistratur* (transaction-file registry), whose mature form is sketched in the final section of this chapter. All registries grew out of earlier practices. In Berlin, as we saw, the framework established under Christoph Schönbeck in the mid-seventeenth century appears to have launched a pathway toward the transaction-file registry, though much research remains to be undertaken. Schönbeck's efforts

---

[1] Drawing on Hochedlinger, *Aktenkunde*, 22.

[2] Italian developments, which are not considered here, are discussed in de Vivo, Guidi, and Silvestri, *Fonti*, and de Vivo, Guidi, and Silvestri, *Archivi e archivisti*. Lazzarini, "Records," argues for the importance of new record-keeping methods for political evolution in Renaissance Italy.

reveal how systems of archiving based on pertinence and classification could also establish a framework congenial to process-oriented records management, encouraged in this case by the institutional relationship between the record-using Secret Council and the archive that Schönbeck supervised.

Two defining features link the cases probed in this chapter. First, in each case, secretaries and archivists developed strategies for tracking important records that extended across multiple governing offices and institutions (however imperfect and incomplete the resulting systems may have been in practice). Second, the structure and architecture of these systems centered increasingly not on the content of records or their formal or legal genre, but rather on the records' place in a larger administrative flow by which specific decisions were reached, affairs managed, and governance implemented.

Defining Registry: Information and the Process of Governance in the German Lands

On the surface, the common medieval perception of stored charters as treasuries of proofs remained important in most thinking about archival records well into the seventeenth century. Most political actors, however, were fully aware that chancelleries and their storage spaces contained much more than charters and verdicts. By the early sixteenth century, as we have seen, larger polities from Portugal to Würzburg had set in motion the systematic bureaucratization of their chancelleries, eager to deploy texts both probative and informational, not to mention the sophisticated information management undertaken by the very well-informed regime of Venice.[3] As Cornelia Vismann argues, a distinctive element in this transition was the increased preservation of documents created in the course of business. Citing Weber's dictum that "collecting rather than registering issued documents provided the foundation for the modern age," Vismann highlights the importance of the systematic preservation of internal records. Preserving internal records together with incoming and outgoing documents, among other things, helped stimulate the projects for copybooks, inventorization, and classification discussed in the preceding chapters, confirming that "The sixteenth century ... is 'that important epoch in which the modern filing system arises.'"[4] Files are subordinate parts of larger record-management systems; they are not single documents but gatherings of records

---

[3] On the latter, see de Vivo, *Information and Communication*.
[4] Vismann, *Files*, 91, citing Max Weber and Ahasver von Brandt.

produced in the process of information-based decision making.[5] The meaning of records documented in files, to a much higher degree than for the charters in an *archivum* or cartulary, therefore depends on the architecture of the entire system and its integration into an administrative apparatus.

For all of the imagination displayed and the hard work put in by the archivists of the first generation of systematization in Europe chancelleries – men such as Tomé Lopez, Wilhelm Putsch, or Diego de Ayala – their efforts nevertheless failed to keep up with the growing intensity of public administration by writing, and the associated proliferation of not just documents, but also files, as we have seen in the case of Simancas.[6] Even the chancelleries of smaller polities like Lucerne found it nearly impossible to manage the materials accumulating in their chancelleries and vaults; larger and composite states, despite pouring greater resources into their chancelleries, found it even harder. This was true even though the underlying media technologies and forms changed very little from around 1450 to around 1600 and beyond.[7] Paper quires inscribed by quill pens, pre-bound or post-bound codex volumes, and armoires containing boxes or bundles or records remained the dominant forms and configurations for record-keeping and storage; bound quire or codex inventories, often with alphabetical or topical indexes, provided the main finding tools. Not the writing and finding technologies themselves, but rather the growing intensity with which texts were circulated and deployed in governance – and in consequence, the growing number of records that *mattered* to rulers and their servants – lay behind the predicament of sixteenth- and seventeenth-century archivists.

The clerks responded, as they had before, with intensifications of their own. In ways initially ad hoc, but eventually more consistent across polities as archival personnel became professionalized, archivists adapted their tools to the evolving paper-based process of governance going on around them. The records management systems that they produced and accessed – above all, registries – were vital to this intensification. Registry helped enable the emergence of bureaucratic states across the Continent,

---

[5] Vismann builds on the German term *Akten,* which is not perfectly translated by "files," especially for pre-modern usage. The collective plural *Akten* is central to modern German archival terminology as a fundamental category of preserved documents – in parallel with *Urkunden* [charters] and *Bücher* [books].

[6] Vismann, *Files,* 96–99, is stimulating, although not all of her generalizations hold up on closer examination.

[7] In Miller's formulation, "The German Registry," 47, the emergence of registry represented "not so much an advance in technology as rather a clearer distinction of recordkeeping functions."

and fundamentally shaped the mass bureaucratic documentary regimes of the nineteenth and twentieth centuries.[8]

The German term *Registratur* lies behind the concept of registry at issue here. It is polysemic, applying equally to (1) institutions for records management intermediate between an administrative office and a passive, storage-oriented archive, (2) the bodies of records that such institutions produced, and (3) the management tools and finding aids that such institutions generated.[9] Related etymologically to the ubiquitous term "register" via the professional designation of some chancellery employees beginning around 1500 as *Registrator* (a Latinate word designating an official responsible for producing registers), *Registratur* slowly evolved as a general term for the specialized office that managed documents. Ultimately, *Registratur* also designated one distinct phase in the life of governmental records, in which the registry office supported decision making specifically by tracking information about documents (rather than information about the world).[10] Specifically, German registries in the nineteenth century managed documents from their initial arrival or production in a chancellery as part of a political transaction (framed as a set of bureaucratic steps), and continuing through the completion of the particular transaction, when the documents could move from the registry to inactive archival storage. There, they would be available only with special effort, and might be used for projects unrelated to political decision making, such as historical argument or genealogical research. In Vismann's apt characterization, "Around 1600, registries that hitherto had acted as specially designated keys to specific little treasure boxes start turning into independent agencies that connect records, their users, the chancery personnel. The registry was an interim zone in which circulating records turned into recorded files."[11]

Another way to understand registries is to consider how administrative decision making evolved through the early modern period.[12] Seen schematically, administrative action was increasingly envisioned as commencing with a text that required action, such as a recorded command from the

---

[8] On later developments, see Kafka, "The Demon of Writing"; Milligan, *Making a Modern Archive*; and Moore, *Restoring Order*.

[9] A full definition is provided in the online glossary of the Archivschule Marburg, Germany. The key phrase reads: "räumliche oder funktionelle Institution für die Verwaltung von Schriftgut."

[10] On the evolution of the terms, see Hochedlinger, *Aktenkunde*, 61.

[11] Vismann, *Files*, 97.

[12] Hochedlinger, *Aktenkunde*, 65–98, provides an ideal-typical description of nineteenth-century Prussian *Registratur*; a concise English description appears in Miller, "The German Registry," 50–51. The theoretical implications of the transaction are probed in Miller, "Action, Transaction, and *Vorgang*."

prince, a suit filed by a litigant, a letter from a neighboring ruler, or a petition from a subject. This reliance on texts distinguished early modern administration from other, coexisting governmental processes, such as the play of personalities in a ruler's court and the exercise of force in the countryside (all of which continued as well, of course). For an administrative action, the triggering text ideally generated investigations into the matter and deliberations about the appropriate response on the part of a polity's functionaries (including those meeting as the council of a prince or of a city). This work was supported by a chancellery that provided both proofs and information from past records, and which kept track of the matter's pathway through the decision-making process.[13] Once reached, a decision – for example, to issue or confirm a privilege, to command an expenditure, or to make an appointment – was documented by means of a charter issued to a petitioner, an order sent to other officers, or the production of some other record. When the transaction had come to an end, the complete documentation from beginning to end – a heterogeneous mass that could include incoming petitions or letters, internal memoranda and protocols of deliberations, and copies or registers of outgoing charters or commands – moved from the active chancellery into the archive.[14]

This last step is of particular importance. Many Late Medieval chancelleries had no specific repository for administrative records per se. Their only permanent repository was a treasury or *archivum*, which largely held charters received from higher instances and other founding documents. For lack of alternatives, administrative records remained in their chancelleries, or in ad hoc storerooms, attics, and basements, as we have seen. When the flow of records increased, accompanied by growing expectations that administrative records, too, would be accessible in the future, this created strong incentives to arrange storage space more systematically. Whether in the *Schatzarchiv* that Putsch inventoried in Innsbruck or the castle archive in Simancas, more documents and raised expectations led to the differentiation of record-keeping spaces and the proliferation of document descriptions. Chancellery cabinets, designated storerooms, and external repositories became separated from the *archivum* of charters and gained their own specialized staff.[15] By the early sixteenth century, the officers in charge of chancellery repositories often

---

[13] For a culturally embedded approach that expands the functionalist sketch here, see Sabean, "Village Court Protocols and Memory" and "Peasant Voices and Bureaucratic Texts."

[14] The tendency for documents generated during a single transaction to remain together – what one might call the "genealogy of the pile" – appeared in all chancelleries once they kept administrative as well as probative documents. See Vismann, *Files*, 95.

[15] The dynamics of such differentiation are described in Head, "Configuring European Archives."

held the title of *Registrator* in the German lands, responsible for both immediate registration of charters and management of the entire records preservation operation. The distinction among a chancellery's active records, its local repository, and more distant separate archives often became blurred, as when Johann Waser described archives sprawled across the "chanceries, the council chambers ... a room in the town hall next to the accounting office ... [and] the old boxes in the Fraumün-ster."[16] Over time, however, the differences between different functional zones where records were kept became clearer, especially after they were codified in such works as Georg Aebbtlin's *Anführung Zu der Registratur-Kunst* of 1669.

Increasing differentiation of records storage, growing specialization of the staff responsible for maintaining each space, and growing intensifica-tion of organizational schemes were common phenomena across Europe. Yet the details in each case could be very different within the shared constraints imposed by paper and quill, codex and armoire. No single path led from the conditions of the fourteenth century, through the innovative developments of the fifteenth century to the seventeenth century, to a single solution to the challenges of state record-keeping in the eighteenth century and beyond. Instead, officers struggled to adapt the available tools, reconfiguring and recombining logical, spatial, and technical tools in frequently unstable ways. Lacking a shared literature for exchanging ideas, change was often local, and innovations spread only slowly until later in the seventeenth century, when resources to train and instruct new archivists began to proliferate. The following case studies of diverse approaches to registry serve to demonstrate the range of possibilities, as well as show how early the basic problems were recognized and how long it took to solve them.

Three Versions of Registry in Europe from the High Middle Ages to 1700

Three key aspects distinguished registry from other approaches to keep-ing and preserving records, particularly in an *archivum*. First, registries sought, increasingly, to arrange documents according to the flow of decision making in specific institutions, rather than primarily by their content or form. Second, they undertook to store *all* the records of an office's transactions as that office produced them (thereby generating a provenance before the term had been invented). Third, they were

---

[16] StAZh Kataloge 11, vi.

oriented toward future document flows as well as toward managing recent accumulation. These three features combined in various early modern repositories in different ways. This should not be surprising, since registry depended closely on decision-making practices using documents, which themselves varied substantially by place and time across early modern Europe.

Urban Book-Form Registries

The first case discussed here, the proto-registries in serial codex form that characterized many early modern self-governing cities (*Amtsbuchregistraturen* in German), illustrates this point. City governments were smaller and more collegial than princely states, with the chancellor typically serving as both political actor and administrative manager. In the Late Middle Ages, German imperial cities began recording transactions and decisions in serial book form, developing a plethora of book series as their business on paper expanded. Codex-based record-keeping of this kind fulfills our definitional criteria for registry in many respects, as shown in the research of Ernst Pitz on German cities and in an examination of the registries of the city of Leiden in the Netherlands. When Dutch administrators turned their attention from local towns to the trade of the Indies, they carried with them practices of forming books or series to track information – for example, into the record-keeping of the Dutch East India Company, which developed a culture of record-keeping in which there were many registries but no archives until long after its founding.[17]

Cities were one of the first European institutions after the church to begin systematic record-keeping that extended beyond preserving charters. Long before most noble families established paper-based administrations, cities used paper records to assist in governing their citizens and territories.[18] Although it may not be apparent at first glance, urban record books also embodied many of the characteristics of registry, and their elaboration and continued use provided models for other administrations as well. Urban record books often began as notes on the decisions taken by urban councils. Since such councils typically decided all sorts of matters, and often returned to issues over time,

[17] The VOC cannot be discussed further here. On the slow and late formation of any central archive, see Pennings, "Geschiedenis van het archiefbeheer," NLNA Inventories, 1.04.02, especially 50–57.

[18] General introductions to codex-based administration are provided in Hartmann, "Amtsbücher," 40–52, and Hochedlinger, *Aktenkunde*, 33–37, 231–35.

councilors soon began recording their decisions for future reference. Lacking either a professional staff or institutional models, early notes of this kind often appeared on single leaves of parchment or in small bundles. Very soon, however, the practice of keeping such records moved to a protocol book kept by the council. Unlike other genres of medieval administrative book, therefore, urban record books typically contained highly heterogeneous serial entries memorializing the specific transactions of a particular body of officers, regardless of content.[19]

Significantly, such books were reserved (like the later registries) primarily for the internal use of the council and city.[20] The entries had no formal probative value, after all, at least not outside the city's walls. During the course of the fourteenth century, such special books for recording the council's actions appeared in many cities north of the Alps. These might consist of pre-formed volumes, in which case an orientation to future records was explicit; in other cases, protocols of a council's or a regularly convened assembly's meetings might long be kept in quire form, only being bound in the course of later reorganizations in the sixteenth or seventeenth centuries.[21] With the expanding availability of paper, and with the growing volume of document-based transactions of all kinds on the part of urban administrations (by now often in the hands of professionalized secretaries), the single "council book" (*Ratsbuch*) first might be divided into various rubrics before giving way to multiple series of volumes, each dedicated to a specific kind of transaction or to a specific institutional actor. Such volumes, kept in the chancellery (or chancelleries) of the city and recording different kinds of transaction, constituted an ad hoc registry plan. As described by Josef Hartmann, one series might record legal titles (thus forming a cartulary for the city), another might record dues and taxes from the city's subjects, and yet another the registration of new citizens or the outcomes of trials and investigations by the city's courts. Somewhat later, books recording the documents kept in chancellery and *archivum* emerged – that is, record books of metadata, providing indexes and guides to the city's other documentary holdings.[22] Taken as a corpus, a city's record books formed a de facto registry: They were comprehensive, with space for records of

---

[19] The earliest codex-form registers in kingdoms such as France were also heterogeneous in content, but only because they were ad hoc collections of records and information that their makers hoped would be useful in the future.

[20] Hochedlinger, *Aktenkunde*, 230.

[21] Archival scientists generally exclude books consisting of loose documents bound together from the genre of *Amtsbücher*; see Hochedlinger, *Aktenkunde*, 33.

[22] Hartmann, "Amtsbücher," especially 41–43. Jürgen Kloosterhuis proposes a typology of four categories: books that fixed or codified the law; books recording the internal

all kinds of transactions; records were allocated to different books according the actions and offices of the city, and retained their organization by provenance in the very structure of the codices; and they were intended to provide a past perspective for future decisions, and to record future decisions in space set aside in each book.

Ernst Pitz's classic study of Cologne, Nuremberg, and Lübeck provides a clear genealogy of the emergence of such urban registries in codex form.[23] Particularly in the first two cities, the beginnings of systematic record-keeping coincided with the emergence of legally established corporate communities. In Cologne, the first records were sporadic notes on leaves of parchment that recorded tax and fiscal notes. Later, around 1320, such records began taking the form of folded bundles of parchment leaves – proto-quires – that eventually became regular parchment books. The content of these quires and books was diverse:

> These leaves and books, which at first had been used only to record statutes, by the fourteenth century began including other kinds of record about the complete legal activity of city officers: about changes in the city's property holdings, leasing and sale of the capital [*Pfründen*] that supported officers, lists naming the masters [of guilds] and officers, council decrees affecting the officers, and notes about their operation.[24]

In Nuremberg, the first surviving evidence of urban record-keeping is the *Achtbuch*, a parchment codex established around 1285 to record the names of exiled citizens, but which soon included all sorts of judicial decisions taken by the city council.[25] After the city's autonomy expanded to include lordly authority in 1298, a new volume was created in 1302 to record all sorts of decisions, thereby acting as a "general council and administrative record book."[26] As in Cologne, various additional books were established over time. All took the form of serial entry of internal records by a single office or authority within the city, with the division between books reflecting the emergence of suboffices that specialized in various matters under the general authority of the council. Administrative evolution and the emergence of a segmented registry thus proceeded hand-in-hand.

---

administration of a city; financial account books; and judicial books recording verdicts and outcomes from the arbitrational authority of the city over its members ("freiwillige Gerichtsbarkeit"). See Hochedlinger, *Aktenkunde*, 34, with further types listed on 231.

[23] Pitz, *Schrift- und Aktenwesen*.

[24] Pitz, *Schrift- und Aktenwesen*, 60. On ordinances as a spur to book formation in fourteenth-century Florence, see Tanzini, "Archives."

[25] Pitz, *Schrift- und Aktenwesen*, 159–60. No earlier internal records not in codex form survive.

[26] Pitz, *Schrift- und Aktenwesen*, 161.

Like the Innsbruck copybooks, and like the loose-document registries discussed later in this chapter, urban record books displayed a chronologically distributed pattern of entries: Rather than being created or copied at one time, the pages of an urban record book filled slowly, entry by entry, over a period of years, decades, or even centuries. Even though they occupied the unified form of a codex, therefore, the individual entries constituted separate records. Later on, chancellery staff began creating indexes to such records, or even indexes spanning a number of volumes, as we saw with Lorenz Fries's work in Würzburg. The Würzburg case also reminds us that many domains (not just towns) made use of serial entry books for managing growing bodies of heterogeneous records that they wished to index and track.

Record-book systems of this kind remained the backbone of much urban administration well into the early modern period.[27] Loose documents accumulated as well – often in unmanageable quantities, as we saw in Lucerne and Zurich – but took a secondary role in urban chancelleries' practices until well into the seventeenth century. However, the Late Medieval urban record books differed in one crucial feature from later registries: The entries on their pages referred to specific events or actions (which left traces in various documentary forms), rather than referring primarily to the *documents* that enacted a transaction. That is, information about events still predominated over information about documents.

The city of Leiden, where archivist Jan van Hout reorganized both the storage of records and the production of record books late in the sixteenth century, shows the separation of the two streams of information in the city's records. Van Hout was appointed city secretary (*stadssecretaris*) in 1564 and served until 1609, albeit with a five-year interruption around 1570 when he was in exile. His career coincided with the intense struggles of the war against the region's Habsburg rulers, which eventually led to the establishment of the Dutch Republic in the northern Netherlands. The Low Countries were a center of intensive commercial innovation and political activity even before war broke out in the 1560s. As Eric Ketelaar puts it, "The expanding scope and differentiation of government functions (*overheidstaken*) repeatedly posed new and higher demands on registries and on the accessibility of probative documents about rights and duties owed the sovereign."[28]

Leiden already possessed a Late Medieval *Stedeboek*, a parchment codex with entries based on council actions, as early as 1394.[29] Its table of

---

[27] Hochedlinger, *Aktenkunde*, 231.   [28] Ketelaar, "Jan van Houts 'Registratuer,'" 401.
[29] The *Stedeboek* is Erfgoed Leiden [formerly RA Leiden], Archief secretarie 1253–1575 (SA I), finding aid nr. 501, inv. nr. 84. The notes here rely on the images of the *Stedeboek* available in the Leiden city archive's reading room.

entries, probably created early in the sixteenth century, shows that it was most active before 1475, with sporadic entries being made until 1522. As the *Stedeboek*'s entries dried up, other books of a more specialized nature came to be established, such as the *Keurboeken*, the *Vroedschapsboeken*, and the *Aflezingboeken*, with new volumes added through the sixteenth century.[30] Up to this point, Leiden's urban record books generally resembled those seen all across the region. The city also held a somewhat chaotic collection of material including charters, other documents, and books, all kept in boxes (*Laden*) or on strings (*Coppels*), as was typical at the time. Van Hout created both inventories and alphabetical indexes to these boxes as part of his work, but his main contribution was his reformation of the book-form registers that tracked the city's business.[31] As noted in his expanded charge or *instructie*, issued by the town council in 1580 (which he no doubt helped to draft), van Hout was commanded to preserve drafts of outgoing documents (copies of which were indeed included after 1581 in a series of books labeled *Missiven*[32]) and to see to the "maintenance of good order in the secretaries' office, with a variety of books and gatherings [*copelen*]."[33] Over his long career, van Hout responded to this charge – and to the challenges of war, social change, and impenetrable accumulations of older records – by thoroughly reforming the city's register books, including splitting some series and creating a large number of new series. Of the thirty-nine record books or book series that van Hout named in a 1596 remonstrance to the city council about his pay, he had created twenty-five himself.[34]

---

[30] Ketelaar, "Jan van Houts 'Registratuer,'" 401. The registers (most of which run until van Hout became city secretary in 1564), are cataloged in Erfgoed Leiden, Archief secretarie 1253–1575, a collection whose history is described in Overvoorde and Verburgt, *Archief der secretarie*; a second section of this collection contains the new series established by van Hout after he entered the archive in 1564.

[31] The index and inventories are preserved as Erfgoed Leiden, Archief secretarie 1253–1575, Leiden 501.2 – Archief der Sekretarie, No. 1 and No. 2, respectively. The former is labeled in van Hout's hand as "Register om de stukken van de stadt te vinden in de houwders in 't vertreck."

[32] Two are preserved as Erfgoed Leiden, Archief secretarie 1253–1575, 501a-298, and Erfgoed Leiden, Archief secretarie 1253–1575, 501a-300. Interestingly, each consists of serial copies in full text, without rubrics, keywords, or an index. The copies are in fairly strict chronological order, which suggests they would be accessed primarily by reference to the date of transactions, which appeared in the mayors' and council's journals. The entirely internal character of these copies – intended only for working reference in the chancellery – is reinforced by the fact that the first thirty-two leaves of Missiven A (501a-298) are copied onto the back side of thirty-two copies of a printed proclamation – a frugal use of resources, indeed.

[33] Maanen, *Inventaris van het Stadsarchief*, xxxiv.

[34] The registers are listed and described in detail in Ketelaar, "Jan van Houts 'Registratuer,'" 405–11.

Most notable among his new creations was a new journal of transactions that van Hout established upon his return from exile in 1574, which he entitled "Journal of all the matters of the new mayors, the court, and the council" (*Journael von alle besonges van den nieuwen burgermeesteren, schepenen ende vroetschap*).[35] After a few years, he divided the business recorded in this journal into two new journals, separating the business undertaken by the mayors from judicial business, and thereby establishing the "skeleton of an archive" in Eric Ketelaar's phrase.[36] The *Burgermeesterendachbouc* (Mayors' Journal) and the *Gerechtsdachbouc* (Justice Journal) both began in 1587. R. C. J. van Maanen speculates that the formation of new registers represented van Hout's way of managing the accumulation of various records in bundles (*liassen*).[37] In framing these record books as journals (*dachbouc*), van Hout captured a shift of archival focus from the substance of transactions to the fact that they *were* transactions. As a 1592 ordinance for the operation of the chancellery put it:

First, the secretary shall hold, or have held by his clerks, two journals or day-books, one with the title of *burgermeesteren dach-bouc,* the other with *gerechts-dachbouc,* in which from day to day are recorded all matters taking place or transacted, in which both the actual and the preparatory things should be included, so that we are keeping all those things of which memory must necessarily be preserved; in the latter, all meetings of those on the *Gerechte,* as schout, mayor and aldermen, and in the former, those of the mayors alone.[38]

What an effective chancellery and administration needed, by the late sixteenth century, was to be able to interrogate its own decision-making process for precedents, information, and other perspectives. To assist in such interrogations, van Hout began giving both book-form registers and individual dossiers of material a number, which was used to refer to them in his alphabetical guide to the entire collection.[39] To be sure, many of van Hout's register series remained oriented to specific materials or specific urban committees, in a continuation of older traditions. But his two central journals, recording the business process of the most important urban authorities, reframed the operation of the entire system – and

---

[35] Ketelaar, "Jan van Houts 'Registratuer,'" 405. In addition to these two new series, van Hout created a new *Vroetschapsboek* in 1577, restarting an older *Vroetschapboek* that had run from 1449 to 1574, and various other series.

[36] Ketelaar, "Jan van Houts 'Registratuer,'" 405, describes these two series of journals, echoing § 20 of the Dutch Manual.

[37] Maanen, *Inventaris van het Stadsarchief,* xxxiv.

[38] Transcription provided by Peter Horsman. "Ordonnantie ende onderrichtinge van de ordre ofte geregeltheyt de van nu voortsaen ter secretarije of schrijf-camere deser stadt Leyden zal werden onderhouden ...," printed in 1592.

[39] Maanen, *Inventaris van het Stadsarchief,* xxxvii.

orienting records to processes and documents, rather than to substance, is one key shift that defines a registry. As Ketelaar concludes in his examination of van Hout's 1596 remonstrance, "new administrative and judicial needs were met by 'originative registry.'"[40] The Leiden material makes this shift – a shift that rested not on new materials, medial forms, or techniques, but rather on new ways of deploying well-tested methods – particularly visible.

The Innsbruck Hofregistratur after 1564

A quite different registry system emerged in Innsbruck in 1564, drawing on both local and Viennese antecedents. The rupture in the Austrian Habsburg succession on the death of Ferdinand I in 1564, when his sons divided his realms into three segments, provided the new Tyrolean Archduke Ferdinand II's administrators with the opportunity to transform the tools they knew from Innsbruck, Vienna, and Prague into a new system. The result was a distinctive registry system of great sophistication, the so-called Hofregistratur,[41] which operated without interruption until 1667, and whose principles continued to shape Austrian registry practice into the twentieth century.[42]

The codex-based record-keeping systems and inventories established in Innsbruck during the 1520s, discussed in Chapters 6 and 8, provided one key source of practices for the Hofregistratur. Of vital importance is that Innsbruck registry in the mid-sixteenth century relied on the seriality of the codex not just for its material form, but also for its logic. Like the codex registries of Late Medieval towns, the Innsbruck system incorporated many features of registry as we have defined it, including systematic entry of diverse kinds of record into future-oriented books. The context of an itinerant emperor and archduke communicating constantly with several central chancelleries left a deep mark on Austrian chancellery practice: Each administrative center kept serial records of this

---

[40] Ketelaar, "Jan van Houts 'Registratuer,'" 421 (English abstract).

[41] The loose records and books containing metadata that made up the Hofregistratur had shifting names from the sixteenth to early twentieth centuries (Stolz, "Archiv- und Registraturwesen," 105); this material was later reorganized and described in Beimrohr, Das Tiroler Landesarchiv, 87–88, under the designation: Landesfürstlichen Kanzleien: Oberösterreichisches Hofrat.

[42] Stolz, "Archiv- und Registraturwesen," 107–113, provides information on the system's genesis and early operation. I have worked with the early volumes in the series to examine the indexing principles. TLA Hofregistratur/Hofrat, Journale/Protokolle, Einkommene [sic] Schriften, Series R, vol. 1; Einkommene Schriften, Series K, vol. 25; Konzeptbücher, Series R, vol. 49; Konzeptbücher, Series K, vol. 73 (all from 1564 to 1566).

correspondence as a separate corpus from the record-keeping on local administration. The Innsbruck copybooks represent a particularly well-articulated and -preserved example of the expansion of Late Medieval registers to cover informational records of multiple types.

The new Innsbruck chancellery established in 1565 also drew on Viennese antecedents as it began business. When Ferdinand II acceded to the Tyrol under the terms of his father's will, masses of documents had to be redistributed to reflect the new organization of the Austrian lands. A substantial body of loose documents from Vienna, gathered chronologically into bundles dating from 1528 to 1564 – that is, from the reign of Ferdinand I – found its way to Innsbruck, and may have provided another model for the *Hofregistratur*.[43] The practice of collecting drafts of outgoing documents (*Copeien,* in Habsburg parlance) and originals of incoming reports, petitions, and supplications (*Missiven*) was first described in the Vienna chancellery ordinance of 1526: Several categories of documents were to be gathered monthly into bundles, the ordinance commanded, while the secretaries were to record the details about both textual and oral transactions – that is, metadata – in "memory books" (*Gedenkbücher, Gedächtnisbücher*) for the benefit of later decisions.[44] The surviving traces show that a system for tracking loose records, stored in monthly bundles, had been maturing in Vienna for some time.[45]

On his accession, Archduke Ferdinand II appointed a court chancellor to manage his Tyrolean affairs, who proceeded to found the new court chancellery and *Hofregistratur*.[46] The latter did not cover the entire Innsbruck administration; instead, as its name suggests, it was the registry of Archduke Ferdinand II's own court (*Hof*), whose chancellery

---

[43] Stolz, "Archiv- und Registraturwesen," 105–8, notes that the modern fascicles holding these documents are products of the nineteenth century. The basic unit of storage and management before that time was the monthly bundle, which had a cover sheet on which the series, month, and year were written in large calligraphic script.

[44] Stolz, "Archiv- und Registraturwesen," 105–6. None of these Vienna memory books or the associated protocols survive. Only a codex from 1554 that provides monthly alphabetical *indexes* to keywords for transactions pertaining to the Tyrolean *Vorlände* is still in existence, along with chronologically ordered codices recording correspondence sent from Vienna to Innsbruck in 1562–1563 and 1563–1564.

[45] The terms *Gedenkbuch* and *Gedächtnisbuch* both appear. I rely on Stolz, "Archiv- und Registraturwesen," for the Vienna materials.

[46] Stolz, "Archiv- und Registraturwesen, 107. There is some confusion about this chancellor's identity, since Stolz refers to him once as Franz Wellinger (86) and once as Johann Wellinger (107). Other sources name Johann von Welsberg, from an old Tyrolean noble family, as a key figure in the establishment of the *Hofkanzlei* in 1564. Welsberg traveled on Ferdinand's behalf arranging the collection of documents, such as in Vienna: TLA Hofregistratur/Hofrat, Konzeptbücher (R), vol. 49, fol. 45^r.

communicated with the separate chancelleries for the administration of the *Vorlände*, and with Vienna, Prague, Graz, Milan, and other Habsburg centers.[47] Correspondingly, the documents that circulated through the new *Hofkanzlei* were extremely diverse in nature. They included diplomatic correspondence, correspondence on Habsburg family affairs, commands and reports from the regional administrations, and personal affairs of the archduke and his court, right down to the inspection of some spoiled wine in his Prague cellars.[48]

The system that the new *Hofkanzlei* established to manage loose records shows clearly that the secretaries wanted to know about and have easy access to both every document that reached them (whether from the territorial chancelleries, from subjects, from other Habsburg centers, or from anyone else) and every document sent out in the archduke's name. To achieve this goal, they recombined elements from diplomatic correspondence registers as found in many administrations, from the existing Innsbruck copybook system and from the Viennese system of bundling documents and recording their contents. Unlike the Innsbruck copybooks, into which secretaries *copied* important incoming and outgoing documents, the *Hofregistratur* was built around preserving and accessing the actual documents. Unlike the flexible Viennese *Gedenkbücher*, however, the new journals were organized as strictly chronological protocols that closely mirrored the arrangements of the documents in storage, and that were provided with detailed alphabetical indexes drafted according to Innsbruck practices.

This Innsbruck project clearly was a registry, as the Habsburgs' own designation suggests. It made heterogeneous documents accessible to support decision making, it was organized according to the flow of documents rather than according to their contents, and it was openended and ready for future document flows. At the same time, the continuity of media technologies and decision-making practices that developed as the *Hofregistratur* evolved left deep traces in its organizational logic and practical operation. Notably, the system's reliance on the codex and the technologies that made it so effective (foliation, rubrication, alphabetical indexing) ensured the dominance of linear and chronological order in both the storage of documents and the construction of finding aids (though exceptions to this logic emerged very early in the *Hofregistratur*'s operation). The adaptation of the Viennese bundle-

---

[47] Archduke Ferdinand II (1529–1595) should not be confused with his better-known nephew, Emperor Ferdinand II (1578–1637).

[48] TLA Hofregistratur/Hofrat, Journale/Protokolle, Einkhommne Schriften (K), vol. 25, fol. 15ᵛ.

and-*Gedenkbuch* approach, meanwhile, freed metadata from document texts, allowing the production of denser finding aids for location in the chancellery, with more intensive use of keyword indexes, while the bulky documents could accumulate in separate repositories.

At the heart of the *Hofregistratur* lay an elegant linkage between structures for storage and finding, on the one hand, and processes of registration and management, on the other hand. Both record storage and finding aids, despite the heterogeneous genres of documents they included, fell primarily into two categories – one for political matters, the other for fiscal affairs – which in turn were divided only into incoming and outgoing chronological series. Documents in each of the four resulting series were stored in monthly bundles, with documents placed by the date of their issue.[49] For incoming documents, the Innsbruck *Hofkanzlei* sent the original document to storage once it had been dealt with by the archduke's court, and once it had been journaled and indexed. For outgoing documents, the chancellery's final draft (the *Konzept*) went to storage after the actual emitted charter or letter was complete. As a consequence, adjacent documents in the main series usually had no connection to one another, since only their date determined their position (as had been the case in the Innsbruck serial copybooks that preceded the *Hofregistratur*). The practice of journaling each document by date, meanwhile, meant that entries in the journals mirrored the sequence of the stored records: The journals thus served as a browsable inventory as well as an indexed protocol to the separate documents in storage.

The journals' indexes provided the primary way to access documents for later use. Indexing allowed users to move from a category of action or actor in which they were interested to a document summary, which could reveal what was involved and whether retrieving the document was worthwhile. If it was, the journal, mirroring the repository, provided access to a document's location. The summaries in the journals were concise – typically three to four entries per quarto page in the journals – and occupied only the right-hand section of each page; in the left-hand section, keywords identified the document's main matters and actors. Each journal entry typically had several keywords, chosen by the *Registrator* at the time of initial entry. These provided the primary index entries, though some entries generated additional index entries for the

---

[49] The sorting was according to a *Vermerk* or annotation made by the chancellery's *Registrator*, on the top or back of each document. For incoming documents, the date was that of the document's production, rather than the date it was received in Innsbruck by the chancellery. See Stolz, "Archiv- und Registraturwesen," 108.

names of persons or places involved, or for other noteworthy keywords from the summary. Just beneath each entry was information about where the document was located. In many cases, this information consisted simply of the document's date (sometimes with the abbreviation *GM*, for *Gemeine Missive*), which was sufficient to identify the monthly bundle and position. Other documents had a rubric category identified next to the date; such a rubric meant that the document had been extracted from chronological order and stored instead in special subseries dedicated to specific topics.

Naturally, this entire system did not begin full operation overnight in 1564. The names of the journal volumes, the number of series (originally five, not four), and other details took several years to work out.[50] A few early journal volumes actually carry the title *Gedenkbuch*, used in Vienna since 1526, helping confirm the influence of Vienna practices in establishing the *Hofregistratur*.[51] Once fully established, though, the system operated seamlessly through the reigns of archdukes Ferdinand II and Maximilian III.

It is worth noting how labor-intensive such a registry was. In Innsbruck, every document had to be analyzed, journaled, indexed, and placed in the right sequence. Ferdinand's personal chancery alone employed a dozen men, including a chancellor, four secretaries, and seven scribes, to keep up with this work.[52]

In addition to the costs involved and the challenges of storing the rapidly accumulating bundles, certain features of this system from the outset began undermining its efficiency.[53] The first problem arose from the use of rubrics to separate certain groups of documents from the main series of *gemeine Missiven*, which were ordered chronologically.[54] Although journaled and indexed with the main series, the documents involved were stored as separate groups. Aside from managing the growing complexity of the document bundles associated with this system, the rubrics undermined the coherence of the chronological system. The rubrics themselves were heterogeneous, including domains and places, people, events, areas of governmental action, and others. As Otto Stolz

---

[50] The fifth series, for outgoing general missives, existed only in 1566 and 1567, after which four series of documents and journals continued. See TLA Repertorium B342, 36–37.

[51] Stolz, "Archiv- und Registraturwesen," 109.

[52] Stolz, "Archiv- und Registraturwesen," 85–86.

[53] The travails of the accumulated documents are traced in Beimrohr, "Die Ehemalige Hofregistratur" (manuscript printed in TLA, 1996), TLA Repertorium B 701/1–13.

[54] See Beimrohr, *Tiroler Landesarchiv*, 100; Stolz, "Archiv- und Registraturwesen," 108–9; TLA Repertorium 701/7, 3. There were eventually some 186 special rubrics, according to Beimrohr's careful count.

notes, "These show no signs of a planned and systematic principle of division, but were only chosen from time to time according to need; once they had been established, however, they were preserved."[55] In effect, the material gathered under rubrics formed a second, content-oriented registry, although the quantity of documents that accumulated under different rubrics varied tremendously. The proliferation of unsystematic rubric categories meant that documents became more burdensome to find as well as easier to misfile upon their return to storage. By 1667, the disorder was sufficient that a special adjunct registrator had to draft a new systematic index for the material held under rubrics.[56]

The rigidity of the *Hofregistratur*'s chronological structure and the resulting proliferation of journal volumes became a second obstacle as the system continued in operation. Searching the journals in the 1570s would have been easy, since only a few volumes existed in each series; thirty years later, the same search might involve searching the indexes of forty or more journals in both incoming and outgoing series. Lacking anything like a card catalog, searching grew ever more burdensome as the system continued to operate.[57] Additionally, the Innsbruck *Registratur* had no way to track the documents produced during internal deliberations within the court, which transaction-file systems kept together with related documents in a file (*Akte*).

Even with these shortcomings, the Innsbruck system remains notable for how clearly it separated the management of information from the management of documents. The *Hofregistratur* absolutely depended on systematic indexing – that is, information about information – to allow its users to move from a category to a summary to a document.

The *Hofregistratur* represents an impressive and innovative secretarial product. Building on the codex-based practices they had already developed to manage governance with an itinerant sovereign, the officials in the new Innsbruck *Hofkanzlei* used the opportunity to create a system for managing documents that their archduke and his council could use in the process of governing. This system rested on a strikingly systematic chronological storage of documents, together with coherent metadata in book form that allowed individual loose documents to be located, at least in theory, with great precision. This comprehensive system needed neither new media nor new technologies to operate: The codex, the bundle,

---

[55] Stolz, "Archiv- und Registraturwesen," 109, with a full list of the rubrics on 116.

[56] In particular, there was a tendency for documents from the chronological series to wander into the rubrics, rendering the journal indexes incorrect. On filing problems, see Stolz, "Archiv- und Registraturwesen," 113; on the 1667 reorganization, see 109.

[57] Stolz, "Archiv- und Registraturwesen," 113, confirms this problem.

and the alphabetical index were familiar and well-honed tools in Vienna and Innsbruck, as they were across sixteenth-century Europe.

Emergence of the German Sachakte and Authority File

To complete our discussion of the systematic and interlocking systems of records, repositories, and metadata that constituted registry, we return to the *Sachaktenregistraturen* (transaction-file registries) that emerged in eighteenth-century Brandenburg–Prussia (with parallels across North Germany). To be sure, this system operated in its fully developed form only well after the period studied here, being a product of the enormous expansion of the Prussian state apparatus during the war-filled seventeenth and eighteenth centuries. From the accession of the Great Elector through the traumatic reconstruction of the Prussian state by Chancellor Karl August von Hardenberg and his contemporaries, a great deal of change took place in record-keeping practices. Nevertheless, the particular importance of this case justifies a brief discussion on the basis of the available literature. The Prussian experience of bureaucratization and administrative consolidation, after all, has long been recognized as paradigmatic (whether positively or negatively), and this experience found its echo in the paperwork practices of the *Sachaktenregistratur* with its *Aktenplan, Referenten,* and highly structured regulations. In turn, the ponderous procedures of Prussian bureaucracy became a vital point of reference for analysis and critique of the modern state, from Max Weber to Michel Foucault to the present. Describing the ideal structure of such an institution, therefore, can help highlight the emergent features of earlier registration practices that both embodied and enabled the particular understanding of documents and files that fully developed registry carried out. In the canonical Prussian form of *Sachaktenregistatur*, each ministry operated its own registry of files (*Akten*), in which individual files pertained to specific transactions (*Sachen*), while access to such files took place through a registry office (*Registratur*), until the latter sent them to the central archive for permanent retention.[58]

A nineteenth-century *Registratur* in this ideal sense was a specific office serving a ministry or administrative division – one of several increasingly differentiated spaces and institutions dedicated not simply to preservation, but also to active preparation, management, and routing of information about identifiable cases or disputes. Incoming correspondence of various

---

[58] The following idealized description rests on Miller, "The German Registry"; Vismann, *Files*; Meisner, *Urkunden- und Aktenlehre*; Papritz, "Neuzeitliche Methoden der archivischen Ordnung"; and Hochedlinger, *Aktenkunde*.

kinds came first to the registry, where its arrival was recorded in an appropriate daily journal (*Geschäftstagebuch*) and each item was given a specific tracking number. Each letter was then forwarded, according to a prearranged plan of competence for various matters, to the appropriate office for action or response.[59] Depending on the issue involved and the wishes of the office that handled the resulting business, the registry could also provide older files (*Vorakten*) relevant to the new business. A matter might move through several offices, lead to a recommendation or a set of options presented to a higher council or to the ruler himself or herself, and produce various internal documents in the form of queries, responses, records of past decisions, suggestions from various administrative quarters, and protocols of council discussions. At each stage of circulation (which could involve multiple documents entering the registry and gaining entries in the *Geschäftstagebuch*, each linked to the opening document by its tracking number), officers put annotations on the documents (*Vermerke*) that indicated who had seen it, which steps had been taken, and so forth. Once the relevant authority had made a final action decision, the entire corpus of documents that had accumulated along the way would return to the registry, where it would be organized into an *Akte*, a file, arranged according to explicit rules for file formation. At one extreme, an *Akte* could consist of a single leaf with a brief annotation – for example, when a petition was received and reviewed by a low-level functionary without further action, and returned to the *Registratur*. At the other extreme, a file could grow to hundreds of pages when a complex matter circulated through multiple offices and involved decisions by the highest instances. Nevertheless, in every case, all of the material in a single *Akte* was supposed to relate to a single administrative transaction (a *Sache*), producing the *Sachakte*.

Whether small or large, the *Akte* formed after a decision had been reached (including copies of any outgoing documentary products) received a place in the registry's own repository according to a systematic plan (the *Aktenplan*), which was organized according to state offices and their spheres of action. Placing the matter *ad acta* ("on file") in the registry meant that the entire file remained readily available for consultation; the registry staff provided files on request and tracked who had borrowed them and when they had been returned. To ensure that the registry could provide relevant files to help guide the disposition of new affairs, the staff also compiled alphabetical indexes of people, places, and actions found in the *Akten*. After some predetermined period – usually at

---

[59] Meisner, *Aktenkunde*, 163, scarcely exaggerated when he proclaimed, "Das Geschäftstagebuch ist die Bibel des Registrators."

least a year, as in Schönbeck's Berlin, but often longer – *Akten* were reviewed, and if no longer active, were transferred to the archive (which in the canonical form of *Registratur* was a separate institution). This transfer, we may note, later provided the paradigm of an archival threshold, as the files changed from sources of information to objects of custody. Typically, the *Akten* in the archive preserved the order established in the registry itself, since archives had little staff to undertake any reorganization, nor any reason for doing so. After all, reorganization of the documents that composed the *Akten* would render the registry's indexes invalid. Such transfers of material in its existing order had probably taken place in earlier times in Simancas, as we have seen, and served as the foundation for later theories of provenance as the only legitimate way to organize political archives. Transfers in registry order also ensured that stored records preserved the architecture and functionality of the offices that produced them – a kind of administrative Veronica's veil that turned the archive into a representation of the state that produced the records in the first place. The archive, in this system, served only as a repository of records *no longer in use,* in complete opposition to the medieval *archivum,* whose contents were conceptualized as permanently consequential.

In one way, the German *Registratur* represented a final formalization of the ad hoc collections of administrative material that had begun accumulating in chancelleries across Europe since the fourteenth and fifteenth centuries, separately from the treasury-*archivum* of older charters stored in some sacral location. From the sixteenth to nineteenth centuries, the gradual consolidation of materials from various classified repositories and registries, as well as from the *archivum,* ultimately produced the modern state archive, which contains both probative and administrative materials. Contemplating the fully developed system, Heinrich Otto Meisner, a pioneer in the systematic study of noncharter records (*Akten*), concluded that "The registry is the preliminary stage of the archive."[60]

The emergence of the registry stage as a distinct phase in the life cycle of a record – as cannot be emphasized enough – corresponded closely to new ways of formalizing administration that relied on intensive use of writing to conduct diplomacy and to administer subjects and territories.[61] As the number of matters subject to written tracking, and thus likely to generate written records, expanded, chancelleries began

---

[60] See Meisner, *Aktenkunde,* cited in Hochedlinger, *Aktenkunde,* 61.
[61] This point is stressed throughout the work of Rodríguez de Diego, and is a core argument in Grebe, *Akten.*

managing the resulting corpus more intensively, along the way transforming their previously disordered repositories into a registries and
archives (in the modern sense). Historically, it is nearly impossible to
draw sharp lines between three categories of accumulated records found
in most early modern governance: the records available in the active
space of the chancellery, the records accessible through a registry, and
the records packed away for purely archival (in the sense of "no longer
active") storage and preservation, justified by often vaguely defined
future value or use. In addition, almost all political entities possessed
an *archivum*, whose identity as a treasury set it apart from all three of the
previously described categories, and which usually represented the oldest
and most distinct repository of them all. The four ideal types here found
reflection in many chancelleries, with identifiable collections of records
falling into each category, though others straddled the categories' boundaries. The differentiation and specialization of storage spaces (and, in
parallel, of the associated offices and personnel) drove the transition from
more limited forms of record-keeping found in the Middle Ages to the
more extensive and ambitious systems we have examined.

Another way to understand registry is to note that, at least in its classic
Prussian and Austrian forms, operating a registry involved systematic
separation of information *about* documents from the documents themselves, and promoted the production of distinct metadata about chancellery records. In contrast to early modern schemes of classification,
documents in fully developed registries could *only* be accessed through
carefully designed finding aids such as the *Geschäftstagebuch* (daily business journal) and *Aktenplan* of the Prussian *Sachaktenregistratur,* or the
Einlaufs- and *Auslaufsprotokolle* (entry and exit protocols) of the Austrian
Serienaktenregistratur. Nevertheless, this compilation of metadata continued to be accomplished with tools that would have been familiar to
any fifteenth-century chancellery employee, including the codex, the
chronological or segmented list, and the alphabetical index. This continuity of technologies made it possible for registry to emerge in small
steps and in various ways in different chancelleries.

The idealized sketch presented here – a sketch simultaneously encom-
passing administrative processes and record-keeping practices – highlights the key features of registry, but developed registry was not the
only endpoint of pre-modern archiving in Europe. As a great deal of
current research makes clear, efficient administration was far from the
only concern of early modern political entities and their rulers.[62] Even

---

[62] For example, see Brendecke, *"Arca, Archivillo, Archive."*

when rulers did turn their attention to securing and administering their privileges and powers, the use of documents was only one approach they could deploy. Finally, even when rulers specifically demanded that their chancelleries keep good order among accumulated records, rulers and their agents alike still thought about documents, records, and their authority in multiple ways. Thus, we should view the intensification of records management and the reorientation of document production, tracking, and storage that accompanied registry as only one possible path in the seventeenth century and later, and as a path with many branches, often taken only partially.

Part IV

Rethinking Records in State Archives (1550–)

The intensification of governance and the institutionalization of public authority that characterized much of Europe after the fifteenth century made chancelleries important sites for the exercise of power, just as the changing nature of warfare added emphasis to financial offices. Both chancellors and treasurers, working in tandem, relied increasingly on written records not only to manage resources and to justify their demands on others, but more generally to administer populations and to manage large undertakings, both peaceful and belligerent, on the basis of the detailed written information that flowed into their offices. Building on a repertoire of secretarial practices and tools for managing knowledge that had initially taken shape in the High Middle Ages, they adapted these imaginatively while expanding their use. The availability of new resources, meanwhile, promoted the differentiation of record-keeping functions and the emergence of specialized offices and spaces dedicated to keeping records safe, ordered, and accessible. Although the underlying medial forms that secretaries and registrators employed changed little from 1450 to 1650, the cases explored so far show that archivists of various stripes were well able to recombine and reconfigure them in ways that responded to the demands they faced and to the resources available for carrying out the endless work of preserving and organizing written material for future use. By the seventeenth century, systematic inventorization, classification, and registry were increasingly common, although the exact practices used widely from situation to situation.

The ongoing process of reconfiguring archival tools was driven by pressures both external and internal to the repositories involved. Not only did the expectations of the rulers who sustained and supported chancelleries and registries change, but so did the education of the secretaries, the discourses of law and politics that underlay their efforts to understand present and future needs, and the practices of reading, writing, and organizing knowledge found among scholars and intellectuals, which fed into archival practice as well. In the very long term, new information technologies – especially printing – transformed how all educated individuals read and remembered, though these shifts were slow and subtle enough that their impact on record-keeping practices is not always easy to discern.

Chapter 13 concentrates on how early modern chancelleries understood record-keeping, looking first at the precocious published works of Jacob von Ramingen from the 1560s and 1570s. Ramingen wrote primarily for petty nobles seeking to protect their patrimonies from the archival arsenals of rapacious early modern states. Study of his publications is followed by a case study of the Zurich regime's changing use of records as evidence from about 1550 to 1650. Even though archival discourses continued to valorize proof by authentic instruments, close reading shows that Zurich's authorities used multiple approaches to gathering evidence and arguing with documents in response to their opponents.

Chapter 14 then examines two theoretical approaches to validating the authenticity and the authority of written records that emerged near the end of the seventeenth century. Whereas scholars and philologists in France and the Low Countries turned to each individual document's signs and context to evaluate its authenticity, a group of secretaries in smaller German states developed an explicit legal theory of *ius archivi* (law of archives) that emphasized the provenance of documents, rather than their material and textual characteristics, as key measures of their value. Each school harmonized with the different political environments its authors faced. These two approaches helped differentiate among approaches to record-keeping in a way that foreshadowed the debate over pertinence and provenance that became explicit in the nineteenth century, when archivistics consolidated as a professional discipline.

13 Understanding Records
New Perspectives and New Readings after 1550

Introduction

The case studies in this book so far have explored in detail how practices of storing, ordering, and finding records changed in tandem with broader processes – commonly labeled the "rise of the (early) modern state" or "bureaucratization" – that transformed governance in Europe after the fourteenth century. The larger phenomena are the subject of an enormous literature that has its origins in the mid-nineteenth century, just as early modern forms of dominion were themselves being replaced by the modern mass bureaucratic state. Comparative studies of archival practice can contribute to this larger literature by illuminating one important site among those that made up the early modern state, focusing on the archives that some contemporaries called the very "heart of the state."[1] Only if we understand the early modern machinery of knowledge management – the media, the technologies, and the practices that they informed – will we fully understand how bureaucratization contributed to larger shifts in the way power was exercised.[2] In parallel with an examination of shifting practices, therefore, it is also important to probe the shifting understanding of their work among chancellors, secretaries, registrators, and all the others involved.

This chapter approaches these issues in two ways. First, in a period when archives expanded their scope while the printing of how-to books became more common, it is not surprising that guides to archival management began appearing, though it is noteworthy that such guides appeared relatively late compared to other areas of practice. The first published guide to establishing and maintaining an effective political-legal record-keeping system appeared in 1571, when Jacob von Ramingen authored three works on the new field he called *Registratur*.

---

[1] De Vivo, "Heart of the State."

[2] Two exemplary studies in this direction are Brewer, *The Sinews of Power*, and Soll, *The Information Master*.

Ramingen's thoughts parallel the simultaneous developments in Simancas in a striking way: He recognized the significance of archives as separate offices in service of state knowledge, yet he also remained entangled in the conviction that an archive's primary purpose was to establish patrimonial possession through the documentation of privileges. Ramingen, like his peers, took it for granted that documents should be arranged by their content, but argued for an inductive approach to classification undertaken by an independent office that served other offices such as chancelleries and treasuries. Here, his clear differentiation of administrative functions into distinct but collaborative offices prefigures the practical development we observed in seventeenth-century Berlin. Among other early archival publications, only the works by Ramingen provide any detail about the relationship of archival functions to other offices of government, and about how to arrange collections of charters and other political records. While it cannot be shown that he exerted much direct influence, the themes found in Ramingen's works highlight the practical solutions his contemporaries were beginning to introduce to address the challenges of expanded record-keeping and of administrative bureaucratization.

Contemporary handbooks and manuals provide one way to understand what chancellery specialists thought they were doing; an equally valuable approach involves studying how particular chancelleries gathered, kept, and used written records in practice. This is a very wide topic, however, and such considerations have rarely been the primary focus of research among early modernists, although medievalists have been publishing inspiring models.[3] The last section of this chapter illustrates how such research might proceed and what results it might deliver. The analysis focuses on the way that chancellery officials in Zurich gathered and used testimony about a specific question – namely, the meaning of a treaty they had concluded with their Swiss Catholic confederates in 1531. Over the course of the century from 1550 to 1650, ongoing debate about the treaty provoked several radically different documentary strategies from Zurich as the city sought to protect its Protestant clients from growing Catholic pressure in the region. One key insight of this case, which could extended by similar research across Europe, is that European legal and political culture in this period did not, in fact, provide a consensual and hegemonic understanding of what made a document effective in pursuing a particular cause. Instead, disputing parties continually reinterpreted and reinscribed texts from

---

[3] This is beginning to change; see, for example, Spohnholz, *The Convent*, and Makleff, "Sovereignty."

their archives – in this case, a passage barely a paragraph in length – into new litigational and negotiating contexts, ascribing novel meanings to the same words on the basis of shifting political contexts and hermeneutic strategies. Such ongoing *bricolage* was always possible, given in Europeans' unstable relationships to the texts they made, stored, and used.

Meaning in Archives: Practices and Manuals

The changing documentary landscape after 1550 included new ambitions for the use of records and new institutional loci for their storage and organization – all tied closely to new forms of governance that emphasized writing and that sought to subject many interactions between rulers and their subjects to written routines. To understand these fundamental shifts, it is not enough to examine how records were arranged and described; we must also consider how they were read and deployed in specific contexts. Medievalists following this issue have shown that it would be a mistake to assume that archival documents' primary use was always as evidence in formal court proceedings. Indeed, both the making and the use of documents involved complex social and political constellations, in which political actors might respond as much to the names of parties, signatories, or witnesses (present or absent) or to the visual elaboration and performative presentation of certain documents as to their texts.[4] As the evidence we have confirms, however, archive users in early modern Europe increasingly placed archival documents in the context of other texts, rather than among performative communities, as had more often been the case in earlier centuries, even if they still imagined they were recovering authentic representations of authoritative acts. The growing practical importance of informational documentation and the routinization of dominion through written procedure represented a real, if slow and incomplete, shift in cultural practice.

New orientations tended to concentrate document users' attention on the words and signs they found when retrieving a document from their repositories. Nevertheless, the way that meaning emerged from the consultation of archival documents – re-semiosis, in Thomas Hildbrand's phrasing – continued to be shaped not only by such texts and signs, but also by cultural expectations about documents that their users sustained. Retrieval mechanisms themselves, including archival products such as

---

[4] See Chapters 3 and 5 for additional discussion. Exemplary studies from medieval Switzerland and beyond include Brun, *Schrift*; Hildbrand, *Herrschaft, Schrift und Gedächtnis*; Ketelaar, "Records Out"; Koziol, *Politics of Memory*; Rauschert, *Herrschaft und Schrift*; Teuscher, "Document Collections"; and Teuscher, *Lords' Rights*.

metadata and finding aids, now increasingly shaped how secretaries understood and presented the records they found in their collections. Equally, users' interpretation and deployment of documents always depended on shifting canons of authentication and attribution of authority, which were undergoing fundamental changes. Thus, we can see that archival documents' interpretation remained subject to shifting communicative contexts, but also that readers and users aspired to continuity and stability in their understanding of what they were doing. Taking this approach allows us to avoid both the Scylla of the empirically reliable Rankean archive and the Charybdis of the post-structuralist archive that testifies only to what its users expect to hear. Close attention to *how* documents could generate meaning is therefore essential when considering the ongoing evolution of archives, as the following discussion seeks to demonstrate, first by looking at expectations, then by probing a particular case of documents' use.

One way to understand how early modern Europeans approached the documents accumulating in rulers' repositories is to examine published books that addressed this question. The first printed books discussing record-keeping for lords and other dominions appeared only in the second half of the sixteenth century; in contrast, in many other areas, including the practice of law, "how-to" guides for both specialists and the wider reading public began appearing nearly a century earlier. Jacob von Ramingen published his three works dedicated specifically to the value and practice of *Registratur* beginning in 1571. Only a few other archival manuals were composed before the 1670s – such as Baldessare Bonifacio's essay *De archivis* and Albertino Barisoni's legalistic essay, *De Archivis Commentarius*, probably composed around 1630 but not printed until well into the eighteenth century.[5] To be sure, the absence of printed literature does not mean that no guidance about archival formation and preservation existed. A broad genre of sample-books can be found in archival contexts going far back into the Middle Ages, which mostly provided the proper forms of address and composition for official letters, but which sometimes commented about how to store and organize material. In addition, formal statutes guiding the establishment of chancelleries – *Kanzleiordnungen* in German, where they are particularly abundant and well studied – appeared all over Europe in the sixteenth century. Such statutes often described the duties of specific officers charged with preserving records, and laid down expectations that chancelleries should be able to produce relevant documents when needed for

---

[5] Bonifacius, *De Archivis*; Barisoni, *Albertini Barisonii*. See also Born, "The de Archivis Commentarius" and "Baldessario Bonifacio."

deliberation within the regime.[6] Before Ramingen, however, all such material remained in manuscript and largely confined to the inner circles of administration, excluded from publication since inside knowledge about archival repositories was "not their least treasure, nor their meanest prize."[7]

The genealogy of Ramingen's work helps explain why such printed manuals appeared primarily in Germany, and to a lesser extent in Italy.[8] Ramingen, the son of a secretary and registrator in Württemberg, described his tracts as resting on his father's "method" for restoring the archives of the duchy of Württemberg after 1519.[9] The son continued in the same career, serving the Habsburgs and later the city of Augsburg as registrator and jurisconsult. In the fragmented political terrain of Germany (as in Italy), many opportunities emerged for experts in documentation to assist the possessors of rights and privileges in asserting claims.[10] After all, the larger regional lords such as the house of Württemberg and the Habsburg officials based in Innsbruck were busy intensifying their own record-keeping in the interest of maximizing their own dynastic claims. In turn, lesser lords, towns, and monasteries faced pressure to identify and authenticate their own privileges, and so turned to both local jurists and handbooks for estate management (known as *Hausvaterbücher* or *Libri Oeconomiae*) that advised lesser lordships on all aspects of managing their patrimony.

Ramingen's first publication was exactly in this genre. In 1566, he published a short volume with a lengthy title aimed at this audience: *On the management of a regime's lands and people, and then of real estate and its rights and benefits.*[11] The petty lords and small towns targeted by this work lived and died on a complex legal and social terrain defined by the

---

[6] A brief overview with dates appears in "Kanzleiordnung, Kanzeleienordnung," *Deutsches Rechtswörterbuch* online. Further discussion of many cases is found in Silagi, *Landesherrlichen Kanzleien.*

[7] Ramingen, *Summarischer Bericht*, a iii[r].

[8] Lodolini, "Giurisprudenza," provides a comprehensive oversight of early works on the theory and operation of archives on 7–9, with works listed in n2.

[9] Biographical information on Ramingen is fragmentary and confusing, with varying life dates because of the several related individuals with this name (Bernhardt, *Die Zentralbehörden*, 2:545; Jenny, "Von Schreiber zu Ritter"). The author of the works discussed here lived from 1510 until after 1582. His father, now referred to as Jacob Schreiber, was city secretary of Stuttgart until 1519, and then served the Habsburgs as archivist when they seized the Duchy of Württemberg that year.

[10] The emergence of professionals who were available to organize an institution's records began very informally in the sixteenth and seventeenth centuries, but became a critical feature of nonstate archives after about 1700. See especially Friedrich, "The Rise of Archival Consciousness."

[11] Ramingen, *Von der Haushaltung.*

intersection of feudal law, administrative and legal pressure from greater lords, and contention with litigious subjects and peers. What Ramingen offered them in his works was access to the archival techniques that great lords had been developing for several generations and were now deploying against them.[12] Ramingen's three subsequent publications in 1571 offered specific help to this audience. The first addressed *Renovatur* – that is, the reorganization of domains and their privileges and boundaries; the second covered *Registratur* – that is, the documentation of privileges and the establishment of a functional archive; while the third went into further detail about how to configure a proper *Registratur* in support of a particular domain.[13]

A fundamental focus on patrimonial possession, and thus on documents as legal proofs to be kept in a treasury, is one dimension of Ramingen's work. The other, quite contrasting position found in these publications is a deep appreciation of record-keeping not as an incidental and passive function, but as a distinct and autonomous necessity for effective governance (typically called *gute Policey* in early modern Germany).[14] This juxtaposition of perspectives makes Ramingen's work particularly interesting, since it so closely matches the similar tensions between the patrimonial treasuries and the flexible, efficiently staffed information managers that we have seen in practice in most of the early modern cases discussed so far. Thanks to his own extensive experience and his father's *methodo,* Ramingen understood that the effective storage and recovery of records required both a theoretical perspective and practical methods. Consequently, he was able to articulate current understandings of archives more clearly than any other contemporary. His work also helps illustrate how bureaucratic logic and impulses could hatch from the needs of neo-feudal law and patrimonial administration in a way significant well beyond the sphere of archival studies.

Ramingen begins his preface to *Von der Registratur* by asking, "What could be more necessary for a lord ... than an artful, diligent and legally valid renovation of his regalia and goods, and the privileges and titles that

---

[12] A vivid portrait of such a lesser dynasty and the records it could produce appears in Bastress-Dukehart, *The Zimmern Chronicle.*

[13] Ramingen repeatedly stresses that Renovatur and Registratur are closely and inherently connected. His three works are (1) *Der rechten künstlichen Renouatur,* which was published as with an extract from Paris de Puteo's late fifteenth-century work on documenting feudal law claims, under the title *Praxis et forma, Renovationis seu Reintegrationis,* making the connection to noble patrimonial issues visible; (2) *Von der Registratur;* and (3) *Wie es mit einer künstlichen und volkomnen Registratur Ein gestalt.*

[14] For an overview see Iseli, *Gute Policey.*

Figure 13.1 Textual graphic by Jacob von Ramingen showing the relationship between a registry, the records it holds, and the domain it serves. This visual representation is accompanied on the same page with more detailed definitions in Latin and then German, flagged by a marginal rubric. From Jacob von Ramingen, *Von der Registratur*, Bayrische Staatsbibliothek München, VD16 R 194, folio A iv[v]. Detail from the digital signature urn:nbn:de:bvb:12-bsb00010487–9.
Reproduced by permission of the Bayerische Staatsbibliothek, Munich, Germany.

pertain to them?"[15] The solution he proposes is registry (*Registratur*). By this term, he means not simply the safe storage and inventorization of titles, but rather the creation of a specific functional office with expert staff that will manage this process for all of a domain's documents and records:

> … namely, that his domain's or lordship's *districts, jurisdictions* and other *regalia* and legal claims [*herrligkeiten*], Item his real property, *domains, servitudes* and *yields* [*proventus*] and his other rights and claims and titles, should be over the course of time diligently searched out, investigated, and analyzed in detail; and then the results of such investigation and discussion *combined* and brought artfully, wisely and skillfully into a *corpus with its members, and their partitions and appropriate necessities*, and then described in an orderly and legal way; and finally that for eternal memory and testimony, authenticated instruments and trustworthy books should be compiled.[16]

Ramingen laid out the relationship he envisioned between a registry and the records it managed in a striking textual graphic that appears in *Von der Registratur* (Figure 13.1). "Our registry," it states, is the "administrator and custodian of the oversight or index of the instruments and other documents and monuments, and the repertory of commentaries and arguments, of any domain, regime, or magistracy."

---

[15] *Von der Registratur*, fol. iii[r], in his typically macaronic German-Latin prose: "Was ist einem Herrn / *quo ad Iura atque bona sua* notwendigers / dann eine gute künstliche / fleissige und rechtmessige Renouatur seiner Regalien und güter / und derselben zugehörigen Rechten und Gerechtigkeiten/."

[16] Ramingen, *Von der Registratur*, fol. iii[r-v].

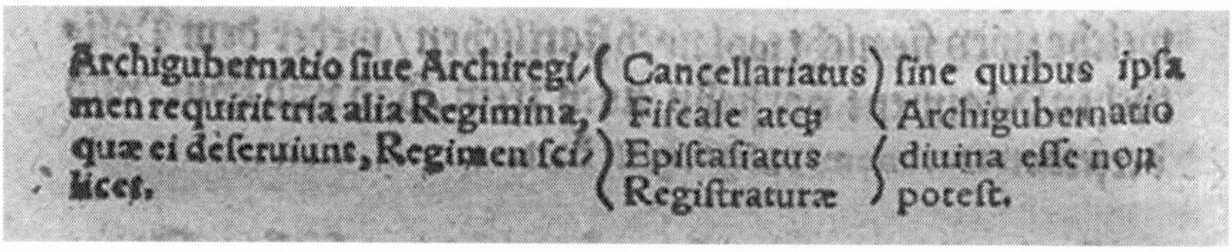

Figure 13.2 Textual graphic showing the "three offices" that Ramingen argued were necessary for every sovereign domain (middle column): a chancellery, a treasury, and a registry, "without which such a supreme government cannot be admirable [*divina esse non potest*]." Ramingen, *Von der Registratur*, Bayrische Staatsbibliothek München, VD16 R 194, folio A iii^v. Detail from the digital signature urn:nbn:de: bvb:12-bsb00010487–9.

Reproduced by permission of the Bayerische Staatsbibliothek, Munich, Germany.

Given these ambitious goals, Ramingen insists that a *Registratur* must be "an office [*Regiment*] that not only serves other offices, but that other offices look to, yea, must look to, according to what they rule over."[17] He thus foreshadows modern archival usage in seeing an archive as a place that comprises the physical fabric of rooms and the collection it contains, as well as the institution and authority that maintains and preserves these. His claims in this area are novel and extensive, considering that in most European states of the time, the functions of registering and preserving old records were subsumed under the chancellery rather than being conceptualized as a separate arm of the state. Only in Spain had the crown moved to create an entirely separate institution for record preservation, and only in 1562 had Philip II finally assigned a secretary specifically to the task of receiving, organizing, and preserving the material that had been accumulating in Simancas castle for a generation, thus separating it conclusively from the royal chancellery in Madrid. Ramingen provides another textual graphic about his "third office" of registry that emphasizes how bold his argument is (Figure 13.2). In it, Ramingen expresses in theory what was beginning to happen in practice, albeit haphazardly. A state's archive should be a separate and vital part of successful administration, he claimed, one that worked with, rather than under, other emerging administrative centers in the chancelleries and treasury.

In his *Von der Registratur*, Ramingen lays out the interior organization of a *Registratur* in broad strokes, dividing it into the *carthophilatium*, which is the actual repository and its contents, and the *tabularium*, which consists of "those books that contain the tenor and arguments, and also

---

[17]   *Von der Registratur*, fol. B i^r.

notes and deliberations about charters."[18] In his *Summarischer Bericht,* he provides additional detail to describe the subdivision of records and their places of storage, using the common Scholastic vocabulary of *partes, membra, classes,* and *stationes* that we have seen, with variations, in other cases. He advised separating matters directly pertaining to the lord from matters from or about his subjects and from outside his domains, and insisted that treasury affairs should have their own subdivision of the repository.[19] Significantly, however, he explicitly refused to go into any greater detail:

> In this situation neither the order nor the scale can be prescribed, nor even less any specific examples and forms be given or precise labels and diagrams be provided. It is daily usage, just as daily praxis, as well as visual inspection and the decisions of those who need to make registers, that provides instruction and teaches these matters.[20]

Again anticipating later developments in archival theory, Ramingen clearly saw that each registry's system of classification and categories, as embodied in divisions and subdivisions of its storage spaces, had to be created inductively on the part of those responsible for making the collection accessible. His perception corresponds to the inductive approach adopted and refined by Zernitz and especially Schönbeck in the Berlin secret archive, which in fact follows the prescriptions found in Ramingen to a surprising degree. Notably, the Berlin archive as it evolved after the 1610s constituted a separate office, parallel and connected to the chancellery of the Secret Council. Additionally, its staff started from a few basic classification techniques, which they deployed to create an inductively based set of categories that were then recorded in inventories, registers, and other finding aids (though never to the detailed degree that Ramingen suggested would be ideal).

Unfortunately, evidence is lacking as to whether Zernitz, Schönbeck, or indeed any seventeenth-century German chancellery personnel were familiar with Ramingen's work. The three booklets were printed only once in 1571, after which they found occasional citation in juristic works; they are not mentioned, to my knowledge, by working chancellery secretaries or archivists in Berlin or anywhere else. Eventually, they became an important foundation for Georg Aebbtlin's 1669 *Anführung zu der Registratur Kunst and* were reprinted (along with Aebbtlin's own

---

[18] *Von der Registratur,* fol. B i[r]. Such appropriation of the term *tabularium* for the repository of cartularies and finding aids is noteworthy.

[19] *Summarischer Bericht,* fols. B ii[r-v]. Much of the *Summarischer Bericht* is dedicated to secrecy, the training of secretaries, and other themes.

[20] *Summarischer Bericht,* fol. B ii[v].

work) in Jacob Wencker's 1713 *Apparatus & Instructus Archivorum ex usu nostri temporis,* ensuring their availability to eighteenth-century jurists and archivists. But even in the absence of evidence for their direct influence, Ramingen's essays are important because they lucidly lay out the core perceptions about records and their organization in the late sixteenth century.

As noted previously, Ramingen followed his milieu in continuing to emphasize patrimonial imperatives to secure, identify, and preserve proofs that could be used against rival claimants or higher instances. Even though this patrimonial element was not always conducive to systematic and transparent organization of collected records, as we have already seen in Simancas, it remained a key ideological cornerstone of political record-keeping all the way to the French Revolution – and in transformed ways, well beyond that era. Ramingen's other, more creative insight was organizational. By the mid-sixteenth century, his work shows, the benefits of delegating the preservation and organization of records to a specific institution with the necessary staff and expertise were becoming visible to those working with records in the courts and the public sphere. Although it took another century for archival functions to become fully differentiated from the broader responsibilities of chancelleries (a development that barely took place in smaller domains), the emergence of archives as institutions, rather than treasuries, had already found a strong advocate in 1571.

The lasting influence of patrimonial understandings of records as proofs and archives as treasuries – even as the forms, content, and volume of records that were produced and kept changed in fundamental ways – raises important questions. It behooves us to take seriously secretaries' and archivists' own frequent statements about the importance of finding records in their repositories. Equally, ubiquitous discourses about how proofs could defend honor, possessions, and income clearly framed the work taking place in many chancelleries. The functions of stored records were of real concern for contemporaries, which justifies our close attention to how such functions were carried out (and how and when they failed). Even so, accepting all these premises does not tell us which uses records actually found use in political and legal contestation. The history of records in use is rich, yet anything but transparent. This reality existed alongside the explicit commitments to proof and functionality that we have seen, and it helped shape archival practices as they changed over the centuries.

The question of how records might be read as evidence, and how changing strategies of reading in turn affected archival priorities and practices, requires close examination of specific cases, because each situation was particular and embedded in cultural and social expect-ations that were not stable. Indeed, that interpretive strategies and com-munities *did* change has been fruitfully explored by medievalists since Brian Stock, and is essential to much scholarship on the Renaissance. When looking at legal documents, however, such issues of documentary hermeneutics have been less developed, especially for the early modern period, though important antecedents do exist. Little has been done, for example, to apply insights from the Cambridge School of contextual analysis of political texts (Quentin Skinner, J. G. A. Pocock[21]) to mun-dane charters, treaties, and agreements, and application of new methods from the history of science to legal practice is just beginning. Yet under-standing the fluidity of all textual knowledge and its dependence on local context when texts reemerged from archival silencing deepens our understanding of what took place in chancelleries and in archives as they confronted a changing world.

Records and Political Knowledge in Transition: A Swiss Case Study

The following case study traces diverse approaches to reading documents in Zurich from the 1550s to the 1630s. Specifically, it asks how magis-trates in Zurich collected, read, and deployed detailed evidence about one Swiss subject territory, the Thurgau, in the course of confessional conflicts with fellow members of the Swiss Confederation. How did magistrates seek out testimony from documents or from persons in the course of political and confessional disputes, how did they read the documents they found or created, and what consequences did their strategies have – which are partially revealed in the documents they used in the process? The discussion here will revolve around the meaning of one particular document – the 1531 Peace of Kappel, known as the second *Landfrieden*, which regulated confessional difference, especially in the Confederation's shared subject territories like the Thurgau. This treaty was read in different ways from the early sixteenth to mid-seventeenth centuries, with each mode of reading corresponding to specific information-gathering and information-using practices, both in the world and in the relevant archives.[22]

---

[21] Classic works include Skinner, *The Foundations*; Pocock, *The Ancient Constitution*; and Pocock, *The Machiavellian Moment*. See also Shapiro, *A Culture of Fact*.

[22] The analysis here was originally developed in Head, "Fragmented Dominion, Fragmented Churches," and "Collecting Testimony and Parsing Texts."

The 1531 *Landfrieden* was a pivotal document for post-Reformation Switzerland.[23] After Martin Luther's and Ulrich Zwingli's challenges to the old church spread across the Swiss Confederation in the early 1520s, religious divergence combined with existing political tensions to trigger tumultuous events from 1529 to 1531. Two short civil wars left the Confederation permanently divided between two confessions, the Catholic and the Reformed or Zwinglian. After Zurich's 1531 defeats at the battles of Kappel and Gubel, the thirteen cantons that constituted the Confederation reestablished peace with a treaty that left each canton free to choose either the "true, undoubted Christian faith" of the eight Catholic cantons or the Zwinglian faith of Zurich and its allies.[24] The treaty that established this outcome, the second *Landfrieden* (territorial peace) of Kappel of November 20, 1531, became part of a de facto system of law that rested on alliances and agreements among the Swiss.[25]

The 1531 *Landfrieden* was particularly important for the Thurgau, a district northeast of Zurich that seven of the cantons had seized from the Habsburgs in 1460. Religious change swept through the Thurgau in the 1520s, supported by the local clergy and backed by Zurich, so that by 1531, a substantial majority of the Thurgau population had opted for Protestant worship.[26] The *Landfrieden* that ended the war in 1531, however, mirrored the new dominance of the Catholic cantons in jointly administered territories like the Thurgau. A single paragraph of the treaty about these joint territories protected existing rights of clerical patronage and allowed individual Catholics to practice (and if necessary to reintroduce) their faith in any church. As a concession to Zurich, Protestants also retained the right to public worship where it was already in place. The treaty therefore ensured biconfessionalism, including the sharing of churches between Catholics and the Reformed population.[27] The administration of the Thurgau subjects remained in the hands of the seven ruling cantons, five of which were Catholic.

Disputes over the Thurgau not only affected local religious practice, but also threatened the stability of the Swiss Confederation as a whole. Tension began to increase in the 1580s, and a major religious riot in

---

[23] General background and narrative can be found in Burnett and Campi, *A Companion to the Swiss Reformation*.

[24] The full 1531 text is published in Walder, *Religionsvergleiche des 16. Jahrhunderts*, 6–14.

[25] Meyer, "Die Durchsetzung eidgenössischen Rechts im Thurgau."

[26] See Kägi, *Die Aufnahme der Reformation*, especially 15–106. Straub, *Rechtsgeschichte der Evangelischen Kirchgemeinden*, 90–91, estimates that in 1540, 2,000–3,000 Catholics faced 30,000–40,000 Protestants.

[27] In general, see Hacke, "Zwischen Konflikt und Konsens." On shared churches, see Brüschweiler, *Die landfriedliche Simultanverhältnisse*.

Gachnang in 1610 marked a first peak.[28] In the 1620s, a second major wave of legal disputes broke out when the Abbot of St. Gallen claimed religious authority over his Reformed subjects and their clergy in the Thurgau and nearby Rhine Valley bailiwicks. A conference of the ruling cantons supported the abbot's claims in 1627, encouraged by Catholic gains in the Thirty Years' War, but a five-year legal campaign by Zurich, aided by the stunning turnaround in the empire after the Swedish entry into the war, reversed this decision.[29] Tensions remained high during the 1630s and 1640s, and finally broke out in a short civil war, the First War of Vilmergen, in 1656.

Although the Thurgau's pattern of recurring religious conflict within a stable political framework encouraged extensive litigation, it was only in the early seventeenth century that authorities in Zurich began drawing systematically on the city's archives in support of their positions. During the sixteenth century, debates over the *Landfrieden* had generally referred not to the text of the peace, but rather to the general principles that the *Landfrieden* authorized.[30] Such authorizing use of a document is the first of three ways of using documents that becomes visible. As the magistrates in Zurich sought more specific evidence they could use, two additional strategies emerged after 1600: the collection and documentation of personal testimony about practices in the Thurgau, and close textual parsing of the *Landfrieden's* exact words so as to argue for the city's interpretation. Each of these three modes made use of written records, but in specific and very different ways. Throughout these developments, the 1531 *Landfrieden* remained the essential point of reference. Mentions of it appear constantly in the entire body of documents that survives, from early arbitrations in 1532 right through to the slightly revised third *Landfrieden* issued after the First Vilmergen War of 1656. All sorts of documents buttressed their claims by stating that they were "according to the *Landfrieden*" – even though the meaning of this phrase steadily evolved.[31]

During the sixteenth century, all parties appealed to the *Landfrieden* by claiming that their demands conformed to what the negotiators had agreed in 1531. Such appeals did not refer to the *Landfrieden*'s text, which had long circulated only among a few actors, almost all of them

---

[28] Stösser, *Der Gachnanger Handel 1610.*
[29] Gallati, *Die Eidgenossenschaft*, provides the only analysis of this conflict.
[30] See Head, "Fragmented Dominion."
[31] The common phrase is "nach lut des landtfridens." An early example from 1532 appears in Strickler, *Actensammlung*, 617–18.

outside the Thurgau. In fact, I have identified only one printed version before 1650, and manuscript copies are not abundant, either.[32] The relative scarcity of copies of the *Landfrieden* suggests that for several generations, most of the actors working out the details of confessional coexistence debated the treaty's meaning without needing or being able to know exactly what it said. Partly as a result, many local outcomes violated the actual terms found in the formal text of the accord. For example, Catholic worship was not introduced everywhere there were Catholic individuals, and the division of parish income often reflected local power relations more than the principles laid down in the treaty. In one typical case, the burghers of Frauenfeld, the Thurgau's chief town, announced in 1606 that "We well know what the *Landfrieden* allows us," before proclaiming a list of demands completely unrelated to the applicable section in the *Landfrieden*'s text.[33]

A second way of arguing about the *Landfrieden* emerged in Zurich after 1600. A generation of growing tension within the Confederation had raised the stakes in the legal maneuvering over religious identity and practice.[34] Additionally, clerical lords in the Thurgau began adopting new legal strategies to put pressure on the Reformed population and their clergy.[35] For example, Zurich learned around 1615 that the (Catholic) Bishop of Constance, who appointed many Thurgau pastors, including Reformed ones, had begun demanding the right to inherit from his appointees in accordance with Catholic canon law.[36] Alarmed, Zurich's authorities ordered the pastor of Weinfelden, Hans Jacob Vogel, to visit his colleagues and examine the agreements they had signed with the bishop in exchange for receiving their share of parish incomes. Lacking information in its own poorly organized archives, the city had to appoint an agent to gather records from local actors. The older pastors' contracts contained no clauses about inheritance, it turned out, but the bishop's demands now made them worried about their employment. As similar

---

[32] *Merckliche und warhafftige geschichten von den Schweytzern* … (n.p., 1532) [ZBZ, Z.XVIII.562.7]. Heinrich Bullinger provided the text in his manuscript chronicle of the Reformation, *Reformationsgeschichte*, 3:247–53 (although the text was copied into Bullinger's manuscript in another hand), as did Johannes Salat in his *Reformationschronik*. Salat's chronicle existed only in five or six copies in the Catholic cantons. See Head, "Thinking with the Thurgau." On the circulation of manuscript chronicles, see Schmid, "Die Chronik im Archiv."

[33] StAZH A 263.1, 1606, "Euangelische zu Frowenfeld."

[34] See, in general, Stadler, "Das Zeitalter."   [35] Z'Graggen, *Tyrannenmord*.

[36] It may seem bizarre that a Catholic bishop appointed Protestant clergy, but his medieval proprietary rights (*Eigenkirchenrecht*) had been protected by the 1531 *Landfrieden*. See Reingrabner, "Zur Rechtsgeschichte."

issues became more salient, the lack of internal documents from the Zurich archive after 1620 provoked a search through old documents elsewhere in order to find possibly relevant material.[37]

In the early 1620s, the Abbot of St. Gallen initiated a similar campaign to gain control over the Reformed congregations he ruled under the 1531 *Landfrieden*. The abbot demanded the exclusive right to appoint pastors in various parishes (rather than collaborating with Zurich's Reformed synod) and insisted that his Thurgau subjects had to attend his (Catholic) consistory court for their marriage disputes. Additionally, his bailiffs received instructions to question local subjects about the content of their pastors' preaching. When Zurich objected to the new measures, the seven cantons who shared rule over the area met in 1627 and approved the abbot's new policies, despite Zurich's vociferous insistence that spiritual matters should not be subject to majority votes.[38]

These struggles greatly increased the demand for accurate political knowledge on all sides – about the Thurgau and what had happened there over the previous century, but also about what previous agreements the parties might have made. Naturally, the abbot and his Catholic allies insisted that their measures simply restored the terms of the original *Landfrieden,* which had been suppressed owing to Zurich's Protestant perfidy. Zurich's defense was inconvenienced because the surviving records generally supported the Catholic position, as even the Zurich authorities acknowledged in internal documents. A report from 1627, for example, noted several passages in the *Landfrieden's* text that supported the Catholic view, and additionally lamented that "many particular contracts and agreements about the division of church endowments will be presented, since we often gave up a good deal for the sake of peace, and there is little we can present from the evangelical side."[39]

Lacking useful documents, the Zurich magistrates turned to a different form of evidence about their clients under the abbot's jurisdiction: *testimony* about actual conditions in the Thurgau and Rheintal, which they hoped would prove that the new demands violated customary practices. The pastors whom the Zurich Reformed church provided for congregations in the Thurgau and Rheintal were the most reliable source for such testimony. To counter the abbot's new measures, the city sought testimonials not just about current conditions, but especially about customs established in earlier times under less confessional tension.

---

[37] The relevant documentation is StAZH A 263.   [38] Gallati, *Die Eidgenossenschaft.*
[39] StAZH A 263.1, "Bedencken ... Anno 1627." This report in the city council's papers likely comes from a secular source.

The clerical archives in Zurich contain a questionnaire circulated to Thurgau pastors around 1629; a similar request went to former pastors who had retired back to Zurich's own territory. The questionnaire asked about both current and old practices regarding spiritual jurisdiction over marriages:

with orderly naming of the parties and the dates if possible, whether [the parties] still live in the territory, whether one heard it directly from them or from other people; and in particular, anything about a case that exists in writing should be transmitted in the original, or also in a copy.[40]

The pastors were asked to describe each clerical position and parish, with special attention paid to local documents: "Should a commune have a recess or an agreement about religious matters since the *Landfrieden*, send a transcription."[41]

Eight clerics who had served in the Thurgau between the 1570s and 1620 replied to this urgent request; some described their appointment and installation in detail, even providing original contracts or consulting personal records about events that lay forty years in the past.[42] Many described working conditions that diverged from the bishop's and abbot's recent demands, even as late as 1620, thereby reinforcing Zurich's argument that the abbot's demands represented an improper innovation. Summoning witnesses with experience reaching as far as possible into the past was a normal legal procedure, so it was no great leap to adapt testimony to the political case that Zurich was preparing against its Catholic rivals. However, the Zurich chancellery also edited such testimonials to make them more effective.

For example, one letter purports to be from the village of Almensberg in October 1627. In fact, the letter was drafted on behalf of the village by Zurich's agent, Melchior Goldin in St. Gallen, who commented on one copy:

The honorable lords and delegates from Zurich are graciously asked to regard my little letter, which I composed for the parishioners in Wertbühl, as if I had also done so for those at Almensberg. There was, alas, too little time, otherwise both those from Wertbühl and from Almensberg would have come to St. Gallen, there to compose requests for assistance.

In short, Goldin was putting words in the Almensbergers' mouths. The Zurich chancellery further edited the original letter by replacing incendiary terms like "papist" with "Catholic," and "fallen away" with "converted to

---

[40] StAZH E II 312, 97–100, here 97.   [41] StAZH E II 312, 98.

[42] The letters from former pastors: StAZH A 264.1, #75, 94, 116, 118, 154, 235, 236, 238, and 239. One pastor sent two responses, leading to nine letters total.

Catholicism." A copy of the modified letter then appeared in a dossier of evidence sent to the Swiss Diet that, in due time, moved into the Zurich archive.

The Zurich magistrates' efforts to collect testimony failed, however, when the city's Catholic rivals brought forth the actual text of the 1531 *Landfrieden* and several subsequent arbitration settlements from their own archives, insisting that specific provisions be observed. Zurich's predicament appears in its rivals' reaffirmation of the Abbot of St. Gallen's aggressive new policies:

> Even though our dear confederates from Zurich ... have presented many various documents and persons who for a long time have attended their consistory court, ... nevertheless, these are entirely contrary to the recesses and mandates for the Rheintal from 1532 and since, [and] the main agreement between the subjects in the Thurgau and the Abbot of St. Gallen in 1532 and the one from 1585, and can in no way bring any disadvantage to our or anyone's privileges and jurisdiction according to the *Landfrieden,* the aforementioned recesses, mandates or agreements.[43]

The exact provisions found in documents outweighed later traditions, the Catholics now insisted, making Zurich's carefully collected evidence from the Thurgau useless.

In 1644, facing a new dispute over religious conversion in the Thurgau, the Zurich synod turned to a third approach to the records in their archives: clerical hermeneutics that relied on close, word-by-word examination of texts to reach a result. The synod began by deploring the *Landfrieden*'s openness to improper interpretation: "With regard to this harmful *Landfrieden* the wisdom of this world's children becomes evident, how they can so plausibly turn all words to their own advantage."[44] Nevertheless, the synod also saw an opportunity in the treaty's otherwise problematic openness, and argued that seemingly unfavorable words could be read differently than the Catholics did. At stake were two words found in the second article of the *Landfrieden*, "should" and "may":

> [b] It has also been clearly discussed and decided among us that if there were any parishes, communes or domains in these same jointly ruled territories, by whatever name they might go, that had accepted the new faith and still wish to remain with it, that they may [*mögen*] well do so. [d] Likewise if there were anyone in the aforementioned territories who had not yet rejected the old faith, in secret or in public, that these same [persons] should [*söllent*] also remain with their old faith unmolested and unhated.[45]

---

[43] StAZH A 264.1, November 9, 1630.   [44] StAZH E II 97, 983.
[45] Walder, *Religionsvergleiche*, 8–9.

By the 1640s, the Catholic cantons were insisting that the words "*should also remain with their old faith*" meant that no additional conversions to the Reformed faith after 1531 were permissible in the Thurgau. Such a legal conclusion would have devastated the Reformed majority's position, and quite possibly forced many parishes to return to exclusively Catholic worship.

In an unusual legal brief of 1645, the Zurich church leadership presented a strategy for how the city could get around "the little word 'should,'" even while conceding that "this bond seems to lie pretty hard."[46] The word "should," they argued,

can be interpreted [*ausgelegt*] and understood to be about the faith that they should stay with, or about the form and manner in which they should stay with it, or about both. That it must be taken neither in the first nor last of these, but rather in a middle sense, namely about the mode in which they should stay by their faith, is demonstrated by the additional little word "also."[47]

The brief's mode of argument was exegetical, making use of precise definitions and logical techniques such as syllogisms. In arguing for a general right to introduce Reformed pastors, for example, the authors first established the general proposition that the *Landfrieden* allowed those who had accepted the new faith to stay with it. They then added the minor premise that "faith is understood to mean either confession or practice," but noted that the *Landfrieden* clearly referred to practice, thus reaching their desired conclusion. The clerical character of this document's hermeneutics becomes evident when we compare it to the Zurich council's reception of it. Although the council scribe did record the brief's emphasis on the "little word 'should,'" the complete analysis found no echo in the council's protocol. Rather, after noting that the treaty did not explicitly prohibit conversions to Protestantism, the council concluded that the whole matter came down to equal privileges for both faiths.[48]

For each of the three documentary strategies discussed here, the Zurich magistrates drew documents from the past into the present, thereby performing a kind of re-semiosis. Each strategy had different implications for archives and the documents in them. With the first approach of relying on a shared discourse of what the document meant without actually referring to its text, the main archival consequence was that the material document remained crucial, since its signatures and

---

[46] The presentation is recorded in two documents: one (StAZH E II 97, 983–996) is in the synod's archives, the other (StAZH E I 5 1b, #69a, January 2, 1645) is an apparently contemporary set of notes made by the city council.

[47] StAZH E II 97, 984–85.   [48] StAZH E I 5 1b, #69a.

seals authenticated the agreement reached by past figures of authority. The text recorded what that agreement had been but did not itself serve as a source of authority. This corresponds very well to the widespread medieval and early modern conception of the archive as treasury whose contents consisted of objects with their authenticating signs; the inscribed texts, in this view, served primarily to explain the underlying act. This understanding of a document's force remained potent in Ramingen's discussion and well into the eighteenth century, as revealed by Zurich's demand in 1712, after the Swiss Reformed cantons decisively defeated their Catholic rivals in the Second War of Vilmergen, that Lucerne relinquish the actual charters recording the 1531 *Landfrieden*; once these were in Zurich's possession, the seals were cut off.

Documents that recorded testimony about particulars possessed a different relationship to the archive. The authority of testimony was different from the authority of a charter, since it rested not on signs about its issuers, but on the closeness of the testifier to the conditions he or she described. Moreover, testimonies had to be managed, as the questionnaires to current and retired Reformed pastors demonstrate. The physical documents that resulted – the actual letters from pastors – were secondary to the information they conveyed, and could readily be edited to ensure that they fit Zurich's needs before being incorporated into dossiers of copied documents for later use (though their inclusion implied that the pastors could be called as witness in person). Once the pastors' letters entered the city's archives, they became important primarily as sources of information, which created incentives to improve the archive's organization and finding tools.

Finally, what impact did close textual analysis have on how archives worked? This approach focused attention on a few critical documents, but shifted emphasis from their external form to the authenticity of their transmission, foreshadowing the emergence of the science of diplomatics later in the seventeenth century. Admittedly, a focus on textual authenticity was slow to emerge in Zurich: Even in the early eighteenth century, a major project to copy old charters did not transcribe the originals, but instead translated the Latin ones into French, and the Middle German ones into modern German.[49] Nevertheless, concern for the security of texts as well as for the integrity of documents was growing. For example, in response to Catholic claims in 1631 about past decisions of the Swiss Diet, the Zurich chancellery drew up a table showing that for some recesses, the versions in the Zurich archives differed from what the

---

[49] Schweizer, "Geschichte," 29, 36.

Catholic cantons reported them to say.[50] This raised questions about how trustworthy the record contained in various archives really was. Not by coincidence, Zurich began demanding to have its own scribe present at meetings of the Swiss Diet, rather than relying on a shared scribe (whose appointment had come firmly into the hands of the Catholic majority).[51]

Conclusion

Even while focusing on the tools that chancellery staff and archivists were developing, it is important to recognize that their efforts were pursuing a moving target. The councils and rulers whom they served viewed archival records as sources of information and ammunition in the endless contestations of early modern politics and, in turn, expected flexibility and creativity from their record-keepers. Given the right perspective, they perceived, all sorts of records might provide evidence. But such flexibility in interpretation made the archivist's or registrator's job much harder. It was already challenging to summarize records in finding aids and to place them appropriately for future use when the legal context was stable. When the forensic and polemical uses of documents became more dynamic, indexing became more uncertain.

The fluid interpretive context of early modern documents had a second dimension: When documents were used in novel ways to argue legal or political cases, the question of their authenticity became ever more salient. After all, it was well known that some old documents were fake. The infamous humanist Lorenzo Valla had demonstrated that the Donation of Constantine – which represented itself as a formal charter – could not possibly have been issued in the fourth century, and Josef Scaliger had demolished the putative authenticity of Annius of Viterbo's alleged Etruscan documents. As antiquarian interest in old documents increased in the seventeenth century, the authenticity of a growing body of material came into question, even as the growing influence of Roman law began casting doubt on the legal validity of the many later charters preserved in noble, urban, and monastic archives. By the end of the seventeenth century, not just the interpretation of documents, but also their authenticity and authority, became a burning question for historians and legists alike. Chapter 14 investigates their debates, and the consequences that their conclusions had for European archives and archival science.

---

[50] StAZH A 264.2, #167.   [51] *Handbuch der Schweizer Geschichte*, 699 n119.

14 New Disciplines of Authenticity and Authority
Mabillon's Diplomatics and the Ius Archivi

Introduction

From the Late Middle Ages through the early modern period, the preservation of political documents was profoundly shaped by a nexus linking such documents to notions of proof and legal procedures, and to the political interests of rulers and subjects. As shown in Chapter 13, proof continued to enjoy great salience in this nexus well into the seventeenth century, even as other ways to read and deploy written evidence spread in practice and through the earliest manuals of archival practice. As chancelleries hived off separate registries and archives with their own spaces and staffs, scholars like Aebbtlin and Bonifacio continued to view the *archivum*, the treasury of probative originals, as the record-keeping heart of states. Nevertheless, starting with Ramingen, such authors also recognized that record-keeping should be a separate institutional function of a well-managed domain, carried out by trained professionals with their own resources and spaces.

In the late seventeenth century, the connections among documents, archives, and proof were also changing across European culture as new approaches to interpretation and intensified public polemics began casting doubt on the contents of archives large and small. This chapter traces shifting conceptions about documents' authenticity and authority in the seventeenth and early eighteenth centuries, which ultimately led to radical new hypotheses about Europe's documentary record. Around 1700, I will argue, the traditional *archivum* – already separated from chancellery registries and growing administrative archives of information – began losing the juristic aura that privileged its contents, opening the path for the emergence of the modern heterogeneous archive as a site of political and historical knowledge judged according to different standards in separate disciplines.

Neo-Roman law continued to evolve throughout the early modern period, becoming more explicit in its prescriptions for legal procedure. In parallel with this evolution, but engendering a far more radical transformation of earlier ideas, European thinkers developed new models for how historical evidence could provide reliable facts and convincing interpretations, a process greatly accelerated by the historical debates triggered by the Protestant Reformation.[1] The resulting interactions of legal, administrative, and historical thinking took distinctive forms in the different national traditions, producing a rich tapestry of positions about the reliability of documentary evidence in various contexts. Particularly in the seventeenth century, historical thinking began impinging on a wide variety of disputes that had previously been contested primarily in juridical terms, ranging from the antiquity of monasteries to the authority of crowns. A wave of erudite *bella diplomatica,* "wars over charters," across Europe provoked original thinking as well as extensive collection, editing, and publication of ancient charters in the context of heated political and ecclesiastical conflicts.[2] Contemporary intellectuals rehearsed their interpretive differences in debates over authority and skepticism, which found their high point in the so-called Pyrrhonist debates about the possibility of secure historical knowledge.[3]

Ultimately, one front of the *bella diplomatica* launched a new scholarly discipline, diplomatics. In France and the Low Countries, a dispute over the authenticity of allegedly Merovingian charters set off by the Jesuit Daniel Papenbroeck eventually triggered the publication of a seminal work on how to authenticate old documents, Jean Mabillon's *De re diplomatica* of 1681. Mabillon's book offered an explicit method for distinguishing authentic documents from the past from the many false ones found in the repositories of monasteries, cities, and crowns, and even in the papal archives. Mabillon's approach privileged the close scrutiny of individual documents in comparison with indubitable specimens, of which the *De re diplomatica* provided a wide range. Mabillon made each individual charter or diploma an object of meticulous and deeply informed analysis of its material and textual form by scholars of broad experience, who could judge whether a charter was authentic, a forgery, or a combination of genuine and spurious elements.

---

[1] The literature is extensive; see, among many others, Grafton, *Defenders of the Text*; Grafton, *What Was History?*; Kelley, *Versions of History*; and Kelley, *Faces of History*. On the specific question of proof, see Grafton and Marchand, *Proof and Persuasion*.

[2] On jurisprudence and Humanist historiography, see Kelley, *The Foundations*; Soll, *The Information Master*; Pocock, *The Ancient Constitution*; Shapiro, *A Culture of Fact*; and Hammerstein, *Jus und Historie*.

[3] Völkel, *"Pyrrhonisumus."* For France, see Bertrand, "Du *De Re*," and Quantin, "Reason and Reasonableness." The philosophical side of history writing in this period will not be a primary focus here.

Mabillon's work generated great praise, but also inspired a series of critical responses, among which I will concentrate on the French Jesuit Bartholomé Germon's *De Veteribus Regum Francorum Diplomatibus* of 1703.[4] Mabillon responded to his critics with a "Supplement" to his magnum opus in 1704, which was soon followed by an anonymous French-language dialogue laying out the various participants' positions.[5] Ultimately, Mabillon's writing inspired intellectual and institutional forces that led to a new discipline, diplomatics, which in turn shaped the discipline of history and the evolution of archivistics in the later eighteenth and nineteenth centuries.

After reviewing the debates over Mabillon, the chapter turns to a contemporary, though much less studied, body of German treatises on archival law, the *ius archivi*, that addressed a narrower question: How were judges to decide which documents deserved credence in the many disputes over sovereignty, jurisdiction, and privileges that occupied the courts of the Holy Roman Empire? The authors involved – most notably Ahasver Fritsch, who published his *Tractatus De Iure Archivi et Cancellarie* in 1664 – took a stance in radical opposition to that championed by Mabillon.[6] Not the careful examination of documents by scholars, they thought, but rather the proper categorization of the *archives* where documents were located provided the key determinant of documents' legal status. Some authors in this tradition went so far as to argue that it did not matter whether records were originals or copies, or whether they still had seals or other marks of authenticity, as long as they came from the right sort of archive. This claim – that the institution that possessed a record mattered more than the features of individual documents – resonated powerfully with the practices of emerging states in the seventeenth and eighteenth centuries. It also supported similar views in archivistics as it, too, emerged as a distinct discipline in the eighteenth and particularly nineteenth centuries. The *ius archivi* thus provides an illuminating foil to Mabillon and the canons of European diplomatics as they took shape, and represents a precursor of state knowledge practices up to the present.

---

[4] Germon, *De veteribus regum Francorum diplomatibus*. Another response with great impact was by the English antiquarian George Hickes. See Hiatt, "Diplomatic Arts."

[5] Mabillon, *Librorum de re diplomatica supplementum*; and the *Histoire des contestations*, anonymous but attributed to either Jacques-Philippe Lallemant (c. 1660–1748) or Gilles-Bernard Raguet (1668–1748).

[6] Fritsch, *Tractatus*. The tract is republished in Fritsch's collected works and in Wencker, *Collecta Archivi*, 13–49.

Standards of Proof: Jurists and Historians in the Early Modern Period

The use of documents to provide proof of legally binding acts, especially on the part of rulers who granted privileges to others, was both a constant and a constantly evolving feature of European law and politics. Public law contestation as well as the antiquarian *bella diplomatica* of the seventeenth century faced a major problem, however, since the majority of old documents – particularly the oldest and potentially most significant ones – did not possess a genealogy that would have justified giving them a priori public faith under Europe's burgeoning neo-Roman law.[7] In the first place, many early charters had not been prepared by the agents whom Roman law demanded, though jurists were generally willing to paper over this point by accepting the involvement of official scribes as fulfilling the necessary criteria, and by treating royal archives and their registers as the equivalent of Late Antique *tabularia* or of notarial registers. As Giuseppi Mascardi put it in his much-republished handbook on proofs, "It is established (*statutum*) about instruments that the term includes all public writings, such as public deeds and archived writings."[8] This concession helped spread the umbrella of public faith more broadly, but still left out many older records, especially north of the Alps. This was because, secondly, no European kingdom could demonstrate that either its treasury of charters or its registers had remained under stable custody since Late Antiquity. The organized *archivum* of the kings of France went back only to the twelfth century, and that of the kings of England perhaps to the eleventh century. The shifting dynasties of the Holy Roman Empire meant that neither emissions registers nor stable repositories survived from before the thirteenth century (aside from a few Sicilian registers of Frederick II), while the Castilian Crown's archives had been massively disrupted as late as the fifteenth century.

Instead, many foundational charters and privileges deployed in territorial or juridical disputes – particularly the oldest ones – came from the archives of monasteries, which could not self-evidently claim *publica fides* for their contents. Mascardi worked around this problem by noting the Roman prescription that very old documents could generally be taken to be authentic, especially if the notary and all the witnesses were deceased.[9] Nevertheless, as the *bella diplomatica* of the seventeenth century gained intensity, the problem of authenticating the oldest documents that lacked

---

[7] On *publica fides* ("public faith"), see Chapter 3.   [8] Mascardi, *Conclusiones*, 1:15.
[9] Mascardi, *Conclusiones*, 2:323–24; 2:326–27, discussing whether antiquity in itself lent documents authenticity, which some authorities denied.

both the formal criteria and the custodial history that Roman law required for *publica fides* became a pressing issue.

Jurists' handbooks had long recognized that false *instrumenta* existed. Indeed, the corrupt notary willing to falsify the record was a stock figure in literature, and legal commentaries provided sensible rules that could help courts prevent forged records from gaining undue force. The focus of such rules was particularistic, however, and left to the judges' discretion decisions about which documents to admit. When disputes arose, the signs found within documents, including witness signatures, seals, and the proper textual forms, took on great importance. Physical flaws such as damage or gaps in a document, erasures, or newer writing on an old substrate were sufficient to cast doubt on an instrument's veracity, and judges could rightly suspect a document that claimed to be old but that had only recently been entered in a notary's register, or a papal letter that did not follow the official curial style of composition.[10] In short, medieval civil and canon lawyers possessed a good practical sense of how to distinguish genuine instruments from spurious ones. As the canon law scholar Huguccio of Pisa (†1210) recommended in his treatise, the document should be examined as a whole from as many aspects as possible.[11]

Privileging the Document: Old Charters in Papenbroeck and Mabillon

By the seventeenth century, a fresh approach to the authenticity of old documents – understood increasingly as historical evidence even while retaining their status as proofs – was emerging. More and more charters circulated in published form, both in polemical dossiers and in increasingly systematic histories of kingdoms, domains, and cities. Antiquarians busily collected and published other historical traces, including coins, inscriptions, and chronicles. Meanwhile, erudite scholars like Joseph Scaliger proved in their treatises that philological analysis resting on close observation could decipher complex issues of chronology and events in the past, while also revealing the spuriousness of previously influential texts.[12]

The Jesuits in Douai and later Antwerp who sought to produce a systematic history of the saints of the Catholic church illustrate this

---

[10] Willett, *The Probative Value*, 9–12, 31; Mascardi, *Conclusiones*, 1:285, 2:132–36, and 2:141 (detailed citations in Head, "Documents").

[11] Paraphrased in Clanchy, *From Memory*, 323–24.

[12] Barret-Kriegel, *Jean Mabillon*, 57; on Scaliger, see Grafton, *Joseph Scaliger*.

phenomenon. The *Acta Sanctorum* devised by Jean Bollande (1596–1665) – and still active today – scoured the libraries and archives of Europe for evidence of the saints' lives and deaths, recording their results in a series of massive volumes organized by the church's calendar of saints. Intent on vindicating holiness against Protestant skepticism, the Bollandists were meticulous about the authenticity of the records they collected, so that their *Acta* could stand fast against the heretics.[13] In 1675, during a debate over a charter attributed to the Merovingian king Dagobert, the Bollandist Daniel Papenbroeck published his "Propylaeum Antiquarium," an essay that offered general principles for how to distinguish authentic charters from spurious ones before postulating that a high proportion of the oldest surviving documents in northern Europe were not, in fact, genuine.[14] His method involved the systematic comparison of a charter under review with other specimens whose authenticity was secure.[15] Papenbroeck's "Propylaeum" unleashed a sustained debate, since it pulled the veil of authority away from the vast body of legally foundational charters found across Europe.[16] Its condemnation of old documents and the beloved saints they helped document not only attracted the opprobrium of monastic orders and churches that his argument touched, but also had deeper significance. If Papenbroeck was right, much of the seemingly most ancient record of the church and of Europe's monarchs and princes lacked authenticity.

The most significant response to Papenbroeck's essay was Mabillon's *De re diplomatica,* which appeared in 1681, six years later.[17] The book, a folio volume divided into six books, is dedicated to Jean-Baptiste Colbert, Louis XIV's chief secretary. In the dedication, Mabillon addressed the problem that Papenbroeck's essay had made unavoidable:

> From this a huge confusion has been born: almost entirely false judgments about true instruments, among inane conjectures about false ones; scarcely any reverence of, nor hardly any authority for quite holy documents, unless perhaps on the part of the more impartial and most erudite, who have purged their spirits of the prejudices of the hypercritical.[18]

---

[13] Sawilla, *Antiquarianismus.*

[14] Papenbroeck, "Ad Tomum II Aprilis Propylaeum," i–lii.

[15] It turns out that Papenbroeck's main specimen in the case involved was itself a fabrication; Sickel, *Urkundenlehre,* 33–34.

[16] Zedelmaier, *Der Anfang.*

[17] See the discussion of the book's genesis in Boutier, "Étienne Baluze." Boutier cites a letter from Mabillon to Thierry Ruinart of May 25, 1679, in which Mabillon announces his intention of "une dissertation touchant les chartes pour distinguer les véritables d'avec les fausses. Le Père Pagebrogue [sic], qui en a donné connexture, m'a donné sujet de réfuter les règles qu'il avance que je trouve fausses."

[18] Mabillon, *De re diplomatica,* a ii^r.

Papenbroeck was only one of Mabillon's targets. Another scholar he viewed as serious, though wrong, was the German jurist Hermann Conring. Conring not only suspected many old French royal documents, but also averred, as a Protestant, that monkish forgeries were a significant cause for the many spurious documents now coming to light.[19] On the other side, as Mabillon knew from responses to the Bollandists' work, many clerical traditionalists believed that critical analysis of Early Medieval texts represented a threat to the authority of the Church Fathers, to the narratives found in the medieval chroniclers of the church's growth, and not least to the specific saints and holy genealogies associated with various monasteries and orders.

The *De re diplomatica*, Mabillon's most influential work by far, had several goals. The first was to refute the "hypercritical" position taken by Papenbroeck and others, which dismissed almost all charters from the Merovingian and Carolingian periods as spurious because they were formally defective or because they lacked a reliable custodial history. Mabillon's second goal was to refine the essentially philological method already suggested by Papenbroeck so that it could produce measured distinctions among true and false documents, distinctions that took full account of historical, chronological, numismatic, and material evidence. The great bulk of the *De re diplomatica* was dedicated to this enterprise by providing lengthy discussions of what authentic Merovingian and Carolingian documents should look like, based on Mabillon's decades of studying the originals at St. Denis.

Mabillon made use of the public faith argument when possible for authenticating old documents and for establishing his early document archetypes.[20] He argued that the papal and episcopal archives were indeed public in the sense understood by the law, even for the earliest periods, and that cartularies and polyptychs from them, like original charters from public archives, could therefore convey public faith (Book 1, Chapter 2; Book 3, Chapter 5). Thus, provenance from a public archive remained an important criterion in his assessment of documents, but his main argument was that in the absence of such provenance, philological analysis could also demonstrate which old documents were truly authentic.

Mabillon's method rested on the comparison of documents in *all* of their characteristics, rather than searching for a single feature that could disqualify them (as Papenbroeck did), or for a single type of authentication

---

[19] Many Protestant critics made this accusation. On Conring, see Stolleis, *Hermann Conring.* and Fasolt, "The Limits."

[20] He deals with this question explicitly in *Librorum de re diplomatica supplementum,* 3–4.

that could guarantee them. Seals, signatures, subscriptions, verbal formulae, materials, inks, and hands all received detailed treatment. At the end of Book 3, Mabillon summarized his approach:

2. Great prudence, erudition, and moderation are the most important requirements as one examines old instruments ...
3. One should always judge in favor where the matter is supported by long possession, as the civil and canon laws enjoin.
4. Pronouncements about ancient charters should not rest simply on the writing, or on any single characteristic, but on all of these at once.[21]

Although skeptics objected – George Hickes called Mabillon's work "nothing less than a manual for the defense, rather than the prosecution, of forgeries"[22] – these principles found immediate resonance among scholars, who have expanded and improved Papenbroeck's and Mabillon's comparative method through the discipline of diplomatics ever since.[23]

In his 1704 response to various critics in his *Supplementum*, Mabillon confronted the philosophical and evidentiary problems that his opponents raised.[24] Two key themes emerged in Mabillon's defense of his method: a trust in expertise and a trust in archives. Mabillon began the *Supplementum*, as he had the *De re diplomatica,* by stressing the damage that a hypercritical approach could do: "Those who seek to lessen the faith and authority of old diplomas and instruments, it seems to me, as they introduce a great bane into letters, so they violate and pervert both public and private law."[25] Mabillon insisted that such evils could be avoided by calling on the experience of experts like himself.[26] His critics might claim that no "indubitable" argument could distinguish true from false charters, but Mabillon maintained that the expert could indeed make such a distinction, "just as an experienced goldsmith can often tell true from false gold simply by touch, the painter an original painting from a copy, or a connoisseur of numismatics the genuine from the spurious on a single glance."[27] Rather than the black-and-white world of the jurist, Mabillon here appealed to the subtle judgments of philological experience as sufficient warrant to authenticate ancient documents.

---

[21] Mabillon, *De re diplomatica*, 241.   [22] Cited in Hiatt, "Diplomatic Arts," 364.
[23] Bertrand, "Du *De re*"; Duranti, "Diplomatics."
[24] See Hiatt, "Diplomatic Arts," especially on Hickes; further discussion appears in Head, "Documents."
[25] Mabillon, *Librorum de re diplomatica supplementum,* 1.
[26] Mabillon, *Librorum de re diplomatica supplementum,* 2.
[27] Mabillon, *Librorum de re diplomatica supplementum,* 2. Mabillon here equates diplomatics with the art of connoisseurship, which was also emerging at this time. I thank Bronwen Wilson for bringing this point to my attention.

The second guarantee of authenticity that Mabillon's *Supplementum* invoked was the continuity of archives. Whereas critics sharply distinguished the genuine *archivum* that conferred authenticity from the mere chests held by private actors, Mabillon used the *Supplementum* to further develop the nuanced position he had laid out in the *De re diplomatica*: "First, I deny that false or interpolated instruments are so common in monasteries or churches, as my opponents accuse."[28] Mabillon dedicated an entire section of the *Supplementum* to demonstrating why this was the case, despite the dangers of fire, barbarians, and especially laymen seeking to seize monastic goods. "Our ancestors' care for archives was great, since the entire fortune of families was contained in them," he noted, and he did his best to show that certain monasteries had indeed provided consistent and lasting care for the documents still found in their archives.[29]

Both Mabillon's methods and his conclusions were congenial to a strong monarchy in firm control of its archives. After all, skeptics threatened to undermine royal authority by rendering foundational proofs spurious, while those who defended documents simply because of their antiquity and their presence in archives created obstacles to royal supremacy. Gallican and Jansenist bishops used papal charters in France to argue for their exemption from royal control and taxation, while German jurists, notably those from the Franco-German borderlands, claimed that the privileges found in the archives of sovereign territories in the empire were *eo ipso* valid, making French claims to supersede such privileges in territories seized from the empire more difficult.[30] Mabillon's method, in contrast, made the authenticity of old documents dependent on the expertise of erudite scholars. It comes as no surprise, then, that Louis XIV's powerful secretary Colbert eagerly sought to employ Mabillon, and avidly supported his research trips to the south of France and to the German lands to gather old charters.[31]

In very same years, a parallel discussion with quite different conclusions was taking place in Germany. Even as many German antiquarians took part in the *bella diplomatica*, learning along the way from

---

[28] Mabillon, *Librorum de re diplomatica supplementum*, 2, under the heading "Archivorum quanta cura."

[29] Mabillon, *Librorum de re diplomatica supplementum*, 5. By emphasizing hazards from such "impetigine quorumdam hominum" over the "ignis, barbari, ac tempus edax," Mabillon undermines his critic Germon's claim that papyrus could not possibly last 800 or 1,000 years.

[30] Barret-Kriegel, *Jean Mabillon*, stresses the monk's close connections with Colbert and the French Crown.

[31] Stockinger, "Factualité historique."

Papenbroeck and Mabillon, a separate group of jurists built on the rapid spread of neo-Roman law in Germany to craft an entirely different approach to the authenticity of ancient documents – one that formalized the argument that legal force depended primarily on documents' presence in the archives of legitimate sovereigns.

The Institutional Approach: Ahasver Fritsch and the German *Ius Archivi*

In Germany, old charters played a considerably different and more important role than in France. Rather than a highly centralized monarchy, Germany was governed by a tapestry of semi-sovereign political entities whose interactions with the monarchy – the Holy Roman Emperors – took place to a significant degree in the empire's various courts. Many imperial estates (from great electoral principalities down to locally privileged domains) were clerical, including three of the seven Electorates as well as numerous sees and abbeys; others were urban, enjoying imperial liberty (*Reichsfreiheit*) owing to their fiercely guarded privileges from former lords or past emperors.

Roman law principles had begun gaining traction in the German lands in the fifteenth century, but the complexity of the jurisdictional fabric as well as German and especially Protestant suspicion that the Roman law favored the Habsburg "Roman" emperors slowed and complicated its influence. By the end of the sixteenth century, Roman law served as a default *ius commune,* but applied only when territorial statute or specific privileges did not supersede it. It gained a stronger foothold in universities, where by the seventeenth century it became the cornerstone of legal education.[32]

By 1600, a burgeoning class of university-trained administrators in the various German territories began fitting the complexity of German legal realities into the Roman-law categories they had learned. Widely circulated handbooks such as Veit Ludwig von Seckendorff's *Teutscher Fürsten-Staat,* along with specific guides such as Ramingen's work discussed in Chapter 13, taught them to pay close attention to both instruments and other written forms of information:

It follows from [chancellors'] obligations that in matters of governance they should diligently read, weigh the information and writings or instruments that lie in the princely archives and repositories or which arrive daily in the chancellery

---

[32] Stolleis, *Geschichte des öffentlichen Rechts*; Strauss, *Law*. On the education of jurists in seventeenth-century Germany, see Weber, *Prudentia gubernatoria*.

and are gathered there, and then faithfully report on or produce from them what they contain, and what pertains to the issue at hand.[33]

The states that these men served wrangled constantly in the imperial courts over their borders, privileges, and control of trade and populations. By the late seventeenth century, the formal rules and logical hierarchies of Roman or Romano-German law increasingly dominated in such litigation, including in the rules of evidence and testimony. As Michael Stolleis has noted, German territorial functionaries and judges therefore also produced ever more treatises on law, evidence, and litigation.[34]

Among such treatises, a number of tracts outlined a *ius archivi* that defined proof by archive (*probatio per archivum*) as a method equivalent to the more traditional proofs by witness testimony, instruments, and so forth.[35] An early coherent treatment of the issue appeared in Rutger Ruland's 1604 handbook, *Tractatus de Commissariis*, on the practice of legal delegation as it considered the value of documents from litigants' archives.[36] In 1658, Nicolaus Myler included the *ius archivi* among the regalian rights enjoyed by German imperial territories in his *De Principibus & Statibus Imperii Rom. Germ ... Succincta Delineatio*.[37] Myler defined the *ius archivi* as a set of procedural rules, resting on sovereignty, that guaranteed the legal validity of the instruments found in princely and urban archives. A few years later, Ahasver Fritsch, chancellor of the small county of Schwarzburg-Rudolstadt, published a more ambitious *Tractatus de iure archivi et cancellariae* that reached similar conclusions, but reframed them to further elevate the importance of a document's provenance over most of its physical or textual characteristics.[38] Fritsch drew directly on neo-Roman law in attributing to the *tabellio* – a term that he and other *ius archivi* thinkers unhesitatingly extended to secretarial officials like themselves – a critical role in establishing whether a document was a *publicum instrumentum* that could rightly enjoy public faith.

The *ius archivi* in effect expanded the definitions of certain key terms, beginning with the word "archive" itself, so as to enhance the authority of the princes its authors served. Fritch and his colleagues assimilated modern

---

[33] Seckendorff, *Teutscher Fürsten-Stat* (1660 edition), 58.

[34] Stolleis, *Geschichte des öffentlichen Rechts*, 1:255.

[35] The literature on the German *ius archivi* is limited: Merzbacher, "Ius Archivi"; Schäfer, "Authentizität"; Vogtherr, "Archivtheorie und Archivpraxis"; Friedrich, "Das Alte Reich." Pitz, "Beiträge zur Geschichte," takes a wider perspective. For a non-German context, see Lodolini, "Giurisprudenza."

[36] Ruland, *Tractatus* (1604).   [37] Mylerus, *De Principibus*, 368–72.

[38] On Fritsch, see Vogtherr, "Archivtheorie," 403–4; and "Fritsch, Ahasver," *Allgemeine Deutsche Biographie*, 8: 108–9.

rulers' archives to the *tabularium* of Roman law by deploying the new and potent concept of sovereignty, which promised those rulers possessing it a wide-ranging authority over all legal matters.[39] Fritsch's first step was to define a true archive under the complex conditions of the Holy Roman Empire and, more importantly, to specify who was authorized to maintain one. From Ruland on, these authors traced the etymology of the word "archive" as a depository of public, and therefore authoritative, documents.[40] Not all collections of documents were archives, then, regardless of whether the individual documents found in them were authentic. As Fritsch's contemporary Nicholas Christoph Lyncker put it, "private cabinets [*privata scrinia*] do not merit the name archive, since they lack public faith."[41] Only a magistrate with sovereign authority, these thinkers argued, provided the public faith that transformed mere collections into archives.

This definitional move denied many political authorities' repositories in Germany the status of public archives, as is emphasized by the amount of detail that Fritsch and his colleagues devoted to specifying which magistrates were entitled to maintain an archive. This was a complex question, since sovereignty in the Holy Roman Empire was shared among many political units that coexisted under the empire's umbrella. The second-longest chapter of Fritsch's *Tractatus* discusses specifically "To whom the *ius archivi* applies."[42] Fritsch began by arguing that "jus scilicet imperii"– that is, sovereignty (*superioritas*) or possession of regalia – was the only essential criterion, and spent the next six pages considering various cases.[43] Counts in the empire and imperial cities enjoyed this right, he argued, even if they did not call their chief administrators "chancellors"; so did the Hanseatic towns. In contrast, any city whose laws required approval by a prince was excluded, as were colleges, universities, and – controversially, if not surprisingly for a Protestant – the church.[44] Imperial knights enjoyed the *ius archivi* collectively for their associations, but individual knights lacked it. These fine distinctions

[39] Ruland, *Tractatus*, 177 (pars II, bk. 5, ch. 4), refers to Bodin in his discussion of "Quinam jus archivi habeant." On the legal implications of sovereignty, see Quaritsch, *Souveränität*.

[40] Ruland, *Tractatus*, 139–41 (pars II, bk. 5, ch. 3), "De etymologia & definitione archiui"; Fritsch, *Tractatus*, 15.

[41] Nicolas Lynker, *De Archivo Imperii* (Jena, 1686), reprinted in Wencker, *Collecta*, 82–109, at 85. Among the authorities Lyncker lists is Mabillon's *De re diplomatica*, bk. 3, ch. 5.

[42] Fritsch, *Tractatus*, 19–26.

[43] Fritsch, *Tractatus*, 20. On using the term "superioritas" for sovereignty, see Quaritsch, *Souveränität*, and Merzbacher, "Ius Archivi," 135–38.

[44] Fritsch, *Tractatus*, chap. III, §§ 5–14. Here, Fritsch took the opposite position from Mabillon, who accorded episcopal archives full public authority, and even sought it selectively for monastic archives.

reflected the institutional structure of the empire as a whole, while also creating a landscape dotted with archives whose status could lend their contents the highest legal authority.

Civil law and the commentators of the sixteenth century, as we have seen, had already recognized the *publica fides* of instruments produced from public archives, and thinkers like Mabillon continued to rely on it in the seventeenth century. Since Fritsch and the other theorists of the *ius archivi* were seeking to enhance the archives in the territories they served, they amplified the existing concept of public faith by expanding the range of material that fit under the definition of an instrument. Fritsch began by making sweeping claims for what should be included in an archive:

What has been discussed so far and experience itself make it clear that the necessity and utility of archives is great in any polity. Many have an interest, truly, that the archive be correctly established. For this it is required, among other things, that it be perfect, that is, that in it every type of document and written monument is placed, the memory of which might have any public or private utility.[45]

Fritsch's longest chapter of the *Tractatus,* chapter VII, followed up on these broad claims under the heading "Concerning faith in archival proofs" (*De Archivali Probationis Fide*).

Fritsch began by denying that there was any legal difference between documents that were in themselves public or private, as long as they derived from a public archive. One section of his chapter, echoing a claim already made by Godefroy and Mascardi, simply asserted that "writings divulged from an archive are included among public instruments."[46] Fritsch's next paragraph expanded on the point:

From which we conclude, moreover, that instruments brought by the parties that are found in a public archive and are authentic – even if they are in and of themselves private – are said to take on a public character ... Thus the primary conclusion: documents [*scripturae*] produced from a public archive, even if they might not be public themselves, routinely generate complete confidence, and prove fully.[47]

As Ernst Pitz noted in an important article, this move resolved a major gap in the legitimation of the German states – namely, that their privileges and authority rested largely on medieval sealed charters. These, according to the Roman law belonged among private (not public) documents, so they had limited probative value.[48] By contrast, Fritsch's

---

[45] Fritsch, *Tractatus,* 33.

[46] Fritsch, *Tractatus,* 37. Also see Godefroy, *Praxis civilis,* 1539.

[47] Fritsch, *Tractatus,* 38–39.

[48] Pitz, "Beiträge zur Geschichte," 284 and n30, notes that university jurisconsults generally treated sealed charters as the equivalent of classical private testimony. In

wholesale upgrading of private charters deposited in sovereign archives rewrote the legitimacy of the German princely states that these authors served.

Once the key question of private versus public authority had been resolved, other limitations on the power of various documents could also be overcome. Fritsch and his Strasbourg contemporary Johannes Schilter, whose brief *Probatio per Archivum* laid out specific rules, sought to include as many documents as possible under the umbrella of archival authenticity. Schilter began by dismissing the obvious objection that the contents of sovereign archives could be produced selectively to favor the archive's possessor, with those documents that the sovereign produced receiving privileged treatment simply because of their source. Despite the potential for abuse this practice created, Schilter nevertheless insisted, "It is also a peculiarity of the *ius archivi* that documents out of their own archive provide proof for those who produced them, against the rules of private law."[49] In essence, a sovereign litigant enjoyed unlimited power to deploy his own archive in court, with no requirement that unfavorable documents be produced.

Archival authority could apply even when documents were missing their seals, were copies, or even were just fragments. Fritsch listed a series of authorities who affirmed the question "whether copies found in a public archive, by the power of the archive, possess the same faith as authentic instruments?" In the end, though, he hesitated to allow archival provenance to substitute for all other requirements for authenticity. "Custody and location cannot alone confer greater faith on a writing," he concluded, though like Mabillon, he also asserted that "antiquity itself recommends faith."[50] Schilter was less hesitant: "Finally, the power of proof also extends to transcripts or copies, even if the original no longer exists, as long as its antiquity is agreed on."[51] Fritsch and Schilter concurred, in any event, that "documents produced from an archive require no other extrinsic proof, nor recognition of the seals."[52] Even official documents that circulated privately, or were not preserved in a formal archive, still deserved greater faith than other private

---

contrast, the functionaries of larger and smaller German states favored an aggressive *ius archivi* that could authenticate the charters that secured each principality's privileges and property.

[49] Schilter, "Probatio per Archivum" (an excerpt from a longer work, his *Institutionum Iuris Publici Romano-Germanis tomi duo* of 1696), reprinted in Wencker, *Collecta*, 50–52, here 50–51. Schilter closely follows Myler's argument here.

[50] Fritsch, *Tractatus*, 45–46.   [51] Schilter, "Probatio per Archivum," 51.

[52] Fritsch, *Tractatus*, 48; Schilter, "Probatio per Archivum," 51, uses nearly identical language. On recognition, see Mascardi, *Conclusiones*, 2:326–27.

instruments.[53] Only documents seized by force should have no effect if used as testimony against their rightful possessors, according to these thinkers – a provision equally useful against external rivals and rebellious subjects.

The law of notaries did provide the *ius archivi* thinkers with certain conditions for a true archive's operation if documents produced from it were to enjoy *publica fides*.[54] Myler, for example, required that "an official should preside over the archive," that instruments proffered in court had to be "stored among other authentic documents," and that the officials in charge should validate the documents' authenticity with their signatures.[55] Fritsch, however, leaned toward minimizing these factors' significance:

... the previously listed requirements are not all precisely necessary for public faith in an archive ... Normally, just one of these requirements seems sufficient by itself, that an archive is well maintained in a public place without suspicion by someone who enjoys the *ius archivi*.[56]

Sovereignty was the key, as its umbrella transformed a wide variety of documents in archives into legally untouchable public testimony. In effect, the *ius archivi* replaced the papyrus or parchment *object* to which Mabillon directed so much attention with *institutionalized* records authorized, partly or completely, by the sovereign power of their possessor.

Conclusion

The theory of "proof by archive" laid out by Fritsch and his colleagues undermined the approach taken by the Belgian and French diplomatists on nearly every point. Rather than the document, the repository and its institutional position became key elements in the Germans' amplified law of archival proof. Whereas diplomatists and antiquarians eagerly cataloged seals, subscriptions, and hands, the *ius archivi* actively denied that such material details were essential to the authority of a document from a sovereign archive. Erudite philology took a place in the *ius archivi* in supporting an expansive definition of the archive founded on learned references to Greek and Roman texts, but played only a minor role when it came to scrutinizing either the texts or the material form of actual instruments.

---

[53] Fritsch, *Tractatus*, 49, citing Rutger Ruland among his authorities.
[54] Compare the rules these thinkers cite with Nussdorfer, *Brokers*, 9–31.
[55] Myler, *De Principibus*, 371.   [56] Fritsch, *Tractatus*, 40–41.

Fritsch et al. were familiar with the *bella diplomatica* and the increasingly detailed examinations of individual charters that the combatants in those wars deployed, and they repeatedly cited Mabillon's *De re diplomatica* after its publication. It seems likely that in addition to their parochial concerns, they saw archival proof as an alternative way to negate the crisis of authority that Papenbroeck had unleashed. As Mareike Menne showed recently, German sovereigns systematically made use of principles similar to those articulated in the *ius archivi* after the Thirty Years' War. Brandenburg agents, once their electoral house had gained control of Ravensberg, Mark, Cleves, and Minden, seized or copied the contents of ecclesiastical, university, guild, and town archives, often transporting them to Berlin even while denying their legal validity before the regime's own administrative tribunals.[57] In France, similar strategies of seizure, copying, and above all deauthorization of uncongenial documents were an integral part of Colbert's efforts on behalf of Louis XIV.[58]

Thus, two divergent responses emerged to the technical crisis of documentary authority in the late seventeenth century: a turn to philological examination of individual documents, as proposed by the founders of modern diplomatics, and a turn to authenticating documents primarily through their archival status, which corresponded to the emerging nineteenth-century discipline of archivistics. Each had profound implications for future developments in record-keeping – particularly state record-keeping, though we must recognize that after 1700, changes in state practices and in media technologies and forms played an equal role in further transforming the nature of European archivality.

[57] Menne, "Confession, Confusion, and Rule."   [58] Soll, *The Information Master*.

15 Conclusion
An Era of Chancellery Books and Beyond

Contexts and Outlook

Over the last two decades, historians and archivists have developed new conceptual approaches to archives as historical subjects as well as sites of practice, as institutions of silence and oppression as well as knowledge and trust, and ultimately as human phenomena worthy of investigation and interpretation rather than as handmaidens either to historical research or to administrative governance. As Alexandra Walsham and Filipo de Vivo each make clear in their introductions to recent collections of research contributions, neither historians' previous understanding of archives as their "factories and laboratories" nor classic archival science's definition of archives as the organized records of their creators' business kept in secure, neutral custody are adequate for this new research.[1] The archives we perceive today are the complex products of long development under constantly changing assumptions and conditions, and took shape among multiple circuits of information that included oral, performative, and printed media, and among social contexts that extended far beyond the forensic and administrative to the erudite, familial, and popular. The new archival history's definitions do not signal the end of a field's emergence, however, but only the end of the beginning. Bolstered by enriched approaches to record-keeping and archives, we are now in a position to begin probing record-making and record-keeping more intensively by looking at archives at specific places and times in much greater detail, seeing these resources as historically and temporally situated variants of processes vital to every historical society.

The preceding chapters have taken up this challenge by focusing on early modern European archivality as one particular historical system. The narrative has concentrated on the accumulation of legal and political records in the possession of political authorities in early modern Europe,

---

[1] Walsham, "The Social History," with quotation from 10; de Vivo, Guidi, and Silvestri, "Archival Transformations."

and the strategies that (mostly unnamed) scribes and secretaries used as part of their responsibility for the resulting masses of documents – which we retrospectively call archives. A relatively constrained evidentiary focus has been balanced by a wide comparative and chronological frame: The juxtaposition of cases, I argue, reveals inflection points and highlights both important continuities and significant changes in the practices and meaning of stored political records, thereby raising new questions for other studies both more particular and more comprehensive. The approach here is historical in the disciplinary sense, while drawing wherever possible on the insights of the new archival science, and benefiting beyond that from studies of communication, rhetoric, political sociology, and many other fields. I hope that these results will prove useful not only to historians delving further into archival histories, but also to practitioners in those other disciplines.

In conclusion, I wish to address three major points. The first two are definitional and interlinked. First, the results here demonstrate that Western European archives and record-keeping practices shared enough underlying logic and continuity to be viewed as *one* cultural system from 1400 to 1700. They participated in a single historically inflected pathway (with great internal variation) that depended on shared practices of governance and domination in the same historical space. Yet this European archivality also possesses larger significance because of its contribution to modern conceptual frameworks for the study and use of archives in general, since deprovincializing and rethinking those frameworks for global societies in a digital age will be easier if we understand the historical particularity of their origins.

The specification of a distinctly European archivality leads to the second point – namely, periodization. The epoch at the heart of this book, with inductively reached endpoints of around 1400 and 1700 and a more diffuse but important inflection around 1550, deserves brief reflection. Addressing the major turning points of the early modern period also highlights some key findings of this book, and points toward areas that seem particularly promising for future research.

Third, in light of my identification of the period around 1700 as a significant milestone, the book ends by looking forward, toward developments in the eighteenth century and beyond. In particular, it addresses the emergence of modern archival theory in the nineteenth century – a development that took place in close connection with both new forms of nationalist historiography and the consolidation of mass bureaucratic states across Europe. These three phenomena seem fundamentally linked by previous developments in the state information systems that they all drew on, and that they all transformed.

European Archivality and Its Periodization

Moving from human record-keeping in general to the analysis of one specific historical system of archiving requires considering which features make it a historical case in the first place or, conversely, which assumptions by scholars make this particular assemblage of material treatable as a whole. Human communities have been making and keeping records for a long time, after all, and systematic record-keeping was ubiquitous in hierarchical agrarian societies all around the globe by 1400. If we accept that Europe after its emergence after 1000 forms a reasonable cultural space for the study of record-keeping, we must remember that not only political activity, but also liturgy, literature, and erudition generated voluminous written materials that began accumulating in various ways. The analysis here rests on defining a subset of that broader accumulation as archival – namely, the preservation of records that were created for intentional use as evidence in the future or to provide future information for rulers.[2] The European archival sphere that follows from this definition was shaped, I argue, by European practices of power, authority, and litigation in ways that set it apart from other genres of text and other practices of accumulation. Its features were also repeatedly inflected by phantoms of Roman law and dominion as imagined by European medieval thinkers and as appropriated (or reinvented) in courts, chancelleries, and universities. Of equal significance was the fragmentation of dominion in practice that characterized medieval Europe. A nexus involving an imagined Roman past and law, fragmented political dominion on the ground, and a political economy that rested on the circulation of privileges documented in writing produced medieval Europe's characteristic landscape of archival treasuries, in which legitimating documentary objects were placed among other sacral possessions in many different domains.[3] These circumstances also lie behind Robert-Henri Bautier's periodization, which distinguished earlier palace archives from the treasury-archives of recipients scattered across Europe in the High and Late Middle Ages, and from the administrative document arsenals of the early modern period.

This study focuses further on archival records in the possession of political actors, since we consistently see such authorities after about 1200 seeking control over knowledge as a way to expand their capacity or to defend their autonomy. Emperor Fredrick II (1194–1250) can

---

[2] The definition of an archival sphere in this way is itself a product of the European history under examination here; there is no escaping the reflexivity involved.

[3] Explored in Potin, "Archives" and "Entre trésor."

stand for this development, since he expanded the sophisticated Mediterranean bureaucracy he inherited in Sicily through his relentless curi-
osity for more knowledge about the world, and deployed documents as
well as armies against an equally scriptocentric papacy. Significantly,
although princes' desire to control knowledge took shape in many different ways, success in this environment required the intensification of
writing and the systematization of record-keeping in ways dependent
on law, which was itself evolving to valorize written procedure and
documentary testimony. In this sense, a broad cultural gradient favored
governance through specialists in writing – "bureaucratization," in academic shorthand – which became the basis for the formation of modern
state systems. In Europe, to put it simply, states became states in part
through their relationships with archival repositories and through their
imagination of archival knowledge (even if this was often largely fantasy).

A series of developments in the thirteenth and fourteenth centuries
that increased the value of writing as a tool for power mark the starting
point of this book. One crucial driver of change seems to have been the
acceleration of record-making at every scale, from mundane contracts –
say, to buy a cat in Siena in 1337 – to political contention at the highest
levels. The increased rate of document production was augmented over
the fourteenth century by the arrival of paper as an inexpensive and
durable medium for record-making. We have seen how the accumulation
of records in political centers at different scales – especially princely
chancelleries and urban centers blessed by fiscal strength and access to
literate staff – led them to expand record-keeping beyond their treasuries
in diverse ways. Royal registers and urban protocol books turned records
into informational resources, using methods eagerly drawn from an
ecclesiastical system that was bureaucratizing in the face of heresy, and
from universities that were systematizing knowledge from Antiquity at an
unprecedented scale. Thus, archival knowledge systems evolved as parts
of a culture-wide transformation in the meaning and use of recorded
information. As such, they can be used to diagnose larger patterns and
their consequences.

The work taking place in chancelleries depended on medial forms that
themselves changed very slowly once paper had become readily available.
We can characterize the period from 1400 to 1700 as the era of the
chancellery book. The codex provided a flexible platform for many
different approaches to records, including copying in cartularies, registering in registers, and indexing in inventories. Open to transformative
configurational change without abandoning the underlying form, the
paper or parchment book remained a key tool for political records
management in European chancelleries until the late seventeenth

century, sandwiched between the golden age of parchment charters that preceded it, and the emergence of card- and file-based archiving that followed it.[4] Technological determinism plays no role here: The codex long preceded paper, and cultural and legal shifts in the High Middle Ages lay behind the intertextual understanding of law and administration that emerged, albeit very unevenly, after 1300, rather than the emissions register or the alphabetical index. Equally, the evolution of registries and the eventual deployment of the card-file responded to major changes in governance – notably, the appearance of bureaucratic surveillance states that responded to overwhelming military pressure by cataloging their subjects and resources in obsessive detail – and in culture, as large libraries of print books, printed encyclopedias, and Baroque copiousness coupled with new sciences transformed intellectual culture.

Between the endpoints of 1400 and 1700, an intermediate turning point in archival practice and consciousness seems to occur around 1550, though it is harder to pin down. One clear marker was the appearance of printed books about making archives, which began with Ramingen's 1571 publications. Another might be the revolution in historiographical methods triggered by the Reformation schisms and embodied in the work of the Magdeburg centuriators. By seeking out primary sources for their revised narrative of Christian history, these polemical thinkers gave the old documents piled up in repositories a new layer of potential meaning, and accelerated the trend toward understanding archives as storerooms for historical as well as juridical and political contention. The late sixteenth century then saw the rise of new forms of historiography, embodied in treatises on the *artes historicae*.[5] In the political world, a new approach to archives as part of larger knowledge networks characterized Juan Páez de Castro's famous 1555 memorial to Philip II of Spain. Philip subsequently sought to place his archives into relationships with libraries, collections, and other forms of knowledge. For each repository, a book that synthesized history from the accumulated material belonged to the plan, thereby moving beyond the juridical and familial goals his father had pursued at the founding of Simancas. Philip wanted to be "fully informed" so that he could dominate his rivals and expand his empire; he wanted to govern on the basis of knowledge.[6] Even if each of these ways of connecting chancellery

---

[4] On managing disaggregated information through slips or cards, considering cognitive as well as practical ramifications, see Blair, *Too Much to Know;* Cevolini, *The Ark*; and Krajewski, *Paper Machines.*

[5] Grafton, *What Was History?*

[6] Brendecke, *Imperium und Empirie*, describes the complex origins and considerable irony in "fully informed" as a legal category.

material to historical thinking had significant antecedents, the constellation that they formed in the mid-sixteenth century seems more than fortuitous, since they all point to an important change in the authority of archives as repositories for specific kinds of knowledge.

By the late seventeenth century, in any event, repositories of political records had moved far beyond the treasure chests in the possession of medieval kings, monasteries, and towns. Preserved records had differentiated into multiple genres, corpora, and streams, directed into spaces articulated by sophisticated conceptual topographies and taxonomies. Specialized chancellery workers mapped record accumulations and indexed material, and were beginning to track files from their delivery, through bureaucratic decision-making processes, and into permanent archives. Rulers' and intellectuals' growing interest in stored records as sources for historical narratives useful for propaganda and political negotiation (as well as for advancing scholarly careers) added a new set of expectations and challenges to the agenda of all sorts of repositories. Intense debates over the authenticity of supposedly ancient documents erupted in the later seventeenth century. Depending on the political situation of the authors and the goals of their patrons, very different ways of approaching records emerged, representing yet another kind of differentiation.

Ultimately, growing external demands for information exceeded the capacity of the long-established medial system of charters, reports, books, and armoires. The result was often dysfunction, as we saw in Lucerne in 1698, but it was sometimes also innovation, however slow and haphazard, as occurred in Berlin. Such innovation, together with the professionalization of archival personnel and their deployment beyond the walls of archives, allowed for new archival developments in the following centuries.

Beyond Early Modern Archives

Major changes characterized the direction taken in political archives from 1700 until the consolidation of modern archival science before 1900. This transitional period also experienced a major divide during the French Revolution and Napoleonic Wars – extremely consequential in archival as in political and cultural history. Since new studies about record-keeping practices and cultures in this period have begun emerging at an accelerating rate, the purpose of the short discussion here is not to report the current state of research.[7] Rather, I seek to connect

---

[7] A few suggestive works: Kafka, "Paperwork"; Milligan, "What Is an Archive?"; Müller, "Die neue Geschichte."

the trajectory of early modern developments traced in this book to questions arising in succeeding periods, with a few final thoughts about how the media revolutions of the twenty-first century might also gain perspective from earlier eras.

The key to post-1700 developments in both archival practice and archival theory lies, I suggest, in the growing resonance among three separate issues. The first is the increasing identification between the state as form of dominion and the nation as ideological framework, knit together by an administrative apparatus that worked bureaucratically through written records. The second is changes in history-writing that increasingly prompted historians to question the origins and legitimacy of the new nation-states. The third is the emergence after 1700, and then much more forcefully after 1819, of national archives completely separated from administrative records, created to be the most trusted locus for finding evidence about each nation-state's past. Each of these processes had many causes, of course, and proceeded in complex and often circuitous ways. At the same time, their intersection was essential for the evolution of both archives and archival science up to the 1890s.

Two contrasting eighteenth-century projects to improve the archival condition of a major state – in Austria under Maria Theresia and in late Bourbon Spain – illustrate both how little and how much had changed since the sixteenth century. In Vienna, archival uncertainties during the Bavarian interregnum (1742–1745) and growing territorial pressure from royal Prussia provoked a project to create a new Habsburg house archive in 1742. Building on earlier proposals, Theodor Anton Taulow von Rosenthal proposed an ambitious unification of Habsburg charters from the family's multiple administrative centers in a new treasury of legitimation to preserve the family patrimony.[8] The similarities with the Simancas project as launched by Charles V in Spain in the 1530s are significant. Indeed, like that project, Rosenthal's endeavor was soon overwhelmed by masses of administrative material, despite his efforts to focus on charters. Important as a new and thoroughly synthetic collection created by seizing or copying material already organized in other Habsburg centers, this archive's founding nevertheless shows the durability of old ideas about archives as treasuries of legitimation.

In Spain, the defense of possessions was also central to the founding of a new synthetic archive in Seville in 1785, the Archivo de Indias. In

---

[8] Rosenthal's 1742 *Memorial* named three key categories of instruments to be collected: actual family records (*Eigentliche Hausakten*), charters about the total state or monarchy (*gesammte Staaten oder Monarchie*), and charters about the individual territorial units. HHStA Kurrentakten K1, bundle 3 (draft of *Ohnmaßgebliche Reflexion* of 1742).

contrast to the Vienna project, founder José de Gálvez y Gallardo wanted to produce authorized *histories* of Spain's conquest and administration in the Americas. For such purposes, the vast accumulations of administrative records in Cádiz were just as important as the charters and council records kept in Simancas and the ministry records from Madrid. All relevant documents from before 1760 were transferred to a new building in Seville, and a historian, Juan Bautista Muñoz, was appointed to arrange them as a historical arsenal for Spain's empire.

The conceptual and real establishment of national archives took off during and after the French Revolution. The central role that the category of nation played during the events leading up to 1789 ensured that the French state's record-keeping would take the form of an explicitly national archive, as ordered by the National Assembly in 1790, and then comprehensively ordained in a decree of 7 *messidor An II* (June 25, 1794). The *messidor* decree also established the right of all French citizens to use the new repository, highlighting how different it was from any early modern archive.[9] The new regime's decree to destroy all feudal titles, meanwhile, led to the obliteration of some 550 tons of paper across France.[10] The vast disruptions of the Napoleonic Wars extended this damage far beyond France. For example, large parts of the pre-war Vatican archives, carried to Paris by Napoleon, were lost during the chaos of the post-war years. Another outcome was the concentration of sovereignty into far fewer national states, especially in the German lands. This development increased pressures for administrative efficiency to support the war machines already built up during the incessant conflicts of the late eighteenth century. In this environment, the rationalization of administrative record-keeping kept intensifying, including through new medial approaches to filing such as printed forms and binders.[11] Meanwhile, following the example already set in the Archivo de Indias, the emerging states began treating their repositories of old records as national patrimonies – still treasuries, in a sense, but now for historians as much as for jurists.[12] Leopold von Ranke's manifesto favoring research based on original sources found in archives appeared in 1824, signaling historians' turn to national archives of administrative records as well as charters.

In a sense, the predicament of early nineteenth-century archivists was that they confronted yet another profound differentiation in the documents

---

[9] Milligan, "What Is an Archive?"   [10] Lokke, "Archives," 30–31.

[11] Vismann, *Files,* especially ch. 4, stating dramatically that after 1806, "Prussian files are, have, and institute the life of the state" (121).

[12] Milligan, *Making a Modern Archive.*

under their charge, as the formerly blurred distinction between historical memory and administrative information became increasingly formal. In its most rigorous form, this differentiation appeared in the scheduled transfer of material from registry to archive, now formally defined as the resting place for documents no longer useful to the state for administrative purposes. Such transfers enabled the concept of an archival threshold, and also raised urgent questions about both appraising the material to determine what should be retained and arranging it for its future users, now imagined as future historians. The urgency of such questions was amplified because the entire accumulated mass of records created up to the Napoleonic Wars was now allocated, in one great lump, to the emerging national archives administrations. What was to be done?

This predicament was the breeding ground of modern archival science. The degree of uncertainty that prevailed in the first decades after the wars ended is noteworthy. In some archives, major efforts to rearrange old records took place, as in Zurich, where the bundled files that had accumulated over centuries of disputes were reformed as chronological bundles organized by subject.[13] The leaders of the new Archives Nationales in Paris established an elaborate classification system for archival corpora, mandatory for provincial archives, although compliance was slow and very uneven. But the possessors of larger collections quickly realized that, even if it were possible to extract and file all charters (for example) in chronological order, applying this approach to the mountains of administrative paperwork tucked into vaults and storerooms not only vastly exceeded the available labor, but also threatened to generate pure chaos. By destroying the fabric of connections between documents that already existed in the forms of inventories and classification systems, many documents' meaning would be lost entirely.

Over the next decades, the emerging concepts of *respect des fonds* and arrangement by provenance provided a practical response to archivists' challenges, and eventually a theoretical justification for leaving material in the order in which it arrived at the archive's door. A great deal of research remains to be done on the period from 1750 to 1850, especially on archival practice, professionalization, new handbooks of practice in the eighteenth century, and the strategies taken before provenance became the core principle of archival organization.

In the late twentieth century, record-makers, record-keepers, and record-users faced an even more profound revolution in medial forms

---

[13] See Schweizer, *Geschichte.*

and configurations than those of the nineteenth century (card catalogs, the telegraph, mechanical print) and early twentieth century (typewriters, telephones). With the spread of desktop computers and the emergence of global data networks, documents began traveling along entirely new circuits and came to be kept and accessed in a bewildering variety of new ways. After 2000, a vast enterprise of digitizing material previously preserved and organized in paper or parchment further complicated the lives of archivists. Even within the confines of state and corporate archives, old maxims quickly became obsolete, provoking new theories such as post-custodial archiving and the records continuum to help the personnel cope. These theoretical accomplishments are likely to continue evolving rapidly.

Not only do archivists and records managers face ongoing technological developments, but they have also been challenged by communities seeking to ensure and protect their own documentation in community archives, and by "big data" institutions that seemingly bypass the old maxims altogether. Yet the profound questions that the new media and new cultural expectations raise still reflect an ongoing conversation about the same fundamental issues: How does writing records relate to memory, and whose memories will be preserved? Who controls the records of the past, and what are their responsibilities? How does the accumulation of inscribed material in technologized forms create contexts for such materials' organization and access that add information beyond what is inscribed by means of ink or bits? And finally, how do organization and access in turn enable (or silence) potential information and diverse knowledge, as users and their questions change? Looking at early modern archives cannot answer these questions directly, but the techniques we develop to understand historical cases can help clarify how we might approach later periods and the conundrums of the present.

Archives Cited

AGI	Archivo General de Indias, Seville, Spain
AGS	Archivo General de Simancas, Simancas, Spain
ANTT	Arquivo Nacional Torre do Tombo, Lisbon, Portugal
Erfgoed Leiden	Erfgoed Leiden en Omstreken (formerly RA Leiden), Leiden, Netherlands
GstA-PK	Geheimes Staatsarchiv Preußischer Kulturbesitz, Berlin (Dahlem), Germany
HHStA	Haus-, Hof- und Staatsarchiv, Vienna, Austria
LN	*Leitura Nova,* 1504–1562 (located at ANTT)
NLNA	Nationaal Archief, The Hague, Netherlands
StABE	Staatsarchiv Bern, Bern, Switzerland
StAGR	Staatsarchiv Graubünden, Chur, Switzerland
StALU	Staatsarchiv Luzern, Lucerne, Switzerland
StAWü	Staatsarchiv Würzburg (Staatliche Archive Bayerns), Würzburg, Germany
StAZH	Staatsarchiv Zürich, Zurich, Switzerland
TLA	Tiroler Landesarchiv, Innsbruck, Austria
ZBZ	Zentalbibliothek Zürich, Zurich, Switzerland

Bibliography

Aebbtlin, Georg. *Anführung Zu der Registratur-Kunst.* Ulm: Christian Balthasar Kühnen, 1669.

Andenmatten, Bernard, and Guido Castelnuovo. "Produzione e conservazione documentarie nel principato sabaudo, XIII–XV secolo." *Bullettino dell'Istituto italiano per il Medio Evo e Archivio Muratoriano* 110, 1 (2008), 279–348.

Anmerckungen Uber die Von dem Wienerischen Hof Der schuldigen Auslieferung Des Reichs-Archivs Entgegen gestellete, Und denen öffentlichen Zeitungen einverleibte Einwendungen. N.p., 1742.

Arendt, Max. *Die brandenburgische Kanzlei, ihr Urkunden- und Registerwesen unter der Regierung des Kurfürsten Johann (1486–99).* Berlin: Blanke, 1913.

Arnold, John H. "Inquisition, Texts and Discourse," in Caterina Bruschi and Peter Biller, eds., *Texts and the Repression of Medieval Heresy*, 63–80. York: York Medieval Press, 2003.

Assmann, Aleida. *Cultural Memory and Western Civilization: Functions, Media, Archives.* Cambridge: Cambridge University Press, 2011 [German original 1992].

Assmann, Jan. *Cultural Memory and Early Civilization: Writing, Remembrance, and Political Imagination.* Cambridge: Cambridge University Press, 2011 [German original 1977].

Azevedo, Pedro A. de, and António Baião. *O Arquivo da Torre do Tombo: Sua história, corpos que o compõem e organização.* Lisbon: Imprensa Commercial, 1905 [reprinted Lisbon: Horizonte, 1989].

Baldwin, John H. *The Government of Philip Augustus: Foundations of French Royal Power in the Middle Ages.* Berkeley: University of California Press, 1986.

Barisoni, Alberto. *Albertini Barisonii episcopi cenetensis de archivis commentarius.* Venice: Jo. Baptista Pasqual, 1737.

Baron, Hans. "Leonardo Bruni: 'Professional Rhetoritician' or 'Civic Humanist'?" *Past and Present* 36 (1967), 21–37.

Barret-Kriegel, Blandine. *Jean Mabillon.* Paris: Presses Universitaires de France, 1988.

Bastian, Jeanette. *Owning Memory: How a Caribbean Community Lost Its Archives and Found Its History.* Westport, CT: Libraries Unlimited, 2003.

Bastress-Dukehart, Erica. *The Zimmern Chronicle: Nobility, Memory and Self-Representation in Sixteenth-Century Germany.* Aldershot: Ashgate, 2002.

Bauer, Wilhelm. "Das Register- und Konzeptwesen in der Reichskanzlei Maximilians I. bis 1502." *Mitteilungen des Instituts für Österreichische Geschichtsforschung* 26 (1905), 247–79.

Baum, Wilhelm. *Sigmund der Münzreiche: Zur Geschichte Tirols und der habsburgischen Länder im Spätmittelalter.* Bolzano: Verlagsanstalt Athesia, 1987.

Bautier, M. Robert-Henri. "La phase cruciale de l'histoire des archives." *Archivum: Revue Internationale des Archives* 18 (1968), 139–49.

Becker, Peter, and William Clark, eds. *Little Tools of Knowledge: Historical Essays on Academic and Bureaucratic Practices.* Ann Arbor: University of Michigan Press, 2001.

Bedos-Rezak, Brigitte. "Towards an Archaeology of the Medieval Charter: Textual Production and Reproduction in Northern France," in Adam Kosto and Anders Winroth, eds. *Charters, Cartularies and Archives: The Preservation and Transmission of Documents in the Medieval West,* 43–60. Toronto: Pontifical Institute of Medieval Studies, 2002.

Beimrohr, Wilfried *Das Tiroler Landesarchiv und seine Bestände.* Innsbruck: Tiroler Landesarchiv, 2002.

Benecke, Gerhard. *Maximilian I (1459–1519): An Analytical Biography.* London: Routledge & Kegan Paul, 1982.

Bernhardt, Walter. *Die Zentralbehörden des Herzogtums Württemberg und ihre Beamten 1520–1569,* 2 vols. Stuttgart: Kohlhammer, 1972.

Bertrand, Paul. *"Du De re diplomatica au Nouveau Traité de diplomatique:* réception des textes fondamentales d'une discipline," in *Dom Jean Mabillon, figure majeure de l'Europe des lettres,* 605–20. Paris: Académie des Inscriptions et Belles-Lettres, 2010.

Bier, Herrman. *Das Urkundenwesen und die Kanzlei der Markgrafen von Brandenburg 1323–1373: I. Teil.* Berlin: Bernhard Paul, 1907.

Biller, Peter, Caterina Bruschi, and Shelagh Sneddon. *Inquisitors and Heretics in Thirteenth-Century Languedoc: Edition and Translation of Toulouse Inquisition Depositions, 1273–1282.* Leiden: Brill, 2011.

Bittner, Ludwig. *Gesamtinventar des Wiener Haus-, Hof- und Staatsarchivs, aufgebaut auf der Geschichte des Archivs und seiner Bestände,* 5 vols. Vienna: Adolf Holzhausens Nachfolger, 1936–1940.

Black's Law Dictionary, 2nd ed. 1910. http://thelawdictionary.org.

Blair, Ann. *Too Much to Know: Managing Scholarly Information before the Modern Age.* New Haven, CT: Yale University Press, 2010.

Blouin, Francis X. Jr., and William G. Rosenberg. *Processing the Past: Contesting Authority in History and the Archives.* Oxford: Oxford University Press, 2011.

Blouin, Francis X. Jr., and William G. Rosenberg. eds. *Archives, Documentation and the Institutions of Social Memory.* Ann Arbor: University of Michigan Press, 2006.

Blumenthal, Uta-Renate. "Päpstliche Urkunden, Briefe, und die europäische Öffentlichkeit," in Klaus Herbers and Ingo Fleisch, *Erinnerung – Niederschrift – Nutzung: Das Papsttum und die Schriftlichkeit im mittelalterlichen Westeuropa,* 11–30. Berlin: De Gruyer, 2011.

Bonifacius, Baldessare. *De archivis liber singularis eiusdem praelectiones et ciuilium institutionum epitome.* Venice: Io. Petrus Pinellus, 1632.

Born, Lester K. "Baldassare Bonifacio and His Essay *De Archivis." American Archivist* 4, 4 (1941), 221–37.

Born, Lester K. ed. "The De Archivis Commentarius of Albertino Barisoni (1587–1667)." *Archivalische Zeitschrift* 50/51 (1955), 13–22.

Bouchard, Constance B. "Monastic Cartularies: Organizing Eternity," in Adam Kosto and Anders Winroth, eds. *Charters, Cartularies and Archives: The Preservation and Transmission of Documents in the Medieval West*, 22–32. Toronto: Pontifical Institute of Medieval Studies, 2002.

Boutier, Jean. "Étienne Baluze et les 'Règles générales pour discerner les anciens titres faux d'avec les véritables'," in Jean Boutier, ed., *Étienne Baluze, 1630–1718: Erudition et pouvoirs dans l'Europe classique*, 315–34. Limoges: Pulim, 2008.

Bouza Alvarez, Fernando. *Del escribano a la biblioteca: La civilización escrita Europea en la alta edad moderna (siglos XV–XVII)*. Madrid: Síntesis, 1997.

Brandstetter, Renward. *Renward Cysat 1545–1614: Der Begründer der schweizerischen Volkskunde*. Lucerne: Buchhandlung Haag, 1909.

Brendecke, Arndt. *"Arca, Archivillo, Archive*: The Keeping, Use, and Status of Historical Documents about the Spanish Conquista." *Archival Science* 10, 3 (2010), 267–83.

Imperium and Empirie: Funktionen des Wissens in der spanischen Kolonialherrschaft. Cologne: Böhlau, 2009. [An abridged English translation, *The Empirical Empire*, trans. Jeremiah Riemer [Berlin: De Gruyter Oldenburg, 2016] appeared after research for this book was complete.]

"Papierfluten: Anwachsende Schriftlichkeit als Pluralisierungsfaktor in der Frühen Neuzeit." *Mitteilungen des Sonderforschungbereichs 573* 1, 1 (2006), 21–30.

Brendecke, Arndt, Markus Friedrich, and Susanne Friedrich, "Information als Kategorie historischer Forschung: Heuristik, Etymologie und Abgrenzung vom Wissensbegriff," in Arndt Brendecke, Markus Friedrich, and Susanne Friedrich, eds., *Information in der Frühen Neuzeit: Status, Bestände, Strategien*, 11–44. Berlin: LIT Verlag, 2008.

Brennecke, Adolf. *Archivkunde: Ein Beitrag zur Theorie und Geschichte des europäischen Archivwesens*, ed. Wolfgang Leesch. Leipzig: Kohler & Amelang, 1953.

Bresslau, Harry. *Handbuch der Urkundenlehre für Deutschland und Italien*, 2nd ed. Leipzig: Veit & Comp. Berlin: Walter de Gruyter, 1912–1931.

Brewer, John. *The Sinews of Power: War, Money, and the English State, 1688–1783*. New York: Alfred A. Knopf. 1989.

Brincken, Anna-Dortheé von den. "Tabula Alphabetica: Von den Anfängen alphabetischer Registerarbeiten zu Geschichtswerken (Vincenz von Beauvais OP, Johnnes von Hautfuney, Palinus Minorita OFM)," in *Festschrift für Hermann Heimpel zum 70. Geburtstag*, 2: 900–23. Göttingen: Max-Planck-Institut für Geschichte, 1972.

Brothman, Brian. "Declining Derrida: Integrity, Tensegrity, and the Preservation of the Archives from Deconstruction." *Archivaria* 48 (1999), 64–89.

Brown, Alison. *Bartolomeo Scala 1430–1497, Chancellor of Florence: The Humanist as Bureaucrat*. Princeton, NJ: Princeton University Press, 1979.

Brown, John Seely, and Paul Duguid. *The Social Life of Information*. Boston: Harvard Business School Press, 2000.

Brown, Warren, Marios Costambeys, Matthew Innes, and Adam J. Kosto, eds. *Documentary Culture and the Laity in the Early Middle Ages*. Cambridge: Cambridge University Press, 2013.

Brun, Peter. *Schrift und politisches Handeln: Eine "zugeschriebene" Geschichte des Aargaus 1415–1425*. Zurich: Chronos, 2006.

Bruschi, Caterina. "'Magna diligentia est habenda per inquisitorem': Precautions before Reading Doat 21–26," in Caterina Bruschi and Peter Biller, eds., *Texts and the Repression of Medieval Heresy*, 81–110. York: York Medieval Press, 2003.

Bruschi, Caterina, and Peter Biller, eds., *Texts and the Repression of Medieval Heresy*. York: York Medieval Press, 2003.

Brüschweiler, Paul. *Die landfriedliche Simultanverhältnisse im Thurgau*. Frauenfeld: Huber, 1932.

Bullinger, Heinrich. *Reformationsgeschichte nach dem Autographon herausgegeben*, vol. 3, ed. J. J. Hottinger and H. H. Vögeli. Frauenfeld: Beyel, 1840.

Burke, Peter. "Commentary" (on special issue: "Towards a Cultural History of Archives"). *Archival Science* 7, 4 (2007), 391–97.
Popular Culture in Early Modern Europe. New York: Harper & Row, 1978.
A Social History of Knowledge: From Gutenberg to Diderot. Cambridge: Polity Press, 2000.

Burnett, Amy N., and Emidio Campi, eds. *A Companion to the Swiss Reformation*. Leiden: Brill, 2016.

Burton, Antoinette, ed. *Archive Stories: Facts, Fictions and the Writing of History*. Durham, NC: Duke University Press, 2005.

Carruthers, Mary. *The Book of Memory: A Study of Memory in Medieval Culture*. Cambridge: Cambridge University Press, 1990.

Casanova, Eugenio. *Archivistica*, 2nd ed. Siena: Lazzeri, 1928.

Castillo Gómez, Antonio. "The Culture of Archives in Spain." *European History Quarterly* 46, 3 (2016), 545–67.

Cevolini, Alberto. *The Ark of Studies: Thomas Harrison*. Turnhout: Brepols, 2017.

Chakrabarty, Dipesh. *Provincializing Europe: Postcolonial Thought and Historical Difference*. Princeton, NJ: Princeton University Press, 2000.

Chancelarias Portuguesas: D. Duarte, 3 vols. Lisbon: Centro de Estudos Históricos, Universidade Nova da Lisboa, 1998–2002.

Clanchy, M. T. *From Memory to Written Record: England, 1066–1307*, 3rd ed. Oxford: Wiley-Blackwell, 2012 [first edition 1979].

Cook, Terry. "What Is Past Is Prologue: A History of Archival Ideas since 1898, and the Future Paradigm Shift." *Archivaria* 43 (1997), 17–63.

Corens, Liesbeth, Kate Peters, and Alexandra Walsham, eds. *Archives and Information in the Early Modern World* (Proceedings of the British Academy, 212). Oxford: Oxford University Press, 2018.

Corpus iuris civilis in IIII. partes distinctum …, ed. Dionysius Godefroy. Lyon: Barthol. Vincentius, 1583.

Cosmar, Carl Wilhelm. *Geschichte des Königlich-Preussischen Geheimen Staats- und Kabinettsarchivs bis 1806*, ed. Meta Kohnke. Cologne: Böhlau, 1993.

Costa, Avelino de Jesus da. "A Chancelaria Real Portuguesa e os seus Registos, de 1217 a 1438." *Revista da Faculdade de Letras: Historia (Porto)* Ser. II, 13 (1996), 71–101.

"La Chancellerie Royale Portugaise jusq'au milieu du XIIIe siècle." *Revista Portuguesa de História* 15 (1975), 143–69.

Costamagna, Giorgio. "I concetti di autenticità e di originalità nel documentazione della Cancelleria genovese nel Medioevo," in Gabriel Silagi, ed., *Landesherrliche Kanzleien im Spätmittelalter*, 2: 485–504. Munich: Arebeo-Gesellschaft, 1984.

Daly, Lloyd W. *Contributions to a History of Alphabetization in Antiquity and the Middle Ages*. Brüssel: Latomus, 1967.

Dames, Nicholas. "The Chapter: A History." *Page-Turner Blog, The New Yorker.* www.newyorker.com/books/page-turner/chapter-history, October 29, 2014.

Daston, Lorraine. "The Sciences of the Archive." *Osiris* 27 (2012), 156–87.

Davis, Natalie Zemon. *Fiction in the Archives: Pardon Tales and Their Tellers in Sixteenth-Century France*. Stanford, CA: Stanford University Press, 1990.

Delaborde, Henri-François. *Étude sur la constitution du Trésor des Chartes*. Paris: Plon-Nourrit, 1909.

"Les Inventaires du Trésor des Chartes Dressés par Gérard de Montaigu," in *Notices et Extraits des Manuscrits de la Bibliothèque Nationale et autres Biblithèques*, vol. 36, pt. 2, 545–98. Paris: Imprimerie Nationale and Librarie C. Klincksieck, 1900.

De la Plaza Bores, Angel. *Archivo General de Simancas: Guia del Investigador*. Valladolid: Dirección General de Archivos y Bibliotecas, 1952.

Delsalle, Paul. *Histoire de l'Archivistique*. Québec: Presses de l'Université du Québec, 1997.

Demougin, Ségolène, ed. *La mémoire perdue: A la recherche des archives oubliées, publiques et privées, de la Rome antique*. Paris: Publications de la Sorbonne, 1994.

Derrida, Jacques, tr. Eric Prenowitz. *Archive Fever: A Freudian Impression*. Chicago: University of Chicago Press, 1996 [French original 1995].

Derrida, Jacques, tr. Rachel Bowlby. *Paper Machine*. Stanford, CA: Stanford University Press, 2005 [French original 2001].

Deswarte, Sylvia. *Les Enluminures de la "Leitura nova": 1504–1552, étude sur la culture artistique au Portugal au temps de l'Humanisme*. Paris: Fundação Calouste Gulbenkian, Centro Cultural Português, 1977.

De Vivo, Filipo. "Archives of Speech: Recording Diplomatic Negotiation in Late Medieval and Early Modern Italy." *European Historical Quarterly* 46, 3 (2016), 519–44.

"Heart of the State, Site of Tension: The Archival Turn Viewed from Venice, ca. 1400–1700." www.cairn-int.info/journal-annales-2013-3-page-699.htm [tr. of "Cœur de l'État, lieu de tension: Le tournant archivistique vu de Venise (XVᵉ–XVIIᵉsiècle)," *Annales: Histoire, Sciences Sociales* 68 (2013), 699–728.]

Information and Communication in Venice: Rethinking Early Modern Politics. Oxford: Oxford University Press, 2007.

"Ordering the Archive in Early Modern Venice (1400–1650)." *Archival Science* 10, 3 (2010), 231–48.

De Vivo, Filipo, Andrea Guidi and Alessandro Silvestri. "Archival Transformations in Early Modern European History." *European Historical Quarterly* 46, 3 (2016), 421–34.

eds. *Archivi e archivisti in Italia tra medioevo ed etá moderna*. Rome: Viella, 2015.

eds. *Fonti per la storia degli archivi degli antichi Stati italiani*. Rome: Ministero dei beni e delle attività culturali e del turismo, 2016.

De Vivo, Filipo, Maria Pia Donato, and Philipp Müller, eds. "Archives and the Writing of History," special section in *Storia della Storiografia* 68, 2 (2015).

Dias, João José Alves. *Portugal do Renascimento à Crise Dinástica* (Nova História de Portugal, vol. 5). Lisbon: Editorial Presença, 1999.

Dinis, António J. Dias, ed. "Relatório do século XVI sobre o Arquivo Nacional da Torre do Tombo." *Anais: Academia Portuguesa da Historia Series II*, 17 (1968), 117–58.

Domeisen, Norbert. *Bürgermeister Johann Heinrich Waser (1600–1669) als Politiker*. Bern/Frankfurt: Herbert Lang/Peter Lang, 1975.

Du Cange, Charles du Fresne sieur. *Glossarium mediae et infimae latinitatis*. Niort: L. Favre, 1883–1887; http://ducange.enc.sorbonne.fr.

Duranti, Luciana. "Archives as a Place." *Archives & Manuscripts* 24, 2 (1996), 242–55.

"Diplomatics: New Uses for an Old Science, Part I" *Archivaria* 28 (1989), 7–27.

Durão, Maria Manuela da Silva. "1471: Um Ano 'Africano' no Desembargo de D. Afonso V." Dissertação de Mestradao, Universidade do Porto, 2002.

Eastwood, Terry. "A Contested Realm: The Nature of Archives and the Orientation of Archival Science," in Terry Eastwood and Heather MacNeil, eds., *Currents of Archival Thinking*, 2nd ed., 3–28. Santa Barbara: Libraries Unlimited, 2017.

Eastwood, Terry, and Heather MacNeil, eds. *Currents of Archival Thinking*, 2nd ed. Santa Barbara: Libraries Unlimited, 2017.

Eckert, Astrid M. *The Struggle for the Files: The Western Allies and the Return of German Archives after World War II*. Cambridge: Cambridge University Press, 2012.

Elliott, J. H. "A Europe of Composite Monarchies." *Past and Present No.* 137 (1992), 48–71.

Esch, Arnold. "Überlieferungs-Chance und Überlieferungs-Zufall als methodisches Problem des Historikers." *Historische Zeitschrift* 240, 3 (1985), 529–70.

Eymerich, Nicolau, and Francisco Peña. *Le manuel des inquisiteurs*, ed. Louis Sala-Molins. Paris: Mouton Éditeur, 1973 [reprint Albin Michel, 2001].

Farge, Arlette, tr. Thomas Scott-Railton. *The Allure of the Archives*. New Haven, CT: Yale Unversity Press, 2013 [French original 1989].

Fasolt, Constantin. "The Limits of History: An Exchange." *Historically Speaking* 6, 5 (2005), 5–17.

Fellner, Thomas, and Heinrich Kretschmayr. *Die Österreichische Zentralverwaltung, Section I: Von Maximilian I. bis zur Vereinigung der österreichischen und böhmischen Hofkanzlei (1749)*. Vienna: Adolf Holzhausen, 1907.

Fianu, Kouky, and DeLloyd Guth, eds. *Écrit et Pouvoir dans les Chancelleries Médiévales: Espace Français, espace Anglais*. Louvain-La-Neuve: Fédération Internationale des Instituts d'Études Médiévales, 1997.

Fichtner, Paula Sutter. *Ferdinand I of Austria: The Politics of Dynasticism in the Age of the Reformation*. Boulder, CO: East European Monographs, 1982.

Foscarini, Fiorella. "Archival Appraisal in Four Paradigms," in Terry Eastwood and Heather MacNeil, eds., *Currents of Archival Thinking*, 2nd ed., 107–33. Santa Barbara: Libraries Unlimited, 2017.

Foucault, Michel, tr. A. M. Sheridan Smith. *The Archaeology of Knowledge and the Discourse on Language*. New York: Pantheon, 1972 [French original 1969].

Freire, Anselmo Braamcamp. "A Chancelaria de D. Afonso V." *Archivo Histórico Portuguez* 2 (1904), 477–87; and 3 (1905), 62–74, 130–54, 212–36, 401–40.

Freitas, Judite Antonieta Gonçalves de. "Chancelarias Régias Quatrocentistas Portuguesas: Produção manuscrita e aproximação político-diplomática." *Revista da Faculdade de Ciências Humanas e Sociais (Porto)* 6 (2009), 136–50.

"The Royal Chancellery at the End of the Portuguese Middle Ages: Diplomacy and Political Society (1970–2005)." *e-Journal of Portuguese History* 7, 2 (2009), www.brown.edu/Departments/Portuguese_Brazilian_Studies/ejph/html/issue14/html/jfreitas.html.

"Tradição legal, codificação e práticas institucionais: um relance pelo Poder Régio no Portugal de Quatrocentos." *Revista da Faculdade de Letras: História (Porto)*, Ser. III, 7 (2006), 51–67.

Frenz, Thomas, "Kanzlei, Registratur und Archiv des Hochstifts Würzburg im 15. Jahrhundert," in Gabriel Silagi, ed., *Landesherrliche Kanzleien im Spätmittelalter*, 2: 39–147. Munich: Arebeo-Gesellschaft, 1984.

Friedrich, Markus. "Das Alte Reich und seine Archive im Spiegel reichspublizistischer und reichrechtlicher Literatur: *Ius archivi*, gerichtliche Beweiskraft und konfessionspolitische Indienstnahme," in Harriet Rudolph and Astrid Schlachta, eds., *Reichsstadt–Reich–Europa: Neue Perspektiven auf den Immerwährenden Reichstag zu Regensburg (1663–1806)*, 411–29. Regensburg: Schnell & Steiner, 2015.

Friedrich, Markus. tr. John Noël Dillon. *The Birth of the Archive: A History of Knowledge*. Ann Arbor: University of Michigan Press, 2018 [German original 2013].

"The Rise of Archival Consciousness in Provincial France: French Feudal Records and Eighteenth-Century Seigneurial Society." *Past and Present Supplement* 11 (2016), 49–70.

Fries, Lorenz. *Chronik der Bischöfe von Würzburg 742–1495*, ed. Ulrike Grosch. Würzburg: Schöningh, 2002.

Die Geschichte des Bauernkrieges in Ostfranken, 2 vols., eds. August Schäffler and Theodor Henner. Aalen: Scientia, 1978.

Fritsch, Ahasver. *Tractatus de iure archivi et cancellarie opera & studio Ahasveri Fritschi iur. doct. consil. Rudelst. Schwb*. Jena: Sengenwald, 1664. [Reprinted in Jacob Wencker, ed. *Collecta archivi et cancellariae jura: quibus accedunt, de archicancellariis, vicecancellariis, cancellariis ac secretariis virorum clarissimorum commentationes*. Strasbourg: Jo. Reinholdi Dulssecker, 1715].

"Fritsch, Ahasver." *Allgemeine Deutsche Biographie*, 8: 108–09. Leipzig: 1875–1912.

Fuchs, Franz, et al., eds. *Lorenz Fries und sein Werk: Bilanz und Einordnung.* Würzburg: Verlag Ferdinand Schöningh, 2014.

Gallati, Frieda. *Die Eidgenossenschaft und der Kaiserhof zur Zeit Ferdinands II. und Ferdinands III. 1619–1657.* Zurich: Leemann and Co., 1932.

Geary, Patrick. "Entre gestion et gesta," in Olivier Guyotjeannin, Laurent Morelle, and Michel Parisse, eds., *Les cartulaires: Actes de la Table ronde (Paris, 5–7 Decembre 1991)*, 13–26. Paris: École des Chartes, 1993.

Phantoms of Remembrance: Memory and Oblivion at the End of the First Millennium. Princeton, NJ: Princeton University Press, 1994.

Genicot, Leopold. *Les Actes Publics* (Typologie des Sources du Moyen Age Occidental, Fasc. 3). Turnhout: Brepols, 1972.

Germon, Bartholomé. *De veteribus regum Francorum diplomatibus, et arte secernendi antiqua diplomata vera à falsis, disceptatio.* Paris: Jean Anisson, 1703.

Giddens, Anthony. *The Nation-State and Violence.* Berkeley: University of California Press, 1985.

Gilliland, Anne J., Sue McKemmish, and Andrew J. Lau, eds. *Research in the Archival Multiverse.* Clayton, Australia: Monash University Publishing, 2017.

Given, James. *Inquisition and Medieval Society: Power, Discipline, and Resistance in Languedoc.* Ithaca, NY: Cornell University Press, 1997.

Glauser, Fritz, et al. *Das Staatsarchiv Luzern im Überblick: ein Archivführer.* Stuttgart/Luzern: Rex Verlag, 1993.

Glénisson, Jean. "Les enquêtes administratives en Europe occidentale aux XIIIe et XIVe siècles," in Werner Paravicini and Karl Ferdinand Werner, eds. *Histoire Comparée de L'Administration (IV–XVIII Siecles)*, 17–25. Munich: Artemis Verlag, 1980.

Godefroy, Dionysius. *Praxis civilis, ex antiqvis et recentioribvs avthoribvs, germanis, italis, gallis, hispanis, belgis, et aliis, qvi de re practica ex professo, nulla tamen vel confusa methodo, scripserunt, collecta.* Frankfurt a.M.: Peter Fischer, 1591.

Goeing, Anja-Silvia. *Storing, Archiving, Organizing: The Changing Dynamics of Scholarly Information Management in Post-Reformation Zurich.* Leiden: Brill, 2017.

Goody, Jack. *The Logic of Writing and the Organization of Society.* Cambridge: Cambridge University Press, 1986.

The Power of the Written Tradition. Washington, DC/London: Smithsonian Institution Press, 2000.

Gordon, Bruce. *The Swiss Reformation.* Manchester: University of Manchester Press, 2002.

Gorecki, Piotr. *The Text and the World: The Henryków Book, Its Authors, and Their Region, 1160–1310.* Oxford: Oxford University Press, 2015.

Gössi, Anton. "Archivordnungen und Kanzleiregistraturen in Luzern bis ins 18. Jh." *Mitteilungen der Vereinigung Schweizerischer Archivare* 27 (1976), 3–25.

Grafton, Anthony. *Defenders of the Text: The Traditions of Scholarship in an Age of Science.* Cambridge: Harvard University Press, 1991.

The Footnote: A Curious History. Cambridge: Harvard University Press, 1997.

"Invention of Traditions and Traditions of Invention in Renaissance Europe: The Strange Case of Annius of Viterbo," in Anthony Grafton and Ann Blair, eds., *The Transmission of Culture in Early Modern Europe*, 8–38. Philadelphia: University of Pennsylvania Press, 1990.

Joseph Scaliger: A Study in the History of Classical Scholarship. Oxford: Clarendon, 1983.

What Was History? The Art of History in Early Modern Europe. Cambridge: Cambridge University Press, 2007.

Grafton, Anthony, and Suzanne L. Marchand, eds. *Proof and Persuasion in History*. Special Issue of *History and Theory* 33, 4 (1994).

Grafton, Anthony, and Glenn W. Most, eds. *Canonical Texts and Scholarly Practices: A Global Comparative Approach*. Cambridge: Cambridge University Press, 2016.

Grafton, Anthony, and Megan Williams. *Christianity and the Transformation of the Book: Origen, Eusebius, and the Library of Caesarea*. Cambridge: Belknap, 2008.

Grebe, Marc-André. *Akten, Archive, Absolutismus? Das Kronarchiv von Simancas im Herrschaftsgefüge der spanischen Habsburger (1540–1598)*. Frankfurt a.M.: Veurvert, 2012.

Groebner, Valentin, tr. Mark Kyburz and John Peck. *Who Are You? Identification, Deception, and Surveillance in Early Modern Europe*. New York: Zone Books, 2007 [German original 2004].

Guidi, Andrea. "The Florentine Archives in Transition: Government, Warfare and Communication (1289–1530 ca.)." *European Historical Quarterly* 46, 3 (2016), 458–79.

Guyotjeannin, Olivier, Laurent Morelle, and Michel Parisse, eds. *Les cartulaires: Actes de la Table ronde (Paris, 5–7 Decembre 1991)*. Paris: École des Chartes, 1993.

Guyotjeannin, Olivier, and Yann Potin. "La Fabrique de la Perpétuité: Le Trésor des Chartes et les Archives du Royaume (XIIIe–XIXe Siècle)," in Étienne Anheim and Olivier Poncet, eds., *Fabrique des archives, fabrique de l'histoire* (Special Issue, *Revue de Synthèse*, Ser. 5, Vol. 125), 15–46.

Hacke, Daniela. "Zwischen Konflikt und Konsens: Zur politisch-konfessionellen Kultur in der Alten Eidgenossenschaft des 16. und 17. Jahrhunderts." *Zeitschrift für Historische Forschung* 32, 4 (2005), 575–604.

Hageneder, Othmar, and Anton Haidacher, eds. *Die Register Innozenz III*. Graz: H. Böhlaus Nachfolger, 1964.

Haidacher, Christoph. "Auf den Spuren des Archivs der Grafen von Görz," in Claudia Sporer-Heis, ed., *Tirol in seinen alten Grenzen*, 123–38. Innsbruck: Wagner, 2008.

"Das Schriftgut der drei 'oberösterreichischen Wesen,'" in Josef Pauser, Martin Scheutz, and Thomas Winkelbauer, eds., *Quellenkunde der Habsburgermonarchie (16.–18. Jahrhundert), Ein exemplarisches Handbuch*, 205–15. Vienna/Munich: R. Oldenbourg Verlag, 2004.

Die älteren Tiroler Rechnungsbücher: Analyse und Edition, 3 vols. Innsbruck: Tiroler Landesarchiv, 1993–2008.

Hallam, Elizabeth, and Judith Everard. *Capetian France 987–1328*, 2nd ed. London: Routledge, 2001.

Hamilton, Carolyn, et al., eds. *Refiguring the Archive*. Dordrecht: Kluwer, 2002.

Hammerstein, Notker. *Jus und Historie: Ein Beitrag zur Geschichte des historischen Denkens an deutschen Universitäten im späten 17. und im 18. Jahrhundert.* Göttingen: Vandenhoeck & Ruprecht, 1972.

Handbuch der Schweizer Geschichte, 2 vols. Zurich: Buchverlag Berichthaus, 1972.

Hartmann, Josef. "Amtsbücher: (a) Allgemeine Entwicklung des Amtsbuchwesens," in Friedrich Beck and Eckart Henning, eds., *Die archivalische Quellen, mit einer Einführung in die Historischen Hilfswissenschaften*, 3rd ed., 40–52. Cologne: Böhlau, 2003.

Head, Randolph C. "Collecting Testimony and Parsing Texts in Zurich: Documentary Strategies for Defending Reformed Identities in the Thurgau, 1600–1656," in Robin Barnes and Marjorie Plummer, eds., *Ideas and Cultural Margins in Early Modern Germany: Essays in Honor of H. C. Erik Midelfort*, 289–305. Aldershot: Ashgate, 2009.

"A Comparative Case-Study Approach to Historical Archives in Europe," in Anne J. Gilliland, Sue McKemmish, and Andrew J. Lau, eds., *Research in the Archival Multiverse*, 433–55. Clayton, Australia: Monash University Publishing, 2017.

"Configuring European Archives: Spaces, Materials and Practices in the Differentiation of Repositories from the Late Middle Ages to 1700." *European History Quarterly* 46, 3 (2016), 498–518.

"Documents, Archives and Proof around 1700." *Historical Journal* 56, 4 (2013), 909–30.

"Empire at Home: European Chancellery Practices and the Challenges of Record Keeping for Early Modern Colonial Enterprises," in Maria Pia Donato, ed., *Pratiques d'archives à l'époque modern: France, mondes coloniaux.* Paris: Editions Classiques Garnier, in press.

"Fragmented Dominion, Fragmented Churches: The Institutionalization of the *Landfrieden* in the Thurgau, 1531–1630." *Archive for Reformation History* 96 (2005), 117–44.

"Knowing Like a State: The Transformation of Political Knowledge in Swiss Archives, 1470–1770." *Journal of Modern History* 75, 4 (2003), 745–82.

"Mirroring Governance: Archives, Inventories and Political Knowledge in Early Modern Switzerland and Europe." *Archival Science* 7 (2007), 317–29.

"Spaces in the Archive, Spaces of the Archive: Material, Topographical and Indexical Articulations of Space in Early Modern Chancery Record Management," in Karin Friedrich, ed., *Opening Spaces: Constructions, Visions and Depictions of Spaces and Boundaries in the Baroque*, 2: 505–19. Wiesbaden: Harrassowitz, 2014.

"Thinking with the Thurgau: Political Pamphlets from the Villmergerkrieg and the Construction of Biconfessional Politics in Switzerland and Europe" in Christopher Ocker et al., eds., *Politics and Reformations: Communities, Polities, Nations, and Empires: Essays in Honour of Thomas A. Brady, Jr.*, 239–58. Leiden: Brill, 2007.

Heidecker, Karl. "30 June 1047: The End of Charters as Legal Evidence in France?" in Petra Schulte, Marco Mostert, and Irene van Renswoude, eds., *Strategies of Writing: Studies on Text and Trust in the Middle Ages*, 85–94. Turnhout: Brepols, 2008.

Heidecker, Karl. ed. *Charters and the Use of the Written Word in Medieval Society.* Turnhout: Brepols, 2000.

Heiler, Thomas. *Die Würzburger Bischofschronik des Lorenz Fries (Gest. 1550): Studien zum historiographischen Werk eines fürstbischöflichen Sekretärs und Archivars.* Würzburg: Verlag F. Schöningh, 2001.

Henny, Sundar. *Vom Leib geschrieben: Der Mikrokosmos Zürich und seine Selbstzeugnisse im 17. Jahrhundert.* Cologne: Böhlau Verlag, 2016.

Hentonnen, Pekka. "Looking at Archival Concepts and Practice in the Light of Speech Act Theory," in Anne J. Gilliland, Sue McKemmish, and Andrew J. Lau, eds., *Research in the Archival Multiverse,* 537–56. Clayton, Australia: Monash University Publishing, 2017.

Herzog, Tamar. *A Short History of European Law: The Last Two and a Half Millennia.* Cambridge, MA: Harvard University Press, 2018.

Heuberger, Richard. "Das Urkunden- und Kanzleiwesen der Grafen von Tirol, Herzöge von Kärnten, aus dem Hause Görz." *Mitteilungen des Instituts für österreichische Geschichtsforschung, Ergänzungsband* 9 (1915), 51–177, 265–394.

Hiatt, Alfred. "Diplomatic Arts: Hickes against Mabillon in the Republic of Letters." *Journal of the History of Ideas* 70, 3 (2009), 351–73.

The Making of Medieval Forgeries: False Documents in Fifteenth-Century England. London/Toronto: British Library and University of Toronto Press, 2004.

Hildbrand, Thomas. *Herrschaft, Schrift und Gedächtnis: Das Kloster Allerheiligen und sein Umgang mit Wissen in Wirtschaft, Recht und Archiv (11.–16. Jahrhundert).* Zurich: Chronos, 1996.

"Quellenkritik in der Zeitdimension: Vom Umgang mit Schriftgut. Anmerkungen zur theoretischen Grundlegung einer Analyse von prozesshaft bedeutungvollem Schriftgut mit zwei Beispielen aus der mittelalterlichen Ostschweiz." *Frühmittelalterliche Studien* 29 (1995), 349–89.

Hirschler, Konrad. "From Archives to Archival Practice: Rethinking the Preservation of Mamluk Administrative Documents." *Journal of the American Oriental Society* 136, 1 (2016), 1–28.

[Hirzel, Samuel]. "Versuch eines Plans zu Eintheilung der gesammelten Urkunden über die Eidgnösische Geschichte." *Verhandlungen der Helvetischen Gesellschaft in Schinznach* (1767), 21–34.

Histoire des contestations sur la diplomatique avec l'analise de cet ouvrage composé par le R.P. Dom. Jean Mabillon. Paris: F. Delalune, 1708. [Attributed either to Jacques-Philippe Lallemant (c. 1660–1748) or to Gilles-Bernard Raguet (1668–1748).]

Hochedlinger, Michael. *Aktenkunde: Urkunden- und Aktenlehre der Neuzeit.* Vienna/Munich: Böhlau Verlag and Oldenbourg Verlag, 2009.

Österreichische Archivgeschichte vom Spätmittelalter bis zum Ende des Papierzeitalters. Vienna/Munich: Böhlau Verlag and Oldenbourg Verlag, 2013.

Horsman, Peter, Eric Ketelaar, and Theo Thomassen. "New Respect for the Old Order: The Context of the Dutch Manual." *American Archivist* 66 (2003), 249–70.

Im Hof, Ulrich, and François de Capitani. *Die Helvetische Gesellschaft: Spätaufklärung und Vorrevolution in der Schweiz,* 2 vols. Frauenfeld/Stuttgart: Huber, 1983.

Iseli, Andrea. *Gute Policey: Öffentliche Ordnung in der Frühen Neuzeit.* Stuttgart: UTB, 2009.

Jenkinson, Hilary. *A Manual of Archive Administration, Including the Problems of War Archives and Archive Making.* Oxford: Clarendon Press, 1922.

Jenny, Beat Rudolf. "Von Schreiber zu Ritter: Jakob von Ramingen 1510 – nach 1582." *Schriften des Vereins für Geschichte und Naturgeschichte der Baar* 26 (1966), 1–66.

Jenny, Rudolf. *Das Staatsarchiv Graubünden in landesgeschichtlicher Schau.* Chur: Calven-Verlag, 1974.

Johanek, Peter. "Methodisches zur Verbreitung und Bekanntmachung von Gesestzen im Spätmittelalter," in Werner Paravicini and Karl Ferdinand Werner, eds. *Histoire Comparée de L'Administration (IV–XVIII Siecles)*, 88–101. Munich: Artemis Verlag, 1980.

Jucker, Michael. *Gesandte, Schreiber, Akten: politische Kommunikation auf eidgenössischen Tagsatzungen im Spätmittelalter.* Zurich: Chronos, 2004.

Kafka, Ben. "The Demon of Writing: Paperwork, Public Safety and the Reign of Terror." *Representations* 98, 1 (2007), 1–24.

"Paperwork: The State of the Discipline." *Book History* 12 (2009), 340–53.

Kagan, Richard. *Clio and the Crown.* Baltimore: Johns Hopkins University Press, 2009.

Kägi, Ursula. *Die Aufnahme der Reformation in den ostschweizerischen Untertanengebieten – der Weg Zürichs zu einem obrigkeitlichen Kirchenregiment bis zum Frühjahr 1529.* Zurich: Juris-Verlag, 1972.

Keller, Hagen, "Vom 'heiligen Buch' zur 'Buchführung': Lebensfunktionen der Schrift im Mittelalter," in Hagen Keller, Klaus Grubmüller, and Nikolaus Staubach, eds., *Pragmatische Schriftlichkeit im Mittelalter: Erscheinungsformen und Entwicklungsstufen*, 1–31. Munich: Wilhelm Fink Verlag, 1992.

Keller, Hagen, and Thomas Behrmann, eds. *Kommunales Schriftgut in Oberitalien: Formen, Funktion, Überlieferung.* Munich: Wilhelm Fink Verlag, 1995.

Keller, Hagen, Klaus Grubmüller, and Nikolaus Staubach, eds. *Pragmatische Schriftlichkeit im Mittelalter: Erscheinungsformen und Entwicklungsstufen.* Munich: Wilhelm Fink Verlag, 1992.

Kelley, Donald. *Faces of History: Historical Inquiry from Herodotus to Herder.* New Haven, CT: Yale University Press, 1998.

The Foundations of Modern Historical Scholarship: Language, Law and History in the French Renaissance. New York: Columbia University Press, 1970.

Versions of History from Antiquity to the Enlightenment, 1450–1800. New Haven, CT: Yale University Press, 1991.

Ketelaar, Eric. "The Archival Image." *American Archivist* 58, 4 (1995), 454–6.

"Archival Turns and Returns," in Anne J. Gilliland, Sue McKemmish, and Andrew J. Lau, eds., *Research in the Archival Multiverse*, 228–68. Clayton, Australia: Monash University Publishing, 2017.

"The Difference Best Postponed? Cultures and Comparative Archival Science." *Archivaria* 44 (1997), 142–48.

"Jan van Houts 'Registratuer'." *Nederlands Archievenblad* 84 (1980), 400–12.

"Records Out and Archives In: Early Modern Cities as Creators of Records and as Communities of Archives." *Archival Science* 10, 3 (2010), 201–10.

Klinkenborg, Melle. *Geschichte des Geheimen Staatsarchivs vom 15. bis zum 18. Jahrhundert*, ed. Jürgen Kloosterhuis. Berlin: Geheimes Staatsarchiv, 2011.

Kloosterhius, Jürgen. "In arduis solertia et fides," in Jürgen Kloosterhius, ed., *Archivarbeit für Preußen*, 421–2. Berlin: Geheimes Staatsarchiv, 2000.

"Mittelalterliche Amtsbücher, Strukturen und Materien," in Friedrich Beck and Eckart Henning, eds., *Die archivalischen Quellen*, 4th ed., 53–73. Stuttgart: UTB, 2004.

"Von der Repositurenvielfalt zur Archiveinheit: Die Etappen der Tektonierung des Geheimen Staatsarchivs," in Jürgen Kloosterhius, ed., *Archivarbeit für Preußen*, 47–70. Berlin: Geheimes Staatsarchiv, 2000.

Koch, Petra. "Die Archivierung kommunaler Bücher in den ober- und mittelitalienischen Städten im 13. und frühen 14. Jahrhundert," in Hagen Keller and Thomas Behrmann, eds., *Kommunales Schriftgut in Oberitalien: Formen, Funktion, Überlieferung*, 19–70. Munich: Wilhelm Fink Verlag, 1995.

Kögl, Werner. "Die Bedeutung des Wilhelm Putsch für die Organisation des Archivwesens unter Ferdinand I." *Mitteilungen des Österreichischen Staatsarchivs* 28 (1975), 197–209.

Kos, Miklo. "Carte sine litteris." *Mitteilungen des Instituts für Österreichische Geschichtsforschung* 62 (1954), 97–100.

Kosto, Adam. *Making Agreements in Medieval Catalonia: Power, Order and the Written Word, 1000–1200*. Cambridge: Cambridge University Press, 2001.

"'Statim invenire ante': Finding aids and research tools in pre-Scholastic legal and administrative manuscripts." *Scriptorium* 70, 2 (2016), 285–309.

Kosto, Adam, and Anders Winroth, eds. *Charters, Cartularies and Archives: The Preservation and Transmission of Documents in the Medieval West*. Toronto: Pontifical Institute of Medieval Studies, 2002.

Koziol, Geoffrey. *The Politics of Memory and Identity in Carolingian Royal Diplomas: The West Frankish Kingdom 840–987*. Turnhout: Brepols, 2012.

Krajewski, Markus, tr. Peter Krapp. *Paper Machines: About Cards & Catalogs, 1548–1929*. Cambridge, MA: MIT Press, 2011 [German original 2002].

Kuchenbuch, Ludolf, and Uta Kleine, eds. *'Textus' im Mittelalter: Komponenten und Situationen des Wortgebrauchs im schriftsemantischen Feld*. Göttingen: Vandenhoek & Ruprecht, 2006.

Lambert, Malcolm. *Medieval Heresy: Popular Movements from the Gregorian Reform to the Reformation*. Oxford: Basil Blackwell, 1992.

La Roi Ladurie, Emmanuel. *Montaillou: The Promised Land of Error*. New York: Vintage Books, 1979.

Lazzarini, Isabella. "Records, Politics and Diplomacy: Secretaries and Chanceries in Renaissance Italy (1350–c. 1520)," in Paul Dover, ed., *Secretaries and Statecraft in the Early Modern World*, 16–36. (Edinburgh: Edinburgh University Press, 2017.

Lehmann, Joachim. "Registraturgeschichtliche und quellenkundliche Aspekte älterer Kanzleiregister." *Archivmitteilungen* 26, 1 (1976), 13–18.

Leonardi, Claudio, Marcello Morelli, and Francesco Santi, eds. *Fabula in Tabula: Una storia degli indici del manoscritto al testo elettronico*. Spoleto: Centro Italiano di Studi Sull'alto Medievo, 1995.

Lepper, Marcel, and Ulrich Raulff. "Erfindung des Archivs," in Marcel Lepper and Ulrich Raulff, eds., *Handbuch Archiv: Geschichte, Aufgaben, Perspektiven*, 1–8. Stuttgart: J. B. Metzler Verlag, 2016.

Lepsius, Susanne, and Thomas Wettstein, eds. *Als die Welt in die Akten kam: Prozeßschriftgut im europäischen Mittelalter*. Frankfurt a.M.: Vittorio Klostermann, 2008.

Levillain, Léon. "Le 'De re diplomatica,'" in *Mélanges et Documents Publiés a l'Occasion du 2e Centenaire de la Mort de Mabillon*, 195–252. Paris: Librairie Honoré Champion, 1908.

Lewinski, Ludwig. *Die Brandenburgische Kanzlei und das Urkundenwesen während der Regierung der beiden ersten Hohenzollerschen Markgrafen (1411–1470)*. Strasbourg: Heitz & Mündel, 1893.

Lodolini, Elio. "Giurisprudenza della Sacra Rota Romana in materia di archivi (secc. XIV–XVIII)." *Rassegna degli archivi di stato* 42 (1982), 7–33.

"The War of Independence of Archivists." *Archivaria* 28 (1989), 36–47.

Lokke, Carl. "Archives and the French Revolution." *American Archivist* 31, 1 (1968), 23–31.

Lowe, Raphael. *The Medieval History of the Latin Vulgate*. Cambridge: Cambridge University Press, 1969.

Lynker, Nicolai Christopher. *De archivo imperii*, reprinted in Jacob Wencker, ed. *Collecta archivi et cancellariae jura: quibus accedunt, de archicancellariis, vicecancellariis, cancellariis ac secretariis virorum clarissimorum commentationes*, 82–109. Strasbourg: Jo. Reinholdi Dulssecker, 1715.

Maanen, Rudi van. *Inventaris van het Stadsarchief van Leiden (1253) 1574–1816 (1897)*. Leiden: Gemeentearchief Leiden, 1986.

Mabillon, Jean. *De re diplomatica libri VI*. Paris: Billaine, 1681.

Librorum de re diplomatica supplementum. Paris: Charles Robustel, 1704 [Also included in the 1708 second edition of *De re diplomatica libri VI*].

Maissen, Thomas. *Die Geburt der Republik: Staatsverständnis und Repräsentation in der frühneuzeitlichen Eidgenossenschaft*. Göttingen: Vandenhoeck & Ruprecht, 2006.

Makleff, Ron. "Sovereignty and Silence: The Creation of a Myth of Archival Destruction, Liège, 1408." *Archive Journal*, August 2017, www.archive journal.net/essays/sovereignty-and-silence.

Mann, Michael. *The Sources of Social Power: Vol. 1: A History of Power from the Beginning to A.D. 1760*. Cambridge: Cambridge University Press, 1986.

Marchal, Guy P. "Das Meisterli von Emmenbrücke oder vom Aussagewert mündlicher Überlieferung: Eine Fallstudie zum Problem Willhelm Tell." *Schweizerische Zeitschrift für Geschichte* 34, 4 (1984), 521–39.

Marques, A. H. de Oliveira, *Portugal na Crise dos Séculos XIV e XV* (Nova História De Portugal, vol. 4). Lisbon: Editorial Presença, 1987.

Martin, Henri-Jean, and Jean Vezin, eds. *Mise en page et mise en texte du livre manuscrit*. Mayenne: Librarie-Promodis, 1990.

Mascardi, Giuseppe. *Conclusiones probationum omnium, quae in vtroque foro versantur…* Venice: Haeredes Damiani Zenarij, 1609.

McDonald, Terrence J., ed. *The Historic Turn in the Human Sciences*. Ann Arbor: University of Michigan, 1996.

McKemmish, Sue. "Recordkeeping in the Continuum," in Anne J. Gilliland, Sue McKemmish, and Andrew J. Lau, eds., *Research in the Archival Multiverse*, 122–60. Clayton, Australia: Monash University Publishing, 2017.

McKemmish, Sue, et al., eds. *Archives: Recordkeeping and Society*. Wagga Wagga: Center for Information Studies, Charles Sturt University, 2005.

McKitterick, Rosalind. *Charlemagne: The Formation of a European Identity*. Cambridge: Cambridge University Press, 2008.

McNeely, Ian. *The Emancipation of Writing: German Civil Society in the Making, 1790s–1820s*. Berkeley: University of California Press, 2003.

McNeely, Ian F., and Lisa Wolverton. *Reinventing Knowledge from Alexandria to the Internet*. New York/London: W. W. Norton, 2008.

Meier, Christel, Dagmar Hüpper, and Hagen Keller, eds. *Der Codex im Gebrauch*. Munich: Wilhelm Fink Verlag, 1996.

Meisner, Heinrich Otto. *Aktenkunde: Ein Handbuch für Archivbenützer, mit besonderer Berücksichtigung Brandenburg-Preußens*. Berlin: E. S. Mittler & Sohn, 1935.

Urkunden- und Aktenlehre der Neuzeit. Leipzig: Koehler & Amelang, 1950.

Menne, Mareike. "Confession, Confusion and Rule in a Box? Archival Accumulation in Northwestern Germany in the Age of Confessionalization." *Archival Science* 10, 3 (2010), 299–314.

Merzbacher, Friedrich. "Ius Archivi: Zum geschichtlichen Archivrecht." *Archivalische Zeitschrift* 75 (1979), 135–47.

Meyer, Bruno. "Die Durchsetzung eidgenössischen Rechts im Thurgau. Studien zum Verfassungsrecht der Eidgenossenschaft des 15. Jahrhunderts," in *Festgabe Hans Nabholz*, 139–69. Aarau: Sauerländer, 1944.

Miller, Frederic. *Arranging and Describing Archives and Manuscripts*. Chicago: Society of American Archivists, 1990.

Miller, Peter. *Peiresc's Europe: Learning and Virtue in the Seventeenth Century*. New Haven, CT: Yale University Press, 2000.

Miller, Thea "Action, Transaction, and *Vorgang*: Gaining New Insights from an Old Practice." *Archival Science* 3, 4 (2003), 413–30.

"The German Registry: The Emergence of a Recordkeeping Model." *Archival Science* 3, 1 (2003), 43–63.

Milligan, Jennifer. "*Making a Modern Archive: The Archives Nationales of France, 1850–1887*." PhD Dissertation, Rutgers University, 2002.

"'What Is an Archive?' in Modern France," in Antoinette Burton, ed., *Archive Stories: Facts, Fictions and the Writing of History*, 159–83. Durham, NC: Duke University Press, 2005.

Moore, G.F. "The Vulgate Chapters and Numbered Verses in the Hebrew Bible." *Journal of Biblical Literature* 12, 1 (1893), 73–78.

Moore, Lara Jennifer. *Restoring Order: The Ecole des Chartes and the Organization of Archives and Libraries in France, 1820–1870*. Duluth: Litwin, 2008.

Moore, R. I. *The Formation of a Persecuting Society: Power and Deviance in Western Europe, 950–1250*. Oxford: Blackwell, 1987.

The Origins of European Dissent. London: Allen Lane/Penguin Books, 1977.

Moraw, Peter. *Von offener Verfassung zur gestalteter Verdichtung: Das Reich im späten Mittelalter 1250 bis 1490*. Berlin: Propyläen Verlag, 1985.

Morelle, Laurent. "De l'original à la copie: Remarques sur l'evaluation des transcriptions dans les cartulaires médiévaux," in Olivier Guyotjeannin, Laurent Morelle, and Michel Parisse, eds., *Les cartulaires: Actes de la Table ronde (Paris, 5–7 Decembre 1991)*, 91–104. Paris: École des Chartes, 1993.

Morsel, Joseph. "En Guise d'Introduction: les chartriers entre 'retour aux sources' et déconstruction des objects historiens," in Philippe Contamine and Laurent Vissière, eds., *Les chartriers seigneuriaux: défendre ses droits, construire sa mémoire, XIII⁴–XXI⁴ siècle*, 9–34. Geneva: Droz, 2010.

Müller, Ernst, and Ernst Posner, *Übersicht über die Bestände des Geheimen Staatsarchivs zu Berlin Dahlem: I. Hauptabteilung*. Leipzig: S. Hirzel, 1934.

Müller, Philipp. "Die neue Geschichte aus dem alten Archiv: Geschichtsforschung und Arkanpolitik in Mitteleuropa, ca. 1800–1850." *Historische Zeitschrift* 299, 1 (2014), 36–69.

Muller, Samuel, J. A. Feith, and R. Fruin, tr. Arthur H. Leavitt. *Manual for the Arrangement and Description of Archives*. New York: H. W. Wilson, 1968 [Dutch original 1898].

Myler, Nicolaus. *De principibus & statibus Imperii Rom. Germ. eorumvè praecipuis juribus succincta delineatio*, 2nd ed. Stuttgart: Johannes Wyrich Rösslin and Wilhelm Serlin, 1658.

Navarro Bonilla, Diego. *Escritura, Poder y Archivo: la organización documental de la Diputación del Reino de Aragón (siglos XV–XVIII)*. Zaragoza: Prensas Universitarias, 2004.

La imagen del archivo: representación y funciones en España (siglos XVI y XVII). Madrid: Trea, 2003.

"El Mundo Como Archivo y Representación: Símbolos e imagen de los poderes de la escritura." *Emblemata* 14 (2008), 19–43.

Nicolaj, Giovanna. "Originale, authenticum, publicum: Una sciarada per il documento diplomatico," in Adam Kosto and Anders Winroth, eds., *Charters, Cartularies and Archives: The Preservation and Transmission of Documents in the Medieval West*, 8–21. Toronto: Pontifical Institute of Medieval Studies, 2002.

Nirenberg, David. "Review of Given, Inquisition." *Speculum* 75, 1 (2000), 182–84.

Noflatscher, Heinz. *Räte und Herrscher: Politische Eliten an den Habsburgerhöfen der österreichischen Länder 1480–1530*. Mainz: Verlag Philipp von Zabern, 1999.

Nussdorfer, Laurie. *Brokers of Public Trust: Notaries in Early Modern Rome*. Baltimore: Johns Hopkins University Press, 2009.

Oberste, Jörg. *Die Dokumente der klösterlichen Visitationen*. Turnhout: Brepols, 1999.

"Normierung und Pragmatik des Schriftgebrauchs im cisterziensischen Visitationsverfahren bis zum beginnenden 14. Jahrhundert." *Historisches Jahrbuch* 114 (1994), 312–48.

Oliver, Gillian. "Managing Records in Current Recordkeeping Environments," in Terry Eastwood and Heather MacNeil, eds., *Currents of Archival Thinking*, 2nd ed., 83–106. Santa Barbara: Libraries Unlimited, 2017.

Ong, Walter. *Orality and Literacy: The Technologizing of the Word*. London/New York: Methuen, 1982.

O'Toole, James M. "Back to the Future: Ernst Posner's *Archives in the Ancient World.*" *American Archivist* 67 (2004), 161–75.

Overvoorde, J. C., and J. W. Verburgt. *Archief der secretarie van de stad Leiden 1253–1575.* Leiden: J. J. Groen & Zoon, 1937.

Pales-Gobilliard, Annette, ed. *Le Livre des sentences de l'inquisiteur Bernard Gui, 1308–1323.* Paris: CNRS, 2002.

Papenbroeck, Daniel. "Ad tomum II Aprilis propylaeum antiquarium circa veri ac falsi discrimen in vetustis membranis," in *Acta sanctorum Aprilis, Vol. 2: Quo medii XI dies continentur,* i–lii. Antwerp: Michaelus Cnobarus, 1675.

Papritz, Johannes. *Archivwissenschaft,* 4 vols. Marburg: Archivschule Marburg, 1983.
    "Neuzeitliche Methoden der archivischen Ordnung: Schriftgut vor 1800." *Archivum* 14 (1964), 13–56.

Paravicini, Werner, and Karl Ferdinand Werner, eds. *Histoire Comparée de L'Administration (IV–XVIII Siecles).* Munich: Artemis Verlag, 1980.

Parker, Geoffrey. *Philip II,* 3rd edition. Chicago: Open Court, 1995.

Parkes, Malcolm. "Folia librorum quaerere: Medieval experience of the problems of hypertext and the index," in Claudi,Leonardi, Marcello Morelli, and Francesco Santi, eds., *Fabula in Tabula: Una storia degli indici del manoscritto al testo elettronico,* 23–41. Spoleto: Centro Italiano di Studi Sull'alto Medievo, 1995.
    "The Influence of the Concepts of *Ordinatio* and *Compilatio* on the Development of the Book," in J. J. G. Alexander and M. T. Gibson, eds., *Medieval Learning and Literature,* 115–41. Oxford: Clarendon Press, 1976.
    Pause and Effect: An Introduction to the History of Punctuation in the West. Berkeley/Los Angeles: University of California Press, 1993.

Patze, Hans. "Die Herrschaftspraxis der deutschen Landesherren während des späten Mittelalters," in Werner Paravicini and Karl Ferdinand Werner, eds., *Histoire Comparée de L'Administration (IV–XVIII Siecles),* 363–91. Munich: Artemis Verlag, 1980.

Pauser, Josef, Martin Scheutz, and Thomas Winkelbauer, eds. *Quellenkunde der Habsburgermonarchie (16.-18. Jahrhundert). Ein exemplarisches Handbuch.* Vienna/Munich: R. Oldenbourg Verlag, 2004.

Pennings, J. C. M. "Geschiednis van het archiefbeheer," in "Inventaris van het archief van de Verenigde Oost-Indiscche Compagnie (VOC), 1602–1795 (1812)," NLNA Inventories, 1.04.02.

Perry, Adele. "The Colonial Archive on Trial: Possession, Dispossession, and History in Delgamuukw v. British Columbia," in Antoinette Burton, ed., *Archive Stories: Facts, Fictions and the Writing of History,* 325–50. Durham, NC: Duke University Press, 2005.

Pessanha, José. "Uma Rehabilitação historica: inventarios da Torre do Tombo no seculo XVI." *Archivo Historico Portuguez* 3 (1905), 287–303.

Peters, Edward. *Heresy and Authority in Medieval Europe: Documents in Translation.* Philadelphia: University of Pennsylvania Press, 1980.
    Inquisition. Berkeley: University of California Press, 1989.

Petersen, Stefan. "Die Hohe Registratur des Lorenz Fries: Ein Kanzleibehelf als Zeugnis effizienter Verwaltung," in Franz Fuchs et al., eds., *Lorenz Fries und sein Werk,* 269–93. Würzburg: Schöningh, 2014.

Pitz, Ernst. "Beiträge zur Geschichte des Ius Archivi."*Der Archivar* 16 (1963), 279–86.

"Diplom und Registereintrag: Über normative und prozessuale Interpretation von Papst- und Königsurkunden und ihre Abhängigkeit von der Form der Überlieferung," in Christel Meier, Dagmar Hüpper, and Hagen Keller, eds., *Der Codex im Gebrauch*, 101–8. Munich: Wilhelm Fink Verlag, 1996.

Schrift- und Aktenwesen der städtischen Verwaltung im Spätmittelalter. Köln–Nürnberg–Lübeck. Cologne: Paul Neubner, 1959.

Pocock, J.G.A. *The Ancient Constitution and the Feudal Law: A Study of English Historical Thought in the Seventeenth Century*, 2nd ed. Cambridge: Cambridge University Press, 1987.

The Machiavellian Moment: Florentine Political Thought and the Atlantic Republican Tradition. Princeton, NJ: Princeton University Press, 1975.

Popkewitz, Thomas, et al. "Debate–Discussion: The Cult of Facts, Romanticizing the Archive, and Ignoring Styles of Reasoning: Delusive Technologies of Conducting Historical Research [includes position paper and six short responses]," *Bildungsgeschichte: International Journal for the Historiography of Education* 8, 2 (2018), 192–220.

Portugal, Fernando. "A Chancelaria de D. Manuel." *Ethnos (Lisbon)* 6 (1970), 261–70.

"Mapa dos anos representados em cada livro da chancelaria de D. Manuel." Typed manuscript, Torre do Tombo (PDF provided to the author by Pedro Pinto).

Posner, Ernst. *Archives in the Ancient World.* Cambridge, MA: Harvard University Press, 1972.

Potin, Yann. "Archives en sacristie: Le trésor est-il un bâtiment d'archives? Le cas du 'Trésor des chartes' des rois de France (XIIIe–XIXe siècle)." *Livraisons d'histoire de l'architecture* 10, 2 (2005), 65–85.

"Entre trésor sacré et vaisselle du prince: Le roi médiéval est-il un collectionneur?" *Hypothèses* 2003, 1 (2003), 45–56.

Quantin, Jean-Louis. "Reason and Reasonableness in French Historical Scholarship." *Huntington Library Quarterly* 74, 3 (2011), 401–436.

Quaritsch, Helmut. *Souveränität. Entstehung und Entwicklung des Begriffs in Frankriech und Deutschland vom 13. Jahrhundert bis 1806.* Berlin: Duncker und Humblot, 1986.

Raible, Wolfgang. *Die Semiotik der Textgestalt: Erscheinungsformen und Folgen eines kulturellen Evolutionsprozesses.* Heidelberg: Carl Winter, 1991.

Ramingen, Jacob von. *Der rechten künstlichen Renouatur/Eigentliche unnd gründtliche Beschreibung.* Heidelberg: Carpentarius, 1571.

Summarischer Bericht/Wie es mit einer künstlichen und volkomnen Registratur Ein gestalt... Heidelberg: Johannes Mayer, 1571.

Von der Haushaltung der Regiment land und Leüt, und dann der ligenden Güter, und ihrer Rechten und Gniessen... Augsburg: Mattheus Franke, 1566.

Von der Registratur/Und ihen Gebäwen und Regimenten... Heidelberg: Johannes Maier, 1571.

Ranke, Leopold von. *Zur Kritik neuerer Geschichtsschreiber.* Leipzig: G. Reimer, 1824.

Rau, Virginia. *A Tôrre do Tombo em 1631.* Lisbon: Bertrand Irmaos, 1945.

Raumer, Georg Wilhelm von, ed. Eckart Henning. "Geschichte des Geheimen Staats- und Cabinets-Archivs zu Berlin bis zum Jahre 1820." *Archivalische Zeitschrift* 72 (1976), 30–75.

Rauschert, Jeanette. *Herrschaft und Schrift: Strategien der Inszenierung und Funktionalisierung von Texten in Luzern und Bern am Ende des Mittelalters.* Berlin/New York: De Gruyter, 2006.

Reingrabner, Gustav. "Zur Rechtsgeschichte des Parochialsystems in der Reformationszeit." *Österreichisches Archiv für Kirchenrecht*, 32, 1–2 (1981), 42–58.

Ribeiro, Fernanda. "Como seria a estrutura primitiva do Arquivo da Casa da Coroa (Torre do Tombo)?" Biblioteca Digital, Faculdade de Letras, Universidade do Porto, http://ler.letras.up.pt/uploads/ficheiros/1240.pdf.

Ridener, John. *From Polders to Postmodernism: A Concise History of Archival Theory.* Duluth: Litwin Books, 2009.

Riedmann, Josef. "Die Rechnungsbücher der Tiroler Landesfürsten," in Gabriel Silagi, ed., *Landesherrliche Kanzleien im Spätmittelalter*, 2: 315–23. Munich: Arebeo-Gesellschaft, 1984.

Rodríguez de Diego, José Luis. "Archivos del Poder, Archivos de la Administración, Archivos de la Historia (s. XVI–XVII)," in Juan José Generelo and Ángeles Moreno López, eds., *Historia de los Archivos y de la Archivistica en España*, 29–42. Valladolid: Secretario de Publicaciones y Intercambio Científico, Universidad de Valladolid, 1998.

"Estudio" in José Luis Rodríguez de Diego, ed., *Instrucción para el gobierno del Archivo de Simancas (Año 1588)*, 10–75. Madrid: Ministerio de Educación y Cultura, 1988.

ed. *Instrucción para el gobierno del Archivo de Simancas (Año 1588).* Madrid: Ministerio de Educación y Cultura, 1988.

"La Formación del Archivo de Simancas en el Siglo XVI," in María Luisa López-Vidriero and Pedro M. Cátedra, eds., *Coleccionismo y Bibliotecas (Siglos XV-XVIII)*, 519–57. Salamanca: Ediciones Universidad de Salamanca, 1998.

"Significado del proyecto archivistico de Felipe II," in Alfredo Alvar Ezquerra, ed., *Imágenes históricos de Felipe II*, 183–96. Madrid: Centro de Estudios Cervantinos, 2000.

Rodríguez de Diego, José Luis, and Julia Rodríguez de Diego. "Un archivo no solo para el rey: Significado social del proyecto simanquino en el siglo XVI," in José Martínez Millán, ed., *Felipe II (1527–1598): Europa y la monarquía católica*, 4: 463–75. Madrid: Parteluz, 1998.

Roe, Kathleen. *Arranging and Describing Archives and Manuscripts (Archival Fundamentals Series II).* Chicago: Society of American Archivists, 2005.

Rosa, Maria de Lurdes. *O morgadio em Portugal, séculos XIV–XV: Modelos e práticas de comportamento linhagístico.* Lisbon: Estampa, 1995.

Rosa, Maria de Lurdes, and Randolph C. Head, eds. *Rethinking the Archive in Pre-Modern Europe: Family Archives and Their Inventories from the 15th to 19th Century.* Lisbon: Instituto de Estudos Medievais, 2015.

Rosenberg, Daniel. "Introduction" (Special section on Information Overload). *Journal of the History of Ideas* 64, 1 (2003), 1–9.

Rosenthal, Eduard. *Die Behördenorganisation Kaiser Ferdinands I.: Das Vorbild der Verwaltungsorganisation in den deutschen Territorien: Ein Beitrag zu Geschichte des Verwaltungsrechts*. Vienna: Carl Gerold's Sohn, 1887.

Rouse, Richard, and Mary Rouse. "Concordances et Index," in Henri-Jean Martin and Jean Vezin, eds., *Mise en page et mise en texte du livre manuscrit*, 219–28. Mayenne: Librarie-Promodis, 1990.

Preachers, Sermons and Florilegia: Studies on the Maniplus florum *of Thomas of Ireland*. Toronto: Pontifical Institute of Medieval Studies, 1979.

"*Statim Invenire*: Schools, Preachers, and New Attitudes to the Page," in Robert L. Benson and Giles Constable, eds., *Renaissance and Renewal in the Twelfth Century*, 201–25. Oxford: Clarendon Press, 1982.

Rück, Peter. "Die Ordnung der herzoglich savoyischen Archive unter Amadeus VIII. (1398–1451)." *Archivalische Zeitschrift* 67 (1971), 11–101.

"Zur Diskussion um die Archivgeschichte: die Anfaenge des Archivwesens in der Schweiz (800–1400)." *Mitteilungen der Vereinigung Schweizerischer Archivare* 26 (1975), 3–40.

Ruland, Rutger. *Tractatus de commissariis, et commissionibus camerae imperialis quadripartitus*. Frankfurt a.M.: Ioannis Sauris, 1604.

Sabean, David W. "Peasant Voices and Bureaucratic Texts: Narrative Structure in Early Modern Protocols," in Peter Becker and William Clark, eds., *Little Tools of Knowledge: Historical Essays on Academic and Bureaucratic Practices*, 67–93. Ann Arbor: University of Michigan Press, 2001.

"Village Court Protocols and Memory," in Heinrich Schmidt, André Holenstein, and Andreas Würgler, eds., *Gemeinde, Reformation und Widerstand. Festschrift für Peter Blickle zum 60. Geburtstag*, 3–23. Tübingen: Bibliotheca Academica, 1998.

Saenger, Paul. "Benito Arias Montana and the Evolving Notion of Locus in Sixteenth-Century Printed Books." *Word & Image* 17, 1–2 (2001), 119–37.

"The Impact of the Early Printed Page on the History of Reading." *Bulletin du Bibliophile* (1996), 2: 237–301.

Space between Words: The Origins of Silent Reading. Stanford, CA: Stanford University Press, 1997.

Salat, Johannes. *Reformationschronik 1517–1534*, ed. Ruth Jörg. Bern: Allgemeine Geschichtsforschende Gesellschaft, 1986.

Sancho Rayon, José, and Francisco de Zabalburu, eds. "Índice de las Escrituras Reales que están en el Archivo de Simancas. Año de 1568," in *Colección de Documentos Ineditos para la Historia de España por el Marqués de la Fuensante del Valle*, 81: 45–153. Madrid: Imprenta de Miguel Ginesta, 1883.

Sawilla, Jan Marco. *Antiquarianismus, Hagiographie und Historie im 17. Jahrhundert: Zum Werk der Bollandisten, Ein wissenschaftshistorischer Versuch*. Tübingen: Max Niemeyer Verlag, 2009.

Saxer, Daniela. "Archival Objects in Motion: Historians' Appropriation of Sources in Nineteenth-Century Austria and Switzerland." *Archival Science* 10, 3 (2010), 315–31.

Die Schärfung des Quellenblicks: Forschungspraktiken in der Geschichtswissenschaft 1840–1914. Berlin: De Gruyter, 2014.

Schäfer, Udo. "Authentizität: Vom Siegel zur digitalen Signatur," in Udo Schäfer and Nicole Bickhoff, eds., *Archivierung elektronischer Unterlagen*, 165–81. Stuttgart: Kohlhammer, 1999.

Schäffler, August. "Die 'hohe Registratur' des Magister Lorenzen Fries." *Archiv des historischen Vereins von Unterfranken und Aschaffenburg* 22, 1 (1874), 1–32.

"Die Urkunden und Archivalbände des hochstiftisch wirzburgischen Archives im 16. Jahrhundert." *Archivalische Zeitschrift* 10 (1885), 141–57.

Schellenberg, Theodor R. *Modern Archives: Principles and Techniques.* Chicago: University of Chicago Press, 1956.

Schenk, Dietmar. "'Archivmacht' und geschichtliche Wahrheit," in Rainer Hering and Dietmar Schenk, eds., *Wie mächtig sind Archive?*, 21–43. Hamburg: Hamburg University Press, 2013.

"Aufheben, was nicht vergessen werden darf": Archive vom alten Europa bis zur digitalen Welt. Stuttgart: Franz Steiner, 2013.

Scherzer, Walter. "Die Anfänge der Archive der Bischofe und des Domkapitels zu Würzburg." *Archivalische Zeitschrift* 73 (1977), 21–40.

Schilter, Johannes. "Probatio per archivum," in Jacob Wencker, ed., *Collecta archivi et cancellariae jura: quibus accedunt, de archicancellariis, vicecancellariis, cancellariis ac secretariis virorum clarissimorum commentationes*, 50–52. Strasbourg: Jo. Reinholdi Dulssecker, 1715.

Schmid, Barbara. "Das Hausbuch als literarische Gattung: Die Aufzeichnungen Johann Heinrich Wasers (1600–1669) und die Zürcher Hausbuchüberlieferung." *Daphnis* 34, 3/5 (2005), 603–56.

Schreiben für Status und Herrschaft: Deutsche Autobiographik in Spätmittelalter und früher Neuzeit. Zurich: Chronos, 2006.

Schmid, Regula. "Die Chronik im Archiv: Amtliche Geschichtsschreibung und ihr Gebrauchspotential im Spätmittelalter und in der Frühen Neuzeit." *Das Mittelalter* 5 (2000), 115–38.

"Fahnengeschichten: Erinnern in der spätmittelalterlichen Gemeinde." *Traverse* (1999), 39–48.

Geschichte im Dienst der Stadt: Amtliche Historie und Politik im Spätmittelalter. Zurich: Chronos, 2009.

Schulte, Petra. "Fides Publica: Die Dekonstruktion eines Forschungsbegriffes," in Petra Schulte, Marco Mostert, and Irene van Renswoude, eds., *Strategies of Writing: Studies on Text and Trust in the Middle Ages*, 15–36. Turnhout: Brepols, 2008.

"Notarial Documents," in Franz-Josef Arlinghaus et al., *Transforming the Medieval World: Uses of Pragmatic Literacy in the Middle Ages*, 197–238. Turnhout: Brepols, 2006.

Scripturae publicae creditur: Das Vertrauen in Notariatsurkunden im kommunalen Italien des 12. und 13. Jahrhunderts. Tübingen: Max Niemeyer Verlag, 2003.

Schulte, Petra, Marco Mostert, and Irene van Renswoude, eds. *Strategies of Writing: Studies on Text and Trust in the Middle Ages.* Turnhout: Brepols, 2008.

Schulze, Winfried. "Die veränderte Bedeutung sozialer Konflikte im 16. und 17. Jahrhundert," in Hans-Ulrich Wehler, *Der deutsche Bauernkrieg 1524–1526*, 277–302. Göttingen: Vandenhoeck & Ruprecht, 1975.

Schwarz, Dietrich W. H. "Zwei gotische Archivschränke aus Zürich." *Mitteilungen der antiquarische Gesellschaft von Zürich* 60 (1993), 81–9.

Schweizer, Paul. "Geschichte des Zürcher Staatsarchivs." *Neujahrsblatt zum Besten des Waisenhauses in Zürich* 116 (1894), 2–40.

Seckendorff, Veit Ludwig von. *Teutscher Fürsten-Stat*. Frankfurt a.M.: Thomas Matthias Götz, 1660.

Senatore, Francesco. *"Uno mundo de carta": Forme e struttura dell'diplomazia sforzesca*. Naples: Liguori, 1998.

Shapiro, Barbara J. *A Culture of Fact: England, 1550–1720*. Ithaca, NY: Cornell University Press, 2000.

Sickel, Theodor. *Urkundenlehre: Lehre von den Urkunden der ersten Karolinger (751–840)*. Vienna: Carl Gerold's Sohn, 1867.

Sickinger, James. *Public Records and Archives in Classical Athens*. Chapel Hill: University of North Carolina Press, 1999.

Silagi, Gabriel, ed. *Landesherrliche Kanzleien im Spätmittelalter*. Munich: Arebeo-Gesellschaft, 1984.

Silvestri, Alessandro. "Archives of the Mediterranean: Governance and Record-Keeping in the Crown of Aragon in the Long Fifteenth Century." *European Historical Quarterly* 46, 3 (2016), 435–57.

Simonett, Jürg, and Roger Sablonier, eds. *Handbuch der Bündner Geschichte, Vol. 2: Frühe Neuzeit*. Chur: Verlag Bündner Monatsblatt, 2000.

Skinner, Quentin. *The Foundations of Modern Political Thought, Vol. 2: The Age of Reformation*. Cambridge: Cambridge University Press, 1978.

Smith, Barry. "Document Acts," in Anita Konzelmann-Ziv and Hans Bernhard Schmid, eds., *Institutions, Emotions and Group Agents: Contributions to Social Ontology*, 19–31. Dordrecht: Springer, 2014.

Soll, Jacob. *The Information Master: Jean-Baptiste Colbert's Secret State Intelligence System*. Ann Arbor: University of Michigan Press, 2009.

The Reckoning: Financial Accountability and the Rise and Fall of Nations. New York: Basic Books, 2014.

Spangenberg, Hans. "Die Kanzleivermerke als Quelle verwaltungsgeschichtlicher Forschung." *Archiv für Urkundenforschung* 10 (1928), 469–525.

Spohnholz, Jesse. *The Convent of Wesel: The Event That Never Was and the Invention of Tradition*. Cambridge: Cambridge University Press, 2017.

Stadler, Peter. "Das Zeitalter der Gegenreformation," in *Handbuch der Schweizer Geschichte*, 1: 571–672. Zurich: Berichthaus, 1972.

Starzer, Albert. *Beiträge zur Geschichte der niederösterreichischen Statthalterei*. Vienna: K. u. K. Niederösterreichische Statthalterei, 1887.

Steedman, Carolyn. *Dust: The Archive and Cultural History*. New Brunswick, NJ: Rutgers University Press, 2002.

Stirnemann, Patricia. "L'Illustration du Cartulaire de Saint-Martin-Du-Canigou," in Olivier Guyotjeannin, Laurent Morelle, and Michel Parisse, eds., *Les cartulaires: Actes de la Table ronde (Paris, 5–7 Decembre 1991)*, 171–78. Paris: École des Chartes, 1993.

Stock, Brian. *The Implications of Literacy: Written Language and Models of Interpretation in the Eleventh and Twelfth Centuries*. Princeton, NJ: Princeton University Press, 1983.

"Schriftgebrauch und Rationalität im Mittelalter," in Wolfgang Schluchter, ed., *Max Webers Sicht des okzidentalen Christentums*, 165–83. Frankfurt: Suhrkamp, 1988.

Stockinger, Thomas. "Factualité historique, preuve juridique, autorité patristique: stratégies d'argumentation dans les controverses érudites en milieu ecclésiastique," in Jean Leclant et al., eds., *Dom Jean Mabillon, figure majeure de l'Europe des lettres*, 709–33. Paris: Académie des Inscriptions et Belles-Lettres, 2010.

Stoler, Laura Ann. *Along the Archival Grain: Epistemic Anxieties and Colonial Common Sense*. Princeton, NJ: Princeton University Press, 2009.

"Colonial Archives and the Arts of Governance." *Archival Science* 2 (2002), 87–109.

Stolleis, Michael. *Geschichte des öffentlichen Rechts in Deutschland, Vol. 1: Reichspublizistik und Policeywissenschaft 1600–1800*. Munich: C. H. Beck, 1988.

ed. *Hermann Conring (1606–1681): Beiträge zu Leben und Werk*. Berlin: Duncker & Humblot, 1983.

Stolz, Otto. "Archiv- und Registraturwesen der oberösterreichischen (tirolisch-schwäbischen) Regierung im 16. Jahrhundert." *Archivalische Zeitschrift* 42/43 (1934), 81–136.

Geschichte und Bestände des Staatlichen Archives zu Innsbruck. Vienna: Adolf Holzhausens Nachfolger, 1938.

Stösser, Heinrich. *Der Gachnanger Handel 1610. Ein Beitrag zur Religionspolitik der Eidgenossenschaft*. Villingen im Schwarzwald: Müller Druck, 1965.

Stowasser, Otto H. "Das Archiv der Herzöge von Österreich." *Mitteilungen des Archivrates* 3, 1 (1919), 15–62.

"Die österreichischen Kanzleibücher vornehmlich des 14. Jahrhunderts und das Aufkommen der Kanzleivermerke." *Mitteilungen des österreichischen Instituts für Geschichtsforschung* 35 (1914), 688–724.

Straub, Conrad. *Rechtsgeschichte der Evangelischen Kirchgemeinden der Landschaft Thurgau unter den eidgenössischen Landfrieden (1529–1792)*. Frauenfeld: Huber, 1902.

Strauss, Gerald. *Law, Resistance and the State: The Opposition to Roman Law in Reformation Germany*. Princeton, NJ: Princeton University Press, 1986.

Strickler, Johannes, ed. *Actensammlung zur Schweizerischen Reformationsgeschichte in den Jahren 1521–1532*. Zurich: Meyer & Zeller, 1881.

Tanzini, Lorenzo. "Archives and the management of public records in 14th-century Florence." Paper delivered at conference on "Politics and the Archives, Politics of the Archives," June 10, 2013, at Birkbeck College, University of London.

"Pratiche guidizarie e documentazione nello Stato fiorentino tra Tre e Quattrocento," in Andrea Giorgio, Stefano Moscadelli and Carla Zarilli, eds., *La documentazione degli organii guidiziari nell'Italia tardo-medievale e moderno*, 785–832. Rome: Archivi di Stato, 2012.

Tennant, Elaine. *The Habsburg Chancellery Language in Perspective*. Berkeley: University of California Press, 1985.

Tessier, Georges. "L'enregistrement." *Moyen Age* 62 (1956), 39–52.

Teuscher, Simon. "Document Collections, Mobilized Regulations, and the Making of Customary Law at the End of the Middle Ages." *Archival Science* 10 (2010), 211–29.

"Kompilation und Mündlichkeit: Herrschaftskultur und Gebrauch von Weis-
tümern im Raum Zürich (14.–15. Jahrhundert)." *Historische Zeitschrift* 273, 2
(2001), 289–333.

Teuscher, Simon. tr. Philip Grace. *Lords' Rights and Peasant Stories: Writing and
the Formation of Tradition in the Later Middle Ages*. Philadelphia: University of
Pennsylvania Press 2012 [German original 2007].

"Textualising Peasant Inquiries: German Weistümer between Orality and
Literacy," in Karl Heidecker, ed., *Charters and the Use of the Written Word
in Medieval Society*, 239–53. Turnhout: Brepols, 2000.

Thomas, David, Simon Fowler, and Valerie Johnson. *The Silence of the Archive*.
Chicago: Neal Schuman, 2017.

Tock, Benoît-Michel. "Les Textes Non Diplomatiques dans les cartulaires de la
province de Reims," in Olivier Guyotjeannin, Laurent Morelle, and Michel
Parisse, eds., *Les cartulaires: Actes de la Table ronde (Paris, 5–7 Decembre
1991)*, 45–58. Paris: École des Chartes, 1993.

Troulliot, Michael. *Silencing the Past: Power and the Production of History*. Boston:
Beacon Press, 1995.

Trusen, Winfried. "Vom Inquisitionsverfahren zum Ketzer- und Hexenprozeß,"
in Dieter Schwab, ed., *Staat, Kirche, Wissenschaft in einer pluralistischen
Gesellschaft: Festschrift zum 65. Geburtstag von Paul Mikat*, 435–50. Berlin:
Duncker & Humblot, 1989.

Van Caenegem, R. C. "Methods of Proof in Western Medieval Law," in R. C.
Van Caenegem, *Legal History: A European Perspective*, 71–114. London:
Hambledon Press, 1991 [Original publication 1965].

Vismann, Cornielia, tr. Geoffrey Winthrop-Young. *Files: Law and Media Technology*. Stanford, CA: Stanford University Press, 2008. [German original
2000].

Vogtherr, Thomas. "Archivtheorie und Archivpraxis im ausgehenden 17. Jahr-
hundert: Ahasver Fritsch, Jacob Bernhard Multz von Oberschönfeld, und
Georg Aebbtlin," in Reiner Cunz, ed., *Fundamenta Historiae: Geschichte im
Spiegel der Numismatik und ihrer Nachbarwissenschaften*, 403–9. Hannover:
Niedersächsisches Landesmuseum, 2004.

Völkel, Markus. *"Pyrrhonisumus historicus" und "fides historica": Die Entwicklung
der deutschen historischen Methodologie unter dem Gesichtspunkt der historischen
Skepsis*. Frankfurt a.M.: Peter Lang, 1987.

Wagner, Kurt. *Das Brandenburgische Kanzlei- und Urkundenwesen zur Zeit des
Kurfürsten Albrecht Achilles (1470–86): Einleitung und Exkurs I. and II.* Berlin:
Blanke, 1911.

Walder, Ernst, ed. *Religionsvergleiche des 16. Jahrhunderts*. Bern: H. Lang, 1945.

Walsham, Alexandra. "The Social History of the Archive: Record-Keeping in
Early Modern Europe." *Past and Present Supplement* 11 (2016), 10–48.

Walther, Andreas. "Kanzleiordnungen Maximilians I., Karls V. und Ferdinands.
I." *Archiv für Urkundenforschung* 2 (1909), 335–406.

Weber, Max. "Politics as a Vocation," in Hans Gerth and C. Wright Mills, ed.
and tr., *From Max Weber*, 77–127. New York: Free Press, 1946.

ed. and tr. Hans Gerth and C. K. Yang. *The Religion of China*. New York: Free
Press, 1951.

Weber, Wolfgang. *Prudentia gubernatoria. Studien zur Herrschaftslehre in der deutschen politischen Wissenschaft des 17. Jahrhunderts.* Tübingen: Max Niemeyer Verlag, 1992.

Weijers, Olga. "Les Index au Moyen Âge: Sont-ils un Genre Littéraire?", in Claudi, Leonardi, Marcello Morelli, and Francesco Santi, eds., *Fabula in Tabula: Una storia degli indici del manoscritto al testo elettronico*, 11–22. Spoleto: Centro Italiano di Studi Sull'alto Medievo, 1995.

Wencker, Jacob, ed. *Apparatus & instructus archivorum ex usu nostri temporis.* Strasbourg: Jo. Reinholdi Dulssecker, 1713.

⸻ ed. *Collecta archivi et cancellariae jura: quibus accedunt, de archicancellariis, vice-cancellariis, cancellariis ac secretariis virorum clarissimorum commentationes.* Strasbourg: Jo. Reinholdi Dulssecker, 1715.

Wiesflecker, Angelika. "Die 'oberösterreichischen' Kammerraitbücher zu Innsbruck 1493–1519: Ein Beitrag zur Wirtschafts-, Finanz- und Kulturgeschichte der oberösterreichischen Ländergruppe." PhD Dissertation, Graz, 1986.

Wild, Joachim. *Beiträge zur Registerführung der bayrischen Klöster und Hochstifte im Mittelalter.* Kallmünz: Verlag Michael Laßleben, 1973.

Willett, Robert A. *The Probative Value of Documents in Ecclesiastical Trials (De Fide Instrumentorum): An Historical Synopsis and Commentary.* Washington, DC: Catholic University Press, 1942.

Williams, Caroline. "Diplomatic Attitudes: From Mabillon to Metadata." *Journal of the Society of Archivists* 26, 1 (2005), 1–24.

Woolf, D. R. "A High Road to the Archives? Rewriting the History of Early Modern English Historical Culture." *Storia della Storiographia* 32 (1997), 33–59.

Yakel, Elizabeth. "Archival Representation," in Francis X. Blouin Jr., and William G. Rosenberg, eds., *Archives, Documentation and the Institutions of Social Memory*, 151–63. Ann Arbor: University of Michigan Press, 2006.

Yale, Elizabeth. "The History of Archives: The State of the Discipline." *Book History* 18 (2015), 332–59.

Yeo, Geoffrey. "Concepts of Record (1): Evidence, Information and Persistent Representations." *American Archivist* 70 (2007), 315–43.

⸻ "Continuing Debates about Description," in Terry Eastwood and Heather MacNeil, eds., *Currents of Archival Thinking*, 2nd ed., 163–92. Santa Barbara: Libraries Unlimited, 2017.

⸻ *Records, Information and Data: Exploring the Role of Record-Keeping in an Information Culture.* London: Facet Publishing, 2018.

Zedelmaier, Helmut. *Der Anfang der Geschichte: Studien zur Ursprungsdebatte im 18. Jahrhundert.* Hamburg: Meiner, 2003.

⸻ "*Facilitas inveniendi*: The Alphabetical Index as a Knowledge Management Tool." *Indexer* 25, 4 (2007), 235–42.

Z'Graggen, Bruno. *Tyrannenmord im Toggenburg. Fürstäbtische Herrschaft und protestantischer Widerstand um 1600.* Zurich: Chronos, 1999.

Zins, Chaim. "Conceptual Approaches for Defining Data, Information and Knowledge." *Journal of the American Society for Information Science and Technology* 58, 4 (2007), 479–93.

Index

Made in the USA
Middletown, DE
09 November 2021

52007156R00205